THE StockTwits® EDGE

Founded in 1807, John Wiley & Sons is the oldest independent publishing company in the United States. With offices in North America, Europe, Australia, and Asia, Wiley is globally committed to developing and marketing print and electronic products and services for our customers' professional and personal knowledge and understanding.

The Wiley Trading series features books by traders who have survived the market's ever changing temperament and have prospered—some by reinventing systems, others by getting back to basics. Whether a novice trader, professional, or somewhere in-between, these books will provide the advice and strategies needed to prosper today and well into the future.

For a list of available titles, please visit our Web site at www.WileyFinance.com.

THE StockTwits® EDGE

Actionable Trade Setups from **Real Market Pros**

Howard Lindzon | Philip Pearlman | Ivaylo Ivanhoff

editors

John Wiley & Sons, Inc.

Published by John Wiley & Sons, Inc., Hoboken, New Jersey.
Published simultaneously in Canada.

Library of Congress Cataloging-in-Publication Data:

Lindzon, Howard.
The stocktwits edge : 40 actionable trade setups from real market pros / Howard Lindzon, Philip Pearlman, Ivaylo Ivanhoff.
p. cm. — (Wiley trading ; 510)
Includes index.
ISBN 978-1-118-02905-3 (cloth); ISBN 978-1-118-08927-9 (ebk);
ISBN 978-1-118-08928-6 (ebk); ISBN 978-1-118-08929-3 (ebk)
1. Foreign exchange market. 2. Foreign exchange futures. 3. Investment analysis.
I. Pearlman, Philip. II. Ivanhoff, Ivaylo. III. Title.
HG3851.L536 2011
332.64—dc22

Printed in the United States of America

10 9 8 7 6 5 4 3 2 1

The StockTwits Edge *is dedicated to our incredible community of traders and investors, who have brought forth the amazing talent in this book.*

Thanks Friends!

Contents

Introduction

At StockTwits, we believe the stock market can be a fun and profitable place. Whenever you bring together a group of highly talented and motivated people chasing profits and ask them to talk about what works for them, you're bound to hit upon some valuable ideas and unforgettable stories. Whether you trade once a year or every day, the learning never stops. And that's one of the key messages of *The StockTwits Edge*. It takes time, repetition, and strict discipline, but if you dedicate yourself to learning, you will discover the true power of money and your inner self.

StockTwits is an online "idea network," a Facebook for finance, an *American Idol* or farm system for traders and investors, a virtual global trading floor. We strive to help people share and receive ideas, discover like-minded people, leverage a community of passionate people, build a publishing and research brand, and help people monetize their work. The community is made up of more than 100,000 people from all corners of the world who trade thousands of instruments. You can customize your StockTwits streams to get the ideas you want from the people you want and about the stocks that matter to you most. You can get them on the web site at http://stocktwits.com, or pushed to you on your phone or e-mail.

The real-time Web has changed many things for stocks, markets, and finance. Rapid connections and the miracle of discovery, curation, and serendipity have made the entire social networking industry difficult to value on Wall Street. I wrote extensively about this in my first book, entitled *The Wallstrip Edge* (Business Plus, 2009). The social Web and technology advances have evolved to create tools and platforms that will fuel finance and the sharing of ideas. With StockTwits, traders and investors are empowered more than ever before to learn and learn quickly through the leverage of others.

And since StockTwits is about crowdsourcing the best ideas and talent, that's just what you'll find in this book. It's our first book and therefore a labor of love. For this book, we invited 46 of our community members who love, live, and breathe the markets to each write a brief chapter in which they detail their favorite setups, including background, rationale, and examples. *The StockTwits Edge* features setups from different time frames, asset classes, and market styles.

Based on our research and thousands of interviews with traders and investors, we came to the conclusion that most successful people specialize in a favorite setup. A setup is a combination of factors that need to align in time and space in order to produce a buy or sell signal. In *The StockTwits Edge*, each trader presents a favorite setup in detail as well as the approach for finding new ideas and managing risk that the trader uses successfully on a daily basis. It is amazing how diverse the chapters are.

Some of the traders you'll meet in this book have been trading for 40 years and others for four, but each has an amazing focus and belief that if you can master one thing well in the markets you can succeed. While all of us may not always practice what we preach, the idea-generation engine of StockTwits makes it that much easier to stay focused and disciplined.

The idea for this book started with Ivaylo Ivanhoff, a community member who was finishing his MBA work in St. Louis when he reached out to me via e-mail. As I normally do when hit with a great idea, I called him directly. Ivanhoff has since come to work at StockTwits (shockingly, he calls it his dream job!) and was instrumental in pulling everything together for this book. My pal Phil Pearlman, head of content at StockTwits, is my trusted source for idea curation and he, too, has been on board since day one. I called the good people at John Wiley & Sons, and they said let's do it.

If you feel like you might be underinvested or that maybe you overtrade, this book is for you. This book is for all of us! It's no secret that I love stocks and I love trading and investing. I also love sharing ideas and, if I can, a few laughs. When I co-founded StockTwits in 2008, I knew it was a big idea and not sure I had the energy to get it off the ground. Over the years, StockTwits has become that perfect platform for me and so many others. Now we are a team of 20 and just plowing ahead into the social Web frontier.

We hope this book is a beginning point on your investing/trading journey. Armed with each contributor's favorite setup, you can visit the StockTwits web site and see the same people sharing live ideas around these setups. You can hold them to their own words. You can become friends and I hope challenge them when they drift from their styles, as we all inevitably do sometimes.

Though I don't believe in tips, I do have one for you here: If you come to the site, don't be concerned with contributing; it's likely that 80 to 90 percent of the audience is just eavesdropping anyway. There is nothing wrong with that. Positive and constructive feedback never hurts, though, and in the social world of the Web you will indeed catch more flies with honey.

We are excited about all the new and young faces that show up on StockTwits every day leveraging their ideas and sharing information. We hope you enjoy this book and get as much out of it as we did in putting it together for you.

A special thanks goes to my friend Doug Estadt, who has championed StockTwits from when he first met me, gave me a big bear hug, and ran to get his checkbook. Doug has been a huge supporter of StockTwits and a mentor to many young traders on the stream. Doug was traveling in China while we finalized chapters. You can follow him on Stocktwits@wsmco.

Because of the intense mentoring that occurs on StockTwits there are new stars discovered each and every day. To taste the true experience of StockTwits, head to the site.

Howard Lindzon
Co-Founder and CEO of StockTwits

THE StockTwits® EDGE

PART I

Trend Following

CHAPTER 1

Find Trends, Ride Them, and Get Off

Howard Lindzon, *@howardlindzon*

LESS IS MORE

In 1987, after earning my undergraduate degree, I took a job in the back office at a small brokerage firm in Toronto called Davidson Partners. I was in order entry. Brokers would fill out tickets and drop them in a box for me, and I would enter the orders to be filled. Two months into my job, the market crashed. I saw people lose everything. I was on the ground floor of a panic, and I was hooked.

It is now 2011 and I do not have the same 24 years to catch up on all my mistakes and wins, so I want this chapter to be about speed. My goal is to get you to an "aha" moment about the value of trend following whereby you can catch big moves in stocks and markets.

I trust everyone and trust no one. I can do that because I have tried just about every type of investing known to man. Today when I invest or trade in the global markets, I am in control. I make every decision. I take responsibility at some level for every made or lost dollar of mine in the markets.

I believe the markets are opportunity machines. We built StockTwits to offer investors and traders an endless supply of ideas with more context and less opinion. It will mean different things to different people, but your goal should always be to seek out investors and traders who make your job easier, and to give back when possible.

I believe investors should swing for the fences. If you invest properly, your best investments will become trades (you can call yourself a trader). If you know how to manage losses, those trades will not become investments; you will kick out losing positions from your portfolio so that you hold only winners and manage profits.

Do anything well for 10 years and you will be a success. If investing is in your 10-year plan, you just need to stay in the game and get started as soon as possible. I wish

I'd had the proper perspective in 1998 when I started my hedge fund. After 20-plus years of stock investing, I can't believe how much time you can spend away from your screens and still be successful as a trader and an investor. In a nutshell, "less is more." The best investors and traders prune, shed, purge, hold, and even add to winners and sometimes start over.

I believe most people will never allocate the proper amount of time to learn how to trade, but all of us can invest. We live in spectacular times. You can leverage the Web in so many ways, especially around knowledge. You can *Do More Faster* (the title of Brad Feld and David Cohen's most excellent book on start-ups [John Wiley & Sons, 2010]) than at any time in the history of mankind. Our community at StockTwits is filled with tens of thousands of traders, a global trading floor that collectively digests and shares prices, ideas, and news.

CATCHING BIG TRENDS

I believe you can outwork everyone to get an edge but don't need inside information to be successful. In fact, I would argue that the further you remove yourself from the worries of all the noise, inside information, and tips, the better your investing results will become. Surround yourself with voices and people you trust and carefully let new voices into your routine over time.

I believe the opportunity of an investing lifestyle is an amazing freedom to pursue. You can learn to watch and enjoy the markets. Knowing what I want to do has helped me focus on a plan. My strength is the network I have built over 12 years as a hedge fund manager, investor, and entrepreneur. I have been very fortunate to benefit from the Internet explosion during the meat of my investing years. Finding mentors has never been easier. I use the term *social leverage* for this phenomenon. You should slip into my social stream if you want to take part in the process. You are not locked in, and that is the power of the Web today.

As a trend investor, I have caught some big moves: Chipotle, Apple, Amazon, Rackspace, Crocs, and many private Internet companies. You did not need inside information to catch 200 points in Apple stock or 100 points in Netflix in 2009 and 2010. I am open-minded, and experience has taught me that patterns exist and they repeat. If you build a daily routine and focus on the right lists, you can learn to catch big stock moves.

To catch a large basket of trends, one should start at the macro level and work to the micro level. My friend Ivan says this about trend following: "Short-term price trends are fueled by momentum, medium-term price trends are fed by earnings-related catalysts, and long-term price trends are sustained by social and business trends."

It also makes sense to focus on your areas of passion. Doing the work necessary to catch trends will be easier if you are immersed in the work you love. And of course, selling is a discipline that must be honed. I am very mechanical when it comes to exiting positions.

I have missed so many winners, and, as all investors do, I never own enough of the winners I do eventually own and ride. I keep on investing because I know a new opportunity is around the corner and I will get better at spotting catalysts that will lead to big moves.

I believe that you should not worry about valuations or price-earnings (P/E) ratios for your liquid investments. Valuation matters when you can't sell a security. I don't think many investors or analysts can successfully determine forward prices. If they could, markets would be way more efficient. Having a defined strategy is all that matters. I am known as an "early seller," but I like the moniker. Being an "early buyer" is a moniker I seek to avoid.

I used to trade and hire traders. Daily performance mattered. Now 10-year performance matters to me. I survived 10 years with pretty much my original limited partners in my hedge fund, despite making every mistake in the book. Daily performance anxiety is the stress of the entire financial industry. It will never disappear. That stress is our opportunity. The louder and more active trading and Wall Street become, the quieter you should become. Technology will continue to make it possible for both sides to do their jobs, cheaper and faster.

SIMPLE IS GOOD

When I read Malcolm Gladwell's *The Tipping Point* (Little, Brown, 2000), I wondered why tipping points were not linked to stock prices. Stocks "tip" just like products and ideas. If you look back at the great stock winners of all time, you can spot a myriad of points where you could have matched "aha" moments with large stock advances.

I believe that if I follow my simple routine, the right stocks will find me. Every Saturday morning, I go to www.stocktwits50.com to get a quick snapshot of money flow and momentum. It saves me time. In 20 minutes I have a good picture of the momentum in the markets.

During the week, I follow Joe Fahmy (@jfahmy), as well as @stocktwits50, @biggercapital, @ivanhoff, and @upsidetrader. Discovery is a fantastic feature of today's social Web platforms, so ask others on the StockTwits streams whom they trust. New voices are constantly surfacing. I check Techmeme at http://techmeme.com and Abnormal Returns at http://abnormalreturns.com and scan the headlines and read many stories. By doing so consistently, you will start to pick up the company and ticker symbols that entrepreneurs, angel investors, financial bloggers, financial journalists, and hedge fund managers are talking about. I read venture capitalist Fred Wilson at www.avc.com, Brad Feld at www.feld.com/blog, and TechCrunch at http://techcrunch.com as well.

UNDERSTANDING MOMENTUM

Momentum is a way of life. It is a style. For most people it's psychologically difficult to embrace momentum. When I launched my daily Web video show called *Wallstrip* in 2006, I wanted to express in a short video format that you only need one good trend idea to change your life. We presented a new stock almost every day, trying to reveal the catalysts behind big price moves.

Price is the ultimate leading indicator. It reflects the collective consciousness of the market. If a stock is trading at a new all-time high, the odds are the underlying company is growing very fast and under accumulation from institutions. When a stock is trading at all-time highs, every holder is in a winning position, and everyone who is short is in a losing position—a powerful combination that is often a recipe for further price appreciation.

Every stock that goes on to make 500 percent passes 100 percent and many new highs along the way. A stock that is breaking out to a new all-time high after a long period of consolidation is always worth further investigation.

However, price is not the only data point for me buying stocks. I like to keep my turnover rate low and I am very picky when it comes to opening new positions. I need to understand the catalysts that will sustain future price appreciation.

Once a stock reaches a new all-time high, I start to follow it. I always do my homework and if I find a strong catalyst that is likely to sustain the price trend, I buy.

I will never pay the lowest price and sometimes do pay the highest price, but I won't let one bad stock or investment wreck my life. There will be times when investing seems easy, but do not confuse a bull market with brains. There are times when most stocks go up as fresh money enters the equity markets and higher prices boost risk appetite.

MACRO TRENDS TODAY

My goal is to own shares in companies that will monetize the big social and business trends of the next decade. As we enter 2011, I can't imagine a world without inflation in commodities and deflation in technology and start-up costs, including talent. In 2010, we saw the continuation of some major trends—cloud computing, the mobile Web, the social Web, and the consumer Internet. Most interesting is the phenomenon I describe as "the $50 club sandwich and the $5 smart phone." While traveling to Paris recently, I encountered the $50 club sandwich at The Four Seasons Hotel and, while not typical, this is surely a sign of the times amid global commodity inflation. As 2011 ends, we will likely see some unbelievably low prices in smart phones as the war heats up among the telecoms, handset makers, and Skype, and as the operating systems of Apple, Google, and Microsoft fight for market share.

EXAMPLES

With the themes I've described in mind, I'll elaborate on three positions of mine (as of January 2011).

Rackspace Hosting, Inc.

When you hear the word *cloud* in the investing space, Amazon may be the first company that comes to mind. But for me it's Rackspace, and I first talked about it on my blog in January 2010. I wrote: "Every smart person says Rackspace is overvalued. I say many smart people go broke on that argument. The cloud is the buzz and Rackspace is the cloud for many institutions that manage money. All roll-ups end badly, but guessing when is too hard. Trend guys are making a killing here as the 'dumb money.'"

I did not wait for an all-time high in this case. I had been following the industry and the stock closely, and when the markets began to streak higher in September 2010, I purchased the stock. (See Figures 1.1 and 1.2.) Rackspace had also recently launched

FIGURE 1.1 RAX Monthly Chart
Source: © StockCharts.com.

FIGURE 1.2 RAX Breaking Out to a New All-Time High at $12, Weekly Chart
Source: © StockCharts.com.

a project called Open Stack that would make the company less focused on acquisitions and more focused on organic growth. I entered just under $20 and while I have sold some stock along the way, the stock today is at $34.

Intuit

Intuit is not a sexy company. They do not seem to care and I like that. Intuit owns the small and medium-sized businesses (SMBs) in the United States when it comes to accounting and tax preparation products. It may not be as sexy as the enterprise or the consumer markets, but profits and market share are super-sexy to institutional investors, and Intuit sells the hammers and the shovels to the SMBs. (See Figure 1.3.)

FIGURE 1.3 INTU Monthly Chart
Source: © StockCharts.com.

Intuit recently spent $170 million to further entrench itself in the consumer market when it purchased Mint.com.

Intuit has not been a rocket ship since hitting all-time highs (see Figure 1.4), but I believe there are catalysts. The company has fantastic margins from recurring revenue, little competition in many areas of its software distribution, and operating leverage.

One area I would love to see Intuit announce expansion into is retail. There should be Mint stores in thousands of towns and cities across the United States. The personal finance industry and SMBs need a fresh, comfortable, and contemporary learning environment to experience Intuit products. I can envision Mint and Quicken "genius bars" in a retail environment that dares to immerse the consumer and SMB in personal finance.

FIGURE 1.4 High-Volume Earnings Breakout to a New All-Time High, INTU Daily Chart
Source: © StockCharts.com.

Ariba, Inc.

I added Ariba to my portfolio in November 2010. Ariba was breaking to six-year highs and I found it by reading the *New York Times*. (See Figure 1.5.)

It is important to note that again awareness and serendipity matter. Checking prices matters. I was not searching for Ariba, but Ariba found me during casual business reading. As you do this more and more, you develop a different level of awareness. Intrigued by the article, I checked the price and the stock was trading at major highs. I liked that Ariba was a marketplace and focused on software and a long-forgotten leader from the Internet bubble.

Within a few days I purchased the stock.

FIGURE 1.5 Ariba (ARBA) Weekly Chart
Source: © StockCharts.com.

HERE COMES THE SUN

I have witnessed four panics and crashes in my investing career. The shortest was in 1987; I had a cigarette and missed it. The 1998 Asian contagion/Long-Term Capital Management crisis lasted a summer and gave way to the spectacular rise and bursting of the Internet bubble in the year 2000. Most recently, there was the mortgage and banking panic of 2008 and 2009. All were messy, all caused great pain, but all the crashes created massive new opportunities. Preserve capital in bad markets, and you will live to ride the next great trends, which are always around the corner.

CHAPTER 2

Trade, Trend, Tail

Keith McCullough, *@KeithMcCullough*

Keith's messages and links on StockTwits have stood out from day one. Most professionals do not think sharing is useful to them, but Keith does and for that our community has embraced him. Keith runs a virtual hedge fund in an innovative way—by offering full-blown research and not trading any positions. His firm's sole focus is to provide investors with deep, knowledgeable research and ideas as if he were running the money himself.

MAKE MONEY OR GO HOME

I didn't learn anything useful about trading markets in school. The proverbial hockey stick in my learning curve came by doing. The only struggle that matters is coming to terms with the reality that trading markets isn't something you learn in a textbook. Experience is earned by making mistakes.

I had spent just enough time on the sell side to realize that I didn't want to be there anymore and was hired by a hedge fund manager by the name of Jon Dawson who was, at the time, breaking up with another hedge fund manager by the name of Art Samberg. As Samberg moved along to start one of the largest hedge funds in the game (Pequot), that left poor Jon saddled with guys like me: inexperienced and aggressive, young and naive. I had the perfect skill set to learn the hard way—by making mistakes using live ammo.

My first three years as an analyst, being groomed to be a portfolio manager (PM) on the buy side, were down markets for stocks—2000, 2001, and 2002—so I effectively learned by doing on the short side. Simple mandate: make money or be fired. That probably explains why I'm much more adept at making sales than chasing rabbits.

I started Hedgeye so that I could learn out in the open. I operate in an open architecture now for anyone in the game to see. I get much more useful feedback this way and, by design, I'm forced to be as honest as my positioning makes me. Essentially I operate a virtual hedge fund, so that I can bring transparency, accountability, and trust to investors at all levels.

PAY ATTENTION TO VOLATILITY

Real-time market prices rule. Everything else is all about storytelling around those prices.

Gains on the short side are meant to be taken. On the long side, pretending you are Captain Stock Picker is fine, as long as volatility is low. In a game of heightened volatility, you need to shorten your holding periods. The plan always needs to be that the plan is going to change, but you have to be duration agnostic so that you can capitalize on playing the game that is in front of you.

BEARISH AND BULLISH FORMATIONS

Our risk management setup is primarily derived by mathematical assumptions in chaos/complexity theory.

Our Trade, Trend, and Tail lines are quantitatively manufactured using a baseline model of 27 global macro factors that span countries, currencies, and commodities market prices. Then we overlay our top-down view with a bottom-up three-factor view of the security in question (price, volume, and volatility).

Trade: an anticipated duration on a portfolio position of three weeks or less.
Trend: an anticipated duration on a portfolio position of three months or more.
Tail: an anticipated duration on a portfolio position of three years or less.

All of our signals (entry/exit) are driven by closing market prices. All durations are measured simultaneously. Violating a Tail level is an explicit sell signal as much as breaking out above a Trade level is a buy signal.

They occur when all three of my risk management durations (Trade, Trend, and Tail) are confirmed by the market's price. In English, a bullish formation means that the Trade line of support is also supported by the Trend and Tail lines.

The logic here is pretty straightforward: All monkeys are in the pool—short-term day traders (Trade), intermediate-term sophisticates who have a good read on things like quarterly analytics (Trend), and long-term Warren Buffett wannabes (Tail) who buy and hold. Nothing perpetuates bullish price momentum like higher highs and higher lows in price from the short term to the long term.

I find these formations with my research team. I have a global macro and quantitative team that screens from the top down while my sector and stock analysts screen from the bottom up. We meet in the middle every morning during our 8:30 A.M. meeting. I have a staff of 40 who are gainfully employed with one objective: all research, all the time. I make all of the calls on entry/exit points.

GET ME SOME GOLD

Being bullish enough on Gold coming out of the August breakout was critical provided that the immediate-term Trade line of support held and both volume and volatility studies confirmed price action across all three durations (i.e., volatility remained low and volume continued to expand). I traded this bullish formation with a bullish bias until the Trade line was violated (see Figure 2.1).

Never start justifying a Trade line breakdown with nonsense like "valuation." Market prices don't lie; people do.

Trade = $1,261
Trend = $1,226
Tail = $1,181

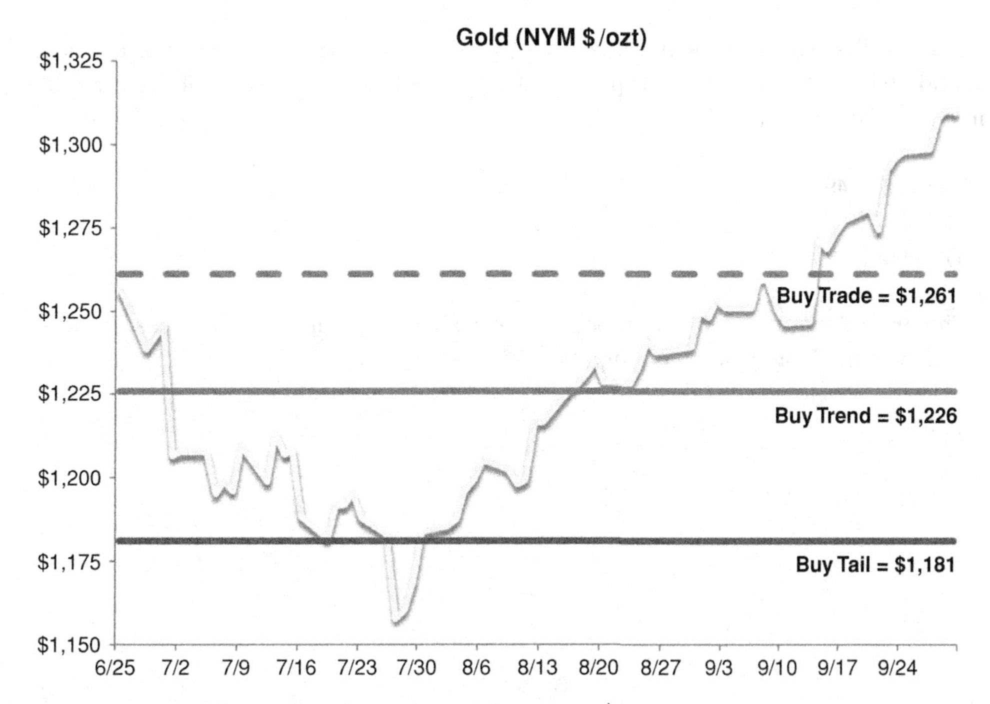

FIGURE 2.1 Gold Is a Buy above the Trade Line at $1,261

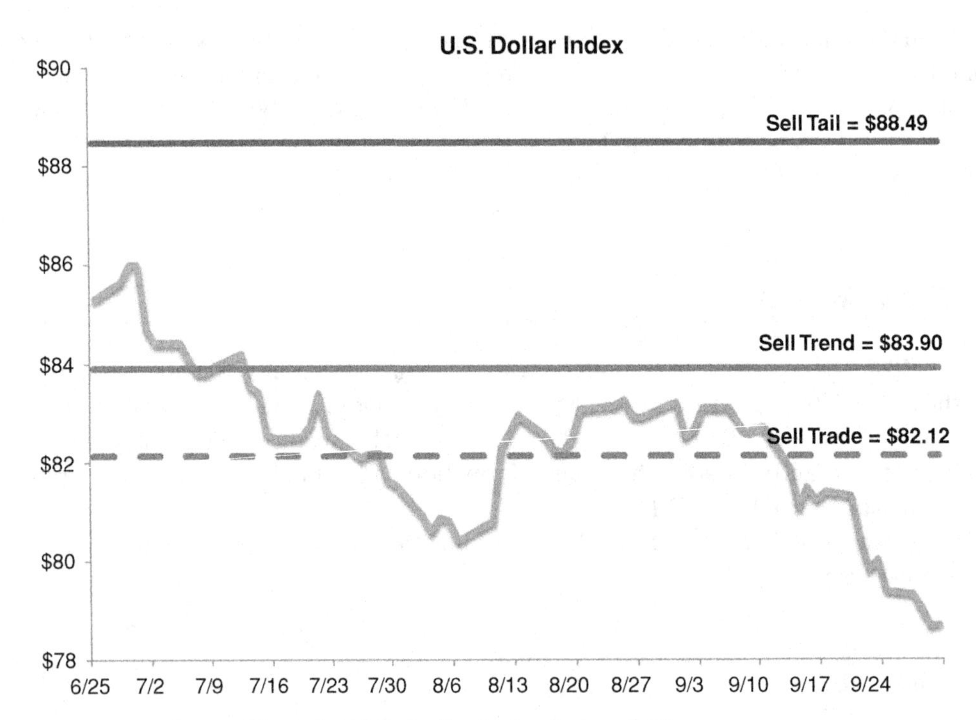

FIGURE 2.2 Going Short the U.S. Dollar Index below $82

The corollary to long Gold has been short the U.S. Dollar Index. We call this a bearish formation where the Tail sits on top of the Trend and Trade, scaring all of the valuation monkeys out of the pool.

Tail = $88.49
Trend = $83.90
Trade = $82.12

The breakdown through $82 in September was an explicit signal to press the short side and be what I call bearish enough (see Figure 2.2).

CHAPTER 3

Don't Quit

Michael K. Dawson, @*TrendRida*

Michael is a skilled trend trader. You might not notice him when you first come to StockTwits, as it is not his style to boast after his winners. Michael will sneak up on you. He is an inspiration to other traders and a model of decorum, so it is no surprise that his words are a testament to persistence, will, and belief in yourself.

The game taught me the game. And it didn't spare me the rod while teaching.
—Jesse Livermore

BURNING DESIRE

On March 31, 2006, I walked away from a 20-year career in engineering, marketing, and sales to trade full-time on my own account. I'd be lying if I said that I didn't miss the sales conferences in Hawaii, building customer relationships on the 19th hole, and most of all the big fat paycheck—all perks of my last job. Many of my friends thought that I was crazy, and to be honest I had a hard time explaining my reasoning. My boss was cool. The pay was great. The work was challenging. So, why quit? It boiled down to this thing that many people have, but most suppress.

In his classic book *Think and Grow Rich*, Napoleon Hill describes an innate characteristic found in successful people. He called it a "burning desire." Essentially, it is an urge, a passion, an inner drive that's so overwhelming that if denied it will make you miserable no matter how much money or prestige you have. This described my situation to the letter.

My initial attempt at addressing my "burning desire" happened four years into my career. After spending countless days and nights pursuing and attaining bachelor's and master's degrees in electrical engineering, I quit a well-paying engineering job to start a video production company. Unfortunately, like most first-time businesses, it crashed and burned.

However, the lessons I learned were invaluable. The most important lesson learned was that if you have something to offer, you can always find another job. As a matter of fact, after my business fizzled I went right back to the same company I had resigned from, this time at a higher salary. From that point on, I had no fear.

Although I may not have had any fear, I did get a little more comfortable as I progressed from engineering to marketing and ultimately to sales with a six-figure salary and an expense account. However, if you truly have the "burning desire," it will not be denied. So, 15 years after the video company debacle, being much better prepared in knowledge and capital, I ventured out again. This time, I would make my way in the financial services business primarily trading stocks in my own account.

I have loved stocks since I made my first trade in 1995. I bought Macromedia and sold it eight months later for a 65 percent gain. I won't mention the name of the penny stock that I discovered in a chat room and started to accumulate around the same time. There was no happy ending to that one. The late 1990s was a great time to be in the stock market. Working in high tech, many of our customers were highfliers like Cisco Systems and Sun Microsystems.

Often my first call after a sales call was to my broker. By December 1999, I had accumulated significant positions in America Online (AOL), Microsoft, Yahoo!, Cisco, CMGI Inc., and others. I was crushing it. I recall, at the ripe old age of 36, thinking that financial freedom was one year away. Then something unbelievable happened. In March 2000, the stock market started to fall. Buying on the dips stopped working as the downward momentum increased. All of the books I had read talked about buying, but no one talked about selling. Frozen like a deer in headlights by the end of 2000, I was nearly wiped out. I had ridden CMGI from $5 to $160 and back down. The same was true with most of the others.

Fortunately, trading was still a part-time endeavor and I had a real job to pay the bills. Scarred and bruised, it would be a few more years before I was active in the markets again. This time I was determined to find a strategy that included that mysterious art of trading called selling.

TOP-DOWN APPROACH

It has taken me years to develop my market philosophy and approach. I continue to refine it based on my experiences. Ideally, I would love to be a big game hunter—spending my days in search of another CMGI, but this time selling at $160. That is a perfectly valid approach, but it is a high-risk and low-probability strategy. When I was playing that game, I had the comfort of a paycheck from a 9-to-5 job. Once I became a full-time trader I had to lower the risk and increase the probability. Occasionally, I may find a CMGI in my portfolio, but I have no allusions of 30-bagger returns.

I define myself as a trend trader—thus, the StockTwits handle @TrendRida. My forte is discovering long-term themes, leveraging them through the stock market, and riding them as long as possible. Currently, I am focused on four trends that have near-term and long-term catalysts:

1. *Mobile and cloud computing (global digital living room).* This is the ability to move and access content anywhere in the world.
2. *Brazil (a subset of the BRIC thesis).* An expanding and prosperous middle class benefits from the country's abundance of natural resources.
3. *LED lighting.* This is a fairly straightforward way to play the move toward energy efficiency.
4. *Precious metals (gold and silver).* There are multiple correlations here. With inflation, the dollar, interest rates, and political uncertainty, precious metals serve as a great diversification tool.

Over time, I have learned that I can manage only 10 to 15 stocks at a time. Thus, scanning a 5,000-stock universe was never a good use of my time. Focusing on stocks within themes has made my life much simpler. Since the themes are in high-growth areas, stocks within each theme provide sufficient opportunities to achieve my goals.

I don't spend much time studying cash flows and price-earnings (P/E) ratios. However, I do prefer stocks with strong fundamental underpinnings. I have found that *Investor's Business Daily* (*IBD*)'s earnings per share (EPS) and relative strength (RS) ranking system is adequate for my needs. I always cross-reference stocks with *IBD* before purchasing.

Since my drubbing in 2000, I have become a believer in technical analysis for devising entry and exit points. If I'd had a simple rule like selling any stock once it broke its 200-day moving average, I still might have been able to hang it up and be financially free at the end of 2000.

I discovered the final cornerstones of my approach in 2003 when I read two books: *Trading for a Living* by Dr. Alexander Elder (John Wiley & Sons, 1992) and *Trade Your Way to Financial Freedom* by Dr. Van Tharp (McGraw-Hill, 1999). Since both were published prior to 2000, once again, I should be writing this from a Caribbean Island. Obviously, I say that in jest; without the loss, I might not have internalized the information in the books anyway. In other words, losses are a part of this game. They are the master teacher.

The books talk about three items that are now integral to my trading strategy:

1. *Psychology*—understanding how you respond to fear and greed. (I have very little fear, and that can be hazardous without #2 and #3.)
2. *Risk management*—how to protect your capital.
3. *Money management*—how much to allocate and when to add more money to a trade. The secret to the market is not only being right, but making a lot of money when you are right. That comes down to money management.

FAVORITE SETUP

A general rule of thumb is that markets trend 15 to 30 percent of the time and they are range-bound the remainder of the time. If this is true, the market will be favorable for trend trading (my preferred style) only two or three times a year. Over the past year, I have observed a couple of traders who are quite successful trading only during this favorable period. Eventually I would like to get to that point, but to date I have been trading both in season and out of season. However, I trade a different setup in a range-bound market than in a trending one.

In a range-bound market, the objective is to buy the dips and sell the rips. Obviously, that's much easier said than done. I have had success using the two-period Relative Strength Index (RSI) as a guide (see Figure 3.1). The objective is to buy when the RSI is below 10 (oversold) and to sell when it is above 90 (overbought). Actually, the more oversold (below 1) or overbought (above 99), the better. This is a modification of the standard 14-period RSI that most traders use.

I discovered this strategy in Larry Connors and Cesar Alvarez's book *Short Term Trading Strategies That Work* (TradingMarkets, 2008). Their studies found that shortening the time frame produced superior results.

Log Me In (LOGM) as shown in Figure 3.2 is a great example of a stock transitioning from a range to a trend trade (my favorite play). It is not overly important to get into the first stocks that move out of the transition. Sometimes they get to the good grass and sometimes the lion eats them. If it is truly a transition to a trending market, many stocks will follow.

Let's break down this play (shown in Figure 3.2) in detail:

1. The 20, 50, and 200 exponential moving averages (EMAs) were in perfect alignment (20EMA > 50EMA > 200EMA) and had been since March. However, the downward-sloping moving average convergence/divergence (MACD) signified that the stock wasn't quite ready to start trending.
2. The bounce off the August 12 low followed by the MACD cross on August 18 were signs that its behavior was changing.
3. On August 27, it was clear that the low (28.63) from the prior three days was a turning point (a pivot low). I love placing stops slightly below pivot lows. With a reasonable place to establish a stop and strong candle intact, August 27 proved to be an ideal buying opportunity (30.46) for a trend trade.
4. As the saying goes, cut your losses quickly and let your winners run. With the initial stop in place, the losses were covered; now it was time to manage the trade, leaving it enough room to run.
5. As the trade developed, my job was to look for opportunities to raise my stop. Each higher low (HL) became an ideal spot to raise the stop. The objective was to simply continue raising the stop until the trade was stopped out. LOGM was looking like a sweet win.

FIGURE 3.1 AAPL Breaks Out from a Long-Term Range
Source: © StockCharts.com.

Now let me address one final detail. In my opinion, it's the most important aspect of trading—risk management. This is not a game to me. If a trade gets too out of control, I may not be able to recover and might have to go back to working 9 to 5. So, before entering a trade, I know exactly where my losses will be cut (initial stop). I like to place this stop slightly below the most recent pivot low. In LOGM's case, the stop was placed a nickel below the August 27 low at 28.58. There are many ways to determine stops, and this is just my personal preference. For many traders, risk mitigation ends with a stop; however, I like to take it one step further by incorporating money management.

FIGURE 3.2 Transition from a Range to a Trend, LOGM Daily Chart
Source: © StockCharts.com.

My preference is to not risk more than 1 to 2 percent of my portfolio on any trade. Thus, \$2,000 would be the most that could be lost on a trade in a \$100,000 portfolio. Often, I will set my initial risk at 1.2 percent or less. Where does the 1.2 percent come from? It's just a level that I have become comfortable with. My stops are often in the 6 percent range, and I like allocating 20 percent to a trade (0.06×0.2). If the stock requires a larger initial stop, I allocate a smaller position (8 percent stop, 15 percent allocation). The converse is also true. A tighter stop will allow a larger position (4 percent stop,

30 percent allocation). If a trade dictates a tighter stop (e.g., 4 percent), I may not allocate the entire 30 percent. I may allocate only 25 percent, thus reducing my overall portfolio risk from 1.2 percent to 1 percent.

Extending this money management concept to LOGM, assuming a portfolio of $100,000 with maximum risk of 1.2 percent per trade:

Initial risk = [(Purchase price/Stop) – 1] = [(30.46/28.58) – 1] = 6.6%
Allocation = 20% (*Note:* Stop was between 6 percent and 8 percent; used discretion to choose 20 percent)
Dollars in trade = 0.2 × $100,000 = $20,000
Shares purchased = $20,000/30.46 = 657 shares

WORDS OF WISDOM

Regardless of what you think of The Donald (Donald Trump), he says some profound stuff from time to time. A quote of his that I think of often is: "Never, ever give up. Never quit. You can never be successful if you give up." I could have easily given up after my failed video production company. I could have given up after the disaster in 2000. I may stumble again and have to go back to working a 9 to 5 job. However, I was also taught at an early age to "rest if you must, but don't you quit." Truer words were never spoken.

CHAPTER 4

Know Thyself

Chris Peruna, @chrisperuna

Chris is a great trend follower with an impressive track record. He keeps investing simple. I have been reading his blog since my Wallstrip.com days, and he is a must-follow on StockTwits. The StockTwits stream is about ideas, but sticking with trends is not an idea that needs constant attention. Less is often more. Chris makes less *great.*

Successful traders always follow the line of least resistance—
follow the trend—the trend is your friend.

—Jesse Livermore

FOLLOWING IN THE STEPS OF MY FATHER

I am a part-time trader with a full-time career in architecture.

As a teenager, I first gained an interest in trading from my father, who also traded stocks and options from the 1970s to the 1990s. My father's specialty was to trend trade the major moving averages with a focus on stocks with strong earnings and sales. To this day, I still trade heavily based on his trending 200-day moving average plays, although I have slightly modified my screening methods to incorporate more technical analysis than fundamental analysis.

I am looking for gains of 25 percent or more and losses no larger than 7 to 10 percent (preferably smaller). Please understand that this 7 to 10 percent loss is calculated into a position sizing spreadsheet that risks only a maximum of 1 to 3 percent of total capital in that account. The foundation of my approach is rooted in the CAN SLIM philosophy, but I developed my system with detailed position-sizing calculations and money management rules from Dr. Van Tharp's teachings and books. (CAN SLIM, developed by *Investor's*

Business Daily editor William O'Neil, stands for Current earnings, Annual earnings, New product or service, Supply and demand, Leader or laggard?, Institutional sponsorship, and Market indexes.)

I am much more consistent and profitable as a medium- and longer-term trend trader than as a day trader (even more so on the long side). I don't need to be everything all the time as long as I continue to focus on the areas that bring me the greatest success. Understanding myself has been my holy grail of understanding how to trade the market with consistency and profitability. I spot a trend, then trade the trend (up or down), and always cut losses before they become damaging.

THE TREND IS YOUR FRIEND

I am a trend trader who looks for opportunities in individual stocks within an intermediate time frame. I am looking to hold a stock anywhere from a few weeks to several months on both the long and the short side (a holding period of a year or longer is not out of the question). I focus on the long side based on my CAN SLIM roots but have become more comfortable placing short trades when the market is trending downward. I will cut a loser in the first day of trading if it shows a loss and won't hesitate to take a profit in as little as a week if it hits my target. My targets and stops are based on risk-to-reward ratios using support and resistance setups derived from technical analysis.

I aim to trade in situations when the odds are in my favor by properly employing risk management strategies such as position sizing and expectancy. My method exclusively uses after-market data, which allows me to focus on the big picture without any noise. I have developed profitable techniques using reliable stock screens that focus on both fundamental and technical criteria.

BASE FORMATIONS ON QUIET VOLUME

I screen for stocks that appear ripe to break out of consolidated bases on above-average volume. These bases show the stock trending upward along or slightly above both the 50-day and 200-day moving averages. Some may refer to these bases as flat patterns, cup-with-handle patterns, or head-and-shoulders patterns (also referred to as the Dow Theory reversal or 1-2-3 setup), but I am just looking for a base formation on quiet volume. It is critical to study the breakouts by reviewing weekly charts, which allows me to establish the accumulation or distribution along with volume confirmation. I favor stocks that are new to the market within the past two years—recent initial public offerings (IPOs). These stocks tend to have increasing earnings, innovative new products, and a chart without overhead resistance or selling pressure.

THE MASTERCARD TRADE

MasterCard (MA) is the perfect example of the typical setup I am looking for. (See Figure 4.1.) The stock debuted in May 2006 and traded sideways for about two months before breaking out and starting its first uptrend. Following a five-month uptrend, the stock started to consolidate and form a new sideways pattern on mostly quiet volume.

The criteria that allow this stock to make my fundamental screens are:

- Earnings per share (EPS) rating is increasing.
- Relative price strength (RS) rating is rising.
- Current price is greater than or equal to $10 per share.
- IPO date: Stock debuted within the past two years.
- Market capitalization is greater than or equal to $100 million.

Note: I use proprietary information for EPS and RS ratings from Daily Graphs.

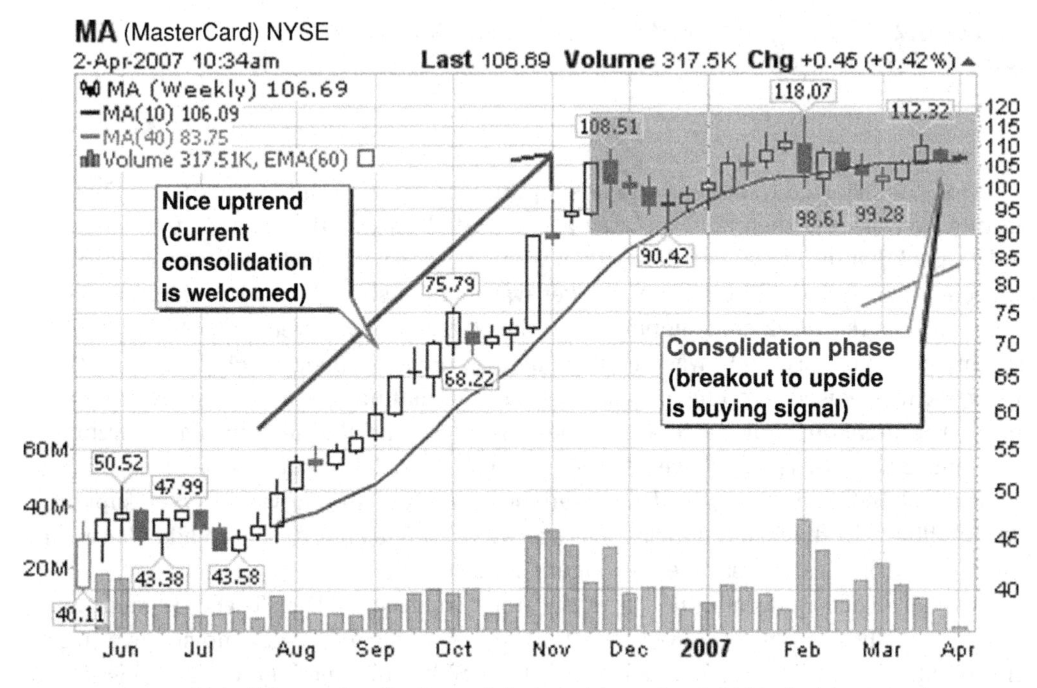

FIGURE 4.1 MA (MasterCard) Consolidating Near Its 10-Week Moving Average, Weekly Chart
Source: © StockCharts.com.

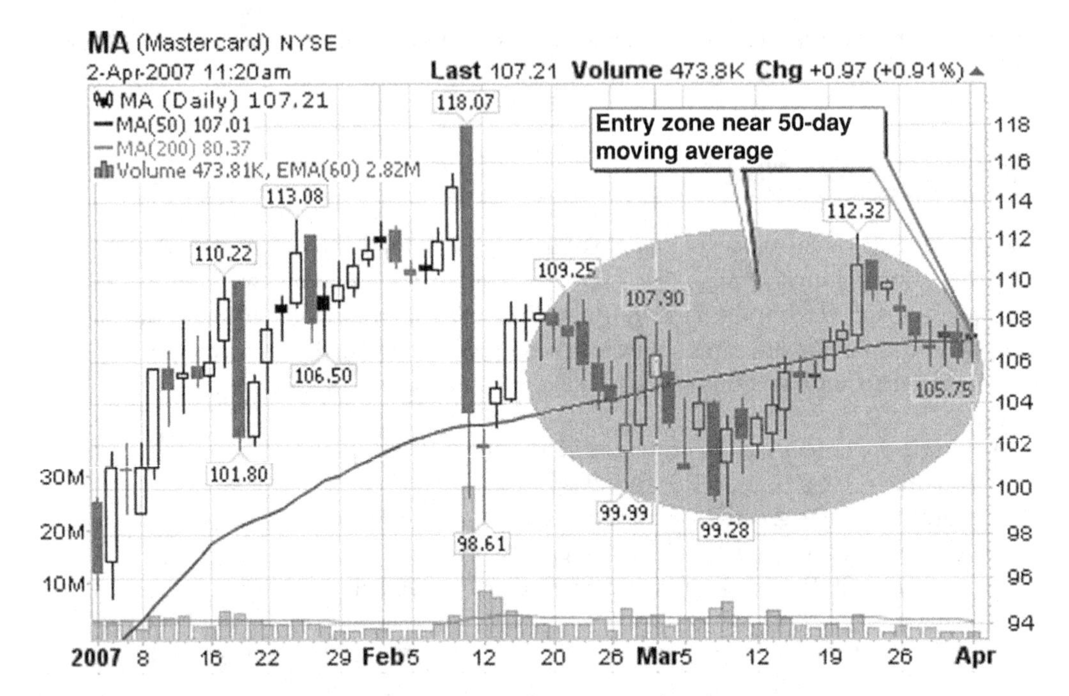

FIGURE 4.2 Going Long MA (MasterCard) Here, Daily Chart
Source: © StockCharts.com.

The stock started to appear on my support screens as it pulled back to the 50-day moving average and then held the area as support. This was the case for four months and a signal that the stock was shaking out weak holders while institutions were starting to accumulate, quietly. The general market was gaining strength, so I decided to place initial buys as the stock held support along the 50-day moving average (see Figure 4.2). The breakout in April 2007 was accompanied by huge volume, which confirmed that the stock was poised to go higher and that institutional investors were supporting the move. The breakout took place above the $118 mark and the new uptrend continued until June 2008 with a peak above $300 per share. The stock had several pullbacks during the uptrend, but it never negatively violated the critical 200-day moving average support. Each pullback to the 50-day moving average was another opportunity to add shares or enter a position for the first time (see Figure 4.3).

The sell signal came later in 2008 as the stock confirmed a Dow Theory reversal and then eventually went on to trade below both the 50-day and 200-day moving averages. This breakdown also took place as the M in CAN SLIM (the market) was showing signs of weakness.

FIGURE 4.3 A High-Volume Breakout above $118
Source: © StockCharts.com.

WORDS OF WISDOM

The beauty of the stock market is that you don't have to be right all the time in order to be profitable. If you learn to focus your investment to the market leaders and manage risk accordingly, you will be well ahead of the crowd. It is just like Bernard Baruch said: "If a speculator is correct half of the time, he is hitting a good average. Even being right 3 or 4 times out of 10 should yield a person a fortune if he has the sense to cut his losses quickly on the ventures where he is wrong."

CHAPTER 5

Insider Information Is Reflected in the Charts

Keith Kern, @stt2318

The most successful traders have simple strategies. Keith understands that less is more and he focuses his efforts where it really matters—price action. He shows up every day on the StockTwits stream and shares an incredible number of ideas. He gets that StockTwits is an "idea network."

There is no substitute for hard work. Hard work creates good luck.
—Thomas Edison

MARKET BIO

I entered the trading business as an investment representative, working briefly for Merrill Lynch and also Edward Jones. As a broker I discovered that a brokerage house focused more on sales than on proper equity selection. I realized that the only way to learn about what drives stock prices is to study market psychology by researching the behavior of thousands of individual stocks in different time frames. My studies led me to technical analysis.

When I became confident enough in my ability to trade based on technical analysis, I left my position at Merrill Lynch in 2001 and began trading my own account full-time. While it was a huge decision to do this while supporting a young family, I quickly realized it was the right one for me. Trading successfully led me to meet others online who were pursuing the same goal but using techniques different from my own. I would say a key milestone in my success has been marrying my own technical skills with those of a fellow trader (full partner since 2006) who uses fundamental stock analysis. I found the combination of technical and fundamental analysis to be powerful in achieving a high success rate of profitable trades.

BREAKOUTS FROM LONG CONSOLIDATION

I target stocks that have patterns of long-term consolidation. I establish long or short positions on initial breaks of these patterns and continue to trade them as they move up or down. A typical position will not exceed 10 percent of my portfolio and I maintain a 50 percent cash position at all times. I am nimble in my trading and do not hold a position if it is not performing as expected. I will sell half of a position on a successful break to lock in a profit and scale out of more of the position as it approaches the target or stops out at or above the initial breakout.

I have found that more often than not that information will seep into a stock's trading pattern long before that information is ever disseminated publicly. This is true for many reasons. For instance, professional analysts or money managers have far greater access to a company than the average investor has. Based on what they learn, they will act accordingly long before their reason is widely known. While the reason for their actions may remain unknown, their behavior will be reflected in the trading volumes and activity of a given stock. This is only one way such information seeps into market action. There are many.

The ability to discern this reflected knowledge gives me a distinct advantage in trading profitably. This advantage is further enhanced by trading with a partner rooted in fundamental analysis.

FIGURE 5.1 Breaking Out after Long Consolidation, FARO Daily Chart
Source: © StockCharts.com.

BREAKOUT FROM A LONG BASE

My favorite setup involves a stock that has been trading sideways for a period of time and has tested resistance many times. I will establish a position as this pattern breaks prior tops when the breakout is accompanied by (and this is most critical) impressive relative volume expansion. I will then trade in and out of these setups as they move higher over time. I will use stops on the way up at prior resistance points, which will then act as new support levels. In addition, I use the Relative Strength Index (RSI) and moving average convergence/divergence (MACD) to look for positive divergences in these setups as they advance.

A typical example of my favorite setup can be seen in Figure 5.1, featuring FARO Technologies (FARO).

Every time when a stock makes a high-volume breakout from a multiyear range, you should pay attention. Something significant has happened, and it has changed the supply/demand dynamics. High volume is an indicator of institutional involvement, and most institutional investors don't start to accumulate positions without doing their homework.

PART II

Value Investing

CHAPTER 6

Margin of Safety

Todd Sullivan, *@toddsullivan*

Todd is a friend so I am a little biased, but I trust him. He actually manages a bit of my money. Value investing is very different from all other investing styles you will read about in this book. It is a different discipline. I am more comfortable investing in start-up Web deals, which are even more illiquid but have a value that is picked out of thin air. There are so many ways to invest capital, but value sounds the simplest. It is *not*. Todd finds value with a hidden catalyst that most would never notice. He digs deep and he's smart. Todd's blog is a great place to watch his game plan unfold daily and to learn from a true professional.

Buy fear and sell greed.

—Warren Buffett

INVESTING BIO

I have owned various businesses my entire life. I was 18 when I started a pool installation company to pay my way through college. As a business owner you gain a unique perspective into operation and business cycles. These experiences led me to value investing and the thought process that buying a stock was not simply buying a piece of paper to trade away; it was buying a real stake in a business. The decision process behind buying a stock of a publicly traded company is no different than buying a local business. I have successfully used the same approach in my investing for the past 15 years.

In January 2007 I started a blog to share my thoughts on investing and the current state of the economy. Having developed a following, in September 2009 I moved the blog over to the StockTwits network and offered a paid model. The success of the blog and the returns generated for its subscribers led to the formation of my hedge fund, Rand Strategic Partners, in December 2009.

HUNTING FOR VALUE

I look for pricing dislocations between the current price of a company and its real value. Buying a stock at a big-enough discount to its actual value gives me a large margin of safety. I use fundamental analysis and focus on a company's balance sheet to determine its financial health. Once I determine that the balance sheet is in good shape, I then look at the company's operations, objectives, management, and products and try to determine why it is trading at such a large discount. If all the parameters just mentioned are in order, I then look for a catalyst that could help to unlock the value of the company.

A good company can remain cheap for years unless there is a catalyst to help unlock that value. It can be a new product, management addition or subtraction, new line of business, or something else. Whatever that upcoming catalyst might be, I need to have a high degree of certainty it will be successful.

Once I determine it is likely to be successful, I set quarterly benchmarks to track the performance of any initiative. As long as the company continues to make progress toward its goals, it remains a holding. If it falters, depending on the reason for the shortcoming, I will sell. Once the goal is met and the company is fairly valued, I sell and look for another opportunity.

FAVORITE SETUP

My ideal setup begins with sheer panic in either an individual stock or the market itself. Unabated selling leads to wonderful opportunities for those willing to look past the price declines to see what the company is worth.

The logic is thus: An event happens that causes market participants to extrapolate a permanent impairment on a company when in reality the condition is only temporary. When the condition is rectified, the company will begin to trade again at its real value. That expectation of permanence, however, causes a large and swift price reduction and creates the value opportunity.

This fits my approach of buying good businesses at great prices. There are many reasons a particular asset may be changing hands at a price well below its true value. Many times those reasons are valid, but sometime they are not. In a short-term perspective, equities prices are heavily impacted by risk appetites and emotions. Because of that we can often find people willing to sell pieces of a company (stocks) at prices that do not reflect their true value.

Where do I find them? The 52-week low list is a good starting point. You can do various stock screens for low price-to-book ratio, low price-earnings (P/E) ratio, and so on. Have a favorite investor? Go to the Securities and Exchange Commission (SEC) web site at www.sec.gov, check out company filings, and see what companies are doing. Then go do your homework on each one. Does the investment make sense to you? Is it still cheap? It might be worth a look. Follow other value investing blogs and read periodicals and the like. The point is that there is no one right way, but the more you look around, the more you increase your chances of finding good value.

Another great way is to simply look around your surroundings. Is there a retailer at the mall that you read was left for dead a year ago and now you see lines out the door? Is there a new tenant that everyone is talking about? Do you find yourself buying products from company A recently when you had always bought from its competitor, company B? Is there a new fast-food chain or retailer coming into your area and opening a bunch of new stores or one there expanding into other towns?

I operate under the "I'm not that different from most folks" mantra. That tells me that if I have made a major purchasing shift for whatever reason, chances are a whole lot of other people have probably done the same. Now, that does not mean the shift is into a cheap company, but if you catch it soon enough, it may very well be cheap relative to its potential value. The analysis of a company whose products you know and use is far easier than starting from scratch.

HOW DO YOU MANAGE RISK?

Risk is controlled by buying the company at a cheap-enough price. If you can buy a company for essentially the market value of its liquid assets—(Cash + Accounts receivable + Inventory) – (Accounts payable + Debt)—then your margin of safety is huge. It is rare for a good company to trade at this level. This offers a large degree of safety regarding any potential downside risk. If your investment thesis turns out to be wrong, the proceeds from an eventual liquidation would offset any potential capital losses.

Positions must be kept manageable at first. When investing in turnarounds, it's important to have a small position initially that could be increased later as certain milestones in management's plan are met. If management has a one-year plan and has made little progress after two quarters, money should not be added to this holding (it may also be the right time to consider exiting). However, if the managers are ahead of their plan and the stock remains cheap, then incremental increases are warranted.

I don't believe in diversification as a way to manage risk. Frankly, the logic escapes me. It essentially says that I ought to own something in a certain sector because I do not own anything in that sector. What if the only stocks in that category worth owning are very expensive? Should I buy them? What if the only stocks there that are cheap are cheap because they are lousy companies? Should I still buy them because they are cheap and I need to own something in that sector? If the best stocks are great companies and very cheap, should I buy only one so I do not become too concentrated in one sector?

It makes far more sense to me to concentrate your portfolio on your "best ideas." When Warren Buffett's Berkshire Hathaway had its best years it held a very concentrated portfolio. Pre-Berkshire (the Buffett Partnership) typically held only a few names. This is not the case today simply because of its size. You cannot run a concentrated portfolio with more than $100 billion to invest. In fact, at one point, Buffett had 40 percent of Berkshire's portfolio in one name—American Express. Today the best mutual fund manager of the past decade, Bruce Berkowitz of the Fairholme Funds, typically holds no more than 10 names. Hedge fund manager Bill Ackman, who has beat the S&P 500 index by earning 298 percent to the S&P's 11 percent since his fund's inception, generally holds six to eight names.

If I own 7 to 10 stocks that I know inside and out and I think are screaming bargains, does it really make sense to buy a home builder because my portfolio lacks one? Now, if owning your 7 to 10 "best ideas" diversifies you across many different categories, then that is wonderful, I guess. The point is, investors should not simply buy something in a particular category because they feel obligated to. They should buy it only if it is a great company trading at a great price.

Further, margin is to be avoided at all costs. It does two things: magnify returns and magnify losses. There is one major rule in value investing—you don't want to become a forced seller. Give your investing thesis enough time to develop. Give Mr. Market enough time to recognize the value of your stocks. By magnifying losses, margin calls also make them permanent. If you are only 80 percent invested, you can never be forced by the gyrations of the market to become a seller. Your losses remain only on paper and your positions are given a chance to recover when the market does so. And if you did your homework, a recovery is to be expected. What margin does is take what may be a temporary drop in a portfolio's value and turn it into a permanent one as you are forced to liquidate stocks at losses to satisfy margin calls. Besides, it is always a good idea to have enough cash on hand to take advantage of new emerging value opportunities. You never know when they will appear.

GOING WITH iGo

I utilize the so-called liquid assets (current assets) approach. I want to know, for every dollar I am spending to purchase shares of a company, what I am getting in terms of its more liquid assets after all liabilities are subtracted. I give no value to property, plant, and equipment, or to other assets like patents and trademarks. While these assets certainly have value, that value is debatable and not easily monetized in a worst-case scenario. Typically if they have to be monetized, it is done at material discount to their carrying value. Because of that, I omit them from the equation and consider whatever value they may bring as a bonus. A company with at least 50 percent of its liquid assets represented in the current share price warrants a far closer look as to its investment suitability.

Here is the formula:

$$[\text{Cash} + (\text{Accounts receivable} * .75 + \text{Inventory} * .75) + \text{Prepaid}]$$
$$-(\text{Accounts payable} + \text{Accrued} + \text{Debt})/\text{Shares}$$

Per Share Analysis			
	Balance Sheet	Value	Current Price
Cash	$33,570,000	$33,570,000	$1.14
Receivables	7,300,000	5,475,000	
Inventory	3,870,000	1,935,000	
Prepaid Expense	480,000	480,000	
		41,460,000	
Payables	4,550,000		Per Share Value
Accrued Expense	2,700,000		$1.06
Debt	0		
		7,250,000	
Shares	32,410,000		% of Share Price
			93%

FIGURE 6.1 Valuation Model
Data as of 6/30/2009 prior to purchase.

It should be noted here that receivables and inventory discounts vary by industry in terms of the likelihood of collections. Let's look at iGo, Inc., which is a company that sells innovative accessories for mobile electronic devices, as an example. Inputting the numbers for iGo gives us the model shown in Figure 6.1.

This gives a liquid value of $1.06 a share versus the $1.14 market price. We are spending 8 cents per share for the rest of the company's business. Risking 8 cents to potentially make 20 to 30 times more? This is what I call a good risk-to-reward ratio.

Once we know the company has a cheap valuation, we then want to find out why and what the company has going on that will cause its real value to be realized.

Why was iGo so cheap?

The short answer is that previous management wasn't the best in class, to put it kindly, and had positioned the company essentially as a producer of chargers for another company, Targus. New management came in, developed its current technology, and began to produce universal chargers under the iGo name. The Targus contract was canceled and the company essentially started over as it worked to get retailers to carry its new product. During this time there was substantial doubt about the company's ability to survive.

What did I expect?

The iGo enterprise had a very strong balance sheet and a product that was unlike anything else on the market at the time. This is still true today (November 2010). After buying and using the product, I came to the conclusion that this company had a unique product that worked as advertised and one that retailers would want to carry.

Soon after our purchase iGo secured retail space in Staples, Office Max, Office Depot, Best Buy airport kiosks, Wal-Mart, and Verizon Wireless. Then its laptop charger won "Best Green Gadget" from *LAPTOP* magazine and its netbook charger was named a *PC* magazine "Best Product."

With these new deals, the stock began to climb. In August 2010, iGo was awarded its first patent for its "Vampire Power" technology, acquired UK-based Adapt Mobile, and began its first TV and radio ad campaign to increase sales.

Fall 2010 brought deals with Cisco Systems for its flip camera and Texas Instruments to develop and market the iGo Green Chip for distribution to original equipment manufacturers (OEMs).

The stock of iGo is still very cheap as of November 2010, and the company presents a strong balance sheet and impressive possibilities. Management has expressed the wish "to aggressively monetize the patent," and the most likely way to do that is through licensing deals. The chip could be embedded in appliances, electronics, and other devices to mitigate their energy consumption, and iGo would simply collect money for the chip's use. I would also expect the current distribution network to expand materially and profits to begin to ramp up.

I expect licensing deals to commence in 2011 with OEMs and the company's bottom line to improve significantly.

CHAPTER 7

The BeanScreen

Daniel Miller and Jason Robinson, @*wallstreetbean*

Daniel and Jason love social media and the intersection of stocks. Daniel and Jason have a great attitude, keep things simple, and, because they believe in the value process of stock picking, have set themselves apart on the stream and built a great audience to hear and discuss their strategies and ideas. As I like to say at StockTwits, it is not about the production and money, but the ideas and the strategy.

As long as we're right with more than half our money, more than half the time, we're good.

—Wall Street Bean

SUCCESSFUL INVESTING REQUIRES DUE DILIGENCE AND TIME

The great tech run of the late 1990s attracted our attention to the stock market initially. Being poor college students at the time, we were amazed and fascinated at how much money was being made in technology companies. For the few years leading up to the peak of the NASDAQ Composite, it appeared anyone could invest in anything and make money. No research or study seemed to be required. Just throw some cash at an Internet start-up and you could double your money in a few months! Watching the NASDAQ reach all-time highs in early 2000 was the catalyst that finally got us to put our own money into the stock market. In hindsight, that was the worst possible time for us to start investing. Without much experience and knowledge of the markets, we made some poor investments. When the tech bubble finally popped and the NASDAQ came crashing back to earth, so did our portfolio. By the time the markets finally bottomed out in October 2002, we had learned a valuable lesson: *Successful investing requires due diligence and time.* From then on, we began to implement a long-term value strategy that approached investing from a fundamental perspective. By the fall of 2003, we had the beginnings of a fundamental screening system in place, focused on evaluating the nuts and bolts of a company's balance sheet and financial health. A few years later, we began to see the fruits of our labor pay off consistently.

My name is Daniel Miller. My father bought me my first lawn mower when I was 12 years old. Growing weary of cutting the family's lawn week after week with nothing to show for it but sweat and grass stains, I decided to take my trusty Murray to the streets of the 'hood. I mowed three or four lawns per weekend for $15 to $20 a pop. This money was deposited into an interest-bearing savings account each Monday until my junior year of high school. Later, led by the desire for a better return on my hard-earned dollars, I put my money in a mutual fund (the Alliance Technology Fund). This was my first foray into the investing world. After about six years of squirreling away dollars in the fund and watching the tech bubble expand month after month, I of course became increasingly interested in the stock market. Though riskier than most mutual funds, the idea of investing in individually strong, well-managed companies with healthy balance sheets became very appealing. If one did his homework, the return on investment could be much greater, and being the lover of number crunching that I am, uncovering and studying the bare-bones fundamentals of a company's balance sheet from an analytical approach sounded like a good time.

My partner in the Wall Street Bean, Jason Robinson, is a lifelong friend of mine. As a child, Jason was a compulsive saver and hard worker. In the fifth grade he once spent an entire weekend slaving away at a nursery, hauling grass pallets for $100. This bought him the Air Jordan sneakers that he had been so coveting that year. In hindsight, he wishes he had bought some Nike shares instead. Jason became interested in the stock market while in college and after graduating began discussing strategies and ideas with me. An avid reader and watcher of financial literature and media, Jason's specialty is studying and interpreting the macroeconomic trends taking shape in the world today, and how they might affect the companies we follow.

THE TORTOISE AND THE HARE

As a child, one of my favorite bedtime readings was from a book of Aesop's fables. Within those wondrous pages resided the classic story of "The Tortoise and the Hare." Whether it had a subliminal effect on my investing philosophy, or life in general, I'll never know for sure, but it is analogous to how Jason and I approach the markets today. Our philosophy is that technical patterns and psychology often dictate the short-term movements in the markets and individual stocks; but the basic, hard-core fundamentals eventually shine through over longer time periods for stocks as the short-term fluctuations are smoothed out.

We are value investors, because this approach makes a lot of sense to us. Over time, market fluctuations based on technicals or psychology will inevitably create oversold conditions for certain sectors, industries, or individual stocks. When the pendulum swings to the oversold end of the spectrum, fundamentally strong companies may become attractive from a valuation standpoint, regardless of the current market sentiment or technicals. Combining solid underlying fundamentals with favorable valuations is key to how we discover stocks with long-term investing potential.

We are not out to make a quick buck on a fast trade. Our goal is to have strong, steady returns over the months and years to come with a "buy and kinda hold" approach. That is to say, we are not against taking profits around a core position in the near term if we are able to realize substantial gains, but generally our strategy is geared toward uncovering companies that are leaders in their industries and exhibit consistently strong fundamentals over intermediate (six-month) to long-term (two-year) time frames. Once we have done that, we look for value. It can be tricky finding the optimal entry point when purchasing a stock, but if a company on our watch list is trading at a discount to most industry average valuations, then we become very interested. Frequently we seek out the advice of a technical trader on the StockTwits stream to determine an ideal entry based on short-term or long-term support levels.

THE BEANSCREEN

After several years of listening to pundits on television hype this or that stock during the height of the dot-com bubble, and reading endless financial articles by so-called stock-picking gurus, we realized that it doesn't take a genius or professional to invest wisely. It just takes some patience, practice, and effort. At that time, none of the online screens that we came across offered the capability of quickly screening a specific company against a customized set of parameters to determine how many of those parameters it passed or failed against. For example, in all the screens we could find, you started the process by selecting a wide range of parameters (e.g., P/E, gross margins, return on equity), with the benchmarks of your choice (e.g., P/E < 12, gross margins $> 50\%$, return on equity $> 20\%$). Next, you hit "enter" and the screens would crank out any number of stocks that met all the criteria you selected. If a stock didn't pass *all* the benchmarks for *all* the parameters selected, then it was not generated in the results. This all-or-none system drove us crazy. We didn't care if some stocks couldn't pass *all* our benchmark requirements for the parameters we selected. We just wanted to know *how many* of the benchmarks it passed. In the fall of 2003, we decided to start doing our own research, and as a result the beginnings of the BeanScreen took shape.

In laying down the foundation of the BeanScreen, we first compiled an array of fundamental parameters into an Excel spreadsheet from six major statistical categories that we found on MSN Money at http://money.msn.com:

1. Growth rates
2. Price ratios
3. Profit margins
4. Financial condition
5. Return on investment
6. Management efficiency

We also tossed in some additional parameters such as relative strength, insider ownership, and institutional ownership.

Next, we set benchmarks for the parameters in each category by which a stock either passed or failed. We also incorporated industry average metrics into the mix, using the same pass or fail system. For example, if a company had a price-to-sales ratio greater than the industry average, then it failed that metric. If that same company had net margins greater than the industry average, then it passed that metric. Then we devised a simple binary scoring system, awarding a stock 1 point for a "pass" and 0 points for a "fail"; thus the more benchmarks a company passed, the higher the score. Any data that might be missing or not currently available for a parameter was assigned 0.25 point. Finally, we decided that keeping a trailing history on select companies' scores would be ideal to detect trends in their fundamental health over time.

So in a nutshell, that is how the BeanScreen was initially conceived and put together. Over the years it has been tweaked and adjusted, with the biggest change being made to how a company's statistical data was uploaded into the screen. What used to be done painstakingly by hand each quarter blessedly became mostly automated in 2008, when my cousin Sean Miller discovered an add-in program for Excel created by Randy Harmelink called the Stock Market Functions Add-In. This program allowed us to upload the statistical data for the parameters we screened against with the click of a button. Sean then created a new spreadsheet design with our binary scoring system incorporated into the screen. In four steps it works like this:

1. A company's ticker is entered into a field.
2. Statistics are generated via the add-in program for selected parameters.
3. Statistics are screened against 80-plus parameter benchmarks set by us.
4. A score is calculated using our pass/fail system.

Since 2003, we have screened thousands of stocks, of which approximately 500 remain on our monthly screening list. If a new stock passes our preliminary screen, it is added to our tracking list. If a stock fails to score well initially, or over time shows a dramatic decrease in fundamental strength, it is kicked out of the BeanScreen until its situation improves. In determining our monthly fundamental strength rankings, stocks are screened and scored on a scale of 0 to 85. Over time, an average score and rank is compiled and calculated for each company. As mentioned, the higher the score, the stronger a company's overall fundamental health. Here is the simple breakdown:

60–85 = Very strong
50–59 = Strong
40–49 = Average
30–39 = Weak
00–29 = Very weak

Our monthly rankings are *not* a "buy" list, but an index of companies that we believe exhibit very healthy fundamentals. We track their performance collectively via our screening model, the WSB20, just to get a feel for how they behave, irrespective of price entry, compared to the broader markets. Whether a stock is at a 52-week high or low, or somewhere in between, does not matter. The index is rebalanced on the first day of each quarter with the new top 20 and tracked solely on fundamental strength, *not* value.

The Wall Street Bean's mission each month is to provide our followers and readers with ideas and opinions from a fundamental perspective to be used as a stepping-stone for further research and analysis. We often seek out advice and information from other investors and technical traders on the Twitter and StockTwits streams, and highly recommend that our readers do the same. Learning about other investing styles and strategies can be a valuable tool in helping investors improve upon their own methods of research and analysis.

EQUITY SELECTION

The underlying logic behind our equity selection process is that if a company exhibits strong overall fundamental strength over time (one to two years), is a consistent leader in its industry, and trades at a relative discount to its peers, then the chances are good that it will outperform the markets over time, especially during periods of broad market rallies. Just because a stock passes most of our screening criteria does not necessarily mean that we believe it will outperform the market. A company may screen well one month, but perform poorly the next. We don't feel comfortable investing in a stock for the long term until we have built up a scoring history based on our screen, generally for one or two years. If a company passes most of our criteria over that time frame, then we feel the odds are better for it to perform well versus the broader markets. This assumption comes from the index we have built based on our screening model, the WSB20. It is based solely on fundamental strength, *not* value. In tracking its performance, each stock was initially given an equal weighting and monitored for three months. It is rebalanced on the first day of each subsequent quarter (9/1, 12/1, 3/1, 6/1), with any gain or loss in value, including dividends, redistributed evenly among the new top 20. Since we began tracking the index on June 1, 2009, it has outperformed the S&P 500 index to date. We believe this is strong evidence that our screen can successfully uncover stocks with market-beating potential. If the WSB20 can outperform the markets over time based on fundamental strength alone, imagine the potential returns one could make by uncovering the best value plays within the group. That is what we aim to do each month with our personal accounts.

The *valuation* criteria we use when selecting a stock investment with strong underlying fundamentals are based on about 15 ratios (mostly price ratios). These ratios and the benchmarks we use to screen them against are generally as follows:

1. Current P/E < 12
2. Current P/E < industry average
3. Forward P/E < 15
4. Price/sales < 2
5. Price/sales < industry average
6. Price/book < 2
7. Price/book < industry average
8. Price/cash flow < 10
9. Price/cash flow < industry average
10. PEG (5-year) < 1
11. PEG (5-year) < industry average
12. Book value/share > 5
13. Book value/share > industry average
14. Enterprise value/EBITDA < 10
15. Enterprise value/revenue < 2

If a stock passes most of these criteria, as well as exhibiting overall healthy fundamentals in the BeanScreen, we will strongly consider taking a position (using buy limit orders). In addition, we often ask the technical analysis experts on the StockTwits stream where they see long- and short-term support levels. This may help us in finding an optimal entry point when placing our buy limit order.

Our ideal setup is to first establish a core list of companies each month that have a history of exhibiting strong fundamentals and are scoring leaders within their respective industries. Next, we'll take a hard look at that list and prune it down to those stocks with the most attractive valuations, especially when compared to their industry averages. Then we set buy limits on the stocks we're interested in and then . . . we wait. We rarely place market orders, so it is not unusual for us to have a few days or even weeks pass before an order is filled . . . or not. If we hit on a buy, great. If a stock takes off and we miss out, it's no big deal. We are patient with our purchases, and if an opportunity passes us by, there is always another great company trading at a discount just around the corner.

RISK MANAGEMENT

To control risk we use three simple strategies:

1. If a stock's *valuation* parameters start to get *expensive* and/or its *price* has a nice *run-up* while remaining fundamentally *strong*, we'll unload some shares using a stop or sell limit and keep a core position.
2. If a stock's *valuation* parameters are *favorable* and its *price declines* dramatically while remaining fundamentally *strong*, we'll add to our position to bring our cost basis down.
3. If a stock's overall fundamentals *weaken* over time, regardless of *valuations* or *price*, we'll set a stop limit 5 to 10 percent below its market price and only raise it (never lower it) if the stock moves north. We will close the position entirely, for a loss if need be, if and when the stop is triggered.

When it comes to position sizing, we generally allocate up to 8 percent of our capital into a single investing idea for those stocks within our top 20 rankings, and up to 5 percent for others. Never using margin, we normally scale into a position over two to four entries (especially with high-beta stocks), but will sometimes take a full position all at once in low-beta names. Our investing style can best be described as "buy and kinda hold." We will often trade around a core position based on its valuation as long the underlying fundamentals remain strong. If a stock goes on a nice run, but begins to look overvalued relative to its industry peers, we will pare down our position by one-third or one-half and let the rest ride.

Our view on diversification is to own 30 to 40 stocks, all of which are fundamentally sound and leaders within their respective industries. By its very nature, the BeanScreen produces a diverse mix of excellent companies each month (both domestic and foreign), covering a wide range of industries. We aren't concerned about being overweight in a particular industry. Sometimes an industry as a whole can be oversold in our opinion, such as the offshore drillers after the BP oil leak in the Gulf of Mexico. In our view, this event created an ideal opportunity to invest heavily in fundamentally sound names trading at a discount. If the fundamentals appear strong and the valuations are attractive for multiple companies within an industry, we might create a basket of four to six stocks. For example, in the oil and gas drilling industry, we have owned the following stocks all at once in the past: NE, DO, ATW, and ESV. We have done the same with retail apparel as well with BKE, TRLG, ARO, and JOSB.

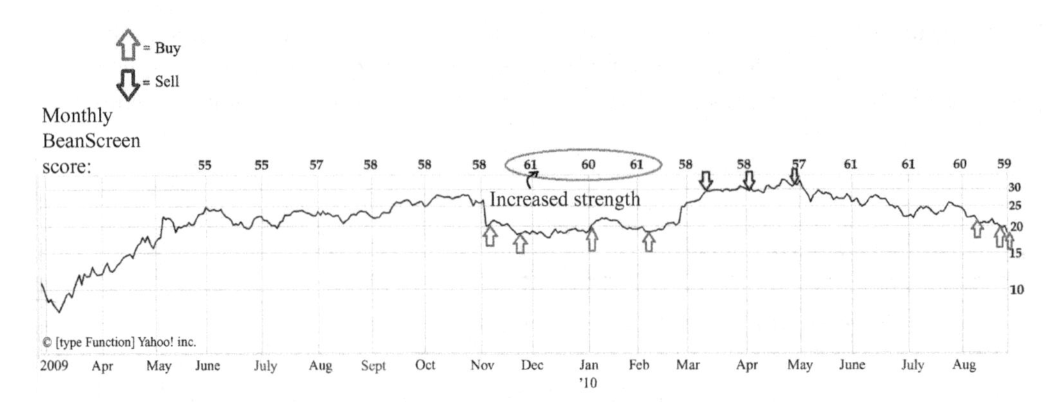

FIGURE 7.1 True Religion (TRLG)
Note the increase in BeanScreen scores after the price drop in November 2009. Valuations became very attractive, prompting us to purchase shares. As the stock price appreciated into the spring of 2010, we sold off shares, then once again bought more in August as the share price fell into our buy range.

HOW THE BEANSCREEN HAS HELPED OUR INVESTING

Now it is time to present a couple of examples of how our "buy and kinda hold" approach to investing, as a function of the BeanScreen, has worked for us in the real world. Figures 7.1 and 7.2 are two charts depicting how our investing strategy has played out with True Religion (TRLG) and Feihe International (formerly called American Dairy) (ADY). With TRLG, we made money along the way and continue to hold shares as of this discussion. With ADY, we lost money as the fundamentals went from great to bad to worse,

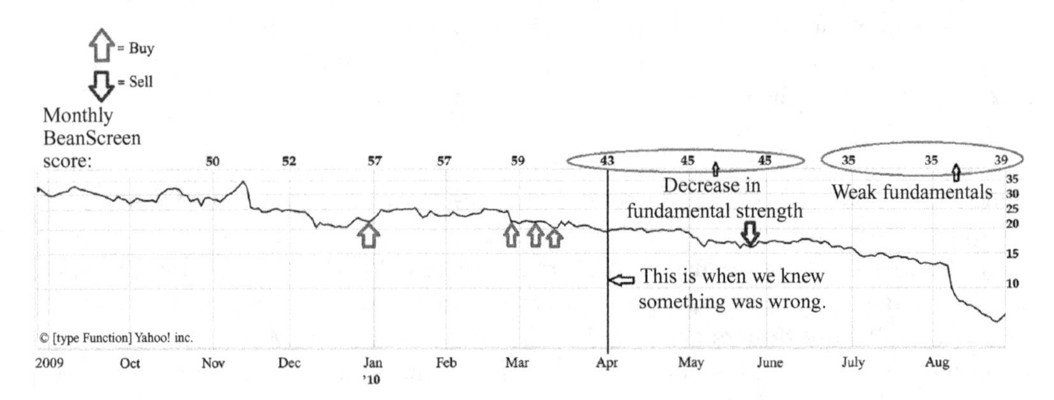

FIGURE 7.2 American Dairy (ADY)
In late March 2010, after a bad earnings report, the fundamentals dropped suddenly to 43 in the BeanScreen, prompting us to close out our position for a loss. Though an unwise investment, the BeanScreen saved us from realizing an even greater loss as the stock price dropped precipitously in August 2010.

but we were able to close out our position before things turned *really* nasty. As with all investments these days, it is important to stay vigilant and to routinely evaluate the fundamentals of a company's balance sheet.

With TRLG, we initiated a position on November 4, 2009, at $20.52 per share (see Figure 7.1). We had been following the company for about 14 months and were impressed with its consistently strong fundamentals. When the stock price dropped suddenly at the start of November, we noticed a jump in the BeanScreen score as valuations became very favorable. We added to our position three more times over the next few months as TRLG's fundamentals remained healthy and valuations stayed attractive. As March 2010 approached, the stock price began its climb toward $30 per share. On March 11, we sold one-fourth of our position at $29.26 as valuations became less attractive. Over the next six to seven weeks we sold off shares two more times at $30 and $32 per share, locking in gains of about 50 percent from our previous entries. Even though the overall fundamentals continued to look strong to us, we felt that it was the right time to take some profits due to the sudden rise in valuations, especially when compared to the industry average. Shortly thereafter, TRLG's stock price began to slide; and as the valuations once again turned favorable while overall fundamentals remained solid, we purchased shares again in August at $21.40, $19.90, and $18.37. Now we sit back, study, and watch!

A different scenario played out with ADY (see Figure 7.2). We initiated a position on December 29, 2009, at $22.50 per share. At that time we had been tracking ADY for only about three months (big mistake!), but its fundamental score was a strong 57 in the BeanScreen. Valuations looked attractive as well, so we figured we'd give it a shot. Over the next few months, we added to our position three more times as the fundamentals remained steady and valuations appealing. In late March 2010, after a bad earnings report, the fundamentals dropped suddenly to 43 in the BeanScreen. That got our attention. Over the next couple of months, the stock price began to slide as we monitored the situation closely. Finally, on May 25, we decided to take our medicine and cash out our entire position at $15.52 for a loss of about $4.50 per share. Though the overall fundamentals weren't terrible in May and June, we did not see foresee them improving anytime soon. As you can see, getting out of ADY when we did turned out to be fortuitous.

In closing, we would like to say there are probably thousands of great trading and investing strategies out there. The key is in finding one that you understand, are familiar with, and are good at—and stick with it! Our fundamentally driven BeanScreen is not a perfect system, but it has been a great stepping-stone and idea creator for us over the years. We have enjoyed sharing the fruits of its labor, as well as our opinions, with the StockTwits community and all our friends and family here at home. We continue to learn, discover, tweak, and adapt with time, hoping to become better, more proficient investors in the future.

CHAPTER 8

Fallen Angels

Michael Bigger, *@biggercapital*

Michael is one of the most experienced guys in the StockTwits community. He has seen it all—the booms and the busts—and has thrived by focusing on the opportunities. He has the rare ability not only to filter the noise but to exploit it to his advantage. He's super-talented.

Bear markets make people a lot of money; they just don't know it at the time.
—Shelby Davis

PROFESSIONAL BACKGROUND

I am an investor and a trader who has been involved with trading technologies for more than 20 years. I received a BS in physics from the University of Québec in Montréal in 1986 and an MBA from York University in Toronto in 1991. In 1992, I joined Citibank as the head trader of U.S. single-stock derivatives, where I managed a $5 billion portfolio of equity derivatives. I traded mostly collars. We were dealing with sizable positions and in many cases we were essentially the market. When you manage big positions, the first thing you learn about is the importance of liquidity.

In 1998, I joined D.E. Shaw & Co., L.P. to trade the U.S. equity derivatives portfolio. This is the place I started to appreciate the power of technology. I realized that when you build a new platform, you should be incremental. Start slowly and evolve one step at a time.

In 2000, I entered into the listed equity options business by establishing KBC Financial Products as one of the three initial market makers of the International Securities Exchange. We built that business into the primary market maker for listed equity options on over 120 companies, with 15 traders executing thousands of trades per day. My work there helped me learn a lot about investor psychology. Most of our clients were much more conservative than they thought they were. In theory, everyone liked volatility, but in practice few were willing to absorb it. In December 2001, I left KBC to start my trading firm, Bigger Capital.

As a private investor in start-up companies, I was among a group of investors who sold Innovative Fibers to Alcatel for $175 million in July 2000.

I wrote *In Praise of Speculation!*, an e-book that evaluates the viability of John Butler's investment philosophy in today's market. The original version of Butler's book was published in 1922. I stumbled upon it by accident and I loved it from a first read. I was amazed by the ingenuity of the concepts that were presented in the book. John Butler was probably one of the first guys in the world who wrote about intrinsic value well before Benjamin Graham. I share my market missives and market commentary at www.thisisbigger.com.

VALUE AND THE BIG MAC THEORY

At Bigger Capital, we run two portfolios: (1) quantitative and (2) investment. In the investment portfolio, we focus on trying to create as much output as possible with relatively little input. Once every three to five years, we buy one stock. We buy a great company at a very cheap price. Cheapness for us means the ability to really buy as much as possible of what we like. Our margin of safety resides in the quality of the business, not so much in the discount to intrinsic value. We aim to make 10 to 100 times our initial investment. This investment model is positioned between a mature investing strategy that mimics the market (about 10 to 13 percent per annum) and a venture capitalist investing model (30 percent or more).

One of the most successful posts on our blog is titled "A Thousandfold Return on Investment." It tells the story of a friend who made more than 1,000 times his investment in McDonald's in the 1960s. As part of that post, I included his field trip report, which he wrote in 1965.

When confronted with making a long-term investment, we always ask ourselves whether there is a little bit of Big Mac in the investment thesis. Does it feel like investing in McDonald's in the 1960s and 1970s? Are customers going bananas over the experience, the operational excellence, the consistency, the product comfort, and so forth?

We won't commit capital to a long-term investment unless there is some Big Mac in the thesis. Over the years, that method led us to the following investments that had a little bit of Big Mac in them:

- Amazon.com, 2001
- Priceline, 2002
- McDonald's, 2003
- Netflix, 2005
- Crocs, 2008

BUYING GREAT COMPANIES AT LOW PRICES

The ability to load up on the exceptional business at cheap prices finds its origin in a big sell-off, be it a sector sell-off or a vicious bear market. We get excited when some outstanding company's securities fall more than 90 percent from their highs. It does happen!

Among the rubble, we go looking for great companies that have very little debt. We prefer to look at companies we know something about, but we will get a quick education if necessary.

We ask ourselves: If the stock goes down further and we had enough money, would we buy the whole company? If the answer is yes, we pull the trigger for size.

THE IMPORTANCE OF MIND SHARE

When we are looking for an investment, we focus first on stocks of companies with a clear mind share, meaning that the company's products and services are well known and liked by a wide audience. The existence of mind share is the biggest margin of safety one investor can ask for. It represents the social trend that ultimately drives any company's earnings.

If the mind share is there, we then focus on valuation. As much as we like a business, we don't like to overpay for it. The potential long-term return tends to be negatively correlated with the price paid. (The lower the price, the bigger the potential return.) We research stocks that have declined 90 to 95 percent from their all-time high price. We have one simple rule of thumb to value a company: If the next five years of expected earnings are equal the current market capitalization, we are interested. Needless to say, such opportunities come only during bear markets.

Most people know about the spectacular collapse of Crocs (CROX) in 2007–2008, shown in Figure 8.1. The company built capacity to meet exploding demand, but when the demand for its iconic shoes declined, the company had way too much inventory on its hands, which caused severe financial stress. The stock slid from $75 to $0.90.

If you typed the term "Crocs" into Twitter's search box during these sad days, you would get a comprehensive overview of what the general public thought about Crocs:

- Crocs are coyote ugly.
- Knockoffs are cheaper; there is no need to buy Crocs.
- Crocs are a short-term fad.
- The company is mismanaged.
- In July 2009, the *Washington Post* reported that Crocs was on its way to bankruptcy. The company was "doomed."

These points illustrate the overall sentiment regarding Crocs at the time. Most investors accepted these ideas, dismissed Crocs, and believed the *Washington Post*'s thesis. However, if you looked closely at the company, a different scenario was unfolding.

FIGURE 8.1 CROX Drops More Than 98 Percent from Its All-Time High, Monthly Chart
Source: © StockCharts.com.

We decided to drill down into each of the above-mentioned issues and find out whether the market was right or wrong about Crocs.

Here is what we wrote about these issues then:

- *Crocs are coyote ugly.*
  Some people like the Crocs clog style; others simply hate it. This is fair. However, a quick look at the Crocs web site will convince you that there is more to Crocs than clogs. Crocs sells comfortable, durable shoes in a wide variety of appealing styles for men, women, and children, and the company offers great value. The naysayers seem to view Crocs merely as a clogs marketer. Nothing could be further from the truth.

The tug-of-war between lovers and haters is polarizing the market and making people talk about the brand. Being talked about on the Internet is an asset.

- *Knockoffs are cheaper; there is no need to buy Crocs.*
Crocs' customers are convinced that imitations do not feel as good as the real Crocs shoes. That is as true with Crocs as it is true for other companies that focus more on quality and experience and less on price. For example, some people will spend much more money on a Tempur-Pedic mattress than on a cheaper imitation. They believe the satisfaction they get from using the real thing surpasses the money they save by using the fake thing. This trade-off is worth it to them. Crocs are no different. Customers are still buying.
As Crocs diversifies its product line into more than the 120 styles currently available, the imitators will have a hard time keeping up with Crocs' pace. As Crocs introduces styles more frequently, its product life cycle shrinks, making it more difficult for imitators to put products on the shelves on a timely basis. The retailers might not want to deal with this complexity for the low-margin product.

- *Crocs are a short-term fad.*
Ever since its shoes became popular, people have labeled Crocs as a fad. However, in a "Best of 2008" list, Crocs appeared in two categories:
    1. Best-Selling Products in the Shoes and Handbags Category (Amazon.com and Endless.com): Crocs Cayman sandal.
    2. Most-Loved Products in the Shoes and Handbags Category (Amazon.com and Endless.com): Crocs Athens thong sandal.

    As of today, Crocs are still at the top of the chart at Amazon.com. The company's second-quarter results confirm that the shoes are selling briskly. For some customers, Crocs are simply an addiction. John Duerden, Crocs' CEO, commented, "There are more than 100 million consumers in 125 countries that love our product. The Crocs brand is only five years old, and already it's almost as well-known as Nike and Adidas. It's an icon and whether people love it or hate it, they talk about it." In short, Crocs has products that resonate with consumers. To put the company's achievement in perspective, it took a hundred years for Citibank to achieve the 100 million customers mark.

    Crocs' customers are going bananas over the experience and there is a little bit of Big Mac in the thesis. With the end of 2010 approaching, Crocs remains at the top of the chart on Amazon.com.

- *The company is mismanaged.*
Crocs' challenges are deeply rooted in the company's torrid growth prior to 2008. Since the company could barely meet demand in 2006 and 2007, management overestimated the amount of inventory needed to satisfy demand. Therefore, when the economy turned south in 2008 and Crocs' clog business matured, sales fell sharply.
To address these issues, on February 25, 2009, Crocs announced that it had appointed John Duerden to serve as the company's president and chief

executive officer. Crocs released this statement: "Duerden has more than 20 years of senior level management experience across a variety of industries, including thirteen years as president or CEO. From 1990 to 1995, Duerden served as president and chief operating officer of Reebok International. During this time, the company's worldwide sales tripled to $3 billion and Reebok became established as a pre-eminent international sports brand."

Duerden quickly took action to address the company's challenges. He focused on aligning its production capacity to meet demand, reducing its overhead expenses and its workforce, paying down debt, and managing its product life cycle tightly.

Duerden's strategy is bearing fruit. The company's inventory, which topped $250 million in 2007, is now standing at $116 million, and it is decreasing.

- *In July 2009, the* Washington Post *reported that Crocs was on its way to bankruptcy. The company was "doomed."*
  Crocs has always been a debt-light company, considering its size. That was the case before the *Washington Post* published its report. While the *Post* was busy writing its article, Crocs was repaying its debt. When Crocs reported second quarter results, it announced it had paid back its debt and had $77 million in cash. Inflammatory headlines sell newspapers and create investment opportunities.

In closing, Crocs enjoys one of the best mind shares in the shoe business. As Crocs successfully overcomes its main challenges, expect the business to thrive. Although I am sure the skepticism about and criticism of the company will continue, at least until such time as it becomes clearer that Crocs' transformation is gaining traction, Crocs' fundamentals are improving. The company is well positioned to succeed and deepen its sustainable advantage. If we had more capital, we would have bought the entire company at the time.

WORDS OF WISDOM

Shelby Davis was a great investor. He died in 1994 with a net worth of more than $900 million, which he made mostly through investing on his own.

Near the end of 2010, it had been two years since we added a new holding to our investment portfolio. That last stock was Crocs, which we started buying on July 8, 2008.

Despite the fact that the S&P 500 index has slid more than 10 percent from its 2010 high reached in April, we don't see much value in the U.S. markets. To us, value means that an investment is trading at a level that can return five times or more our investment over a three- to five-year period.

It is hard to find securities with that potential investment payoff at the moment. Therefore, we will just sit tight and wait. We are building our cash war chest, and we will be ready to pounce on serious weaknesses. They always come around.

CHAPTER 9

Dividends Don't Lie

Eddy Elfenbein, *@crossingwallstreet*

Crossing Wall Street was one of the first blogs I discovered about markets back in 2005. Eddy has always had a clear voice and knows how to explain trends and other complicated financial topics in a digestible way. He's got a great sense of humor as well. He is a veteran in all the good ways, and his blog is a must-read.

In the short run, the market is a voting machine.
In the long run, it's a weighing machine.
—Benjamin Graham

MY PROFESSORS WERE WRONG

When I was in graduate school pursuing my MBA, my professors lectured me about the efficient markets hypothesis (EMH). This is the idea that capital markets work so well that they incorporate all known information about a stock. As a result, it's impossible for an investor to outperform the market consistently.

Sure, some people could beat the market for a while, but that was all a matter of dumb luck. A successful investor, the professors said, is no more talented at investing than a coin flipper is at flipping coins. Oh, please! I knew this was nonsense. Later on, when I worked in finance as a professional, I saw how good investors routinely beat the market. Not just once or twice, but again and again and again.

Still, the EMH crowd never lets up. Funny, we never hear that it's impossible for an investor to *lose* to the market consistently. But that's what the EMH implies as well. No, we're told only that it's about failing to beat the market. What a bunch of rubbish! This is one of those dumb ideas that only an intellectual could believe.

I was so disgusted by the advice I saw investors getting that I started my own investing blog. With a little help from some of my techie friends, I started Crossing Wall Street in the summer of 2005.

With my blog, I wanted to prove that anyone—yes, *anyone*—can beat the market consistently. All you need is a little homework and a lot of patience. In my blog, I tracked my recommended stocks to see how well they did against the broader market. This is my Buy List, and it's the cornerstone of Crossing Wall Street.

I even went so far as to say that I would keep trading in my Buy List to the bare minimum. Each year, I pick 20 stocks for the list. According to my rules, I can't change any of the stocks for the entire year. Once the Buy List is chosen, it's set in stone for the entire year. Too much trading, in my opinion, is the bane of the successful investor.

At the end of each year, I change only five stocks. That's just one-quarter of the portfolio. That kind of slow-motion strategy would send lot of professional mutual fund and hedge fund guys over the edge. Nevertheless, I was determined to show people how to invest successfully.

One more thing—my blog is totally free. The Buy List is open to everyone and you can see how well (or poorly) I'm doing at any time during the day. I'm happy to say that my Buy List is well on its way toward beating the S&P 500 for the fourth straight year—and I've done it with less volatility as well. As of November 5, 2010, the Buy List has gained 33.36 percent compared with 8.77 percent for the S&P 500.

My professors were wrong. The market can be beaten, and I'll show you how.

THE KIND OF STOCKS I LIKE: ONLY THE HIGHEST QUALITY

So how does one go about beating the market? My investing philosophy is remarkably simple: I look for great companies and wait until the share prices drop to a good bargain. It's that simple. I don't use any fancy software or stock screens. I don't use any formulas. Thankfully, there are no Greek letters floating around my investment decisions.

I simply follow a list of about 40 stocks of very, very high-quality companies. Think of it this way: Even if we narrow the market to the 3,000 stocks on the Russell 3000, that means that nearly 99 percent of the stock market doesn't make it past my first cut.

By high quality, I mean companies with consistently strong operating histories, high returns on equity (ROEs), and strong cash flows—especially free cash. Nothing fancy here. I like good, solid companies that keep costs low and have a strong position in their markets. The kind of math I use was taught in the third grade.

I especially like companies that have proven track records of growing earnings in good times and bad times. Since I can't know every move management makes, a long stretch of superior ROE tells me that the management team probably knows what it's doing.

I prefer to find stocks that pay strong dividends. The reason is that dividends don't lie. Companies can fudge just about any number they want to. The secret scandal of accounting isn't what companies do that's wrong; it's what they do that the rules allow.

AFLAC, THE DUCK STOCK

In 1970, John Amos visited the World's Fair in Osaka, Japan. When he got there, he was astounded by the number of people who walked around the crowded cities wearing surgical masks. Amos instantly recognized a golden business opportunity. Amos, along with his two brothers, ran a small insurance company based in Columbus, Georgia, called the American Family Life Assurance Company. He figured that if people in surgical masks won't buy insurance, no one will.

For many years, American Family had been a pioneer in the insurance industry. It was the first company to offer cancer insurance. The company also decided to focus on insurance in the workplace. Almost all its policies are funded by payroll deductions.

In 1974, the Japanese government awarded American Family a monopoly on Japanese cancer insurance. It is rare for the Japanese to recognize gaijin—or foreigners—in this way, and the only reason American Family got it was because no Japanese firms were interested. Today, 95 percent of all the listed companies in Japan offer American Family's products.

Despite all of its success, no one had heard of American Family. The company's name recognition was at 2 percent. How do you get the public interested is something as dull as supplemental life insurance? The company's advertising firm noticed that American Family's nickname sounded almost like a . . . duck. Ten years later, Aflac's name recognition is over 90 percent.

The commercials are silly, but they're a brilliant way for people to remember the company's name. Most people don't realize how profitable Aflac has been. The company just ended its very impressive streak of dividend increases of 10 percent or more. I've searched and searched and haven't been able to find any company that has had a longer streak.

This performance has made me a very big fan of Aflac's management, and they've earned my trust. During the summer of 2010, it seemed like the European economy was heading over the cliff. Shares of Aflac plunged over concerns that the company held lots of investments in troubled economies like Ireland and Greece.

Aflac publicly said that it did indeed have some exposure to those trouble spots, but reassured investors that its overall business was just dandy. I was amazed by this reaction. Here we saw the company tell investors not to worry, yet the stock was going for about *seven times earnings*.

Once earnings came out, investors saw that the company was telling the truth, and the short sellers got squeezed hard. In July, the company said that it expected earnings per share to rise by 10 percent, which translated to $5.34 per share. At the time, the stock was going for $50 a share. Aflac's stock was an amazing value and it was hidden in plain sight. From early June to early November, the stock rallied over 40 percent. It was some of the easiest money I ever made.

The lesson is to spot a great company. Wait for a minor or transitory problem to scare investors away. As the price drops, get ready to swoop in and wait for the market to come to its senses. Benjamin Graham famously said: "In the short run, the market is a voting machine. In the long run, it's a weighing machine."

ORPHAN STOCKS: THE SHARES OVERLOOKED BY WALL STREET

Another set of stocks I like are orphan stocks. These are stocks that aren't followed by a single analyst on Wall Street. You'd never know from watching CNBC or perusing investing message boards but there are lots of great companies that are completely unknown on Wall Street. Some are too small. Others are too boring. Some people shy away from investing in little-known companies. Me, I love orphan stocks.

If you do a little homework, you can be as well-informed as anyone on a small stock. Most investors never think of calling the company and asking questions. Well, you're the owner! You're certainly allowed. A lot of times, managements of good companies are more than happy to discuss their business. (How often does someone call you asking about your job?)

The best part is that Wall Street has dramatically cut back on its research departments over the past few years, so there are even more orphan stocks out there. There are hordes of analysts who follow the superstar stocks like Apple (AAPL) or Google (GOOG). More than 30 analysts follow Google, and more than 40 follow Apple. That's why I don't even bother with them—it's too hard to get an edge on other investors.

But if you spend a little time, you can find great companies that no one knows about. With fewer eyes on these stocks, it's easier to find mispriced companies, which means more opportunities to find cheap stocks. This is exactly what my professors said couldn't happen.

I'll give you a great example of an orphan stock, little Hawkins Corporation (HWKN) of Minneapolis, Minnesota. Never heard of them? Don't worry, neither has the rest of Wall Street. Hawkins is a specialty chemical company for the Upper Midwest. So if you're in, say, Fargo and you need a shipment of sodium hydroxide, well, these are the boys to call. They've been around for many years and the company is largely in family hands. It's not the sexiest business but they do what they do, and they do it well.

At last check, Hawkins has fewer than 300 employees and a market value around $400 million. To put that in context, Exxon Mobil (XOM) is worth about 1,000 times Hawkins. Last year, Hawkins had revenue of $257 million. Wal-Mart (WMT) generates that in about five hours.

The odd thing about Hawkins is that it used to split the stock almost every year, but by small amounts. You'd get a 10 percent, 15 percent, or 20 percent stock dividend each year. As a result, the nominal share and dividend price didn't move much, but the stock really did very well.

Over the years, Hawkins has been an outstanding performer. Since 1980, this little orphan stock has beaten market stalwarts Coca-Cola (KO) and Disney (DIS). It has even beaten tech powerhouses like Intel (INTC). And still no one on Wall Street follows the stock!

One great orphan stock came to me from a reader who wanted to know my opinion on Nicholas Financial (NICK). I had never heard of it, so that afternoon I did a little homework. I called the company, spoke to the CFO (always go to the finance guys first), and soon I was sold.

Nicholas Financial is in the unexciting field of making loans for used cars. The hitch is that it is very careful about the loans. What Nicholas does that really caught my attention is that it doesn't sell the loans like all those subprime lenders do. Nicholas does the revolutionary act of holding on to its customers' loans until they're paid off. My word! If the mortgage industry had done the same, maybe we wouldn't be in such a mess today.

Nicholas gets most of its loans by buying them right from dealers. It generates some of its own in-house, but most loans don't begin with Nicholas. Since these are loans for used cars, most people assume that Nicholas is a subprime lender, and that's how the market treated its stock. Shares of NICK peaked at over $13 in 2006. By 2009, the stock was going for $1.65 per share. Ouch!

Here's the hard part to explain: Yes, the rough economy was harsh on NICK's customers. Yes, lots of loans went bad. But no, the company wasn't going bankrupt. In fact, it wasn't even close to going bankrupt. Anyone who just looked at the numbers could plainly see that once the economy stopped cratering, Nicholas would be just fine.

Here are some numbers: NICK's earnings per share dropped from 85 cents in 2008 to 50 cents in 2009 (the fiscal year ends in March). In other words, the stock was going for about three times earnings! By 2010, the company's profit rebounded to 87 cents per share, and in October shares of Nicholas crossed $10. Again, all it took was a little homework and some patience. This was another value hidden in plain sight.

DEEP TRUTHS ABOUT THE MARKETS AND INVESTING

In his 1988 *Baseball Abstract*, Bill James, the famous statistical guru, listed a number of lessons he had learned so far through his study of baseball statistics. In that vein, I'll list some observations that I've learned over the years:

The Federal Reserve isn't nearly as powerful as is commonly believed.

There isn't a person or group of people in charge of the market.

There's no such thing as a "healthy correction."

Good stocks can go down for no reason.

Bad stocks can go up for no reason.

A trend can last much longer than you thought possible.

Stocks don't know you own them.

The market doesn't care about politics.

The most important variable to the stock market, by far, is the direction of long-term interest rates.

The stock market hates inflation. The only thing it hates more is deflation. The best environment for stocks is a low, stable inflation rate.

PART III

Day Trading

CHAPTER 10

Only Price Pays

Brian Shannon, *@alphatrends*

Brian and I go way back. Brian used to write blog posts about the stocks we covered in our daily Wallstrip.com video show. When I started StockTwits, I called Brian and told him what we were going to do and he instantly wrote a check to invest. Brian is not only a super-successful trader, but also an avid teacher of technical analysis. It is not an accident that about one-third of the traders featured in this book point to Brian as the mentor who has had the biggest impact on their market careers.

LEARNING THE HARD WAY

A few weeks before I made the transition from a retail stockbroker to full-time trader, I learned that the market doesn't care about my opinion. Of course, I learned this lesson the same way everyone else does, the hard way! I had been trading a company called Chantal Pharmaceuticals (CHTL) really well for a few weeks and held a larger position than I should have over the weekend. My confidence was high and the company had a "miracle wrinkle-removing skin cream" that seemed to be selling very well and getting a lot of positive press. Well, *Barron's* exposed the company for what it was (a fraud), and the next Monday the stock opened down 30 to 40 percent or so. I sold the stock and was mentally crushed, but it was a great lesson in risk management and proper position sizing. I think it was about six months later when the company filed for bankruptcy. The setback delayed my transition to full-time trader as I built my equity back up. Looking back, it was the best time to learn that lesson, because it taught me to be skeptical and careful about my risk management.

I started as a retail stockbroker in Boston, and it didn't take me long to realize that the job was a glorified telemarketing position. I learned a lot as a retail broker about sales, people, and some stock strategies, but it wasn't where my heart was. I was fortunate to have the brokerage experience because it allowed me to realize how markets operated while I controlled other people's money and did not have the emotional attachment that comes with your own equity. It allowed me to appreciate the value of managing positions versus the buy-and-hold mentality that was so popular with retail brokerage firms; it helped me identify my niche.

After a few years as a broker I found a New York City firm that let me trade its capital remotely. This experience got me started in full-time trading and really fired my passion for learning more about the markets and implementing new strategies. After trading from home for about a year with that firm, I opened a trading office with a partner in downtown Denver. This office was similar to many of the trading offices in the early and mid-1990s where customers came in to trade on our equipment in exchange for a piece of the brokerage commissions they paid. This was a nice setup, and we kept at that for about two years until a competing firm approached us to join up with them. That firm was Market Wise Securities, and with it we had the opportunity to trade larger accounts at great commission rates and did not have to bother with the day-to-day operations that my partner and I were not very enthusiastic about.

I stayed at Market Wise for about five years, and it was there that I realized that in addition to being the most profitable trader at the firm, I could also do an effective job of teaching others the principles of trading; I had a talent for explaining the way markets operate. Teaching about the markets is something that sped up my own learning curve, and it allowed me to realize that "the simplicity of the markets is their greatest disguise," as the owner of Market Wise, David Nassar, liked to say.

I left Market Wise in 2004 and since then I have written my book *Technical Analysis Using Multiple Timeframes* (LifeVest Publishing, 2008) and started a subscription product with StockTwits. My passion has always been trading, and I continue to evolve and hone my approach. The biggest thing I continue to realize about attaining success in the markets is that it is a simple approach combined with a clear mind and strong money management principles that reward participants most frequently.

THE TRUE VALUE OF TECHNICAL ANALYSIS

Technical analysis gets a lot of criticism from people who do not fully appreciate the level of simplicity and ingenuity that it can offer in the right hands. I believe that terms like Hindenburg omen, death cross, golden cross, Fibonacci level, Adams pitchfork, lunar cycle, and so on are largely a distraction from the true value of technical analysis: simple recognition of trend, timing, and risk management. I would never say that some of those indicators are worthless, but there is only one thing that pays us or punishes us in the market and that is price action. Only price pays! So doesn't it stand to reason that we should focus our attention on price action? That is what this chapter is about. If you are looking for any new science in technical analysis or a cleverly named pattern, flip to another chapter. If you are interested in how to utilize stock charts to find low-risk/high-potential trade ideas and manage risk, let's get started.

Many people mistakenly use technical analysis as a system: buying moving average (MA) crossovers, or shorting when an indicator flashes "oversold." Technical analysis should be used as a framework to form our analysis, which starts with a simple understanding of market structure. When we analyze the market based on listening to its message, we can assess probabilities of success and risk objectively and plan our trades without the damaging influence of emotions. Many experts will tell you to control your emotions, which is obviously easier said than done. It is better to have a plan of action laid out in advance to minimize the chances of emotions coming into the decision-making process.

We know that stocks are either advancing, declining, or in a neutral period. Cyclical analysis recognizes there are four stages of a stock's life cycle: Stage 1—accumulation, Stage 2—markup, Stage 3—distribution, and Stage 4—decline. Putting labels on the stages of the life cycle allows us not only to easily recognize and scan for opportunities, but also to recognize times of uncertainty so we can step aside and have the safety of cash as a position. Generally speaking, trend traders want to be long stocks in Stage 2, to be short in Stage 4, and to avoid the neutral Stages 1 and 3.

TREND ALIGNMENT

Trading and investing sound easy with phrases like "the trend is your friend"; just buy a stock in an uptrend and sell when it stops going up, right? The problem is that there can be several trends present that send conflicting messages. The longer term may be in a solid uptrend, but in the short term the stock may be experiencing a normal, but brutal, bout of profit taking. These pullbacks can be the beginning of the end, or they may just be the pause that refreshes before the stock is able to continue on to new highs. The fact is that at the time the stock is undergoing short-term profit taking, the uncertainty can be high and if you buy the stock just as it begins to correct, you can experience large losses in the short term while still being correct about the longer-term trend. If your timing is off, you may be stopped out of what might have been a good trade. In order to stack the odds of success in your favor, analysis of multiple time frames will allow you to make much better decisions on the timing of your entries, which puts you in a position of strength right from the beginning of your trade.

When we analyze a stock with charts, we should use a minimum of three different time frames. Just as Charles Dow recognized three different trends, we should start with those as a minimum. For this example we will consider the goal of finding a good swing trade candidate. To start our analysis, we should begin with a longer-term time frame. In this case that will be a chart with daily candles that shows approximately one year of data. Using just price, volume, and a 50-day moving average, we should be able to figure out what the primary trend is. A very quick way to sum up the trend here is to observe the location of the stock in relation to the 50-day moving average and what the slope of that moving average is. Generally, we will consider the stock "innocent until proven guilty" if it has a pattern of higher highs and higher lows above a rising 50-day moving average and "guilty until proven innocent" if it shows lower highs and lower lows below a declining 50-day moving average. When analyzing volume, we want to see a pattern of expanding volume in the direction of the trend followed by lighter volume as volatility contracts and short-term corrections ensue. Assuming that we are looking for a long-side trade, we will start with a stock in an uptrend and then drill down our analysis to a shorter-term time frame.

The intermediate-term time frame a swing trader will want to consider is a chart constructed with 65- or 30-minute candles. We will generally observe 20 to 30 days for this time frame. The 65- and 30-minute time frames are ideal here because they allow us to look at the data without it being scrunched up if we were using a shorter-term time frame for this many days. It is also important to make sure that we have the data presented with an equal number of candles for each day. With 390 minutes in a trading day, if we were using 60-minute candles, there would be six candles with 60 minutes of data and one candle with 30 minutes of trading data; this is similar to comparing six apples to one orange. It is more accurate to observe six equal periods of 65-minute data or 13 periods of 30-minute data. I think the absolute best moving average (MA) to use on this time frame is a 5-day MA. Be careful not to enter a 5-"period" MA, because it will follow right on top of the candles and will not provide a useful reference point. In order to look at a 5-*day* MA, we need to consider some simple math. Each day the market is open for 13 individual 30-minute periods. Over five days, there are 65 30-minute periods, so if we place a 65-period MA on the 30-minute time frame, we are looking at a dynamic 5-day moving average price of the stock. For a 65-minute chart, the 5-day MA is represented with a 30-period MA. Long trades should typically be entered as the stock is above a 5-day MA that is just starting to slope upward and is acting as support. Short sales should be placed as the stock is under a 5-day MA that is just beginning to decline and act as resistance.

What we want to observe on the intermediate-term time frame is where the stock is in relation to the 5-day MA, the slope of the 5-day MA, and where the important support and resistance levels reside. This is the time to ask two questions:

One, where has the stock come from? Meaning, has it rallied the past three days and is now extended from an important level of support? If so, we may be late to the movement and the chances of a correction (by price or through time) may be too great to justify taking a position. If instead the stock has experienced a short-term pullback and has found support, it is likely a great stock to stalk for strength with a stop just below the consolidation area. This is how we determine the potential for price risk and stop placement on the trade.

The second question we want to answer on this time frame is: Where does the stock have the potential to go? Put simply, does it appear that there will be enough profit potential relative to the risk we have perceived? If the stock appears to have a prior important level of resistance just above where it is trading, the potential for profit may not justify taking an actual trade.

The answers to these two questions allow us to determine our risk/reward profile. A commonly accepted risk-reward ratio is 1:3, meaning that you would be willing to risk one dollar to make three dollars. A ratio like this means that you could lose on two trades and still come out ahead if you made three dollars on a third trade. Trading isn't about being right all the time; it is about managing risk so you can consistently come out ahead.

Short-term analysis can be taken as deep as you like, but there is the danger that if you look too closely, you will lose sight of the forest by focusing on the trees. In other words, the shorter the time frames you look at, the greater the likelihood of micromanaging the trade becomes and you may lose out on the bigger profit opportunities observed on the intermediate-term time frame. We will continue with our swing trade example and use either a 5- or a 10-minute time frame (I like to switch between the two for more clarity; it is a way to avoid the compression of data) to get a closer look at the action. A look at shorter-term trends gives us clues for when to enter the trade and how to manage it.

For a bullish example, we will look at 15 days' worth of 10-minute data to see the four stages repeated within the longer bullish Stage 2 action. When looking at the data for approximately 15 days, we can see shorter-term cycles; and here is how we want to approach these trends with the goal of entering a stock as the trend becomes aligned. If we have bullish daily chart, the action of a swing trader should be dictated by where the stock is in the shorter-term cycle.

When we have a longer-term Stage 2 markup and the shorter-term trend is:

- *Stage 1—accumulation.* This is where we do our planning; we observe, analyze, and *anticipate* the point where buyers will take control, and we think of our price objectives and stop levels.
- *Stage 2—markup.* As the stock makes a short-term higher high, we want to buy the stock. We want to *participate* in what appears to be a developing trend. Stage 2 is also where we manage our winners by raising the stop up under higher lows.
- *Stage 3—distribution.* The stock is now showing signs of fatigue and may be in need of a correction through time; this is a good point to *exit* the position or to lock in at least partial profits.
- *Stage 4—decline.* When the primary trend is higher, this is likely just a pullback and the odds do not favor profitable short sales; it is better to *avoid* these stocks and look for better setups where trends are coming into alignment.

When we have a longer-term Stage 4 decline and the shorter-term trend is:

- *Stage 3—distribution.* This is where we do our planning; we observe, analyze, and *anticipate* the point where sellers will take control, and we think of our price objectives and stop levels.
- *Stage 4—decline.* As the stock makes a short-term lower low, we want to enter our short position. We want to *participate* in what appears to be a developing trend. Stage 4 is also where we manage our winners by lowering the stops up above the lower highs.

- *Stage 1—accumulation.* The sellers are now showing signs of fatigue and the stock may be in need of a correction through time; this is a good point to *exit* the position or to lock in at least partial profits.
- *Stage 2—markup.* When the primary trend is lower, this is likely just a short-term bout of strength and the odds do not favor profitable long trades; it is better to *avoid* these stocks and look for better setups where trends are coming into alignment.

There is no perfect time frame to trade on, as people all have different goals, levels of patience, capital resources, amounts of time they can commit to the market, and so on. The idea of trend alignment can be utilized by anyone from longer-term investors down to day traders. The value of technical analysis is to provide our framework so we can enter our trades or investments at a time that makes sense based on the cyclical flow of capital through markets.

CHAPTER 11

Intraday Earnings Momentum Gap Trade

John Lee, *@weeklyTA*

John is too young to be as passionate and smart about stocks and markets as he is. You can get this way only from lots and lots of hard work. His students and the broader StockTwits community are unanimous in their praise of his expertise, attention to detail, and willingness to share his knowledge. John's focus on managing money, not just entries into stocks, will make him a great mentor for any beginner and really for any trader who wants to improve and add weapons to the trading arsenal.

Success always comes when preparation meets opportunity.

—Henry Hartman

FINDING THE RIGHT APPROACH

I started investing at the age of 13. Almost every night, my dad brought home annual reports and *Wall Street Journal*s and I gradually became interested in the stock market. At that time, I adopted a conventional fundamental buy-and-hold strategy in Dow stocks and avoided the NASDAQ mania and crash. During my first year at Valley Forge Military College in 2002, I started to learn more about the dynamics of the market and gradually began educating myself.

But it wasn't until I was 17 that I adopted a swing trading strategy based on technical analysis that was an early version to my current approach. I switched my market philosophy due to time constraints. Also, I was dissatisfied with the performance of the buy-and-hold Dow stocks strategy. I could no longer withstand large drawdowns simply because I was supposed to "hold" and ignore market cycles.

I knew I could do better.

I came to realize that I am not great at dissecting fundamental reports and that my personality fits better with a shorter holding period. I am more of a visual person and I excel at short-term technical analysis with an emphasis on candlestick trading. Being aware of my own strengths and weaknesses was a critical step toward finding the right market approach for me. In retrospect, this was huge.

I served in the U.S. Army Reserves and Maryland National Guard from 2002 to 2008. My military experience is likely the single most significant contributing factor in how I stay disciplined, focused, and prepared in trading. Even today, I apply this instilled discipline to every single trade I make. I could never stress enough to my students the importance of mastering disciplines away from trading, whether it is training for a marathon or military training. This will prepare you for the commitment required to be a successful trader.

At the University of Maryland in 2005, I won first place in the annual stock picking contest and started a stock newsletter for the Smith School of Business. That was the first year I taught a friend how to trade and discovered that I had a gift for sharing my knowledge and helping others. In addition, it made me realize that the more I teach, the more I learn.

I have never stopped learning. In the past five years, I have read hundreds of books and currently possess over 1,200 publications in my personal library. I also review approximately 300 to 500 charts daily. Consistently acquiring knowledge, analyzing charts, and applying both have exponentially shortened my learning curve. I did not have a mentor when I started trading, but I made sure that I took something valuable out of almost every book I read.

During my first two years, my performance was lackluster even though I had a natural eye for setups. I did not become consistently profitable until I developed a disciplined risk/money management system that utilized buy/sell stops and brackets designed to significantly limit losses. The ability to cut losses short differentiates successful professionals from developing traders.

Once I figured out the importance of discipline and began incorporating it into my trading strategies, I started having significant success. This is around the time I started managing my family's money. In 2005 I doubled my capital and I have never performed worse since then.

In 2008 I began blogging after a friend had lost the majority of his equity during the devastating financial crisis and was in dire need of help. I started my blog just to share my ideas with him and never thought that it would become something thousands would read.

Since then, my interest and involvement in blogging have increased substantially. I continue to love helping others sharpen their skills, and as my audience increases, I experience both a greater sense of responsibility as well as more satisfaction.

I have also added a private coaching program and train over hundreds of students worldwide. I run ChartsGoneWild.com, host Charts Gone Wild on StockTwits TV, and manage my own trading account.

TECHNICAL ANALYSIS RULES

As a day and swing trader, I believe in constantly adapting to the changing market environment by taking advantage of short-term price swings through the use of systematic and discretionary technical analysis. My philosophy is to keep things simple, which is clearly demonstrated by adopting only the basic and most important aspects of technical analysis, including price, volume, moving averages (MAs), support/resistance, candlestick charting, and chart pattern recognition.

I know when to stay in cash to avoid potentially damaging situations. The ability to preserve capital through vigilant risk management is crucial to trading success and a rewarding career. I strive to maintain the highest standards of discipline by consistently going over the same preparation routine every day. I meticulously analyze my trades in an attempt to better understand my strengths and weaknesses. You have to know yourself before you try to understand the psychology of other market participants.

TRADING EARNINGS MOMENTUM

I have many favorite setups, but here is a day trading technique that works best during earnings season. No, we don't get in before earnings and gamble on the outcome. Instead, we trade the reaction to earnings the next morning. This is a variation of the "postearnings reaction premarket momentum play."

For day trades, I like to trade earnings reactions and play momentum in continuation and breakaway gaps. Statistically, continuation and breakaway gaps do not fade nearly as often as area gaps. In addition, finding the best setups involves analyzing their precise locations and plotting them on the daily charts during the premarket session. Many of these intraday breakout plays resemble the pattern in Figure 11.1.

For this intraday earnings momentum gap trade, the perfect long scenario occurs when a stock is automatically above a major resistance area on a powerful catalyst on high premarket volume. However, this alone does not guarantee success. Instead, to increase the probabilities of a continuation, I observe the first 2 to 10 minutes of the day for a break of the day's high on the 1-minute intraday chart. If you use a 5-minute chart, you are highly likely to miss the initial morning entry; therefore, the shortest time frame must be used to correctly time your entry. If the market is also up, the chance for failure decreases significantly. While most traders shy away from the first half hour of the day, that is typically where the majority of my profits come from.

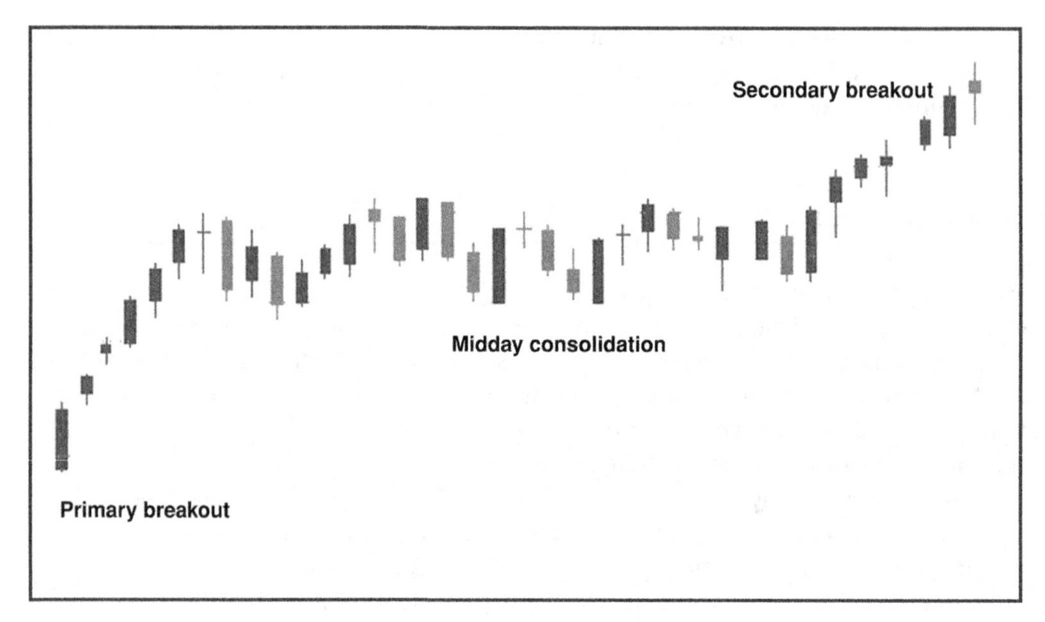

FIGURE 11.1 Typical Intraday Move in a Trending Stock

The best place to find premarket movers is to visit the NASDAQ home page at www.nasdaq.com and view the "Extended Trading" tab. I prefer to focus more on NASDAQ stocks because they provide more momentum than New York Stock Exchange stocks on average. During earnings season, you should also check every liquid stock that reported earnings during the previous day's after-hours session and the current day's premarket session. You will have candidates to choose from on a near daily basis.

Typically, I use a 5 percent position size up to a maximum allotment of 10 percent. Due to the high frequency of the pattern seen in Figure 11.1, a trader would typically have an initial entry point in the morning and a second entry point in the afternoon. If a secondary target (explained later) is not met but the stock is in a bullish consolidation, then the trader has the option to scale in another 5 percent prior to the secondary breakout. Normally, I will not add to an existing position more than once. A process of scaling out may be used when initial and secondary targets are met. You will see an example of initial and secondary targets and the locations of where a trader will have the option of scaling out.

Here are the four initial premarket criteria I look for in these plays (see Figure 11.2). To keep things simple, I will refer only to long setups:

1. *Gap location.* Where is the gap located? Is it above a known resistance level?
2. *Premarket volume.* Is the stock trading 5,000 shares (bad) or 50,000 shares (good)?

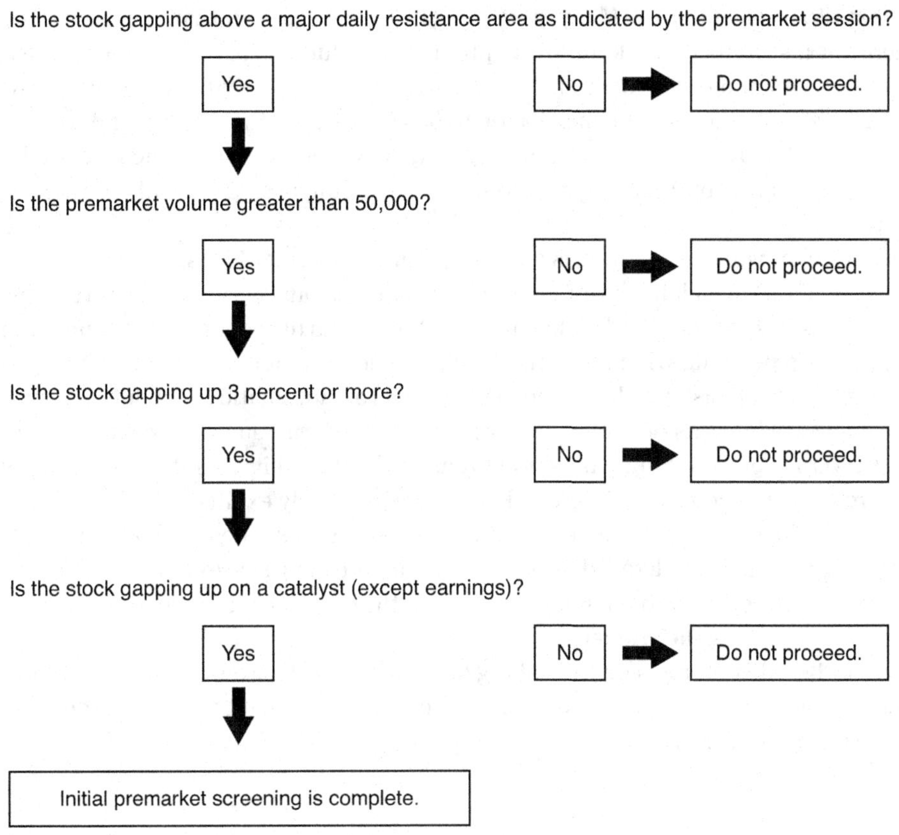

Is the stock gapping above a major daily resistance area as indicated by the premarket session?

Yes | No → Do not proceed.

Is the premarket volume greater than 50,000?

Yes | No → Do not proceed.

Is the stock gapping up 3 percent or more?

Yes | No → Do not proceed.

Is the stock gapping up on a catalyst (except earnings)?

Yes | No → Do not proceed.

Initial premarket screening is complete.

FIGURE 11.2 Screening Process

3. *Gap magnitude.* How large is the gap by percentage?
4. *Catalyst-driven.* Why is it gapping?

Keep in mind that we are not trading the actual earnings number. Instead, we are focusing on the reaction to the earnings number. We trade earnings gaps because the vast majority of the daily continuation and breakaway gaps are a result of earnings catalysts and these gaps have a high probability of starting new trends or continuing existing trends. We also trade postearnings reactions because these stocks will always trade at above-average volume, many times trading at 2 to 10 times the average daily volume. This makes the stock very liquid and easy to enter and exit versus trading a thin, illiquid stock and having difficulty with order fills.

Particularly if a stock posts a positive earnings surprise, then institutions are more likely to accumulate the stock over time. This type of buying provides a floor on the daily chart. If a stock gaps without a news catalyst, then traders should absolutely avoid that stock at any cost. Many times, a gap that is up less than 3 percent is not sufficient for a sustained breakout. If the premarket volume is 50,000 shares or greater, then there is genuine excitement and interest and you are likely to see heavy activity. Many times, a stock can gap up on 5,000 or 10,000 shares, but those gaps tend to be area gaps. Statistically, over 90 percent of area gaps fade within five days. Since we are looking for strength and continuation, we do not want fading area gaps with high chances of failure.

On a psychological level, there is a mix of buying, covering shorts, taking profits, and letting cash sit on the sidelines waiting to make a move. During the first 2 to 10 minutes of the day, it is easy to tell which side will win. During this ultrashort time frame, market participants are deciding which way the stock should continue. If a stock gaps above a short- or long-term resistance level, then that signals an automatic breakout above a key technical level. When this occurs, a higher proportion of true buying and short covering will occur versus profit taking. The initial break in the day's high results from additional buying pressure and continued interest. People are genuinely excited. If a stock does not meet our criteria, it has a high chance of fading. When a stock fades, then the buyers lose control and the sellers will likely dominate the entire morning session. Before the market opens, we use our criteria to eliminate the stocks that are likely to fade, thus increasing our chances of picking the winners.

I stack the odds on my side by making sure that criteria are met on every level. By playing only the best and highest-probability setups, I ensure that I will make significantly more correct calls over time.

FSYS IS GAPPING UP ON A STRONG EARNINGS REPORT

Let's take a look at an example of a postearnings reaction premarket momentum play on August 5, 2010. Figures 11.3, 11.4, and 11.5 are charts of Fuel Systems Solutions Inc. (NASDAQ: FSYS) on the daily, 5-minute, and 1-minute time frames, respectively.

Prior to the open, the premarket session indicated that FSYS had a high probability of gapping above the $31.45 short-term resistance level at the August 2nd high. This is the first criterion that must be met. If a stock cannot gap above an important resistance level, then the stock has a high probability of fading to the downside. Because FSYS was a candidate, we marked the major daily resistance levels: $32.83 and $33. These were our initial target levels. We also marked the approximate March and April peaks at $34.89 as well as the 200-day moving average (MA) at $34.45. This provided the road map for the entire day.

Did you notice how we didn't use any advanced indicators or anything else that could have cluttered up our charts? Keeping it simple ensures that you are not distracted. Trading is already difficult enough; why make it more difficult?

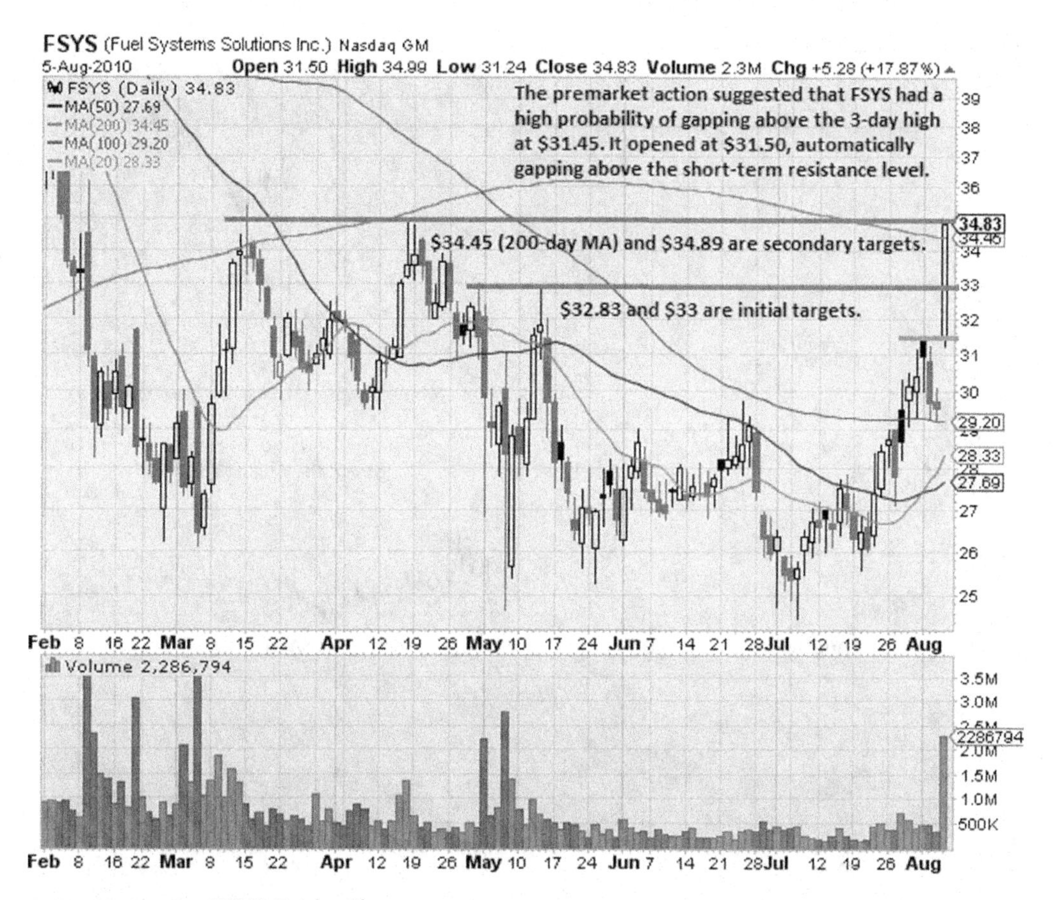

FIGURE 11.3 FSYS Daily Chart
Source: © StockCharts.com.

Now that we had our targets ready before the open, we were prepared. If a stock fails in the first 5 to 10 minutes, I get out immediately. Why? If a stock gaps above resistance and fails, it is a sure sign of weakness.

In Figure 11.3, we can clearly see that the stock will gap above $34.45, as shown in Figure 11.4. You might ask if 5 cents makes a difference. My answer? Every penny counts.

We did not want to get in immediately at 9:30 A.M. because we needed confirmation of strength. We waited at least two minutes for a daily high to establish on the 1-minute chart (Figure 11.5). We would have our confirmation of strength at any point at which the stock broke out of the day's high.

It broke out of the day's high within five minutes of the open on extremely high volume. This characteristic also favorably increased our odds of a continuation. We wanted to get in on the break of the day's high around $32.20. Now we looked for our initial targets of $32.83 and $33. We wanted to set a stop at the day's low at $31.45, which was

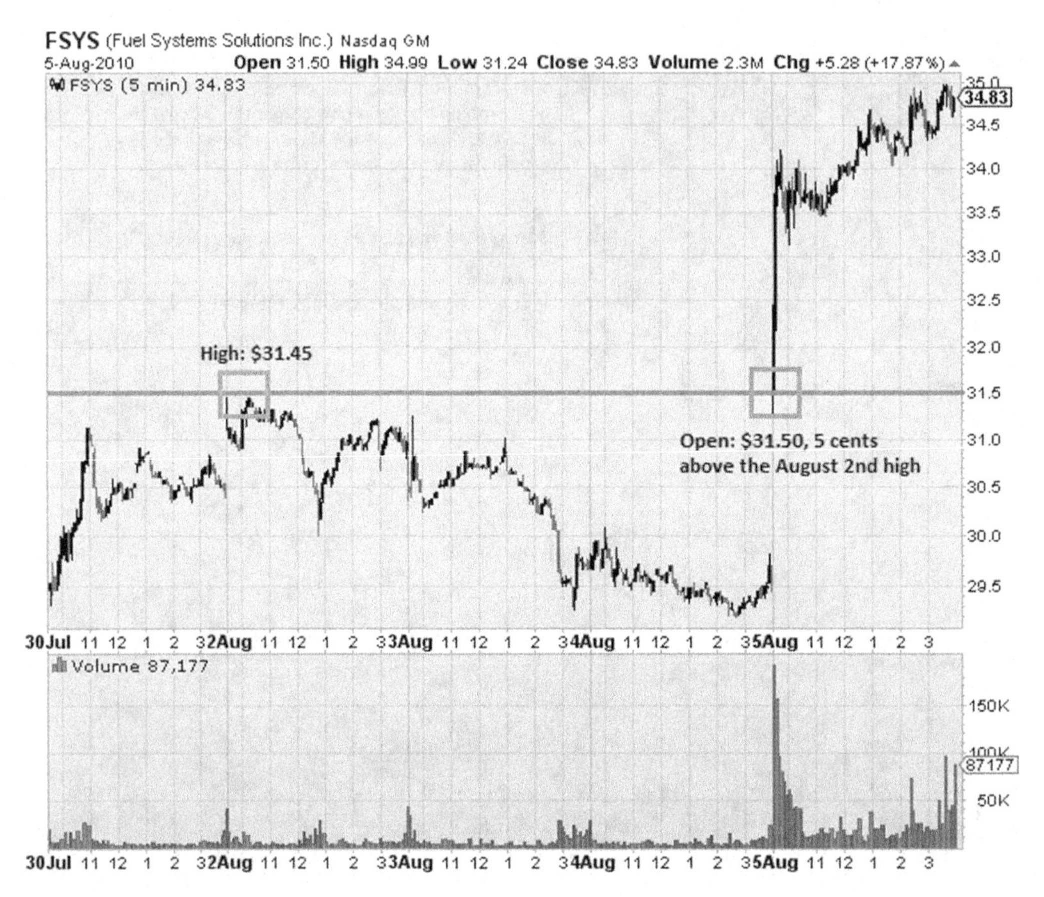

FIGURE 11.4 FSYS 5-Minute Chart
Source: © StockCharts.com.

slightly below the day's open. We were risking 2 percent on this trade to potentially make 7 percent.

The momentum in FSYS was so powerful that it blasted right through these levels. We wanted to keep these levels in case profit taking pulled the stock lower. FSYS held throughout the morning by trading above the $33 level, using prior resistance as support. At this point, I would raise my stop to $32.80, which is slightly below the initial targets of $32.83 and $33. Everything would be profit from here on out and we were now risking 0 percent.

Our secondary targets were at $34.45 and $34.89. We again broke through the day's high and reached $34.45. This would provide an opportunity for traders to take part of their profits through scaling out or to take all of their profits. Since the 200-day MA ($34.45) was the most powerful moving average on the daily chart, it was advisable to take profits here. If we entered at $32.20 and sold at $34.45, we made a profit of $2.25 per share, or 7 percent, in just three hours.

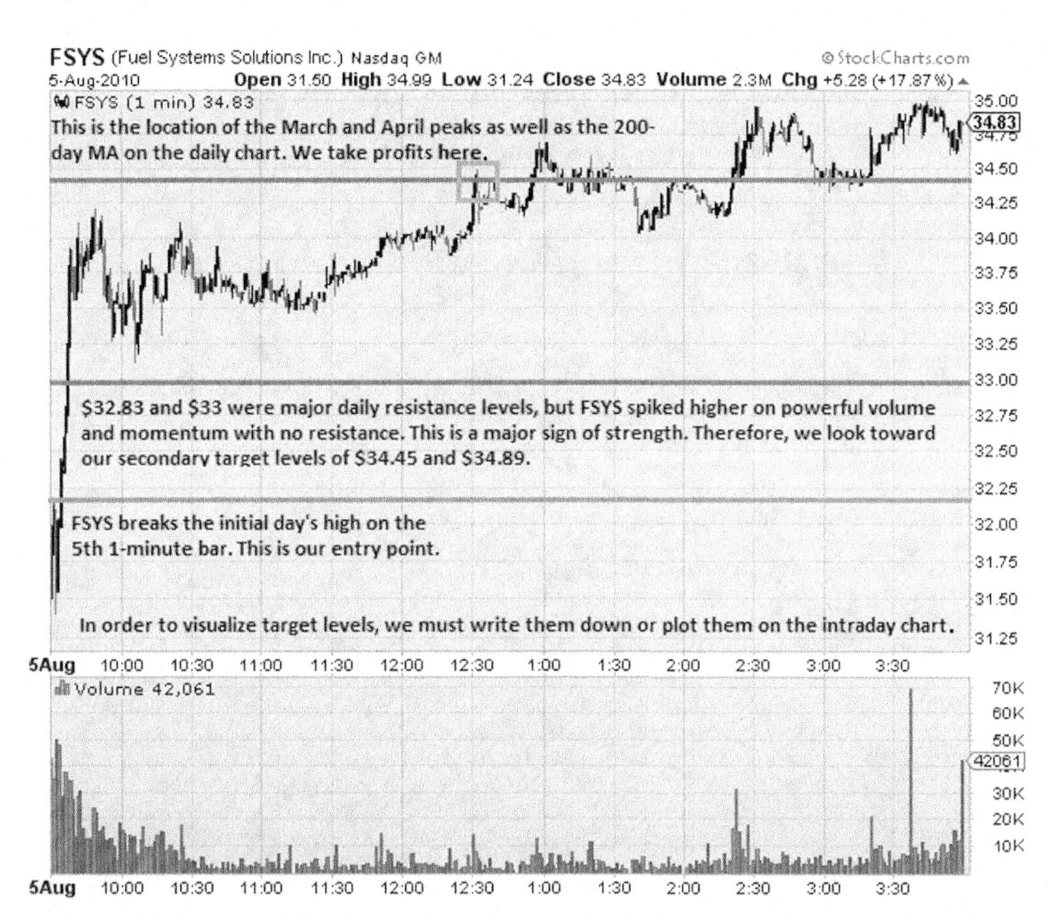

FIGURE 11.5 FSYS 1-Minute Chart
Source: © StockCharts.com.

Due to the high frequency of these gaps during earnings season, you can potentially play one or more of these setups nearly every day. These setups are considered high-probability plays and also carry a lower-risk/higher-reward profile. Most important, I would like to stress that if a stock misses even one requirement, then you should disregard the trade. If you know that the odds will decrease when a stock does not fit your requirements, then why trade the higher-risk setup? We wouldn't.

If you're looking for a way to play earnings through a low-risk approach, then I highly recommend this day trading method for you.

CHAPTER 12

Trading the News

Mike Bellafiore, *@smbcapital*

Trading is an extremely difficult career and lifestyle, but Mike and his team at SMB Capital believe they can teach traders how to succeed. And this focus on mentorship is really paying off—their students and customers are thrilled with the results they're getting. As the economy has changed and young people find it difficult to get started on careers, the art of trading will become a more requested skill. I also believe that trading, like fishing, can be learned and the skills are great ones to have no matter what business you end up pursuing.

I know of no more encouraging fact than the unquestionable ability of man to elevate his life by conscious endeavor.

—Henry David Thoreau

THE PROPRIETARY TRADER

I thought I wanted to be a lawyer. I was clerking for a federal magistrate in Connecticut during my first year in law school, driving my worthless Honda Civic back and forth between Bridgeport and West Hartford. I remember saying to myself: *I don't want to do this. All these people are really nice, and bright, and hardworking, but this is just not for me.* To me being a lawyer was like having a book report due every day. And who ever liked that?

So for my last two years in law school I was exploring what else I could do except be a lawyer. One evening I drove down to Stamford and hopped on the Metro North to New York City for a visit with my best friend from home, Steve Spencer. It was someone's birthday, maybe his cousin's or a friend's, or heck, maybe his. At some point after too many imported bottled beers and an overconsumption of family-style Italian, Steve and his roommate from Wharton approached me: "Why don't you come and trade with us after you graduate? In your first year you can make $200K. The hours are pretty good and it's fun." This all made a lot of sense to me.

When I first started trading in the late 1990s, you sat behind an experienced trader for five days. As we chuckle remembering, you learned through osmosis. You asked questions when the trader appeared to have time, which was almost never. I learned from one of the top 50 greatest day traders of all time (if such a list exists). He traded $10K lots of five different positions at a time. I could tell when things were going bad when he muttered to himself: "Fu$king market makers. Take my stock." I didn't know the difference between a bid and an ask, and here I was commuting 90 minutes each way from southern Connecticut, with no market background other than being long INTC and MSFT like the rest of the universe, trying to follow this legend. He was often so busy that his lunch sat on his desk cold and unfinished until after the close.

My first nine months of trading were a disaster. I was down $36K, with little reason to think I would start getting better, and drowning like many other intraday traders in the Asian financial crisis. For the first time in our firm's history there were firings. Draws were cut routinely, which was the nicer way of letting you go. But then Al Gore created the Internet and everything changed. I walked into a market of opportunity.

Fast-forward to the following year and I had made enough to trade my own money. Back in the day, you got to keep 10 to 30 percent of what you made for the firm, but my take was more than enough to open my own retail trading account flush with enough BP (buying power) with which to trade. I've traded my own money ever since.

There were many different markets after the Internet boom: the bursting of the Internet bubble, the year of the Federal Reserve cuts in 2001 (11 cuts), the bottoming of the burst, and then a range-bound market.

Steve and I were sitting at a proprietary trading desk at the firm of some friends. And one day they closed the prop desk. Some suit I had never seen before paraded in, did his best incompetent CEO routine, and demanded we all be out of the office by the end of the day as security guards stood behind him. We had nowhere to trade in the office. We were forced to find a new home, but this new desk was just a loose collaboration of independent traders doing their own thing. Steve and I missed the interaction with professional traders and idea generation.

Also around us, literally, were self-proclaimed prop shops sprouting up asking people for money ("a capital contribution"), letting newbies trade without any training or a professional trading environment. I watched the seats being filled, emptied, filled, and emptied as trader after trader washed out. It wasn't the failing that bothered me. That is an unfortunate yet real part of the trading game. It was that in this new, more complicated market these new traders had no chance. That wasn't right.

I started thinking what if. What if we, Steve and I, built our own firm? What if we offered new and developing traders a world-class training program? Could we build a firm on these principles? I approached Steve with this idea and immediately he responded, "Why would I want to do that?" I could sense his brain calculating the lost trading income due to training traders, as he had previous experience with this. But I nevertheless started putting the pieces in place to start a firm, and eventually there were just too many pieces to ignore. One day there was SMB Capital, with a mission to offer the best equities training program on the Street.

STOCKS IN PLAY

I am a short-term, intraday, active trader. I trade stocks with fresh news; we say they are in play. We use three factors to make our trading decisions: (1) intraday fundamentals—stocks in play; (2) reading the tape—an old-school trading technique that very few teach; and (3) technical analysis—yes, charts. We look for in-play stocks to trend intraday, and we take positions following this trend.

Why stocks in play? Let's visit the "Traders Ask" section of the SMB Blog for the answer.

Hi Mike,

I hope that my e-mail finds you well. I have a question about trading stocks that are in play. I've studied several approaches to game planning.

1. *Come in with 10 to 20 stocks that have potentially good daily setups, and wait for good intraday price action to confirm that a stock is worth trading. I've found that this approach has led me to overtrade, and jump around from stock to stock. I particularly like to be focused, so this approach has hurt my trading.*
2. *Come in with two or three ideas that are technically sound. Have a deep understanding of the levels and wait for the stock to come into your level or price action to confirm. I've found that with this approach, I can come in with two or three ideas; however, those stocks may or may not have good price action on that particular day. Just because I planned for it, this does not mean that the next day it will have money flowing in or out of it. I could technically come into the office and have nothing to trade because the intraday action is not there.*
3. *Am I better off coming in each morning and looking for stocks that have fresh news or earnings (i.e., a catalyst)? I've heard of this approach; however, it seems like with this approach you really won't prepare well, because you won't know what to trade until the last minute.*

Mike, it's imperative that as short-term traders we're involved where the money is at. How can I better prepare, so I can locate the money and get involved in high-probability stocks? In this particular sense, are scanners a better tool than a watch list game plan?

Too many times I've found myself trading stocks where money is not coming into them, stocks that are not in play, and stocks that have too many candlesticks with tails instead of solid candles.

What do you suggest is the best approach?

I responded with the following:

I love your observation about the wicks in stocks sans fresh news. So true. And so this is not where I want to start for my stock selection. Great job working on your game here to improve your stock selection. It's all stock selection these days!

There is not a right approach for EVERYONE. But there is a right approach FOR YOU. I do have an opinion on the right approach for most traders, and this is what we teach.

We trade the stocks in play:

1. *Stocks with fresh news.*
2. *Stocks with unexpected news.*
3. *Stocks that have moved plus or minus 3 percent on the open.*
4. *Stocks with news that will cause a significant intraday move.*
5. *Handily beats on revenues for the full year, improved margins or market share, new drug, new product—these are key words that catch my attention.*

Why do we trade these stocks?

1. *They offer more intraday opportunities.*
2. *They tend to trend cleaner intraday (bye-bye wicks).*
3. *They are more liquid so you can trade them with more size (ever meet a trader who doesn't want to trade with more size?).*
4. *They move more than other nonnews stocks intraday (efficiency of capital).*
5. *The order flow, reading the tape, is easier to read.*

Okay, I am going to stop here as you have gotten the point. Second-day plays are excellent as well in this trading environment. I will not pass on a stock that has found a very important technical level sans fresh news. We have built the SMB Radar, a proprietary trading tool, which helps us find stocks intraday that move like stocks in play.

But my first choice is a stock with fresh news.

MY "A" SETUP

As I mentioned, we make trading decisions based on three factors: intraday fundamentals (stocks in play), reading the tape, and technical analysis. Picture a big circle with each of these factors occupying a section. My A setups are present when the intraday fundamentals, the tape, and the technicals all point in the same direction. I will place my maximum risk when such an opportunity presents itself.

How do we find a stock that it is likely to move a lot intraday?

- Find a stock with significant fresh news (like earnings).

  See the "Traders Ask" blog postings in the preceding section.
- Find a stock that on our long-term charts has a clear path ahead.

  We do not want to get long a stock that has overhead resistance in 30 cents. Why get long for such a play? Our risk/reward profile is not sufficient. It's better to wait until our stock has cleared very significant longer-term levels so we can be in the real move, where new buyers enter and shorts scramble to cover.
- Wait for the stock to start trending intraday.

  The trend is your friend, as the trading saying goes. We want to trade stocks that are trending intraday and follow this trend. Again, this is how we get in the bigger move. These are the moves traders with earned nicknames like "Iceman" love. Seriously, does it get any cooler than guys calling you Iceman?
- Wait till the open has ended, usually around 10:15 A.M. ET.

  In this market as I write, big and clean moves have been occurring after the open. Wait until the nonsense on the open ends. And then get on board the real order flow that has been entering the market after the open.
- See the stock hold above an important level on the tape.

  Reading the tape (the order flow) gives us confirmation that our stock will head in a certain direction. Remember, we want to be in the real moves, like Iceman. And to be in such a move and hold, we need to be confident in our play. The tape offers us more confidence that in fact we are on the right side and a big move is about to visit. So we wait until there is a held bid or offer on the tape or strength or weakness on the tape that confirms our position. When we spot this on the tape, this is another check in our favor foreshadowing the possibility that a big order may have entered the market. So we pounce!
- Hold until there is a reason to exit.

Cortez, a nontraditional college student, was not a fan of the misinformation being spread about trading on his campus. He was just as disappointed with the sparse selection of trading lectures at his school. You might say he was downright pissed. So he made it happen. He reached out to a proprietary firm (SMB), convinced me to visit and address some future traders, organized multiple student organizations to spread the word of a visiting trader (not easy), and hit up some internal departments (even harder).

At Rutgers-Newark I offered this most important tip for holding this trade: Don't be a wuss! If I were some political pollster, that line would have ranked as most favorite with this college crowd. Don't be a wuss! Hold the position until there is a real reason to exit—as if the market sends you signals to exit that are so clear that it is like someone is jumping out from your computer, shaking you, slapping you upside the head, and saying, "Okay, jackass, now you can exit."

SHORTING TOYOTA MOTOR CORPORATION

One trading session, Toyota (stock symbol TM) had a full-blown crisis on its hands. As had been widely reported, sticking gas pedals and potentially dangerous floor mats had caused TM to recall 5.3 million vehicles since the fall of 2009, including some of its most popular models. TM was gapping down.

During this intraday session while I was babysitting LXK (a stock my brain refuses to allow me to verbalize correctly), Sweetness (because he is built like an NFL running back), one our hardworking new traders, called out TM. Quietly he asserted, "Watch TM—it is below 75." This was a most important longer-term technical level that our firm had discussed during our morning meeting. Opportunity had just entered stage left.

I punched up TM (see Figure 12.1). Below 75 was broken on the long-term and intraday charts. We had fresh news with Toyota's recent large-scale recall and uncertainty as to how devastating this would be to the company. Steve Spencer, my trading partner and best friend since grade school, chirped that 70 was a downside possibility. But TM would not trade below 74.75 on the tape. A significant buyer (piker?) was supporting TM, though broken and fighting awful breaking news (see the left side of Figure 12.2).

Finally, the buyer left (came to his senses?) and I started a Trade2Hold short, meaning I wasn't covering until TM broke its downtrend or some other major event materialized. It was sit back, relax, and don't wuss out by covering too early. What happened?

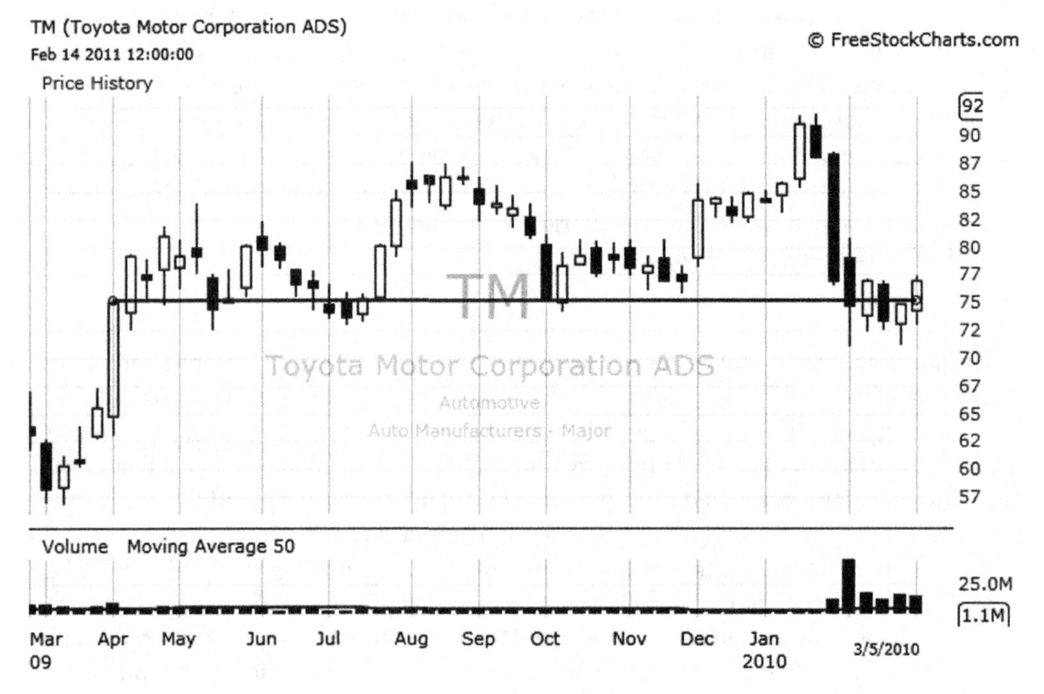

FIGURE 12.1 TM Long-Term Support Level Breaks
Chart courtesy of FreeStockCharts.com.

FIGURE 12.2 TM Intraday Chart Broken below 75
Chart courtesy of FreeStockCharts.com.

Three points of trending downside opportunity followed (see Figure 12.3). We say this is a chop!

After the Open

"I do not make a trade until 10 A.M."

"I don't trade the open."

"The open is too fast and crazy for me."

These are all past chirps from SMB traders. I am not a fan of sitting out the open and missing opening drive setups, fading overdone moves, spotting easy range plays, and so on, but there are many who do not thrive on the open. First you ought to work on your open game with small size in setups with which you are most comfortable. But also this play, my favorite A setup, is a play you can master and do very well with as an intraday trader.

After the open, when a stock starts to trend and has fresh news behind it, you can catch clean, significant, all-day moves in stocks. I was giving a talk in one of those warm-winter locations you get invited to and instantly clear your calendar for when a futures trader asked, "How many of these trades do you see a day?" I responded, "Five or six—more on a great day, and fewer on a slower day." But we do see them every day.

FIGURE 12.3 TM Intraday Downtrend Broken
Chart courtesy of FreeStockCharts.com.

They offer us a downside of 1 and an upside of 10-plus continually. You can make your month just watching, waiting, and making this trade your own.

Cover When the Intraday Downtrend Is Broken

Where do you cover? This depends on the trader. For me I cover such a play if:

1. The intraday downtrend is broken.
2. The stock reaches an important technical support level. In the Toyota case that would have been 70.
3. The corresponding futures significantly change. I would watch the futures and SPDR S&P 500 ETF (SPY) to make sure the market was not exploding. If the market became ultrastrong I might cover.
4. The clear seller disappears on the tape. If a seller was walking the stock down, I could clearly identify her, and then she fled, I might cover.
5. A huge buyer appears on the tape. If I see a price that cannot be violated with a repeating buyer at the same price and the same price and the same price I may cover.

6. The down move is too steep such that my risk/reward is now poor. A steep down move can be a sign of the bottom. The steeper the down move, the more I may have to consider covering, or at a minimum taking some off the table and perhaps reshorting into the next up move.
7. There is breaking positive news in the stock. Well, certainly if news broke that the recall was a hoax I would cover; or if a tier 1 firm upgraded TM with knowledge that the damage was manageable, or if the company offered some significant news that mitigated the harm, that might cause me to stroke my buy button.

As you can see in Figure 12.3, I covered TM when it broke the intraday downtrend. So we didn't get 70, but I cannot control the movement of my stocks. All I can do is enter excellent risk/reward opportunities, trade to my plan, and execute. Still, this was an intraday chop! Thank you, Sweetness.

That is my A setup. Perhaps you can make this setup your own!

CHAPTER 13

Intraday Momentum

Steven Spencer, @sspencer_smb

Steven is a cream-of-the-crop day trader, a true professional. He is aggressive yet minimizes risk. He's the complete package. Steven loves to share, so he is constantly paying it forward with the StockTwits community.

PROFITABLE BY MONTH FOUR

My interest in the stock market began at the age of eight when I was visiting my great-uncle in Greenwich, Connecticut. I discovered that he had made a fortune buying stocks in the 1930s during the Great Depression. It seems like yesterday that he told me the story of how he loaded up on shares of Chrysler at a dollar each because he was certain the government would bail the carmaker out. He turned out to be correct, and in 2008 history repeated itself as the government decided to bail out American car manufacturers once again.

My interest in the market grew further at the age of 10 when my fifth grade teacher explained to our class how stock prices would fluctuate and that it was possible to place a wager on the future direction of a stock via an option without actually owning any shares of a company.

I placed my first trade at the age of 13 when I bought shares of TWA (Trans World Airlines). I don't remember my reason for buying shares at the time, but looking back on it I was lucky to escape with a small profit. The airline industry has been a great destroyer of public wealth for the past several decades, although there is recent evidence that finally this trend has changed.

I made only a couple of trades over the next few years, buying shares of Apple (pre-Mac) as well as shares in a technology start-up called Chopp Computer that was going to revolutionize the PC market with something called "parallel processing." I eventually sold Apple for a profit, but Chopp became a penny stock, virtually worthless.

My interest in the market waned in junior high school as I became focused on the idea of becoming either a defense attorney or a prosecutor after participating in a mock trial in my social studies class.

More than a decade later while attending law school my interest again turned to the market. My college roommate had left his job as a CPA and was working for a firm that traded NASDAQ stocks on a short-term basis. He explained to me that his firm was using state-of-the-art technology to buy and sell shares more quickly than many of the established players on Wall Street.

I was offered a trading position at my friend's firm, so I switched to the evening division of my law school and began trading full-time in March 1996. I was profitable by my fourth month, and by my eighth month I started trading my own account.

One of the greatest obstacles I faced when I began my short-term trading career was putting aside my fundamental knowledge of companies while trading them on an intraday basis. I quickly learned that fading stocks because I thought they had moved up or down too quickly or were not at fair value was a very low-reward, high-risk strategy. That lesson learned very early in my career has strongly influenced my mentoring of young traders today.

At the beginning of my career my focus was almost exclusively on trading technology stocks. This was not by design but rather based on the fact that the NASDAQ market (the firm's focus) was the exchange that listed the vast majority of technology companies. I did also trade some retailers and smaller regional banks, but when a nontechnology company became large enough it would often move its listing to the New York Stock Exchange (NYSE).

The firm where I was learning to trade taught a momentum style of trading that stated if something was moving higher you bought and if it was moving lower you sold. We did little if any premarket preparation and simply would pick stocks that were moving on a particular day, or if the market overall was making a large move we would buy the leaders in each technology subsector.

During the first two years of my career, I had enough success to build up my account to a level that allowed me to start taking larger positions over longer time frames. One such position made me briefly consider leaving trading. In October 1998, I was long about $200K worth of a small assisted-living stock. When I arrived at the office one morning my position had been marked down about $100K. I thought to myself that I should simply liquidate my remaining positions and put my equity into some municipal bonds that would give me safe, tax-free returns.

But as luck would have it, the market bottomed about one week later and then went on a dizzying 18-month rise. I made back the $100K rip I took in less than a week and in the final two months of the year made more money than during my entire first two and a half years of trading. And this was prior to the Internet bubble getting started!

EMBRACE MOMENTUM

My market philosophy is that the efficient markets hypothesis (EMH) is a load of bunk. Warren Buffett eloquently refuted this idea back in the 1970s but for whatever reason it is still a widely held belief. The EMH states that stocks are priced rationally based on the fact that market participants all have access to the same information and will make rational decisions based on that information.

I think that anyone who has been involved in the market for a period of years understands that the market is not efficient. Therefore, many opportunities to exploit the mispricing of securities on every time frame exist. After the run-up of the NASDAQ from 1,200 to 5,000 and then back down to 1,100, I decided that I would sleep much easier at night without longer-term positions. As a result, I infrequently hold overnight.

I believe that there is a small group of people and institutions, mainly momentum hedge funds, that leave an indelible mark on stocks on a daily basis. Over many years, I have become accustomed to how these hedge funds buy and sell their positions, and that impacts both my stock selection and how I will trade stocks on a daily basis.

I spend most of my time trading stocks that I believe these momentum players are buying or selling on longer time frames. Their involvement creates greater liquidity and also makes it easier to spot technical setups. Examples of such stocks in 2010 have been BIDU, RVBD, CMG, and NFLX.

TRADING THE NEWS

My favorite setup involves trading a stock that has fresh news that leads to a clear technical pattern. What I mean by "technical pattern" is price action that I recognize as generally leading to a very significant move the majority of the time. This particular setup can be executed only by someone who has a direct-access trading platform and has the ability to track pre- and postmarket trading. This setup emerges most frequently during earnings season, which occurs four times per year.

Here are some bullet points outlining possible characteristics of this setup:

Fresh News

- There is news that causes a major move in either direction.
- News is released after the market closes and there is after-hours trading in the stock.
- The next morning there is premarket trading confirming a strong sentiment in the stock.

Types of News

- Earnings warning.
- Earnings release with major shift in guidance.
- The Food and Drug Administration (FDA) says no.
- The FDA says yes.
- Hostile takeover bid.

Structure of the Trade

- Strong initial reaction in the after-hours trading.
- Next morning premarket reaction confirms after-hours action by moving further in the direction of the initial move or it has a very small retracement.

Trade Execution

- Initial entry possibilities:
  - Bottom of consolidation in premarket if stock has gapped higher.
  - Top of consolidation in premarket if stock has gapped lower.
  - Above after-hours high.
  - Above premarket high.
  - Below after-hours low.
  - Below premarket low.
- Position sizing:
  - One lot for initial entry.
  - Second lot upon confirmation after market opens.
  - Lots three and four if the stock consolidates near the top or bottom of its opening range and then breaks on significant volume.

CONFIRMING BULLISHNESS OF FUNDAMENTAL HEADLINES

One recent example of this setup involved Riverbed Technology (RVBD). On October 21, 2010, RVBD released earnings well ahead of analysts' estimates and guided higher going forward. This immediately put RVBD on my radar as a potential trade candidate. But what actually moved it from potential candidate to a real trade was the price action that followed. It traded up four points from 46 to 50 in the after-hours. The next morning it was trading two points above its after-hours high. The price action was confirming the bullishness of the fundamental headlines.

Generally, when a stock gaps up as significantly as RVBD did, you would expect some profit taking right when the market opens. This profit taking should cause the stock to drop quickly. If the stock does not drop too severely when the market opens and immediately trades above its opening price and premarket high, it is an excellent candidate to trade significantly higher.

In the case of RVBD, it dropped about one point after the market opened, which was fairly minor considering the six points it had gapped higher. It quickly rebounded, trading up to about 53.50; and when it pulled back, it held support right at its premarket high.

There were several ways to trade this setup, from most aggressive to most conservative. The most aggressive approach I would recommend for only a professional trader with many years of trading experience. This would involve buying one lot after the initial profit taking subsided and RVBD began to trade higher. The danger with this approach is that during price discovery right on the open, a stock can change direction very quickly and less experienced traders might find themselves quickly out-of-the-money on a position.

A less aggressive approach would require the trader to wait for the stock to trade above its premarket high before buying an initial lot. Also, if the stock were to fail to hold above its premarket high, the trader would quickly exit the position. In the case of RVBD, it momentarily traded above its premarket high on the open before there was some profit taking. A trader who entered above the premarket high would have been quickly stopped out of the position.

The most conservative approach would require a trader waiting for the stock to move significantly above its premarket high before opening a position. A powerful move above the premarket high would establish an even greater likelihood of the stock's trend for the day and also would allow the trader to clearly define his risk down to the premarket high. In the case of RVBD, once it moved away from its premarket high, it never traded below this level again. It established clear support at this key price on the five-minute chart before beginning a multiple-point uptrend.

RISK MANAGEMENT

I wanted to make a couple of points about risk-reward ratio and position management. At SMB Capital, we teach our traders to look for trades where the risk is one unit and the reward is five. These trades occur on a daily basis. I have found that most of my top trade ideas have risk-reward ratios far better than 1:5. RVBD fits well into this category. If I were to buy it above the premarket high of 52.30, my position would be completely flat below 52. This would represent total risk of about 35 cents. My estimation of the potential reward buying above the premarket high would be 2 to 4 points based on the size of the gap from the prior day. The actual reward ended up being about 2.5 points, which equates to a risk-reward ratio of about 1:7.

In terms of position management, I will almost never allow my entire position to trade all the way through my stop-loss point. I will close 25 to 50 percent of the position

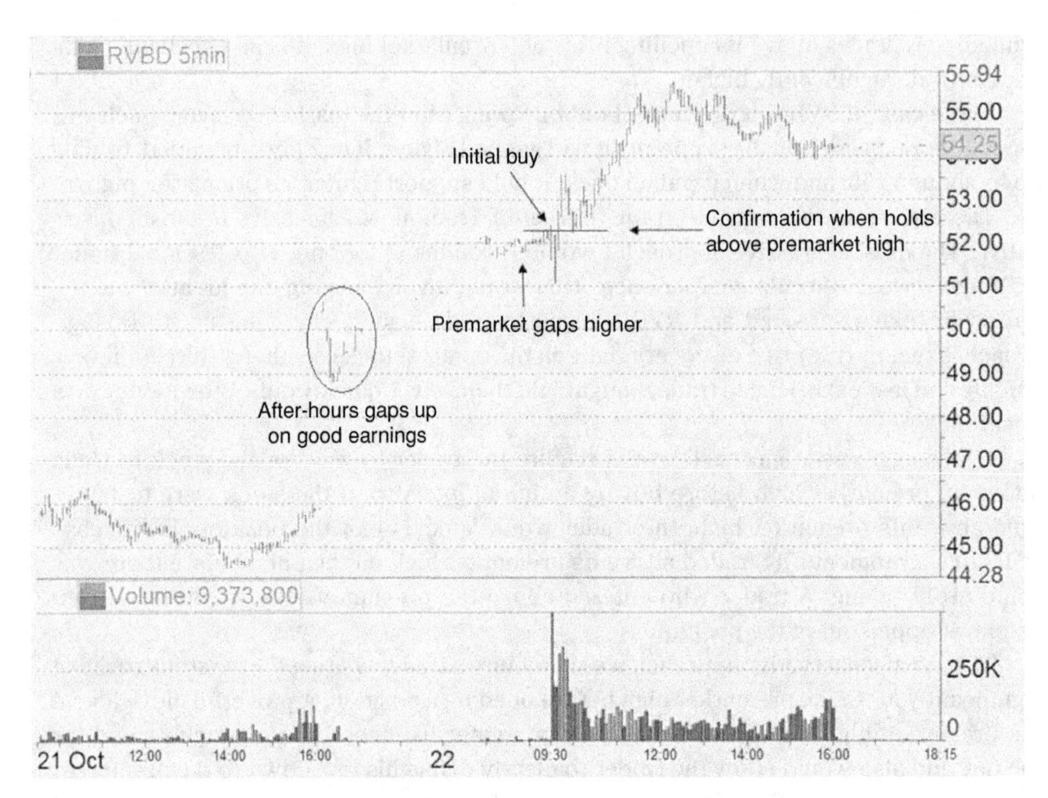

FIGURE 13.1 RVBD Trending Up the Whole Day, 5-Minute Chart

if the trade moves against me right away. This in essence lowers my risk because the average loss I will suffer on the entire position will be lowered. It is important to remember, if you do get stopped out of some of a position if it initially trades against you, that you can buy back the shares you sold if the trade ultimately starts to work.

I have marked up the chart shown in Figure 13.1 to give you some more ideas on how I would manage this position.

CHAPTER 14

The Underlying Psychology of Large Players

Gilbert Mendez, *@smbcapital*

Gilbert has taken tape reading to a whole new level of understanding and insights. He speaks a different language than many of us, so start learning today. He is wicked smart and has a really solid understanding of market psychology.

The price of anything is the amount of life you exchange for it.
—Henry David Thoreau

BURN THE SHIPS

In the early sixteenth century, a Spanish conquistador named Hernan Cortez led an epic odyssey that caused the downfall of the Aztec empire. It has been said that upon reaching new land, Cortez told his crew to burn the boats since there would be victory or death but no going back. I "burned my boats" early on in my career and have not looked back since.

After graduating from college, I did a very short stint at a tier 1 bank and realized that I was not cut out for the corporate world. I decided to be a trader. Here I was, an Ivy Leaguer who turned down a great job to struggle making a penny trading real capital and taking real risk. In addition, my parents were not very happy about it, and it was frustrating to see graduates from my class starting to enjoy the fruits of their 120-hour-a-week jobs. It was not all fun and good times during my first two years of trading. My learning curve was quite extensive.

I must confess, I have read only two books (cover to cover) on trading: Brian Shannon's book on technical analysis and most recently Mike Bellafiore's *One Good Trade* (John Wiley & Sons, 2010). I have attempted to read many others, but somewhere in the first 20 pages I realized that many of the patterns lacked sufficient interpretation and many of the authors had not traded in years.

During those first two years, I spent a ridiculous amount of time back-testing indicators and analyzing chart patterns, and found there was no secret sauce to this game. I had to make plays my own. Trying to copy plays from others was just pointless. I had to put in the time developing trading skills. I had to develop a way of tracking my performance, working on my execution skills, reading the psychology of the market players, getting fast on the keys, and all the many other skills necessary to take money out of the market every day.

Just like a young, aspiring athlete hoping to make it to the big time league, I knew I had to put in the time . . . and that I did. I spent more time thinking about the market, crunching stats about my trading, watching the tape, writing in my journal, and just obsessing about getting better that I can't even remember how I went through it. But there is one memorable story that sticks in my head.

About six months into trading with SMB Capital, I was not sure I was cut out for all-discretionary trading. My black box had recently taken a monster hit off a silly coding glitch. Mind you, I had financed my black box with credit card debt. Smart . . . not really; ballsy . . . you know it! Our trading platform was very unstable and I was getting cracked with the constant outings, I was working another gig to pay the bills, the parents were nagging on the phone on a daily basis, and my girlfriend was not happy with the lifestyle. I had had it. I walked into Mike and Steve's office determined to quit, but they would not let me. They offered some suggestions and I went back at it. That's all I remember. Then about two months later, the market started kicking and the switch turned on.

Knowing that trading was the only career path I wanted to follow, I had no choice but to figure it out. Not surprisingly, my biggest enemy was and still is the emotional monkey within me. I have been able to navigate these very interesting markets by learning to control it. I am looking forward to many more years of fun in this business.

FEAR AND GREED

Not to sound like a cliché, but I do believe the market is driven by fear and greed. This is manifested in a greater way when you look at the markets intraday. Market participants with the big money move around stocks trying to position themselves and they, too, suffer emotional ups and downs.

My way of looking at the market is not that of a fundamentalist or a technician. I am more of a psychologist, if you will. I try to read the underlying psychology of the large players behind a chart and Level II. My edge is found in the overreactions that come from their emotional and irrational responses to fear and greed.

Of course my trading is complemented heavily by having an understanding of the intraday fundamentals and overall technical picture, but I've found that if I trade based on just one of these elements alone, I do not feel in control of my trades.

THE BALANCE BETWEEN BUYERS AND SELLERS

My favorite setup is playing for the second leg of a large move out of a consolidation. When a stock makes a substantial move and it fails to come off its highs and spends enough time there, it gives the buyers a chance to regroup. It gives them a chance to party for a second time as the selling pressure was unable to counter the move. Yet there is one more piece of this play that makes it ideal for my trading approach. Having that tight balance of price action between the buyers and sellers gives players a chance to get bigger than they should, and this causes an emotional imbalance if the stock doesn't follow through as they had expected.

Think of a stock that drives up multiples of its average true range on some volume. Many market participants may think the stock is overdone and the buyers have paid too much for it, giving plenty of fuel to the bears. But after the stock hangs near highs a while without showing weakness, this makes shorts uncomfortable but not panicky yet. But think about what happens when any type of weakness is shown, giving the sellers some hope and a chance to add to their positions. Further, it gives weak buyers the opportunity to throw their positions and even switch their bias. Then if the stock quickly reverses its course and makes new highs, many are trapped. Shorts scramble to cover, weak hands pound back in, those flat want to party as well, and those in control want to press. Now you have a recipe for really panicky buying, and thus paying those new highs creates a very high probability of a second leg higher. The risk is very easy to control as those swing lows will surely be met with buying from those trapped. Having a protective stop right below those lows guarantees that when you are out, you are just wrong in your thesis.

JUNIPER NETWORKS

As way of example I wanted to discuss my favorite setup, seen in Juniper Networks (JNPR) on November 4 and 5, 2010. We have a product called the SMB Radar that filters the tradable universe of stocks in play (due to news and events). Throughout the day, I keep going through this list trying to find a setup that I can take advantage of. Some plays may take place intraday and some may just happen to play out over the course of a couple of days, depending on the time frame in which they occur. In this case, the play happened to take place in a 15-minute chart toward the end of the day, and the trade took two days to play out.

Juniper reported strong earnings on November 4 and the market reacted very positively to the news, as seen in the hourly chart in the top-left corner of Figure 14.1. I did not participate in that up move but wanted to find a spot where I could position myself for a second leg.

Zooming into the 15-minute chart (lower left), we can see a bit of a consolidation and accumulation taking place around 33.80 to 34.00 after noon. The tape indicated strong

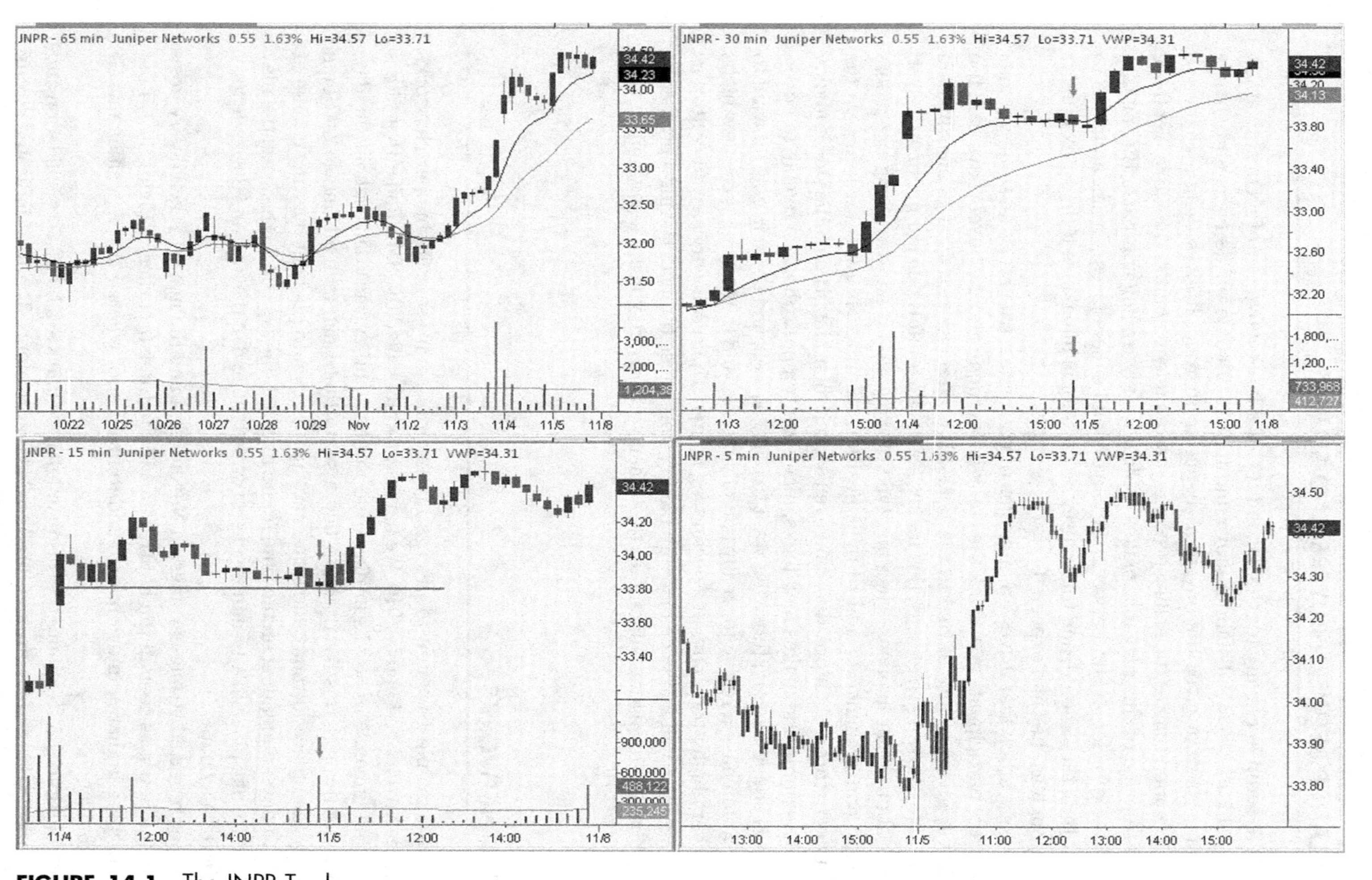

FIGURE 14.1 The JNPR Trade
Charts courtesy of TradeStation.

buying early in the afternoon of the 4th. I sat on my tier 1 position that whole afternoon. As we approached 3 P.M., I added to the position, thinking that the stock was holding up strong and the buyers were not interested in dropping the 33.80 area. I had a protective stop for the extra shares right below the area of buying and a stop for my initial shares below the opening prints below 33.50.

The play, however, didn't materialize into the closing session, so I took my feeler position home that night after selling the extra one right before the close. Coming into Friday, November 5, right on the open I knew there was an argument to be made for either position. If you were long you should be concerned that the stock had no follow-through on the previous day's close, given all the strong buying. If you were short you would be feeling comfortable as the stock couldn't make a push with all that buying and you never felt much pain in that consolidation. The stock needed to trade below 33.80 to give the sellers a reason to press and the buyers a reason to panic and get out of their longs. And above 34.00, it would give the sellers a reason to cover and the buyers a reason to add to their existing longs. Those waiting on the sidelines would just play either break, so naturally some order flow was expected at those levels.

Right on the open on Friday, the stock quickly traded below 33.80 on some significant volume, as pointed out in the 15-minute chart. You could tell there was a healthy number of sell stops that went off below that level. You could see it clearly on the tape. But the stock had no follow-through to the downside and then just as quickly traded back above 33.80 and eventually through 34.00. You could tell people were trapped and the volatility picked up compared to that of the previous day's close. I added to my long above 34.00 and placed my protective stops for both of my lots below that swing low established early in the day. I knew that I could expect a drive similar to that of the previous day (33.50 to 34.25), so I had about 75 cents of upside from my original entry.

Many would trade that same setup differently. I think paying through the second day's high at 34.25 would have been a good trade with a stop below the previous day's low. That play clearly offers more risk to the trader, but I would not really know where to take my profits. I consider that the pay, pray, and walk away play. And I am just not into that. Happy trading.

PART IV

Swing Trading

CHAPTER 15

Flags and Wedges

Joe Donohue, *@upsidetrader*

If I were to pick one guy to trade me off a desert island, Joe would be the one. If I had to pick an old fart to be stuck with on a desert island, Joe would be that man, too. Joe eats, sleeps, and drinks the market and I always trust his instincts. You can't be the best without a work ethic like Joe's. We are glad to have him as an investor, contributor, and partner at StockTwits.

When I am long of stocks it is because my reading of conditions has made me bullish. But you find many people, reputed to be intelligent, who are bullish because they have stocks. I do not allow my possessions—or my prepossessions either—to do any thinking for me. That is why I repeat that I never argue with the tape.

—Jesse Livermore

SERVING CHIVAS TO THE WALL STREET SHARKS

I was about 22 years old and I was just starting my senior year in college when a good pal and classmate walked over to me in a beautiful suit, dressed like Gordon Gekko. I asked him where he worked and he told me he was an apprentice at Bear Stearns. He said he was a "cold caller." I was clueless. Evidently it was the process of talking to very high-net-worth folks and gathering information on their investment approaches so the partner could sell them stocks. He got me an interview, and I too began working for a partner who was formerly from Lehman Brothers. Within the first week I spoke to T. Boone Pickens, Lee Iacocca, Frank Perdue, and many other notable CEOs. I was green and scared, but they took my calls. I was hooked. Four months into my Bear Stearns experience, the Christmas party came along. Due to blizzardlike conditions, some of the caterers just could not get there. Wall Street legend and CEO Ace Greenberg walked into my bosses' office and said they were shorthanded and needed help. I volunteered and ended up bartending that night in the partners' dining room. I had the chance to serve Chivas to guys I had only read about in the *Wall Street Journal*. Rainmakers were everywhere. I thought I was in Pandora before the bad guys showed up. I knew I had to do this with the rest of my life.

My career took me in some different directions: retail, institutional corporate bond trading, capital markets, and the hedge fund business. All of these places were part of a journey, during which I was taught many things and I also taught things to others. Through all of this, the underlying constant for me was the stock market. I could never leave it, and at times when I thought I would never come back, well, that thought never lasted long.

I TRY TO BE WHERE THE MONEY IS

My market philosophy couldn't be simpler. Following the money flow is the key for me. I have a technical approach to trading, but market psychology, momentum, and sentiment are just as important to me. The market is driven by fear and greed, especially after the crash of 2008 and the ensuing process of deleveraging in the developed world. The playbook has changed as "buy and hold" has become as hated as Bernie Madoff. Fear took the market down in 2008, not earnings misses. Greed took us up from the S&P 500 being at 666, not Cisco beating analyst expectations. I have thrown out the playbook and accepted the new normal.

There are many approaches to trading, maybe thousands. I don't use moving average convergence/divergence (MACD), stochastics, Bollinger bands, Fibonacci, or relative strength. There is nothing wrong with those indicators at all. In fact, I know traders who make a fortune using them; they are just not a part of my approach. My own strategy involves extensive analysis of daily and weekly charts, and then I drill down to the 10-minute chart where I use the 10-, 20-, 50-, and 200-period moving averages as support and resistance levels almost exclusively. I trade ranges; I buy strength and short weakness. I try to be where the money is. I buy dips on strong stocks, meaning they are still in an uptrend but they have pulled back on light volume. I short bounces in weak stocks, meaning they are still in a downtrend but have moved higher on light volume.

EXPERIENCE CAN'T BE BOUGHT

People ask me all the time what it takes to be a great trader. My answer consists of two words: screen hours. You can read books or watch DVDs, but unless you study the market with intense passion and have money on the line, it is probably fair to say that you won't become proficient at the game—and yes, it is a game. Even Jesse Livermore said, "It took me five years to play the game intelligently enough to make big money when I was right." I think it is fair to say that most traders lose money. Being a great trader, however, does not need to be inherent in your DNA; it can be learned, but time must be committed.

There is no holy grail to trading, so another good idea is to find a mentor or someone who has earned his stripes, has fought the wars, and has time to teach you. It obviously doesn't have to be a one-on-one situation.

Being a good stock picker is great, but not sufficient for consistent market success. Knowing when to sell or how to build a position based on the size of your portfolio is probably even more important. Risk management is essential.

This may be an extreme example, but how would you have felt if you were pressed fully long the morning of the famous flash crash when we imploded a fast 1,000 points? Extreme, yes, but you get the point. On a less extreme note, perhaps you are very net short going into an event, perhaps a Federal Reserve meeting or maybe an earnings report (I never have more than a one-third position long or short going into a specific earnings report; I consider that riverboat gambling and not trading), but the meeting outcome or the report is not favorable for your position. If you are not hedged, you are in trouble. My best advice if you are leaning substantially one way or the other (short or long) is to be hedged. A smart use of options or exchange-traded funds (ETFs) will get you a seat at the table and help your sleep process that night.

Diversification is key; sprinkle the infield as best you can with your allocated capital. Never go all-in on anything. The market doesn't care what you think and will be happy to make you look like a complete fool in nanoseconds. Your best idea, which could be the result of hours of due diligence and research, can be turned to pixie dust quickly.

USE STOPS OR DON'T BOTHER TRADING

I look at my trading screen and I am always present in my trading foxhole, but I always use stops. Some are mental stops because I am diligently watching, but many have been entered on my platform. I can trade 10 names in a day, get stopped on six of them, and still do very well with the remaining four. It's the commonsense part of trading that many people still have difficulty implementing. Never let a gain turn into a loss.

Selling strength in a name is good. One thing I have tried to drill into my subscribers' heads is selling partial positions into strength while at the same time raising your stop. If I buy a stock at $40 and it trades to $43, I sell one-third and raise my stop to $41. If it continues to $45, I sell another third and raise my stop to $43. This has served me well over the years, as a news event in the economy can flip the market and erase gains quickly. By using this approach, I almost always make money, as the remaining balance of the trade will stop for a profit. Gains are so hard to come by; don't give them back to the market.

Don't be a street sign named "One Way"; try to understand both sides of the market. I would say that 90 percent of people who are trying to learn to trade have never shorted a stock. You need to follow and be active in the ebb and flow of the market. Trading long only unless you are a hedge fund with that dedicated strategy is silly. It's like trading only on sunny days.

It's a different world today, so you must have an edge. Volatility has consumed this market as a result of quantitative and flash trading. The market used to trade in fractions and at a much slower pace; now it is in decimals. Setups were easier to find and understand; now about 70 percent of all trading has become automated. This can be intimidating to any new trader. It is true that there is still a buyer for every seller, but now there is usually a machine on the other end. Swings have become unforgiving and the choppiness some days is just amazing, driving even the pros to the point of extreme frustration.

THE FALLING WEDGE

The bullish or falling wedge is one of my favorite patterns that I look for on a daily basis. You can find them on many time frames, too. The key for me is to see the stock correct

FIGURE 15.1 AAPL Bouncing from Its Rising 20-Day MA, Daily Chart
Source: © StockCharts.com.

FIGURE 15.2 MOTR Bouncing from Its Rising 20-Day MA, Daily Chart
Source: © StockCharts.com.

within an uptrend on lighter volume. In the examples shown in Figures 15.1 and 15.2 the stocks retreated to rising moving average support on modest volume, a bullish formation. Notice the bounces of these stocks after the pullback to the moving average.

CAN YOU STILL WIN THE GAME, OR IS IT RIGGED?

The jaded skeptic in me thinks that everything is rigged to a degree. We know it's stacked against us the minute we walk into the Bellagio in Vegas, but we still rush to the table. The markets have been rigged to some degree since their inception. I'm sure there was funky action going on beneath the Buttonwood tree back in the day.

The answer to the question is yes, you can win the game, but it takes work, study, passion, and an intense desire to beat the other guy, even though the other guy may now be a robot. I believe in the system and believe that if you can develop that edge, whatever it may be, you can win the game.

CHAPTER 16

Breakout from a Tight Base

chessNwine, @chessNwine

The thing I admire about chessNwine is his calm and rational decision-making ability, even when a trade is not going his way. He just seems to do the right thing, the smart thing. It's no surprise he is a successful poker and chess player. It makes perfect sense.

If you personalize losses, you can't trade.

—Bruce Kovner

IT IS LIKE A CHESS STRATEGY

After the 9/11 attacks, I was glued to the television set watching nonstop news coverage. I came across CNBC. Up until that point, I could not differentiate between a livestock and a common stock. I saw the commentators asking guests whether they planned to sell or buy stocks when the markets were scheduled to reopen after 9/11. I was fascinated by the conversation. I intuitively thought that there would be a sharp, fear-based sell-off, which would be a great buying opportunity. I realized that I had no knowledge of how the stock market game worked, so I thought it was probably too obvious to think that. However, I enjoyed the mental stimulation, and it reminded me of a chess strategy.

After that point, I started to educate myself about stocks and investing. Whenever I went to the bookstore, I wandered over to the investing and personal finance section. I started watching CNBC more and I regularly read the *Wall Street Journal*. In essence, I incorporated the stock market into my daily routine.

Reading *Confessions of a Street Addict* by Jim Cramer (Simon & Schuster, 2002) gave me the motivation to make the transition from student of the market to an actual participant in 2003. I must say, however, that *Reminiscences of a Stock Operator* by Jesse Livermore was by far the most influential book on my trading style. The momentum type of trading fits much better with my personality than Benjamin Graham's style of deep value investing.

I am a licensed attorney and I have a background playing poker professionally. I was also a tournament chess player from an early age. Combine all of that with my experience and fascination with the coaching aspect of football and basketball, and you can see that I am attracted to the application of analytical thinking in terms of strategy as well as sound gambling concepts.

While in law school, I traded sparsely during my first year. During my second and third years, however, I had some more time on my hands and became a profitable trader. I believe that I was fortunate to begin trading just as the market was beginning its bull move from 2003 to 2007. I have been a profitable trader since 2004, and I have been trading full-time since 2006. I am primarily a swing trader, with a holding period of anywhere from a few days to several months.

LOOKING FOR AN EDGE

As an individual retail trader, I firmly believe that my advantage is not going to come from trading based on news flow or channel checks with relevant industry sources. I will let others play the fundamentals game, competing against the vast research arms of Wall Street banking houses. Instead, I believe that my edge comes from rigorous daily analysis of the price action and trading volumes of individual issues, sectors, and indexes. I am looking to allocate capital only when I notice a chart pattern that gives me a discernible edge. Without it, I just sit on my hands. As an individual trader, I use this ability to be nimble and selective to my advantage.

I always need to consider any individual stock, as enticing as the chart may be, within the context of the broad market. I am always asking myself three questions:

1. Is the broad market healthy? Is the 200-day moving average of the S&P 500 rising? Are we above the 50-day moving average? Those are two broad signs of general health. For me, the type of market that offers highest-probability setups is one that is steadily trending higher.
2. Is there a clear group of stocks leading us higher? If so, this reinforces the idea that we are in a healthy market. Moreover, I want to identify and participate in the moves of those leadership stocks.
3. Beyond the obvious leadership stocks, are there other stocks or sectors that are on the verge of breaking out to higher prices as well? This requires many hours of research and looking at countless charts, but it is by far the most profitable aspect of trading. You are looking for under-the-radar stocks before they have made their big moves. Again, if the broad market is healthy, the probability that more and more stocks will break higher increases.

BREAKOUT FROM A TIGHT BASE

My favorite setup is called a breakout from a tight base. The odds of this type of setup being successful increase significantly when the broad market is healthy.

This setup is formed when a stock settles into a tight price range after a prior period of volatility expansion. As the price swings and volume contracts, I put the stock on a list of scans, where I am basically stalking its every movement. At a certain point, the pattern will resolve itself, because the presumption is that one side will emerge victorious in the battle between bulls and bears. If the previous overall trend has been up and the consolidation period has been benign in terms of price and volume, then I become confident that the resolution will be a powerful move higher and the bulls will win. The quiet period of trading is usually bullish, because it indicates that traders have accepted a certain price level with ease, and higher prices are likely to come. You can see this type of action in bullish flag patterns, as well as in lateral bases.

As confident as I may be in a pattern resolving in my favor, I am always considering potential stop-loss zones before I hit the bid. In general, I prefer a 7 or 8 percent trailing stop loss. You simply must have a price level where you are willing to admit that you were wrong in your thesis. Not doing so is an egregious display of hubris, as well as a long-term money-losing strategy (the two often go hand in hand).

FOLLOWING MY PLAN

A specific example of a trade that I made, based on the setup just mentioned, was in General Steel Holdings, Inc. (GSI). I had the stock on my list of scans over the weekend of July 31, 2010. Figure 16.1 shows the chart I was looking at.

On Monday, August 2, I saw an uptick in buying volume in the morning, indicating the stock was starting to perk up. Because I had been expecting this tight base to resolve higher, I was prepared to act decisively. I tweeted out to the StockTwits community at lunchtime that I had bought a full position at $2.99 (time-stamped over at iBankCoin.com, where I blog). The stock went parabolic over the next two days. By Wednesday of that week, I was up over 10 percent and decided to scale out of my position. The stock had begun to lose momentum, and I had no interest in giving back my profits (see Figure 16.2).

After I was out of the trade, the stock actually gave back all of those gains, and then some. If I had been greedy and overstayed my welcome, or if I had missed my initial entry point and chased price higher, I would have been severely punished. Thus, the trade reinforced how important preparation, timing, and discipline are to being a successful trader.

In the case of GSI, my buy point was at $2.99, and I set my stop loss at $2.79, which was just below the low end of the base that it had previously formed. I set my stop loss there because if the stock fell below the base it had been forming, then my thesis would

FIGURE 16.1 Volatility Expansion Followed by Range Contraction
Chart courtesy of FreeStockCharts.com. © FreeStockCharts.com.

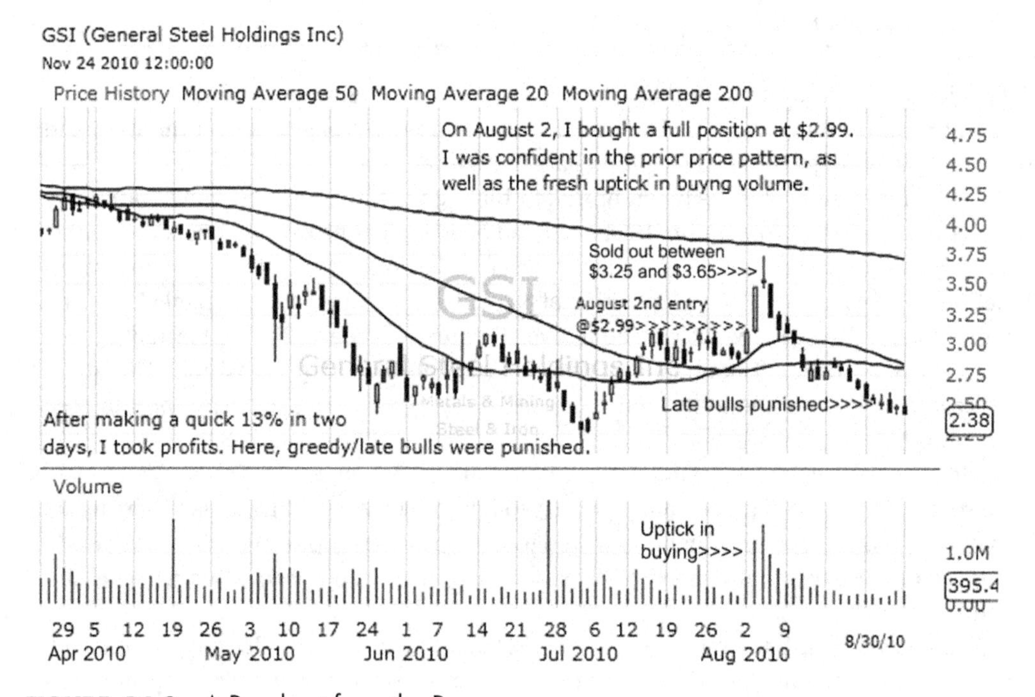

FIGURE 16.2 A Breakout from the Range
Chart courtesy of FreeStockCharts.com. © FreeStockCharts.com.

have been wrong. If that happened, I would have simply cut my losses and moved on to the next trade. I allocated 8 percent of my portfolio to this stock, which is almost always the maximum percentage of my capital that I will use for one position as a rule of managing risk.

I had confidence in the short-term success of the trade (two to three days), and I was prepared to act swiftly, so I bought a full position in the name instead of gradually building one. One of the reasons why I quickly and correctly took profits after two days was because the broad market was on shaky ground. In a healthier broad market, I would have probably held my position longer. In fact, I might have added to it on any type of pullback. However, my mind-set was to take profits and to not be greedy. When the broad market is not healthy, discipline will be your saving grace. Take profits just as quickly as you cut losing positions, and you will keep your head above water in choppy markets.

WORDS OF WISDOM

To paraphrase Paul Tudor Jones, losers average down losers; winners add to winners. Those words of wisdom have served me well. Adding to losing positions is by far the most common way that traders damage their portfolios. It seems quite simple to discuss these risk management concepts in the abstract, but one of the main reasons why so many traders average down on bad trades is because they personalize their losses by allowing them to lower their self-image. Simply put, taking losses is part of trading, regardless of how good you are. As Bruce Kovner says, "If you personalize losses, you can't trade."

CHAPTER 17

The Base Is Everything

HCPG, *@HCPG*

The HCPG team is totally professional. Their mantra—"The base is everything"—just works and you can see it in their solid trades on the StockTwits stream over and over again. They have a consistent, focused game plan around this thinking, and it makes trading easier. The elimination of ideas is as important as the addition of them.

SURVIVING THE CRASH

We are three traders who started trading in the late 1990s. It was a different time back then—everyone talked about stocks; they were in the air you breathed. You went to your family physician for a checkup and he would tell you about some tech stock he had just bought. You would go to your dentist for cleaning and she would tell you about some initial public offering (IPO) a patient had gotten her into.

The three of us went through various undergraduate and graduate schools that didn't have much to do with stock trading before we started. We were young, thought we were smart, and were ready to make some money. We started out as retail traders who simply bought and sold momentum stocks. Back then you couldn't lose money, as everything just went up until, of course, the crash.

The bear market was vicious, especially in 2002. Today we realize how little we knew back then. We shudder when we think about the type of cowboy trading we used to do in the early days. There were some wild fluctuations in our accounts from 1997 to 2002. It was a do-or-die time, and thankfully we adapted and survived.

The positive part of trading in the NASDAQ crash is that it opened our eyes to the importance of risk management and discipline. Today we diligently do our homework, and we risk capital only when we have an edge. Having learned the lessons of the tech crash, we were prepared for the 2007–2009 financial crisis and guided ourselves and our subscribers well through the mess.

Even though we started out as momentum traders (what else was there to do in the late 1990s?), as the years passed we became general technical traders with two main strategies:

1. Trend trading breakout and breakdown strategies (momentum trading).
2. Range-bound strategies buying dips on support and shorting rallies to resistance (reversion to the mean).

We don't trade for home runs but rather for consistency, day in and day out. In 2006, we launched the HighChartPatterns.com newsletter service and became known as HCPG. We started the newsletter for fun and never expected it to take off as it has over the past few years. It was just a way of sharing our homework with a larger audience. We figured if it was going to grow, it would do so organically through word of mouth.

COMBINING TIME FRAMES: THE INTRADAY AND THE DAILY

Even though we're always fine-tuning our trading strategies in order to stay on top of opportunities, the central premise of how we trade, something now that we have used for over a decade, never changes. We combine two different time frames, the daily chart (usually a 3- to 6-month time frame) and the intraday chart (usually 5-minute). When these two coincide, we enter a trade. Everything we do focuses on support and resistance on the daily and intraday charts. Every trade we make is close to either support or resistance. Our belief is that the easiest and fastest way to become a failed trader is to enter after an extended move (and have it reverse on you) or enter in a no-man's-land that has very little edge. Why? Because even if you are right about the direction, you will often get stopped out before you're proven right. We are mostly day traders who look for average 1 to 4 percent gains and with stops usually around 0.5 to 1 percent. However, we also often engage in swing trading from time to time, especially in volatile markets that do not lend themselves to tight stops. We don't rely on any fad strategies or fancy indicators. We just trade around support and resistance like the first technical traders in the early twentieth century did.

OUR UNIQUE MARKET APPROACH

To prepare for the trading day, every evening we go through a master list of around 300 stocks. The stocks are split up into different sectors (for example, oil and gas, coal, financials, technology), and they are stocks we know very well. Most of them we have been trading for over a decade. When new momentum candidates emerge, we add those to our lists. We also go through a list of exchange-traded funds (ETFs) that correspond to the major sectors in the market. Sometimes, especially in volatile markets, the only setups we see are in the ETFs and not individual stocks, and in those situations we just trade the E-mini S&P futures, OIH, XME, and IYR. On the whole, the sector we know best and trade best is the commodity sector, and we have special strategies we use when we trade certain stocks in specific sectors. For example, our rule of thumb is to buy strength in momentum stocks but buy pullbacks on commodities, and that has worked well for us over the years.

We don't do any scans. We like to get to know our stocks well. As every active trader will tell you, there are stocks that simply don't trade well, and the only way to identify them is to get to know their price behavior. Another important part of our trading strategy is to always have an eye for the current leading tell, be it copper futures, crude futures, currencies such as the euro or the yen, or, as we have witnessed lately, Treasuries. If, for example, we go into the day with breakout alerts but notice Treasuries are gaining momentum, we step back and reassess, knowing that the chance of breakout success will diminish with any bond rally. These market tells change from time to time (for example, for large parts of 2008 and 2009 the financials were the tell of the day), and we're always looking to see what the next market tell will be—they greatly influence how we trade.

When we find a chart of interest (usually a base on a daily chart or an imminent trend-line break) we place our alerts at the important price. Our favorite setup is the base and break. We started writing about it in 2006 and it's now used by many traders. Basically a base and break (often called a "b and b" by traders) consists of the following four steps (using a hypothetical example):

1. We go through charts every night looking for stocks that have formed good bases for potential breakouts. We place alerts on these stocks; for example, stock ABCD at 50 breaks out of a two-week base. Often the type of stocks we trade, high-beta stocks, actually start their move before the alert—50 cents to 1 point below the alert everyone has on their screens from the daily chart.
2. The next day we notice stock ABCD has very good volume and relative strength from the open and start stalking it—the stock forming an intraday base on the 5-minute chart between 49.3 and 49.5, riding up an ascending 20-day exponential moving average (EMA), and often basing under R1, the first resistance level.
3. We plan to buy the break of 49.5 if volume comes in on the break—this is what happens a few minutes later and we are filled at 49.54. A base and break on a momentum stock should either go right away or form another base above the current base but never return to the one below it. A return and undercut of the base or EMA is considered a failure and would be our stop.
4. Stock ABCD picks up volume and heads up to 50—our original alert. At 50 the stock is quite extended (having run 50 cents in eight minutes). If we had not caught

the original base and break we would not buy here, even though we have an alert at this price, as our number one rule in trading is to never enter a move extended from the base. We watch 50 and are ready to take some off in case the stock has run out of steam. Stock ABCD now chops around 50 and digests the move. At this point we're not in danger of getting stopped out since we have a comfortable cushion. A while later the 20-day EMA (5-minute chart) starts catching up and the stock starts grinding higher. Our exits are either when the stock becomes extended from the EMA/base or at the next resistance level on the daily chart. If the stock closes well we sometimes swing a partial amount.

Buying close to a base gives protection. The biggest mistake novice day traders make is to buy after an extended vertical move away from any base or 20-day EMA (5-minute chart). When the price reverses, it has no base to fall into and enters a price vacuum. As a consequence, losses come at a much faster rate than if a stock is close to a base. The base provides a natural, logical place to put a stop. It's your safety net.

Everything we do is defined by the base. If we short extended stocks, that means they are extended from the base/moving averages on the daily chart and are extended from the 20-day EMA on the 5-minute intraday chart. Our long entries are never on top of extended moves. We buy near a base, we add on dips near base support zones, and if the base goes, we take the loss. If we're in a friendly tape where things work as they should, our stops are tight. In more choppy, range-bound markets we reduce size in order to widen the stop and give the trade room.

When a trade goes against us we don't freeze, hesitate, or change our strategy. We take the stop and move on without any problem. Why? Because this is how we think: 10 ninjas surround you and give you two options: They will cut off your little finger or they'll cut off your legs and arms. As much as we hate the thought of the loss of our pinkie, we don't hesitate in our decision. Ninjas, thank you for giving us a choice. Please proceed in cutting off our finger. That's how we view day trade stops. They are the lesser evil that we have to accept in order to live to trade another day.

DAILY BREAKOUT SETUP

In healthy trending markets, base and break setups occur on a daily basis. Let's take a look at a typical base and break from November 2010.

In Figure 17.1, we have a standard setup at 86 on OXY, one of our favorite commodity stocks. Oil and gas stocks were acting well and we liked how the stock was setting up at 86. We placed an alert at 86 and included it in the newsletter for our readers.

The next day, a typical base and break alert occurs at 86. In Figure 17.2, note the volume surge on the break of 86—that is the entry. At this point, the stop is just below the rising 20-day EMA on the 5-minute chart, or 85.60.

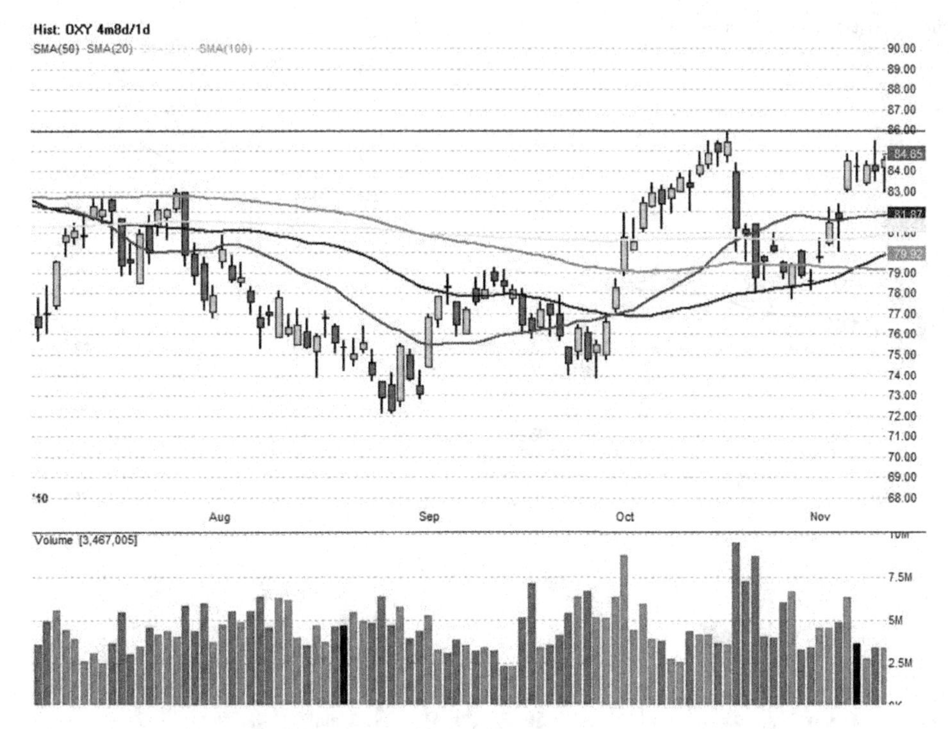

FIGURE 17.1 Breakout Setup, OXY Daily Chart
Source: © TD Ameritrade, Inc. Used with permission. For illustrative purposes only.

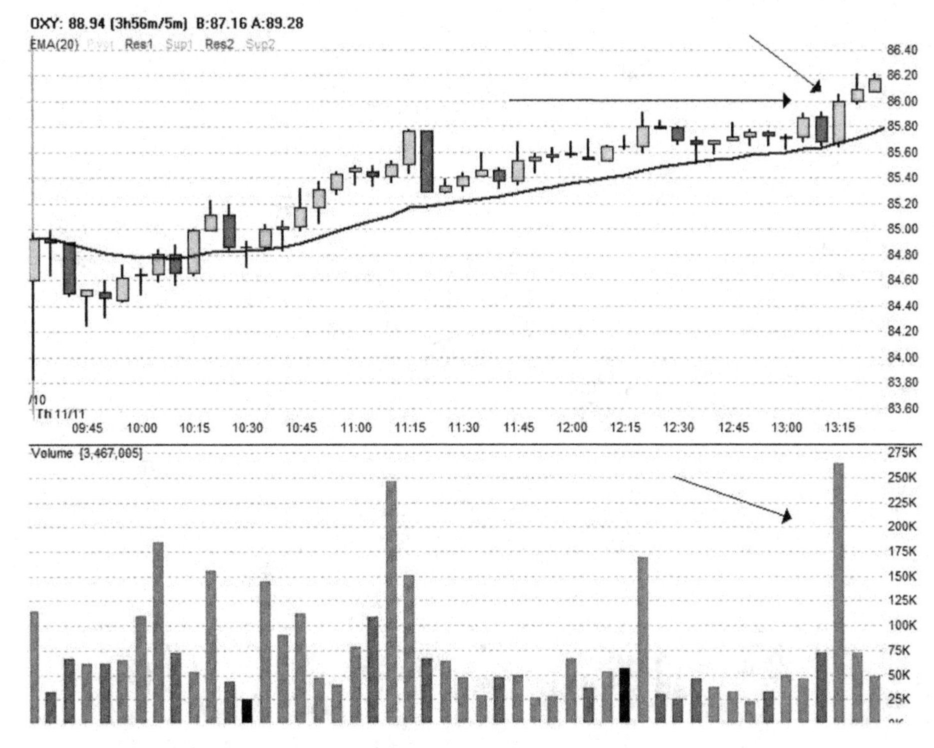

FIGURE 17.2 The Breakout Occurs, OXY 5-Minute Chart
Source: © TD Ameritrade, Inc. Used with permission. For illustrative purposes only.

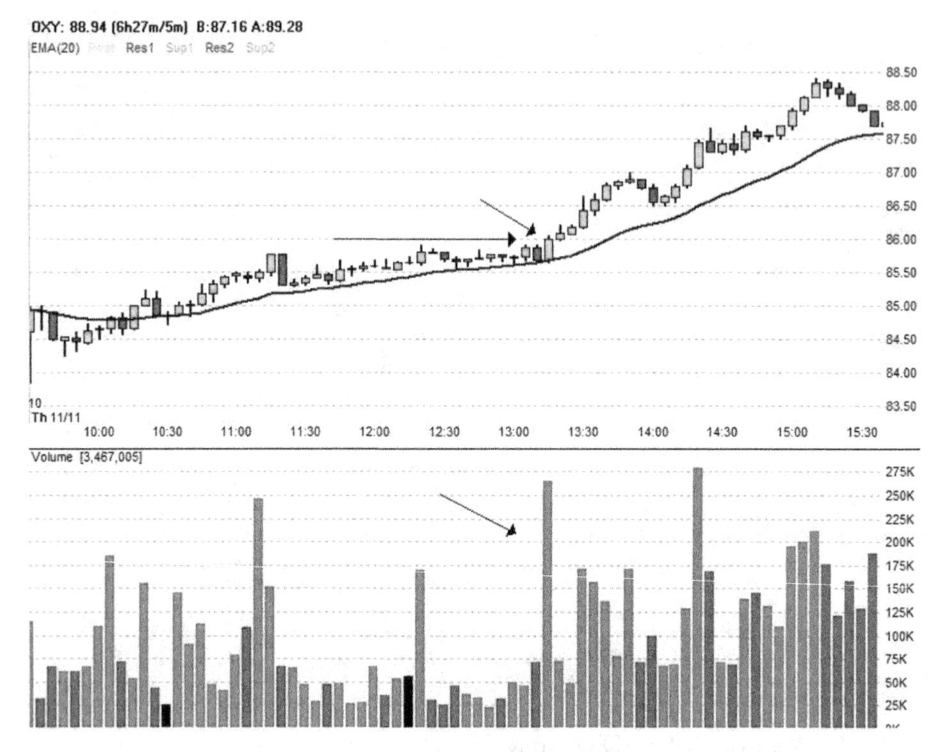

FIGURE 17.3 Taking Partial Profits, OXY 5-Minute Chart
Source: © TD Ameritrade, Inc. Used with permission. For illustrative purposes only.

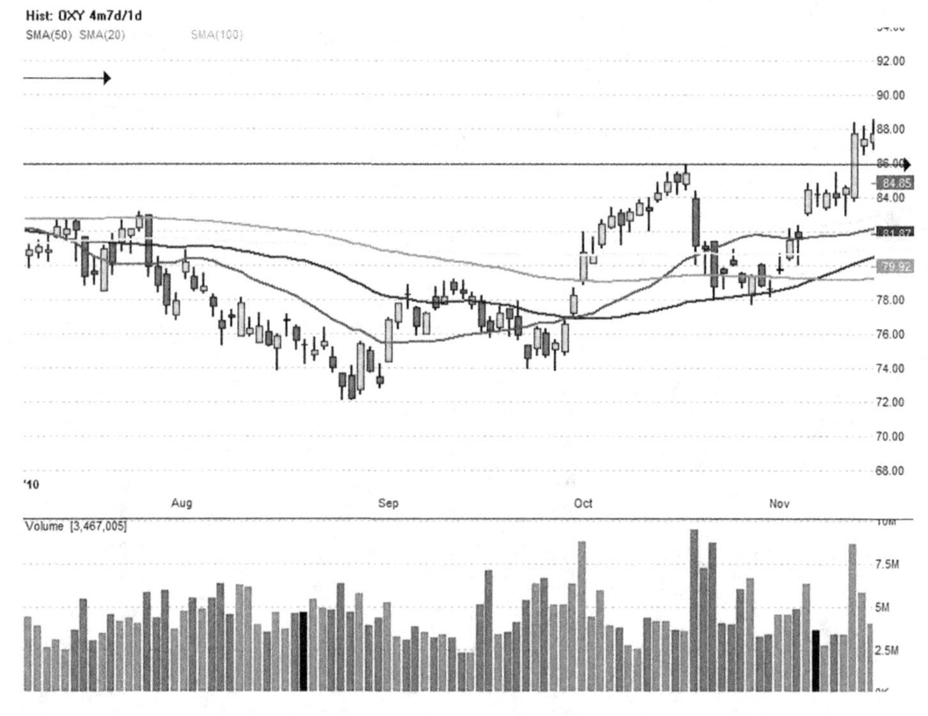

FIGURE 17.4 Keeping a Swing Candidate Overnight, OXY Daily Chart
Source: © TD Ameritrade, Inc. Used with permission. For illustrative purposes only.

An initial partial exit could be around 1 point with the original stop being 40 cents. Ideally we like to have exits *at least* two times that of our original risk. However, in this case there is no reason to have a set stop as the stock is nicely working higher on top of the 20-day EMA (5-minute chart). The EMA thus can become the trailing stop unless the stock starts running extended away from the EMA, which is what occurs right after 3 P.M. when it briefly goes over 88 (see Figure 17.3). That's a great day trade exit. Buy near a base and exit on an extended move away from the base for over 2 points profit with 40 cents risk—excellent risk/reward. OXY was also a good swing candidate for those who preferred to keep the stock overnight, as shown in Figure 17.4.

The base and break strategy is not difficult to learn; however, learning to be patient enough in order to sit and wait for the conditions to be fulfilled before you enter a trade takes a while to master.

CHAPTER 18

Trading People, Not Stocks

Joey Fundora, *@downtowntrader*

Joey Downtown is a solid-as-a-rock trader. He has a great eye and he's patient. He's aggressive when the time calls for it and he goes to play golf when the market is choppy and erratic. He sets stops and sticks to them. But most important, he knows himself and he knows the setups that he plays best. Absorbing his sense of self-awareness is likely his greatest lesson and may be more important than any specific trade that any of us will share on these pages.

When you are trading shorter time frames, you're trading people, not stocks!
—Joey Fundora

FROM ENGINEER TO FULL-TIME TRADER

I started out as an investor, primarily with a focus on technology stocks. My background is in the information technology (IT) field, and I have been involved with that area for almost 20 years. I felt that my expertise in that arena would help me as an investor, and though I did latch onto some winners, I quickly learned that there isn't always a positive correlation between great products and great stock performance. I realized that on shorter time frames, investors' psychology is more important than the underlying fundamentals in a stock. For instance, Apple is a great stock and company, but in a five-day window, market sentiment is infinitely more important to fluctuations in its stock price than the fundamental story behind it. In the long term, the fundamentals should eventually carry the stock, but as a short-term trader I focus on interpreting the actions of market participants. When you are trading shorter time frames, you are really trading people, not stocks. I have always felt this to be the case, and therefore I focus primarily on the actions of others in an effort to increase my odds.

In 2006, I started to blog about stocks as a way to share ideas with other traders and as a way to keep myself honest to my trading. Writing about trading setups forces you to really think through each step in the process, and it is a great way to organize your thoughts. All traders should review their trades and attempt to put their trading ideas to paper, even if only as a mental exercise. Documenting each trading setup helps traders clearly define why they were in a trade and what their expectations were. Following that up by reviewing their trading results helps traders ingrain what they learned from each trade to memory. This is probably the most important thing traders can do to help speed up the learning process in their quest to become consistently profitable. This is why I diligently update my trading journal on a daily basis.

An extremely valuable benefit to keeping a trading journal is collecting the statistics to validate the success or failure of each trading setup. Do you know your win rate for each of your trading setups? Do you know your trading expectancy for long trades? Do you know if you perform better on certain days of the week? Understanding your performance as a trader greatly increases not only the speed of your education as a trader, but also the quality of your trading. If you don't know your performance for each setup, then how can you be sure of what your edge is in the markets? Keeping a detailed trading journal forces a trader to view trades objectively, rather than attempting to invoke a memory of a trade that is most likely skewed by a variety of emotions. A journal allows a trader to step back and view the trades as a whole, rather than individual trades subject to the randomness of the markets. Knowing which component of your trading methodology is working well and which isn't allows a trader to target specific areas to improve, rather than try to work on a vague idea of trading better. Once traders have a good history of what works for them, they can begin to develop a trading methodology that is unique to them. The biggest turning point in my trading career occurred when I became serious about tracking my performance.

TRADE THE TRADERS

I am primarily a swing trader and I focus on the 2- to 10-day target time frame. I trade purely by using technical analysis and I use stock charts to help me analyze what market participants are doing in a given stock. While many traders in this area focus on trading mechanical systems or have a plethora of conditions they are looking for, I really consider myself more of a discretionary trader. I use the indicators on my charts as a filtering system to keep me in the right stocks, but prefer to watch price action at certain levels in order to make my trading decisions. I am also a firm believer in paying attention to intermarket dependencies and correlations. Institutions typically trade baskets of stocks, so I will often look at an entire sector when a single stock is performing well. More often than not, several stocks in a sector will show similar patterns, allowing traders to focus on the best fit for their trading methodology. Once I narrow my universe of stocks down to a few hundred, I will then review them nightly as I look for patterns to develop in the markets. I constantly add and remove stocks from my universe as I see money rotate from one group to another.

While having a well-thought-out equity selection approach is necessary, it is insufficient by itself for consistent success in the market. Managing risk is the single most important component of a trading system. It's not as sexy as a fancy indicator or market scan, but how you manage your risk is what separates successful traders from failed traders. Because we are dealing with an infinite number of variables and human emotions, there is no trading system that is foolproof. Every trading system will suffer losses and drawdowns, and traders must be willing to accept these losses as a cost of doing business. Trading is much like poker in this regard. It doesn't matter how much the odds stack up in your favor; there will be times that the market doesn't react in the way you expect. The best traders minimize the damage when a trade moves against them and then seek to maximize their benefit when the trade moves in their favor. While it's difficult in practice, the concept is really as simple as that.

SWING TRADING REQUIRES SPECIFIC WAY OF THINKING

My main style of trading is swing trading for a single leg up or down. I've found over the years through monitoring my trades that this is my sweet spot. This keeps most of my trades in the 2- to 10-day time frame, but my holding times will sometimes be longer in a trending market. I also prefer to trade in sync with the longer-term trend in a stock. I have found that attempting to trade against the grain, so to speak, is more difficult and is littered with more failed moves.

I start the search for my favorite setup by screening for stocks that are near the end of a consolidation within a longer-term uptrend. Retail traders will often exit an otherwise healthy stock when the first sign of weakness appears. The fear of losing their profits is often stronger than the greed for more. This is why so many traders sell their winners so fast.

Once the scared money has exited, the stock will often resume its uptrend and provide a low-risk opportunity for traders to take advantage of. Stocks need these consolidations in order to fuel sustained moves higher. They also offer traders a great way to manage risk. While a trader can often buy a stock well into a move up and be correct, buying stocks that are extended from a base makes it very difficult to manage risk. If a trader has a poor entry, it makes it much more difficult to manage the trade through normal fluctuations in the stock's price.

The way I recognize stocks near the end of their consolidation is by looking for narrowing in the daily range. Often a stock will have large swings as market participants attempt to find a fair price after a trend move. As market participants reach equilibrium, the stock's price will narrow in range, typically on contracting volume. Once a stock begins to emerge from this range, it often offers a great risk-to-reward trading setup. By waiting for narrow-range candles, a trader can greatly minimize risk by placing the stop closer to the price action. Then, by waiting for the stock to emerge from the consolidation, a trader can increase the odds by letting the market confirm strength rather than attempting to guess the next direction. Once I find this setup, I set my stop under the narrow-range candles accordingly, making sure that a reasonable target is at least three times my defined risk.

One of the most commonly overlooked components to a trading system is the importance of choosing a stop-loss method that is compatible with your profit-taking strategy. The easiest way to accomplish this is to marry the two to a given time frame. If you are focusing on a 10-day window, then your stop should not be at a 3-month low or an intraday 15-minute low. Because my trading methodology is focused on the initial break from a narrow-range consolidation, I prefer to set my stop just under the narrow-range candles used for a trading decision. If the stock drops below these candles, my entire reasoning for the trade is invalidated, so I just exit the trade.

Position sizing is another important component to managing risk, and I always risk the same amount per trade. The way I do this is by using the concept of a risk unit or *R*. *R* is a percentage of my overall portfolio that I risk on a typical trade. Some commonly used values can vary from 0.5 percent to 3 percent, but I typically set it to approximately 1 percent of my portfolio. For a $100,000 trading account, this would equate to risking $1,000 on each trade. I use this method because it allows me to adapt to stocks that fluctuate more wildly than others by decreasing my position size in order to keep dollar risk constant. Once I set my stop and size my position in order to risk only one *R*, I then ensure that a reasonable target is at least three *R*s away. This allows me to trade profitably, even with a winning percentage under 50 percent. This position sizing is described in greater detail in the popular book *Trade Your Way to Financial Freedom* by Van K. Tharp (McGraw-Hill, 1999; 2nd ed. 2007).

The specific setup conditions I am looking for are:

- Find stocks near the end of a consolidation in an uptrend (for my typical time frame an uptrend is defined as stocks trading above their 20- and 50-day simple moving averages).
- Use candlestick charts and pay close attention to the patterns they form, as they reveal market participants' sentiment.
- Look for divergences in the MACD histogram, which can reveal slowing momentum in the countertrend move.
- Watch Bollinger bands for tight contraction, confirming that the consolidation may be near an end.
- Watch volume patterns to gauge the urgency of market participants.
- Set stops under narrow-range candles in order to keep risk manageable.
- Ensure that a reasonable target is at least three *R*s away.

I will scale out into strength as a stock approaches my defined target. I will then look for selling patterns to appear before exiting the remaining shares. If the stock settles into a second consolidation, I will exit any remaining shares if the stock closes under its 9-day exponential moving average. Because I am looking for a single leg up, this simple stop keeps me out of stalling or weakening stocks.

While I focused on buying stocks in uptrending markets, this approach also works in reverse for downtrending markets as well.

NU SKIN ENTERPRISES, INC.

A great example of this setup is a swing trade I took in Nu Skin Enterprises, Inc. (ticker: NUS) in April 2010. I actually profiled this trade in the April 15, 2010, edition of the StockTwits "Talk Your Book" show, and the accompanying video can still be found in the archives.

NUS began building a base in October 2010, consolidating the prior long-term uptrend. There was clear support in the $23 area on the few pullbacks it had, and sellers consistently stepped in when NUS approached the $28 level. These two levels would be considered the boundaries of the base.

NUS eventually cleared the base and then settled into a narrow range consolidation just above prior resistance. It pulled back toward its prior breakout and respected this level as support. As volatility in NUS began to decline, it started trading in small doji candles as buyers and sellers reached an equilibrium point. Once NUS began to emerge from these small candles, it offered an opportunity to get long with a very tight stop.

The entry was at $29.35 on April 12, as NUS cleared two small candles that had tested the 20-day simple moving average. The stop was placed just under the small doji candles at $28.44 and offered a risk of $0.91 per share on the trade. The estimated target was anywhere from $32 to $35 based on a few different techniques. One method for estimating a target is to subtract the top level of the base from the bottom ($28 – $23 = $5), and then add that total to the breakout point. This would yield a target of $33 ($28 + $5 = $33). Another possible target was a measured move taken from the late February low to the March high and then added to the breakout area. In either case, all of the possible targets were in the $33 to $35 area and offered over a 3-to-1 risk-to-reward ratio (see Figure 18.1).

This trade happened to move in my favor quite quickly, and NUS rocketed higher a couple of days after the entry (see Figure 18.2). After the initial thrust to the $31 area, NUS pulled back for a retest of the March high. Notice the long bottoming tails in the two candles on April 16 and 19, hinting that buyers were coming in after initial selling in the day. After this brief pause, NUS resumed the move higher and almost hit $34 per share. I closed half my position at $33.37 on April 23. NUS had already reached my target, but was also becoming extended, which skewed the running risk-to-reward ratio. I typically

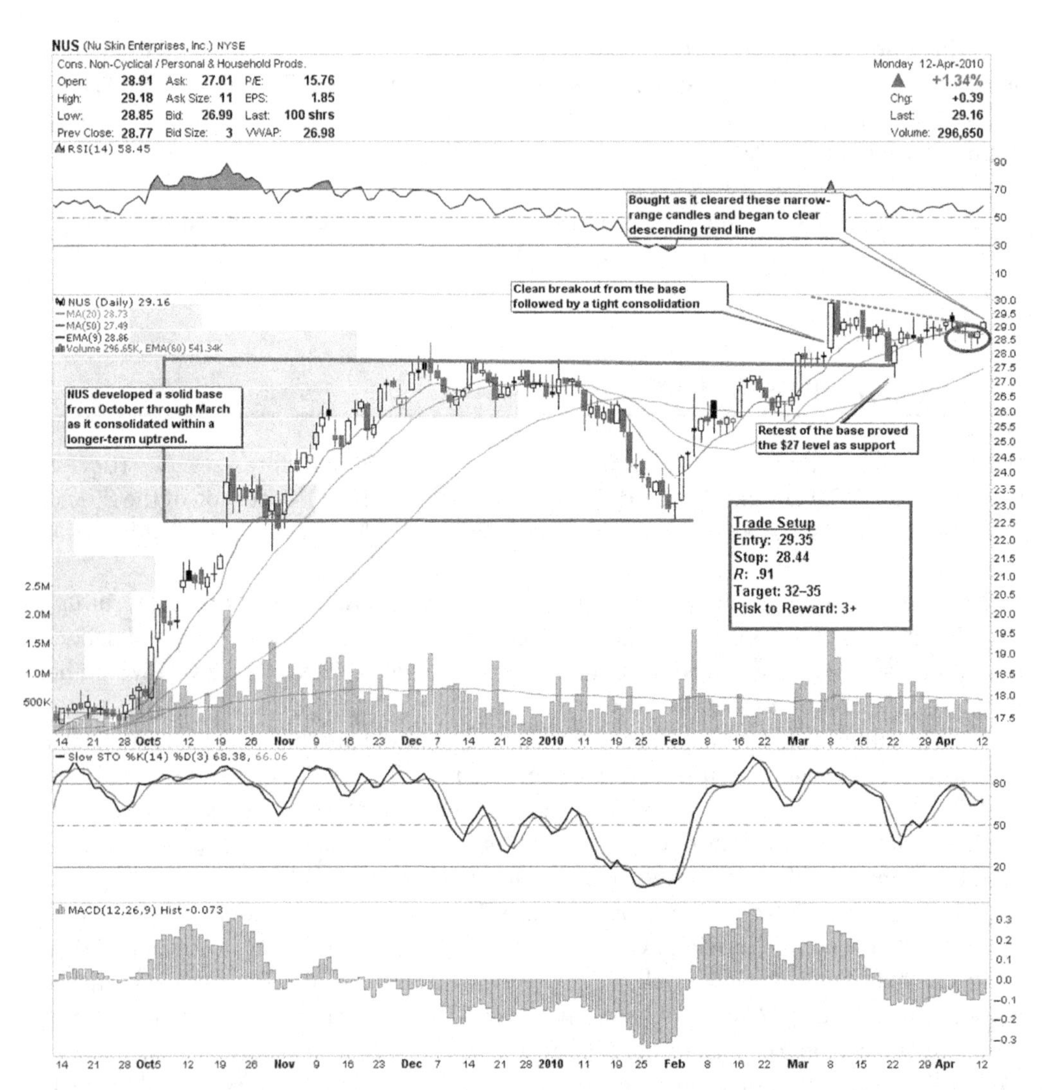

FIGURE 18.1 Breaking Out from a Tight Range, April 12, 2010, NUS Daily Chart
Source: © StockCharts.com.

scale out the first half into strength on my swing trades and then try to squeeze more out of the second half. If a shallow pullback offers another opportunity, I may add the other half back.

One of the indicators I watch is the 9-day exponential moving average, and I usually will exit this trade setup once it appears that the stock will close below this level (see Figure 18.2). While it may seem arbitrary, this setup is predicated on a fast move higher, and a stock that is under this level is showing weakness. NUS reversed sharply off the

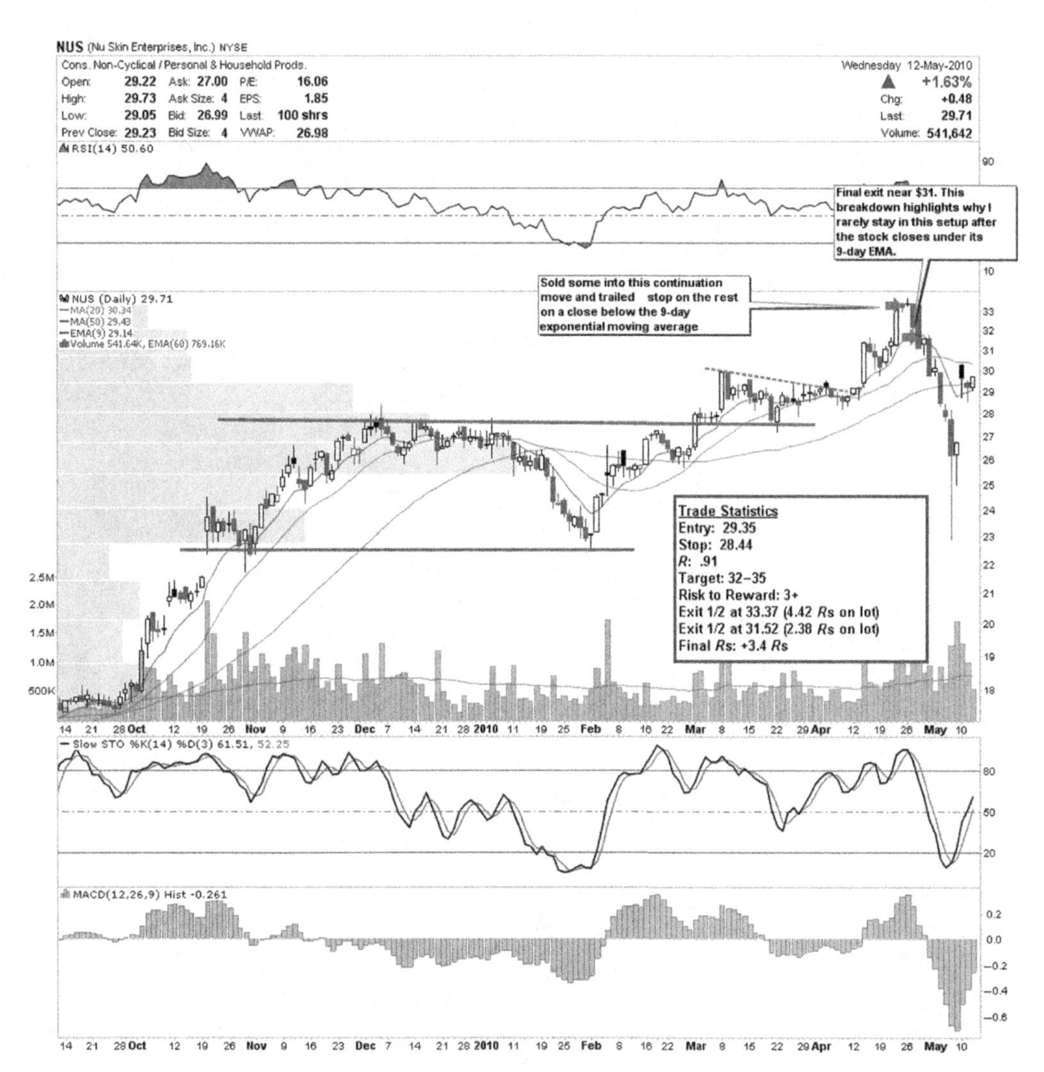

FIGURE 18.2 Scaling Out: Half Position at $33.37 and Half below the 9-Day EMA, NUS Daily Chart
Source: © StockCharts.com.

push to new highs and I sold the remaining portion as it looked like it would close below the 9-day EMA. More important than the fact that it was closing below the moving average, the pattern of buyers supporting the stock on intraday pullbacks disappeared. It is important to understand your intended time frame, and because I am trying to capture a single swing, I will exit at any sign of weakness. As you can see, this simple rule kept me out of harm's way over the next few trading sessions.

CHAPTER 19

The Top-Down Technician

Greg Harmon, @*harmongreg*

Greg has distilled a world of exceptional experiences into a strategy that is simply profitable. While it appears as though he operates effortlessly in the world of technical analysis, it turns out that he has made it to this point only by working so hard for so long. This chapter, along with his blog, DragonflyCap.com, is truly a hidden gem and a boon for those who aspire to be more sophisticated technicians.

The best preparation for tomorrow is doing your best today.
—H. Jackson Brown Jr.

ALL ROADS LEAD TO TECHNICAL ANALYSIS

In 1986, I started working in finance in the securities lending/repo market at Chase Manhattan Bank, where I quickly learned about liquidity and credit spreads. In those days, we would put U.S. Treasury bonds out on repo and buy A1/P1+ commercial paper, both on an overnight basis, for 25 basis points (bps) or more. After five years, I moved to Boston to trade the same market and start international business for State Street. Shortly after my arrival, the equity team left and I added that to my responsibilities and thus had my first opportunity to deal in the equity finance space. The next seven years were a global cavalcade of merger arbitrage, tax arbitrage, dividend arbitrage, yield curve plays, futures arbitrage, covered interest rate arbitrage, and just outright short selling. The involvement in so many different asset classes and markets helped me to build my understanding of intermarket correlations and the major driving forces in capital markets, how securities are settled, and the costs and the risks involved.

After two years in London, I started exploring the hedge fund space. Hedge funds had indirectly been my customers, and in 1999 it was time to dig deeper. I pushed State

Street to start a prime broker and set off on building it. This gave me even greater insight into hedge fund strategies, as well as an introduction to other derivatives hedge funds used, specifically swaps. Three and a half years into it, the company decided against the business on the day I was about to print the first ticket. That's Boston politics in the business world.

I left and went to BNP Paribas in New York to build synthetic prime brokerage and trade portfolio swaps. My customers were some of the biggest hedge funds on the planet, so it was very active. This is the time when I started to pay more attention to technical analysis (TA). The process of hedging my swaps gradually revealed how important technical analysis can be on a shorter time frame. The trader I was working with, Matt Flannery (ex–Deutsche Bank), would talk about DeMark indicators all the time—good stuff but pretty complicated. I wanted something simpler.

One day, I stumbled upon Japanese candlesticks. They are so much more than just bar charts but still pretty simple. I read Steve Nison's book *Japanese Candlestick Charting Techniques* (Prentice Hall, 2nd ed. 2001) and I was hooked. He is the god of Japanese candlesticks. I had always kept up the learning to stay sharp and increase my knowledge and already had an MBA, as well as CFA and CAIA designations, so reading more came naturally. This was where I wanted to be. Doing this at a French bank, where every Frenchman had graduated the equivalent of magna cum laude from an elite quantitative school, made it equally enlightening to me that TA is an art, not a science. What I mean is that the quants ran their models all day and to great precision, but they traded with about a quarter of the frequency of our book. I am not knocking their plan or preparation, but it was a learning experience for me that you may not always be right to the penny but if you hold out for that last penny you will miss a lot of trades. That life ended when the French decided to abandon the synthetic business and strap on the bricks-and-mortar prime brokerage business by purchasing it from Bank of America at the end of 2008. This left me free to focus in depth on refining my understanding of technical analysis.

FROM BROAD TRENDS TO SPECIFIC PICKS

I look for stocks that have the potential to move a lot over the next five days. My philosophy is grounded in trend analysis, starting from the macro level and working downward. It is not totally technical; I do read the papers and review analysis from other traders and some analysts, but my approach is definitely heavily weighted to TA now.

I begin the preparation for each week on Friday afternoon at 4:30 P.M., by reviewing the charts of the major macro indicators I follow gold, oil, the dollar, bonds, and volatility, as well as the major equity indexes—the S&P 500, Russell 2000, and NASDAQ-100—on both a daily and a weekly time frame. This review adds to my understanding of the current trend in the equity markets on two separate time frames, as well as the trend of those intermarket macro factors that influence equities. Armed with this information,

I then do some sector analysis using the SPDR S&P 500 sector exchange-traded funds (ETFs) to get a flavor of what has been driving the indexes and what may drive them in the short term.

Finally, I spend upwards of 10 hours looking at individual charts. I do not use a screener, just my eyeballs. Upwards of 500 names have the potential to make my watch list, and I am looking for the 25 or so names that have potential for big moves within the coming week. I am looking for chart patterns, continuations of trends, and tests of channels. I seek stocks that are near support or resistance areas, using simple moving averages, historical trade activity, and Fibonacci retracement levels and projections. This analysis tells me if a stock has the potential to run 5 or 10 percent or if there are several layers of support or resistance to work through, which may take time.

If a stock looks interesting from a first glance, I then move to looking at the volume, momentum, and stochastic indicators. I keep it simple—just the Relative Strength Index (RSI) and moving average convergence/divergence (MACD). Once I have the potential movers, I tie it all together with the macro and sector analysis to get the top 10 trade ideas for the week. I keep them weighted to the strong sectors and consider how the picks relate to the prevailing trends. I also diversify them so that I am ready to catch moves in multiple sectors as they might occur. These 10 ideas make it to their own page on my screen by Sunday night. The remaining movers that did not make the initial cut may be added later if any of the initial 10 either turn out to be duds or reach their potential. I will give these ideas up to a week for a strong focus, but generally, due to the nature of the selection process, they trigger quickly or not at all.

STRONG TREND LINES AND THE ROOM TO RUN

My favorite setup is a test of a previous trend line that has been support and resistance several times in the past and where the next level of support or resistance is far from that level. In many instances, these setups give you a potential to make money in both directions, so each setup is a two-for-one deal.

I use three tools to control risk: stop losses, controlled position sizes, and options. I combine the first two to determine the maximum amount of money I am willing to lose. Stops are always initially placed at my maximum loss away from the trigger. As a stock moves through a new level of support or resistance I will move my stop with it to protect some profits. For example, if I plan to go long a stock on a hold of resistance at 38, upon my entry at, say, 38.05, my stop might be placed at 37.90. As the stock rises and bases at 39 for some time and then jumps to 39.50, I would raise my stop to just under 39. As the stock approaches my target, I will prepare to exit on a pullback.

I use options sometimes, mainly call and put spreads, when I feel an idea has merit but might take some time. This limits my exposure to the option premium and, since they are spreads, minimizes the time decay.

APPLICATION OF THE SETUP

Let's take a look at Figure 19.1, featuring Anadarko Petroleum Corporation (symbol APC), to reveal my thought process behind managing one of my favorite setups.

The details:

1. August 2, 2010, 9:32 A.M.: Bought APC @ $50.70 after an open above $50.52 resistance/support and a test and hold with a stop loss at $50.35, risking 35 cents.
2. Stock runs up and rests at $51.50, then flags and jumps again. On the jump-off from $51.50, moved stop to $51.50 to lock in 80 cents.
3. Stock continues run into close. Moved stop to $52.00.
4. August 3: Watched the first 30 minutes and saw a hold $52.24. On a lift above $52.50, moved stop to $52.20, just under support.

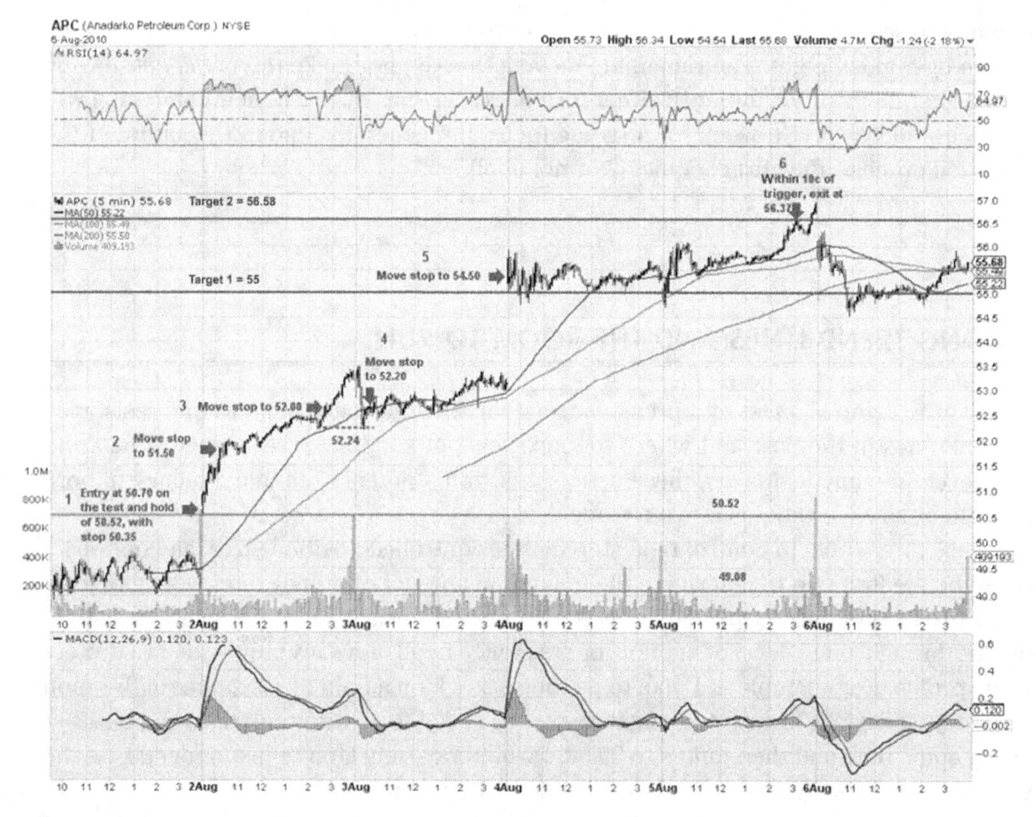

FIGURE 19.1 The Game Plan, APC 5-Minute Chart
Source: © StockCharts.com.

5. August 4: Big gap-up open above first target of $55.00. Moved stop to $54.50.
6. August 5: Just after 3:10 P.M., the stock topped within 10 cents of my second target of $56.58. I placed a sell order and was stopped out at $56.37 at 3:14 P.M.

It is not often that a trade like this comes along. In a good week five or six of my 10 trade ideas trigger, and maybe two of them pay off better than 2 percent. For one trade to move more than 10 percent is something you remember. But I would never have noticed it without doing all the homework.

CHAPTER 20

Identifying Trend Shifts

Derek Hernquist, *@derekhernquist*

Derek is a serious student of the history and psychology of markets, and he is a thoughtful and responsible money manager. He is a big contributor to our StockTwits U blog and always on the stream chipping in with his knowledge. It seems like the more he shares, the deeper he gets.

The usual bull market successfully weathers a number of tests until it is considered invulnerable, at which time it is ripe for a bust.
—George Soros

LEARNING FROM THE MASTERS

I fell in love with the markets at the University of Arizona in 1989, upon entering *USA Today*'s Collegiate Investment Challenge. After years analyzing sports statistics and match-ups, I had found my calling. My breaks were now spent reading *Investor's Business Daily* and logging into Prodigy for stock quotes.

Upon graduation, I jumped into the brokerage field, thinking that was the way to expand my knowledge of investing. I quickly learned that while it gave me the chance to explore new and better ways of allocating money, it was primarily a sales job, which was not my passion. Gradually, I overcame my sales shortcomings and found myself managing an office at the age of 21. Instead of spending my time reading sales and management books, however, I was drawn to learning more and more about the underlying dynamics of capital markets.

First it was Fred C. Kelly's *Why You Win or Lose: The Psychology of Speculation* (www.therichestmaninbabylon.org), an obscure little book that had a huge influence on my thinking. Like many of my books, I lent it out and haven't seen it since, but I clearly remember the lesson. He talked of a farmer with a chicken coop. The farmer had amassed 12 chickens, but then one slipped out of a trapdoor. Then another and another. "I'll stop trying to gather chickens as soon as those three come back," said the farmer. Then two more escaped, and his goal was now to leave with 10 of the original 12. As more kept escaping, he lowered his goal of how many to take home until finally all of the chickens were gone.

As a broker, I had seen this play out repeatedly. Accounts transferred in with thousands of shares of some dog, often a penny stock sold by the scoundrels of that era. People were just not willing to sell those until they got back to even—not necessarily the $5 they originally paid on the initial public offering (IPO), but whatever their new cost was after averaging down a couple of times.

So, "sell your losers" and "never average down" became instant lessons for me, ones I haven't had much trouble with in the 15+ years since. There are many factors that determine what a stock is worth when we make a sell decision, but the price paid should not be one of them. It is a sunk cost that unfortunately bears an outsized psychological trap for many.

The next book that shaped my thinking is *Reminiscences of a Stock Operator* by Edwin Lefèvre. What a book! I've probably read it 15 times. Sure, Jesse Livermore suffered wild swings in his fortunes and ultimately couldn't separate his trade from his self-worth, but boy, did he know markets. I was so enthralled by his ability to effortlessly swing from bullish to bearish based on the prevailing trend and his ability to sit with winning ideas. It was this book that converted me from trying to pick bottoms and tops to getting more in line with what he called the "path of least resistance."

To bring it all together, I needed a way to apply timeless concepts to modern markets. This is where William O'Neil's *How to Make Money in Stocks* (McGraw-Hill, 1988) came in. I had read *Investor's Business Daily* (*IBD*) religiously for years, but did not properly follow its method. I dug deep for stocks with high earnings per share (EPS) rankings and low relative strength (RS). A winning combo, right? I quickly learned just how faulty this was, as high-RS stocks like Cisco Systems and Microsoft and Oracle powered ahead, while I bought junk like Novell and Waste Management whose numbers were good but whose best days were behind them.

I never became a full devotee of the CAN SLIM methods of *IBD*, but the concept of relative strength became the cornerstone of my approach and it is still such today. It is my belief that relative strength precedes absolute price strength, which precedes fundamental news flow. By focusing in on the area that first reveals emerging trends, I am able to combine my respect for trend with my desire to arrive before the party is too obvious.

To this day, I find most in common with the old sages of the early twentieth century, like Livermore and Dow and Wyckoff and Baruch and Watts. While modern tools allow us to study many more opportunities, I think the lessons offered in that era regarding human nature are invaluable and timeless.

EMOTIONS DRIVE PRICES

I'm a believer that markets are constantly seeking the proper price, and this transition from one phase to another is where we can find opportunity. While some think you can plug in numbers and spit out a stock's true value, the reality is that human emotion drives the trending and correcting processes, which occur over and over again. This constant under- and overreacting presents opportunities when prices tend to move from one perception of fair value to another.

THE NEWS ABSORPTION TRADE

My setups are based on the following logic: buy panic after a long downtrend, buy disbelief on a range breakout, buy worry in an uptrend. Conversely, short euphoria after a long uptrend, short belief on a range breakdown, short hope in a downtrend. These are six types of trades, but I will use this forum to discuss just one and its counterpart. I call them my "news absorption" strategies, and while they are countertrend I believe they adhere to the principles of prudent speculation and risk management.

Consider a long uptrend, with quarter after quarter of good news and a reputation for delivering flawless results. Since good news begets more good news (and bad news begets more bad news), we see a positive feedback loop that leaves prudent sellers behind and crushes anyone trying to short the stock. The stock appears indestructible, and gains a manic legion of devoted shareholders. Another great result comes out, and the stock gaps up again—but it doesn't stay up. In fact, it gives up its entire gain and goes negative. This is the point where news reaction has finally caught up with news flow. It does not mean that news flow has to turn bad from there, but if that news could not take the stock higher, what news could?

On the other hand, consider a long downtrend with multiple quarters of disastrous results. The stock has attracted early value buyers along the way, but the feedback loop crushes them quarter after quarter. It is on the trash heap, and preannounces bad earnings again. After a brief sell-off, the stock closes higher. How could this be?

In these two cases, we are witnessing the great discounting mechanism that is the market. It doesn't look in the rearview mirror; it looks six to nine months out. This is why markets pull out of a bear market long before an economic recovery is apparent, and why stocks peak when they are most popular among retail market participants. So when can we move against the prevailing technical and fundamental trends instead of sticking with them?

I start by creating a watch list each day of mid- and large-cap stocks making new 21-day highs or lows on expanded range and double their median volume of the past seven days. You can tweak these numbers to make them your own, but this puts me in position to find the following:

- Popular stocks with new buyers, and hated stocks with new sellers.
- High emotion as noted by larger volume and range.
- News event to be assessed.

I can now evaluate the strength of the reaction to tell me whether (1) the price has caught up with expectations or (2) perception of business strength or weakness may have run ahead of the corporate reality. If it has, we will see the following three types of activity upon these new highs (or lows):

1. Inability for price to stay near its highs or lows.
2. Tendency to open strong and close weak or open weak and close strong.
3. Larger volume on down days than on up days or vice versa.

PRICE BATTLE FOR WHIRLPOOL

First, let's look at a major high in Whirlpool Corporation. The stage was set in April 2010 when a steady uptrend accelerated into an 8-point push higher ahead of an earnings report. Then, a stellar earnings report created a 15-point gap higher. The stock was the toast of its industry following a fivefold move in a year (see Figure 20.1).

We now watch the price battle, as the outcome of a significant event is among the best indicators of direction for the quarter ahead. The chase and short squeeze peaked into the opening levels, as the market rallied along without Whirlpool extending its gains. This was a subtle message that Whirlpool was no longer a high-alpha stock but simply along for the market's beta ride. Confirming its shift from leader to market stock is the large percentage of stocks making 21-day highs along with Whirlpool, a crowded total of 40 percent.

This was not some software or medical device company emerging into new price territory, but an established large-cap company with price memory. It had traded in the 100 to 105 range back in 2007 (see Figure 20.2). Without that longer-term look, we'd have no clue where sellers may be aggressive. With it, we can lean on that area as long as the short-term action suggests the event has triggered selling instead of buying. We short the next day when the stock fails to make another high, with a stop above the event-day high of $118.44 and a target near the quarterly low of $74.

These reactions occur rarely, but when they do a strong message is served that investors are anticipating peaking growth for recent winners or troughing contraction for recent losers. Simply watching this heavy turnover can provide major clues that the stock is leaving strong hands and headed into weak hands or vice versa.

FIGURE 20.1 WHR Gaps Up on a Good Earnings Report and Sells Off, Daily Chart
Source: © StockCharts.com.

IMPORTANCE OF SENTIMENT AND FUNDAMENTAL SHIFTS

Fundamentally driven investors may scoff at the focus on the reaction to news rather than the news itself. While I use price data to find and execute these opportunities, it is sentiment and, yes, fundamentals that I believe drive the process. I find corporate leverage to be the most underrated factor in the pricing of stocks. We are aware that financial leverage can create and destroy wealth on the thinnest of adjustments, but bear with me as I get fundamental.

A growing company makes hires to keep up with its exciting new product line. It still has pricing power due to early entry, and the new employees are young and hungry. This sounds like a recipe for expanding profit margins. Decent growth plus expanding profit margins equals explosive earnings growth, and analysts cannot keep up due to their fixation on prior estimates and fear of going out on a limb.

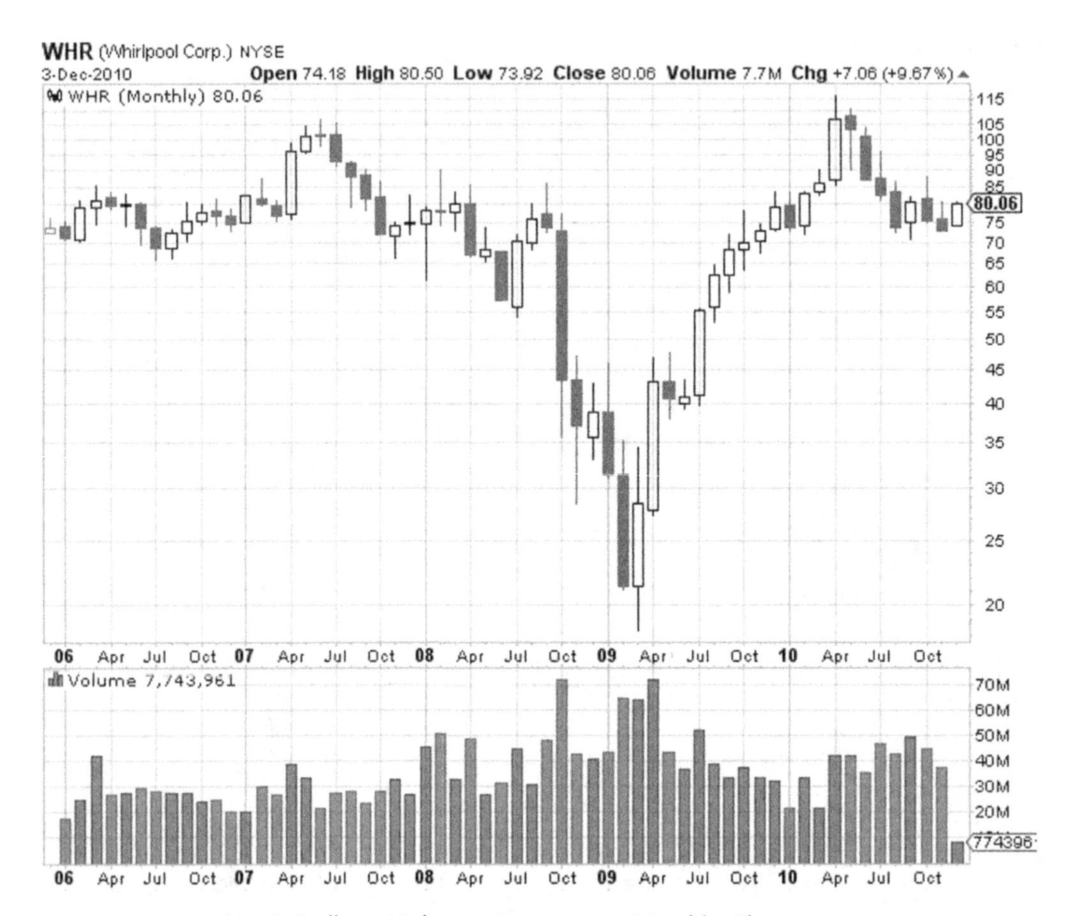

FIGURE 20.2 WHR Stalls at Multiyear Resistance, Monthly Chart
Source: © StockCharts.com.

Contrast this with a company having already experienced major growth, and now facing the inevitable competition that comes with recognition of success. It has higher fixed costs as salespeople have moved into management, new plants and distribution centers have been added, and inventory has been built. As opposed to the lean machine in the preceding example, this company suffers from relative bloat and is one competitor or economic slowdown away from suffering margin pressure.

Management, being optimistic by nature, cannot possibly trim fixed costs fast enough to become lean, and analysts again are too slow to include the impact of this bloated cost structure on earnings forecasts.

I hope I have expressed the opportunity to use price analysis to measure the sentiment and fundamental shifts that may be at play when these factors come together. I don't believe the technicals have some magic power of prediction, but they can objectively reveal what we may not see ourselves if we focus exclusively on the fundamental story.

In the worst case, we've put the risk of major fundamental news behind us. Sure, a takeover can always occur, but with one major opportunity every three months to present their case, both the executives and the analysts following the stock will address the most important issues, and stockholders have a chance to react. We cannot ensure that the reaction tells the story perfectly, but at least we have a few days to act without fear of a corporate development out of left field.

For these reasons, I consider the news absorption trade among the best reward/risk opportunities a speculator can make. In terms of both time and price, these events give us a chance to study while all major players are there to act, and we have that action to lean on as we craft our strategy.

CHAPTER 21

A Chart Will Never Lie to You

Sunrise Trader, @SunriseTrader

Our friend Sunrise has a great philosophical view on trading and investing. Sunrise strives for work and trading balance. Passionate traders find it difficult to pull themselves away from the screens, because there is an endless waterfall of ideas and opportunities. Sunrise understands the power of social leverage and continues to pay it forward on StockTwits. We appreciate it.

A chart will never lie to you. The trick is not lying to yourself about what you see in it.

—@theEquilibrium

JOURNALING TO STAY ACCOUNTABLE

My personal definition of a trader is someone who holds on to stocks for a short period of time from minutes to no longer than a quarter (the time between two earnings reports). In September 2005, I became a trader. I began using technical analysis as my primary way to trade the stock market. I read countless books, attended seminars, watched numerous videos on the Internet, and listened to radio shows hosted by traders and stock market gurus. I was a sponge absorbing anything and everything stock market related to help me with my quest to become a successful trader.

It was during this time that I started to track my progress using a notebook to journal and an Excel spreadsheet to easily calculate and track profit/loss. The column headings on the spreadsheet included the following: stock name, symbol, date purchased, quantity, purchase price, date sold, sales price, net profit/loss after fees and commissions, percentage made/lost, and the number of days I held the position. In the journal I would log more information: why I bought, why I sold, charts, market conditions, support and resistance levels, and more. This may sound cumbersome, but I believe it was and still is the right way to run my trading business.

By my third year of trading, the systems I had in place to track my progress had begun to pay off. This information told me the obvious—amount made or lost and percent made or lost. What it also told me was the information that helped me to better my trading plan. It told me the reason I bought or sold, using charts and explanations of my thought process before, during, and after the trade. The real pot of gold was the knowledge gained by studying my own journal. I had made numerous trades for numerous reasons and with varied outcomes. I was then able to take the information and clearly see my strengths and weaknesses.

There were many struggles and victories, all logged into my journal and spreadsheet. One area that was of interest to me was the number of days I held on to a position. I found those that I held for four days or less had my highest percentage of winning trades. Those I held for 27 days or longer were my most profitable. This group also showed a high percentage of winning trades. I found in the 27-day or longer group that I was letting my winners run, raising my stops along the way but giving enough room so the stock price could pull back some to digest gains as it formed a new base before continuing higher.

The growth came in learning from my mistakes on positions. For example, I quickly saw that I was not cutting my losses soon enough (novice mistake number one). Another beginner's mistake I made was selling a *total* winning position quickly. Yes, I made money, but could I have let the stock work harder for me? I now ask myself a few simple questions: If I sell this position and take my profits, what stock am I going to replace it with? Does this replacement stock have a better setup or reward attached? Is the market still giving me opportunity, or is it appropriate to be in cash? Is it time to be patient, sit in cash, and wait for a pullback? Pullbacks afford opportunity if you have the guts to pull the handle.

One last note from reading my early trading journals is a basic one. My daily comments on open long positions often read, "The stock is making higher highs," and again the next day, "The stock is making higher highs." You cannot get more basic than this, but I will tell you many new traders do not ask themselves this simple question when going long: Is the stock making higher highs? When I started to see my notes say, "The stock is going sideways" or "The stock is making lower lows," I tightened stops or took profits. My journal was helping me make unemotional and logical decisions.

Keep a simple trading journal. Mine helps me to stay accountable. I use it for self-coaching and research. A review from time to time lets me evaluate past trades: what went right, what went wrong, what type of chart setup was used, stops, how profits were taken, and so on. In the end it helps me hone my skills and develop future trading plans.

I could tell you of more struggles and victories, but the bottom line is that my journal, spreadsheet, and charts have all taught me the very thing many expert traders have taught me. Mentors are important, but so is keeping yourself accountable, and a simple trading journal can really help.

HAVING A PLAN

I trade with a strict discipline and my own set of rules. I no longer hold stocks into earnings. I spend many hours studying charts and completing homework to be prepared for the next opportunity. I plan my trades by asking myself a few simple questions: What is the trend? What are the charts telling me? What are the charts telling me when I use multiple time frames? What is the setup? Where has the stock been, and where do the charts tell me it is likely to go? What is the downside (the risk)? What is the goal (the reward)? Then I ask "if this, then that" questions.

Example: *If* price is at support, *then* what is likely to happen? *If* price is at resistance, *then* what is likely to happen? *If* the market gaps up, *then* what am I going to do? There are endless "if this, then that" questions that can be asked. Bottom line: These questions help me anticipate and plan so I can act and not react. I am ready to trade.

I have chosen a profit trading style of laddering out of winning trades. I like to enter a trade and take partial amounts off the table as the price climbs. The first partial position is removed quickly. This gives me a payday and instant gratification. At the same time I will then raise my mental stop. I rarely use a hard stop anymore. That is just my preference, as I am available to watch my positions during the trading day. If you have trouble cutting losses or you cannot watch your positions, hard stops may be the appropriate way for you to trade. I will continue to pay myself as the stock climbs by taking additional partial profits. The last rung of the ladder I let ride until my trailing stop is hit or market conditions suggest a total removal would be prudent.

There are many possible guidelines on raising stops. As a stock moves higher and clears a key resistance level, that level will often get a back test. The stock should find good support on any dip back to that prior resistance area. The stop can be moved to a spot just below that former resistance (now current support) area. As the price continues to break resistance levels, the stop can be adjusted again and again.

Position traders are good at letting their winners ride and moving stops along the way, often having no particular topside in mind. They stay in the position until the chart gives a definite sell signal. Position trading is a new area for me. I have recently started to adapt this style on some trades but am still experimenting and working on skill development.

I always say more green than red. We all lose and make trades that go against us. All traders, if they are honest with themselves, have been there and done that. When this happens you must pull away from the market, take a breath, and start anew. That might mean a few moments to a few days. Remember that cash is a position.

Go back to the basics, do your homework, and trade very lightly. You can also do what I like to call "batting practice" and paper trade. You must be patient, patient, patient. Did I say you must be patient? Yes, you must be patient, with yourself and mostly with the market. Let the market and the charts come to you. They will if you wait for the setups and have a plan.

I have found that if I have a clear plan (trend identified, chart setup, risk/reward, stop, etc.) prior to the execution of any trade and follow the plan, it is much easier regardless of the outcome. The most important thing is to preserve your financial and mental capital so you can trade another day. You must manage risk.

THE STOCK MARKET REFLECTS HUMAN EMOTIONS

I trade with a strict discipline, and to this day if any negative thoughts creep in too much I close out all positions I have in the market and make myself walk away from trading for the time being. You notice I said "too much"; we are all human and emotions are a wonderful part of living. This may sound ridiculous and not very macho, but it works. Leave your emotions outside the trading door and save them for other parts of your life.

I believe the stock market reflects human emotions as much as it reflects fundamental or technical values. I further believe that most of the fundamentals are already baked into the stock charts. Technical analysis is the study of price, time, and sentiment of an index, sector, or individual equity. Technical analysis helps me read the message of the market by identifying the trend and seeing price action. It draws a picture. Technical analysis is a predictor of what's coming. It shows me what the market knows and what I don't. I use technical analysis to guide my decision process.

My market approach is simple; first and foremost my job is to manage risk.

Next it is to identify the different cycles and stages of the market. The key is to identify and recognize which stage of a cycle a stock is experiencing and select accordingly.

A component to cycles of the market and being a trader is identifying support and resistance. Support and resistance can be defined as action and reaction or supply and demand. These two factors are the result of the interaction between fear and greed. Once you determine the preceding you can continue on and look for particular chart patterns and setups that have the best odds for success.

When a clear trend is established, whether it be an uptrend or a downtrend, position sizing is a key factor to either making some money or making the big money. What I mean by this is that when a market gives you clear direction of the trend you must be willing to trade larger positions than when a market is in a channel or basing. Establishing position sizing rules for various market conditions will elevate you from novice to expert trader level in no time.

I keep my exposure to the market, including position size and number of positions, consistent with my overall market analysis. As the market becomes overbought or extended my cash level increases. Then as the market gets oversold and undervalued, I look for opportunities to increase my market exposure. I seldom have more than 10 individual positions at one time. I am most comfortable with five to seven positions.

My charts are simple, with few indicators. When swing trading I use the daily chart with price history and a moving average or two. I also use a volume indicator with a 21-day moving average. Price is what pays (as Brian Shannon would say) and should always be your first indicator. Volume should be used as a way of confirming the price action. I often use two secondary indicators, moving average convergence/divergence (MACD) and Relative Strength Index (RSI). In the interest of space I won't go into a long discussion about either of these. Keep in mind they are secondary indicators. I find them particularly useful when making entry and exit decisions. Always remember that price trumps all.

When a stock is falling there is a tendency to think it is on sale. Don't jump in until a stock gives a good technical signal to buy. Look at the chart and find the area of support, both short-term and long-term. Is the stock basing? Is the selling volume drying up? Is the setup there? If not, move on. If so, put the chart on your watch list and set some alerts.

TRADE STOCKS THAT ARE LEADERS IN THE SECTOR

I have many favorite setups or technical chart patterns that I like to look for and use. I prefer to trade stocks that are leaders in their respective sectors. I like stocks that break to new highs early in a market uptrend, because they often become leaders. I like patterns that base and continue, base and continue. Examples include but are not limited to: continuation flags, continuation pennants, high and tight flags, channel breakouts, and triangle setups in a bullish trend that have touched the top of their base at least three times and begin to base around the 50-day moving average. Wash, rinse, repeat.

I work hard at reading the "right side" of the chart—you know, the blank side, the side yet to be determined. This is another area where the "if this, then that" question can help you be prepared. I will always be on the Yellow Brick Road, slouching toward the Emerald City of the Land of Oz, allowing the charts to tell me their story.

THE DESCENDING TRIANGLE

One of my favorite formations has only an average success rate when all market conditions are considered. Yet in an uptrending market it has a much greater success rate. It is a descending triangle with a bullish upside breakout. Triangles are considered continuation patterns and often break in the direction of the current market trend.

A descending triangle is a price pattern that is confined by two trend lines. The top line is downward sloping and the bottom is a horizontal line. The price trend can come from any direction. This is key; the price must touch each trend line at least twice as distinct peaks and valleys. In other words, it should bounce from line to line making plenty of crossings. I particularly like it when it "knocks three times" or "the third time is the charm"; in other words, it touches three times before breaking out and not just twice. Price must cross the pattern from trend line to trend line, nearly filling the space each time. Volume should decline as it fills the apex of the triangle just before the breakout. The pattern is confirmed once the breakout occurs and *closes* outside the downward-sloping trend lines.

When the break occurs because of a gap up in price, I have found this pattern to have a higher success rate for me. Gap-ups off downtrend moves will often trap traders holding short positions. This makes for a good prescription if you are long. I also like when the pattern is near or at the 50-day moving average. I look for the RSI to be in the neutral zone near the 50 mark and the MACD to be near the zero line. When in the neutral zone, the RSI and MACD have plenty of room to run to the upside before elevating to overbought conditions. If the MACD is showing a positive divergence, that is icing on the cake and the odds are stacked more in favor of the breakout. Remember that RSI and MACD are secondary. Price pays and volume confirms price.

The pattern is not foolproof and is best suited to those who can monitor their stocks closely. Stops should be placed just below the breakout and be raised as price moves up.

Another way to trade this pattern successfully is after a false breakdown occurs. The breakdown should not move the price down much, maybe 5 to 10 percent, and it cannot trade under the triangle for very many days.

After the price closes below the bottom trend line, look for the price to reenter the triangle and break up and through the top trend line. Price must close above the top trend line with conviction. Good volume should accompany this breakout. After the upward breakout, price tends to have a healthy run to the upside. Once again, stops can be placed just below the breakout.

As a side note, this pattern can be used for short trades when the trend is down. It has a better-than-average success rate when used in a downtrending market. I prefer the bullish upside breakout, but have successfully used this pattern on the first retest of the breakdown to position on the short side. In other words, the price breaks below the horizontal line, bases, and successfully retests the breakdown *without* crossing back up and through the horizontal line. A position short taken at the first retest is often successful.

I have traded this pattern many times using one of the three variations described earlier. It is one that I can recognize quickly and enjoy trading as it is a "trade the trader" or "shake the weak hands out" type of trade. Don't get me wrong; I am not being arrogant here, as it has done exactly that to me. It is a pattern that requires patience and timing. It is a pattern I can recognize and embrace. When I see its setup, I trade it.

THE THOUGHT PROCESS BEHIND MY TRADES

Most of the following examples were actual trades made this year.

The chart in Figure 21.1 shows that AAPL formed a descending triangle. Price touched the top and bottom trend lines more than two times, moving back and forth within the triangle. The breakout occurred on a gap up above the 50-day moving average, volume confirmed the price movement, RSI was in the neutral zone, and MACD was positive and moving upward.

In Figure 21.2 (AKAM), the first descending triangle shows you an example of a false breakdown. You see how the price dropped below the bottom trend line and then broke up and out of the triangle on explosive volume.

The second descending triangle shows you that the price was crossing back and forth in the pattern, touching the upper and lower trend lines in a nice tight pattern. Price was

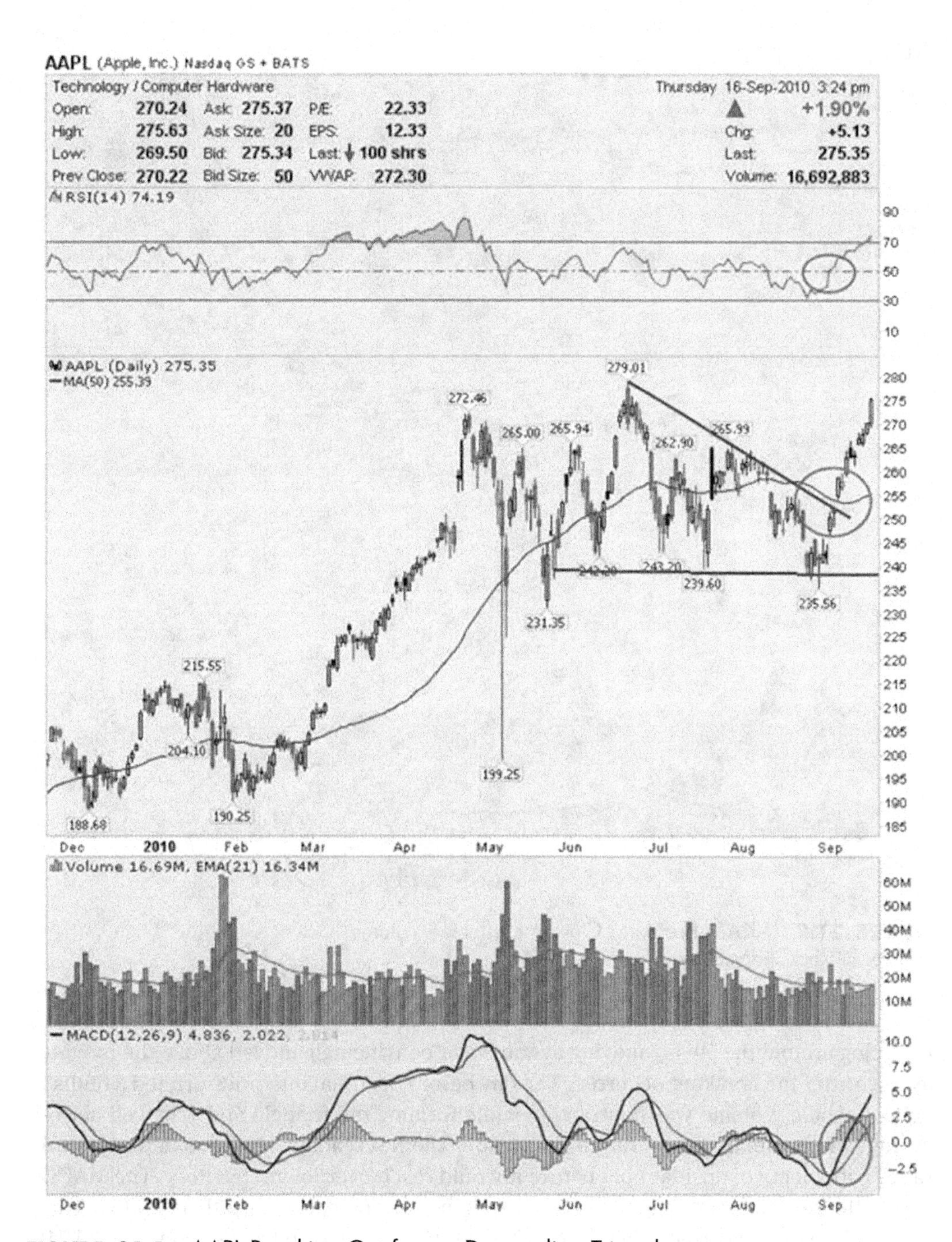

FIGURE 21.1 AAPL Breaking Out from a Descending Triangle
Source: © StockCharts.com.

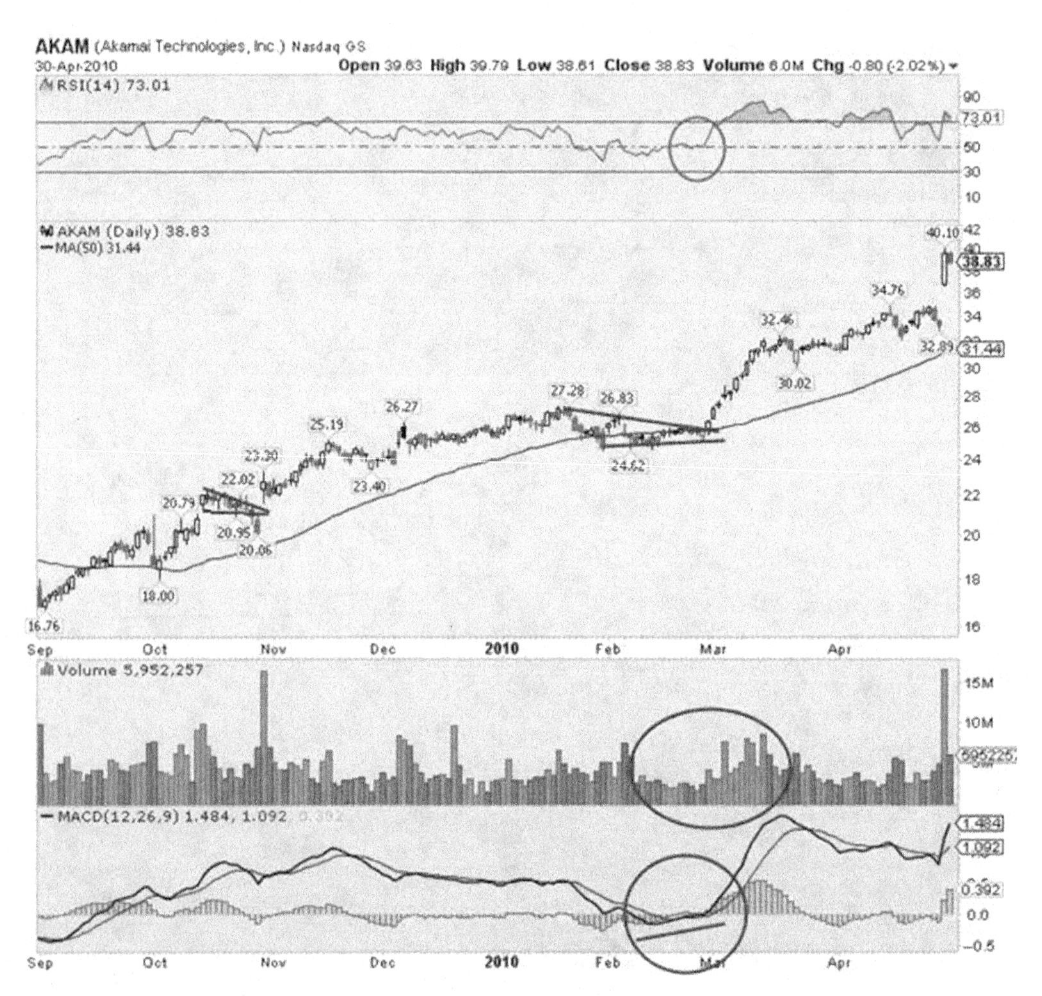

FIGURE 21.2 AKAM Breaking Out on Explosive Volume
Source: © StockCharts.com.

bouncing around the 50-day moving average and convincingly moved above the moving average after the breakout occurred. The day before the breakout, price printed a bullish hollow candle. Volume was contracting while forming the triangle and was well above average on the breakout and run to the upside. The RSI reading of 50 was in the neutral range with plenty of upside room before it would reach overbought territory. The MACD was at the zero line, showing a positive divergence with plenty of upside potential. This setup was textbook perfect. On February 26 the stock opened above the triangle at 25.74, closed the day at 26.30, and ran up to the 32+ area before it started a new base by consolidating and digesting the prior gains. Here were two more successful trades.

The chart in Figure 21.3 shows YUM forming a descending triangle. The top line, while not quite as steep as some, is downward sloping, and the bottom line is horizontal.

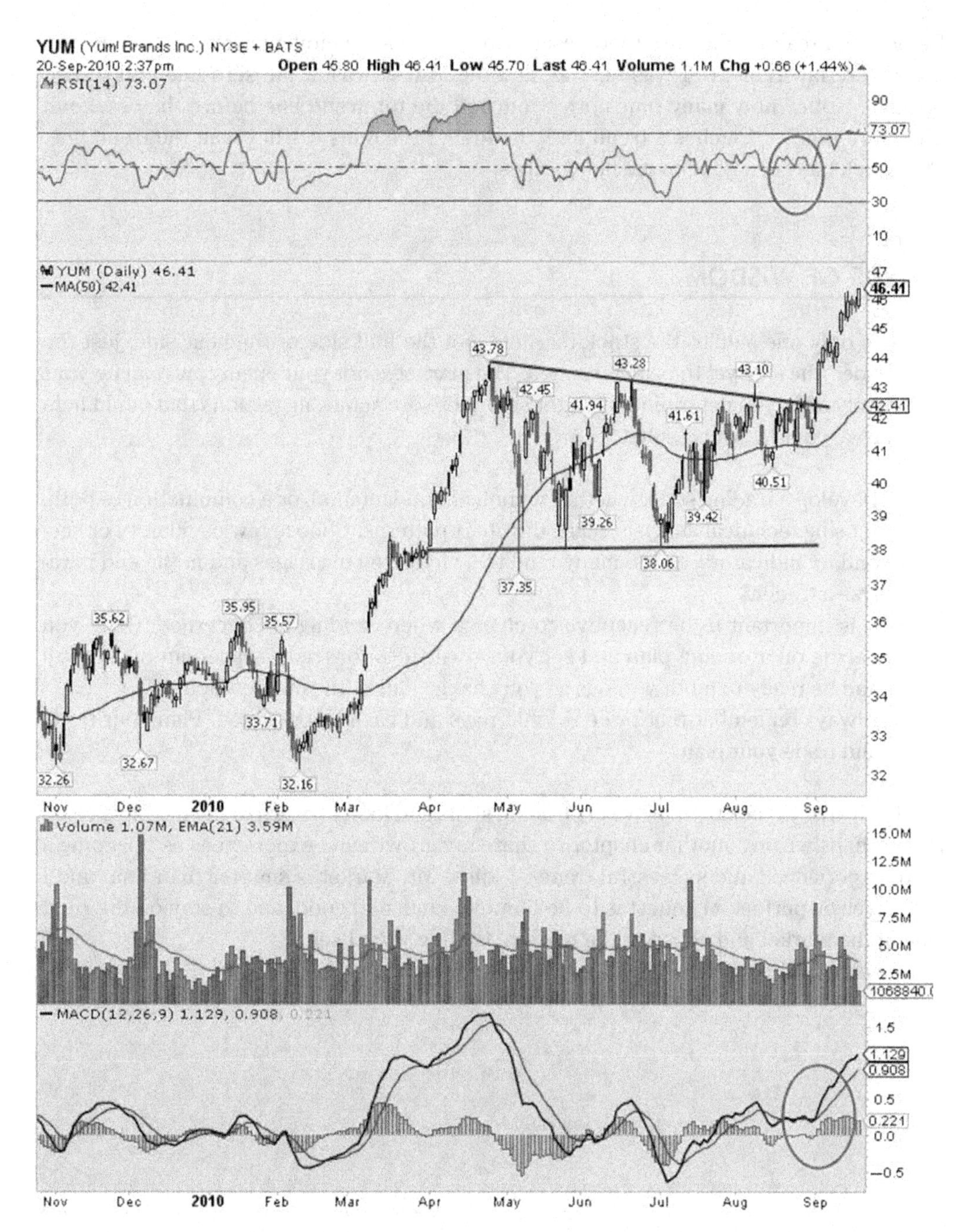

FIGURE 21.3 YUM Breaking Out
Source: © StockCharts.com.

Before the breakout the patterned based above the 50-day moving average, volume patterns were favorable, RSI was neutral, and the MACD was at the zero line and turned positive. Notice how many times price touched the top trend line before the breakout. The more times it touches a trend line, the higher the odds it will break the trend line. This stock has been good to me many times.

WORDS OF WISDOM

There is only one side to the stock market—not the bull side or the bear side, just the "right side," the side yet to be determined. The market is not your enemy and can be your friend only after you determine the right side. Here are some suggestions that could help to improve your trading results:

- Develop a trading style, whether technical, fundamental, or a combination of both. If using technical analysis, learn the chart patterns. Choose few oscillators or secondary indicators, as too many tend to send mixed messages and in the end paralyze a trader.
- It is important to be receptive to change where trading is concerned. Once you decide on a trading plan and set your own rules for trading, keep an open mind and be ready to modify things as you change and as the market dictates.
- Always remember that price is what pays and cash is a position. Plan your trade and trade your plan.

I will always seek to improve my trading skills and look forward to the next five years and perhaps writing another chapter to share my growth and experiences as I become a more experienced and successful trader. I know Mr. Market is smarter than I am and I will never be perfect. My quest is to be humble, kind, and good, and to stay on the right side of the market and ahead of the masses, trading what I see.

Be safe, and be well.

CHAPTER 22

The Short Squeeze Trade

Frank Zorrila, *@zortrades*

Frank is sharing ideas every trading day of the year. He is good-looking for a trader, is married (sorry, ladies), and has the best voice on StockTwits TV. I met him randomly on a subway train and in a rare moment of fame he recognized me. We have been friends ever since, and I believe he is progressing fast as a successful trader and investor.

THE COLD CALLER

It was the summer of 1997 when a friend of mine suggested that I apply as a "cold caller" at a small brokerage firm. The benefits: a two-week trial period, no pay, and no guarantee that it would amount to anything. I interviewed for the internship and was approved. I knew nothing about Wall Street other than it is the street of dreams where a lot of money can be made. As a cold caller, my only job was to make phone calls from 7:30 A.M. until 9:00 P.M.—smile and dial.

In the summer of 1998, I passed my Series 7 exam to become a licensed broker. I am not going to lie. Despite the certificate, I still had no clue about stocks or the market, fundamentals or technicals. My only concern back then was how many dials I was making, how many presentations I was giving on a daily basis, and how many accounts I was opening. The retail brokerage industry for the most part is all about the numbers: commissions, money under management, and accounts being opened.

PHIL, THE MENTOR

One day, a gentleman who had come out of retirement took over the small firm I was working for. Since I don't have permission to mention his name, I am going to refer to him as Phil. When I met Phil, he already had the extensive experience of more than 30 years managing sales and equity trading for various world-renowned companies. At that time, I still had no idea about the market. Again, what I was taught was how to sell a stock with a sexy story, and that I did well. After wiping out my business on a few stocks that the firm investment banking team and the sales manager were pushing because they were fundamentally sound, I told myself there had to be a better way (the cheaper the stock became, the more attractive it was to the analyst: MXIP $4, $28, $0; FTET 90 cents, $4, back to $0; GNBT, NTFY, MGIC, and countless others were some of the supposedly fundamentally sound, buy-and-hold, average-down stocks that led me to technical analysis). Phil was a technician who was always on top of everything that was going on in the world, and while he had an opinion on what was going on at a macro level, he let the charts be his guide. This is when my world started to be more than just dials, accounts, money under management, and commissions. Every morning, Phil would print out his trading ideas, normally 10 charts or so, five longs and five shorts, so no matter what direction the market went—up or down—we had an idea for either direction.

At this point I still had no understanding of the underlying forces in the stock market, but I knew a few things:

1. The market goes up *and* down, not up *or* down (hence the saying "I don't care what the market does—I just want to be on the right side").
2. I did not need the market to go up to make my clients money; I just had to be on the right side.
3. Stocks go down a lot faster than they go up.
4. I enjoyed looking at charts and playing what was moving now, rather than following some analysts who were giving me a guesstimate about what a company was going to earn next year.

Phil would normally get into the office around 7 A.M. Every morning, I would walk into his office with my cup of coffee, take a seat in one of his comfy conference chairs, and ask questions about the charts and his views on the markets. He had a tight grasp on what was going on at the macro level and had many great war stories to tell. There is a massive delusion that technicians only look at charts and know nothing about the events that impact price action. On the contrary, most of us know what is going on around the world but we trade what we see on the charts, not what we think is happening. Today's market is a perfect example. I read all the bearish arguments and not only do I know them but I actually believe most of them. Despite all the scary headlines on the front pages of the mass media, the market has been in an uptrend for over a year now, and making trading decisions based on what is going on in the real world has been a losing bet.

I was Phil's gofer; every day I was in charge of handing out the charts that he printed out for all the brokers. Not only was I trading his picks, but I was also keeping track of his win-loss ratio, which was amazing, and I was starting to pick up on chart patterns. As time went by, I started to build a preference for certain chart patterns. By the year

2000, when Phil went back into retirement, I knew a bunch of stocks but I did not know companies. In other words, I can tell you where the stock was trading and whether it was above the 50-day and 200-day moving averages, but I could not tell you much about what the company did, who its competitors were, or its price-earnings (P/E) ratio. I was comfortable with my understanding, because Phil taught me that stocks are nothing but letters, numbers, and pieces of paper. When a stock goes up 5 to 10 percent in a day on no news it is not because they rang the register today more than they did yesterday; it's because today for some reason there were more buyers of the stock than sellers.

THE IMPORTANCE OF RISK MANAGEMENT

Stock selection is very important in the game of trading, but equally important is risk management. You could be right only five out of 10 times and still be very profitable. Without risk management you are not going to last in this business. I am not a fan of using a certain percentage as a stop, like let's say 9 percent, because what happens if 9 percent below your purchase price is a major support level? Then what? Are you going to get stopped out at the support level? No. So when thinking about risk, I first want to know what my current feeling for the market is. Do I feel like this is the beginning of a bull market where I want to risk 1 to 2 percent of my total account per trade, or are we in the late stage of a rally where I only want to risk 0.25 percent to 0.50 percent of my account per trade? This is something that I recently picked up from great traders like Tickerville (see Chapter 36) and Stockbee (see Chapter 26).

To better control risk, I use a simple position-sizing technique. For example, your account is worth $100K and you like the market here; therefore, you want to risk 1 percent per trade, which equals $1,000. The stock that you are watching is trading at $50. You believe that the stop should be placed at $49.25, so you're risking 75 cents per share. Since you are risking only $1,000 per trade, you can buy only 1,333 shares (1,000/.75 = 1,333). That is the first part of my risk management approach. The second part involves making sure that I am getting involved in only those stocks that offer at least 2:1 reward-to-risk ratio. In other words, the first potential target is at least double the amount I am risking. Defining price targets depends on various factors: stock selection, stage in the price cycle of the stock, float, and general market strength. With all other things being equal, the smaller the float, the faster and the bigger the potential move.

THE ART OF CONTRARY THINKING

At this point I loved my charts but I was still looking for more. What made a stock move more than another? That is when I started to learn about the amount of shares in the float, how many shares were currently short, and how many days it would take to buy back all the shorts. I came across a great web site, Schaeffer's Investment Research at www.schaeffersresearch.com. While nowadays I do not frequent the site like I did before, it had a big influence on me. Schaeffer's brought in the sentiment side of the equation, which I believe is the most powerful tool in this business. At the Schaeffer's site is where I got acquainted with the art of contrary thinking. I realized that heavily shorted stocks trading near their 52-week highs were capable of making huge runs in the short term if a short squeeze was put into effect.

Stocks that had heavy put buying trading near their 52-week highs were also prone to big moves, and sometimes very little selling. If you are long a stock and you bought a put to protect yourself, chances are that you will not be shaken out on a pullback because you have some insurance in the way of the put. Also, if the stock is trading by the 52-week high and people are betting against it, they themselves could be the buyers who will continue to propel the stock to 52-week highs because the stock price (moving up) could turn those nonbelievers into believers. That is when I started to favor stocks that were technically intact and heavily shorted, with a small float and very little analyst coverage.

I did not care whether Goldman Sachs, Merrill Lynch, or any other major firm's analyst was recommending the stock. I knew that many fundamental analysts paid attention to price, so if a certain stock in their universe was printing new 52-week highs on a consistent basis, it was only a matter of time before they or their manager came to the realization that the hold rating had to be turned into a buy rating. The upgrade could be the fuel that sparked the shorts to cover the small float.

Netflix is a stock that comes to mind that had all those ingredients. I remember when Netflix was a $28 stock, and I never, ever thought that its business model was incredible or that the stock was going to be a $200 stock, but what I did know was that the company was growing rapidly, the stock was heavily shorted, and it had a very small float and very little to almost no analyst coverage. The stock was trading near its 52-week high and the insiders were aggressively buying back stocks. These are the attributes of a typical winner.

The debate over fundamentals versus technicals is something that many people wrestle with as far as an investing approach is concerned. I say that you need to use both with a twist of sentiment analysis. While I am not a fundamental guy, I like to buy stocks that have rapid sales and earnings per share (EPS) growth acceleration, because that is what Wall Street wants. What do you think a Wall Street hotshot would rather drive, the ultrasafe Volvo or a super-fast Ferrari? But I also realize that it would be foolish of me to even try to think that I could do the same fundamental analysis that a mutual fund or hedge fund with 100 times more resources than I have could do. That is why sales and EPS growth is as far as I like to go when looking at the fundamentals.

The way I look at it is the following: Let's say that a billion-dollar hedge fund that has multiple analysts at its disposal sends one of them to visit and analyze a company. The analyst visits the company and talks to the president of the company, the CFO, and the plant manager; he studies its competitors; he does the entire top-down fundamental approach. Now he gets back to the office and says to his boss (hedge fund manager): "I love the company because of this and that and that and this." What do you think the manager is going to do? More than likely, the hedge fund will buy the stock, and, my friend, big elephants leave big footprints, and sometimes you will see the volume start to increase, and you will start to notice what is called linearity, where a stock is just in a perfect tight ascending pattern with very little in the way of violent down moves. Look at the Priceline (PCLN) weekly chart from the end of 2008 until the beginning of 2010, or AAPL, BIDU, or NFLX.

An easy way to follow my approach is by using the following four filters:

1. Stocks with a market cap of $2 billion or less.
2. Stocks within 0 to 5 percent of their 52-week highs.
3. Quarter-over-quarter earnings and sales growth above 25 percent.
4. Short float of at least 10 percent.

FIGURE 22.1 AHT Breaking Out to a New 52-Week High, 18 Percent of Its Float Short, 23 Days of Short Interest Ratio, Daily Chart
Source: © StockCharts.com.

As of this writing (October 23, 2010), applying those filters narrows your watch list to six names (ECHO, FIRE, HOGS, OVTI, PODD, and SFSF). The next step is to sit and patiently wait for a good risk/reward setup on the stock.

TYPICAL SHORT SQUEEZE TRADE

Stocks tend to move in groups. In March 2010, I noticed that most casino stocks were breaking out to new 52-week highs. Casinos are essentially hotels in disguise. At that time Ashford Hospitality Trust Inc. (AHT) appeared on my screens (see Figure 22.1). It is a real estate investment trust (REIT) that has invested in 102 hotels (Marriott, Hyatt, and Hilton) with about 23,000 rooms. It was a $6 stock with $3 cash in the bank; 18 percent of its float was short, which represented 23 times the average daily volume. I started to build a position in the 6.25s as AHT was breaking out to a new 52-week high.

Psychology plays an enormous role in market participants' decision making. A combination of close proximity to the 52-week high price and a high short ratio is a recipe for a short squeeze, which means high potential for a big move in a short period of time. Today's short positions are a major source of tomorrow's demand.

CHAPTER 23

The Price Tells the Story

Derald Muniz, @1nvestor

Derald is among the hardest-working traders on the stream. He truly understands market structure and cycles. Switching from long to short setups is second nature to him. He generously shares ideas and always calls his trades on the stream in real time.

The quality of a person's life is in direct proportion to their commitment to excellence, regardless of their chosen field of endeavor.
—Vince Lombardi

MY TRADING JOURNEY

In the early 1990s I worked in an information technology (IT) job with several individuals who were very active in stock trading, and they often shared their experiences with me. They were quite a bit older and had a lot to share. This was my first real exposure to the public stock market and all the various moving parts. I was fascinated and certainly curious, but given my nature, I took many baby steps in the education process of understanding how the markets really worked at a fundamental level. I read hundreds of books on the subject.

Initially I paper traded for a long period of time as I educated myself on many of the various chart and tape reading strategies. I recall focusing mainly on bar charts. I spent an enormous amount of time learning about fundamental analysis. I read several hundred 10-K documents during this early decade, often having to study up on various components to better understand what I was reading. This part of my education process was the most time-consuming, but a worthwhile effort in my view.

Once I felt that it was time to make the move into trading a real money account, I signed up for a Charles Schwab account at a local office. I vividly remember starting out with $1,500 in my account, but then taking several weeks before I was mentally prepared and ready to do my first real trade. I don't mind admitting that I was terrified, excited, and nervous all at the same time. What a thrill.

My first trade ever—I bought five shares of Microsoft. I remember staring at those stock certificates with awe. Now what? After the initial thrill wore off, I remember thinking that it seemed somewhat unsatisfying after a while. Now I just had some paper with writing on it. I soon realized a common problem for early investors, I suspect: With a limited trading account, it seemed like I was not participating in a significant way. I only had five shares; big deal.

Because of this feeling, I had to consider venturing into many of the lower-priced stocks that were available to trade. I had numerous conversations with those around me regarding the pros and cons of taking this approach, including the fact that many of these carried a lot of extra dangers. My rationale seemed to make sense and was simple: I felt that I needed to buy a larger number of shares. I wanted to participate in what I thought was a more significant way. I would learn later that this way of thinking had major flaws, as I realized that higher-priced stocks are that way for a reason—someone thinks they are worth that price indeed. Conversely, lower-priced stocks are that way for a reason—no one wants to pay more for the stock.

My initial experience with a low-priced stock was IDID. I remember all the euphoria surrounding the prospects of the company and I learned early just how important volume was. This stock traded massive volume every day, and I focused on this early in my trading career. Although the trade worked out incredibly well in terms of the return, I could not help but feel that it seemed unusual—sort of too good to be true. At the time, I just could not believe that something could increase in value so rapidly. I soon realized that this is far from the norm. The educational value of this experience was immense—on so many levels. It was during this time that I truly began to understand and reflect on the concept of the risk/reward trade-off.

After my investment in IDID, there was a period of several years when I traded just a few times a month as my turnover was low. I was comfortable with that style and strategy. I looked for value in lower-priced stocks and held them for an extended amount of time. I had learned that it was very important to understand what sort of trades fit my personality, matched my trading skills (at the time), and made sense given my current financial situation. Over time, I grew restless as I began to desire more risk taking, and I wanted to explore other strategies that might suit me—other strategies that I had not yet explored or known about.

During this stage in my trading experience, I expanded my investing into private equity (angel investing), which led me to my first real exposure to an initial public offering (IPO) from the insiders' side. The conversion of private stock to publicly traded stock opened up a whole new avenue to me in terms of risk/reward scenarios. It certainly helped me to understand the enormous potential for profits that could be achieved in the stock market.

I don't have a precise recollection on the development of my profit and loss (P&L), but I believe that it took me more than six months of trading to achieve a profitable account. Most of my missteps had to do with my ill-timed entries into stocks, as I was not aware of so many of the important aspects of trading—like short selling, for example; I had no idea what that meant. Didn't stocks just go up?

My relative success in angel investing changed my financial situation significantly, which certainly impacted by trading approach. I had the means to fund a larger account and I could make trading decisions, namely position sizing decisions that were unthinkable to me just a few years before. I had a six-figure trading account to put to work. The real work began as I had to reformulate so much of my trading plan, update my goals, and think hard about having different accounts that could be utilized for different strategies. I rolled up my sleeves.

The timing was also excellent, given the fact the Internet euphoria was really taking hold, so there were many new, exciting, and relevant opportunities to put money to work. During the late 1990s, I traded YHOO almost daily in significant size, and recall numerous days where the return would exceed $20,000 from one trade. Of course those around me who were participating in the stock market had similar stories, which made it all the more exciting. I just expected it to go up every day, and it did.

At the start of 2000, I was involved with a company as a co-founder, so I focused a lot less on my stock portfolio. In addition, the Internet bubble was close to the burst stage, so in hindsight the timing was likely very good for me. The stock setup opportunities seemed few and far between, but, looking back, this was more due to the fact that I was still so one-dimensional in my trading. Up to that point, I was always *long* a stock. It was time for me to wake up here and realize that traders must know something that I didn't, as many were still making money trading. I remember searching for and finding a book at a local bookstore that centered on trading strategies with a focus on *options* and *short* selling. What a real eye-opener it was for me, in so many ways. In all the time spent with others I knew, no one shorted stock. Also, no one I knew had any idea what options were or how they worked. I remember feeling at that time that I really did not know anything, and it was time to broaden my understanding of trading strategies in a meaningful way. I thought I had spent many years educating myself on stock trading, but had been too narrow-minded in my focus. This would change.

I worked through the next few years learning more and more on shorting stock as well as the use of options not only as protection of long positions, but also as a trade itself. This was a time of a lot of paper trading as I learned all the aspects of selling a stock short. I recall doing my first short sale in 2007 on General Motors (GM), but it was such an odd feeling. It would be quite some time (and many additional trades) before I finally got comfortable with being short a stock. Of course I now view this as a very important tool and do this type of trade frequently.

As for stock options, well, that is another story entirely. Even with the amount of time I've spent learning all the facets of trading options, I would still classify myself as a beginner. Although I have executed over 200 options trades up to this point, even some quite sophisticated, I feel that I've barely scratched the surface. Now that weekly options are available on some stocks, I feel that the opportunities in option trading have become a lot more enhanced—at least in those stocks where weekly options are available. It is simply amazing. I would say that my option trading has improved significantly in the past two years. I have increased my premium selling this year greatly. I also sell calls against a lot of my long-term holdings each month, and will sell puts with great frequency on stocks that are struggling on a particular day.

In terms of time spent trading stocks, I have devoted at least 50 percent of my time since 2008 to trading. I have developed into a swing trader, as it fits my current personality, trading style, and market approach. I typically make 200 trades a year on average, and use E*Trade and thinkorswim as my trading platform. I do keep a trading journal, which I review thoroughly at the end of each month. I spend a lot of time reviewing losing trades, poor exits, and so on in order to hone my skills but more importantly to make improvements in areas where I am failing.

PRICE TELLS THE STORY

I believe that every sector does move in a cycle. Market participation by traders is fair for most participants, but far from perfect. I certainly try to be mindful of the many concepts of manipulation—things like rumor spreading, for example. I've just learned to filter the noise. I am a believer in data, raw data, and feel that in most cases I can decipher things for myself. The price tells the story, plain and simple. You can watch many of the available indicators for a stock, but price is what I care about.

A lot of my research time and reading is spent analyzing what could be moving prices in stocks, up or down. I consider myself a momentum swing trader so it is critical for me to be in a constant mode of watching those indicators that may cause price to move. I do understand the possible catalysts that exist for price movement, like earnings reports. For my style of trading, patience is key—but I also must be disciplined in my exit strategy for the trade. My philosophy is that I do not trade on hope. I lay out my risk/reward profile for each trade and execute those trades that meet my criteria.

Obviously there are often examples of situations where someone (or some entity) has somehow gained an unfair edge that could affect future prices, but I view this as something that will always exist despite the best efforts by those put in place to prevent such occurrences. I still try to trade what I see in the charts, not what I think. I am okay with the notion that some gain an unfair advantage over me at times, or have access to information in a more timely fashion than I do. I view this in a way that I have found to be comfortable for me—I can find opportunities every day despite these unfair advantages that others may have, so I tend to not dwell on it.

Now, the recent hoopla over the role that high-frequency trading (HFT) systems play in the market is of concern. I am still formulating a view on this. For now, I like my advantage over them in that I can think and maneuver with greater ease. I can also accept multiple sources and types of varying data to analyze and make decisions on at any given time. The HFT systems will certainly be something that I will continue to pay attention to, but for now I am okay with their involvement. Providing liquidity is certainly important.

THE WEDGE PLAY

I have several favorite setups that I rely on with great frequency—and see consistent results from. I like wedge plays, gap fill plays, knife catch plays, support buys, and breakout/breakdown plays. However, for the sake of this chapter, I will focus on the wedge.

So why do I like this type of setup? It is the continued tightening range as the bulls and bears battle it out. This range-tightening action clearly demonstrates an exertion of a lot of energy by both sides involved in the trade. I believe at some point within the wedge, the stock moves into the apex of the wedge. At that point one side or the other will have to relent. It is a given and expected result, a reality if you will. It simply will have to break up through the descending trend line above or break down through the ascending trend line below.

This coil is going to uncoil in one direction or the other with force. It is my task to determine which direction, and be prepared (once I determine that I am taking the setup). With this setup, I typically review the daily chart for the wedge pattern, and then use the 15-minute chart to watch price action on the stock. I will also review the weekly chart, and at times will review a monthly chart. I do use Fibonacci levels in a lot of my charts as I look for horizontal support lines. Depending on what the stock has been doing of late, I will look at additional indicators like these six:

1. Relative Strength Index (RSI)
2. Money Flow Index (MFI)
3. Williams %R
4. Moving average convergence/divergence (MACD)
5. Average true range
6. Volume at price

For this trade to get to a point where it is a high-quality setup, there are some basic elements that must be in place first:

1. There must be a cooperating market (it is hard to do this in a market that is down 200 points, for example, unless the plan is to short the stock). You must know the trend, and not fight it.
2. One must pay attention to the industry that the stock is in to ensure that no significant movements are occurring that could overemphasize a movement against you.
3. This trade setup type does take patience at times, as the stock may coil for an extended time. I am fine with that. As a swing trader, I accept that it is simply part of the process in getting prepared to execute the setup.

When putting a setup in motion, I am looking for candles that are tightening up (shrinking in their height). This demonstrates to me that the bulls and bears are standing their ground. I typically do these trades with an anticipatory "first leg in" entry, and then scale in on confirmation (or close the trade at failure).

So, how do I find these setups in the first place? Where is that magical web site that lists the setups for me? Not so fast. Here is where I think a distinct advantage comes into play for successful traders. It is called hard work, and this is where I spend my efforts:

1. I keep an active setup list, focusing on keeping the list under 20 quality stocks at all times. This means there is a constant filtering process going on. Once the filtering is complete, I do consider the entries that remain as being high-quality setups.
2. I build this list using many sources such as traditional stock screeners within my trading platforms, as well as others like StockFetcher. I rely on FINVIZ.com at http://finviz.com as well for a lot of data needs.
3. Of course I use the StockTwits community, and those whom I specifically follow, for idea generation/sharing and to build a solid starting list. I do mean solid. This community is simply invaluable for idea generation and debate.

The filtering process can take quite some time, as you can imagine, as I work through my own emphasis on what I view as key to each particular setup. I will do six things:

1. Review recent volume levels.
2. Try to understand where the relevant moving averages are in relation to price.
3. Check the industry and sector data and check data on a few peers.
4. Spend time reviewing the actual chart (on *multiple* time frames, which is key here).
5. Look for MACD cross events.
6. Look for RSI bottoming or topping.

Although I do a tremendous amount of chart work, I absolutely pay attention to the fundamentals. I will, however, in most cases make my decision to enter (or exit) a trade based on the chart action. The chart tells me what everyone thinks (everyone who is trading the stock). I post my charts on at web site at http://chart.ly/users/1nvestor.

Since I am now comfortable being *long* or *short* a stock, there are times when I am in a setup because I expect a failure. Shorting stock is certainly part of what keeps the market healthy, in my view, and needs to occur to keep that health in place.

RECENT TRADE IN CAB

I will highlight a recent trade here in CAB (Cabela's Inc.) as a wedge play that gave me all the components that I look for in a wedge (or coil) trade. The stock had been coiling for a while as the candles continued to wedge just under 20. Also, the 20-day moving average (MA) continued to rise up in to the price.

On October 25, 2010, the CAB stock showed up in one of my scans. After reviewing the chart, I determined that it was in fact a great wedge candidate (it had been having this coiling effect for several days, churning in the 19.50 range).

After a review of the basic fundamentals of the stock, earnings schedule, and a few peer stocks, I opened a position. Figure 23.1 shows the chart posted near the time of my entry.

In this particular trade, I set my trailing stop at the 20-day moving average (19 at this point). This was a normal position size for me ($50K) and was not done on margin, as

FIGURE 23.1 CAB Approaching a Breakout Zone, Daily Chart
Source: © StockCharts.com.

there was sufficient cash that was not deployed at the time. I did this trade in two legs, about two hours apart.

I will note here that since my plan was to do a swing trade, I used my swing account. I do run four trading accounts:

1. Day trade account, which is used for intraday trades only. In this account, I trade equity and options.
2. Long-term account for stock that I expect to hold for more than 12 months. This account contains holdings that may or may not pay dividends. I sell calls against many of these holdings each month.
3. Options account for trades involving only options. I usually use this account to put on risk reversals, call spreads, and put spreads.
4. Swing account for trades that I expect to hold more than two days but less than a year. It is my most active account by far.

FIGURE 23.2 High-Volume Breakout above the Upper Bollinger Band
Source: © StockCharts.com.

Back to the CAB trade. On November 2, 2010, a significant increase in volume in the shares helped drive the price up more than 20 percent from then-current levels: a true breakout (B/O), as I note in Figures 23.1 and 23.2. At the time I believed that the breakout was in fact imminent and the thesis turned out to be true. During this initial breakout day, I did sell partials of the position into the strength, ending the day with a half position left. On November 3, 2010, I did not sell any additional shares as the stock continued to show amazing strength. A trailing stop was set at 22, which corresponds to the near high-of-day (HOD) price for the November 2, 2010, candle.

On November 3, 2010, I did exit the position balance at 22.75 as the stock began to show signs of exhaustion from the bulls. I have my gains, and if it runs further, so be it.

CHAPTER 24

Force Confirmations, Not Trades

Nick Fenton, *@nickfenton*

Nick is an extremely talented young trader who was schooled by my good friends Andy and Landon Swan. They taught him well, as Nick strikes one after another profitable trade on the StockTwits stream in real time. He is probably the best trader among all rappers and the best rapper among all traders.

Shoot for the moon. Even if you miss, you'll land among the stars.
—Les Brown

BACKGROUND

My name is Nick Fenton or Fentoni for short. I am 30 years young, and an avid trader of equities, options, and futures. When I'm not trading or reading about financial markets, I am doing one or more of the following: drinking the finest bourbon Kentucky has to offer, creating music (my rap group is called Backroad—we are working on our third album), listening to music (Pink Floyd is my all-time favorite), fine-tuning my golf skills, or hunting for my next pair of limited-edition sneakers.

My interest in financial markets was sparked when I won the Kentucky State Stock Market Challenge in seventh grade. The prize was $100, a T-shirt (still have it), and an appearance on the local news. Winning the competition was awesome, but that was nothing compared to the doors that opened as a result of participating. From that point, I began reading about long- and short-term trading strategies. I started paper trading based on quotes in the local newspaper's business section. As a high school graduation gift, my father gave me $6,000 to open an online brokerage account and begin trading. By the time I was midway through college, I had turned the $6,000 into $25,000. Unfortunately, that $25,000 turned into $10,000 before I sold everything and began to reevaluate my strategy.

After selling everything, I took a break from trading to focus on school. I finally started taking classes in my finance major. There were two classes in particular that had a heavy focus on options and futures trading—just basic stuff, nothing analytical. I had read about options and futures and always found interest in them, but this gave me a chance to really understand the fundamentals. I aced both classes and continued to educate myself on these financial instruments, but was not comfortable implementing my knowledge in real trading because I felt something was missing. To me, these were short-term instruments and my method of analysis at the time was based on fundamentals. Regardless, I knew this information was valuable and would come into play in the future, so I continued to learn.

Once I had graduated from college I took a job as a mortgage broker. These days "mortgage broker" has a somewhat negative connotation, but I would not trade that experience for anything. The position allowed me to gain a firm understanding of the variations of loan offerings (which have greatly diminished since as a result of the financial crisis) and the fluctuation of mortgage loan rates. Once I learned that the 10-year U.S. Treasury is the benchmark for mortgage rates, I became obsessed with monitoring the yield curve on Bloomberg's Rates & Bonds page at www.bloomberg.com. I began sending analytical e-mails to the group of 15 brokers in my local office. The e-mails touched on trends I was seeing in rates, 10-year Treasury yield trend observations, real estate news, and anything else I felt was related to rate fluctuations. The e-mails started to catch on, and within a month I received a call from the CFO of the company. I was promoted to Manager of Secondary Markets in the Lending Division, and began sending companywide e-mails twice a week. I also hosted several conference calls throughout the week with the offices located around the United States, sharing my thoughts on rates and lending practices and teaching others my methods of observation and analysis. The CFO knew I loved the stock market and encouraged me to monitor financial markets any chance I got. I began monitoring the markets daily, and was quickly reminded of my love for trading. I would sneak trades here and there when no one was paying attention (shhhh), and began making money.

THE SWAN BROTHERS

I was once again obsessed, and watched CNBC every chance I got just like I had in the past. One day while watching CNBC during my lunch break, I saw a guy named Andy Swan on CNBC talking about Google. It noted that Andy was representing Daytrade-Team, based in Louisville, Kentucky. I live in Louisville and thought to myself, "Whaaa? Louisville, Kentucky?! There's a trading firm right here in my country-ass town? I have to get on board with this company!"

I visited the site at http://daytradeteam.com and got the customer service e-mail address. Next, I updated my resume and sent it, coupled with my story and why they should hire me, to the e-mail address I found on the site. I was contacted within a week and asked to come in for an interview. This was the first time I met Andy and Landon Swan.

I'll admit that I was a bit nervous when I first met Andy, who stood a towering six feet nine, and Landon, a beastly six feet seven. I refrained from any questions about height because I was sure they had heard enough of them in their lifetimes. We got down to business and I quickly realized just how little I really knew about trading. These guys were on another level and I could feel my odds of getting hired worsening by the minute. Nonetheless, I was called back, then called back again! After three interviews and an IQ test, I was offered a position as a junior analyst. I had no idea what I was in for, but I had never been more excited about a job in my life!

This opportunity was basically the beginning of the trader I am today. Andy and Landon introduced me to technical analysis, which really got me excited. Technical analysis opened many doors for me. It gave me the ability to manage trades with precision, spot trends and price patterns, and feel more confident about my overall trading abilities. It also answered the question that had been sitting in the back of my mind for years, which was: "How am I supposed to trade short-term options, options spreads, and futures when most fundamental analysis–based trades take so long to come to fruition?"

After a about a year of reading, testing, coaching, and paper trading technical methods, I began to trade everything from equities to options and futures using technical analysis as my primary method of analysis. I still use both fundamental and technical analysis, but I tend to lean toward technical analysis. It is a much more time-efficient method of analysis, and I have found great success using it, especially for shorter-time-frame trades (intraday and one- to six-week swings).

The Swan brothers later informed me that they were not looking to hire when I sent the e-mail. They simply liked the e-mail and wanted to meet me with no real intention of creating a position for me. To me, the fact that they hired me knowing that is the ultimate compliment!

With the knowledge I gained at DaytradeTeam, I focused all of my time and energy on trading. I have been an advanced trader since 2006, and cannot see myself doing anything else for the rest of my life.

FORCE CONFIRMATIONS, NOT TRADES

My most important trading rule is to learn something new every day. If you ever meet a trader who claims to know everything there is to know about the market, run as fast as you can in the opposite direction.

With regard to trade philosophy, I like to go by a saying I coined a while ago: "Force confirmations, not trades." I am very patient with trades, and rarely rush a situation. I seek top-quality technical setups, and I don't act until price action and volume have confirmed a price pattern. This results in lower trade activity, but considering my strong win percentage I'm perfectly fine with less activity.

Speaking of win percentage, my month-to-month win percentage goal is 60 percent. That said, sometimes I fall short of that goal and sometimes I exceed it. Generally I'm able to have a profitable month if I stay above approximately 45 percent, the reason being proper trade management. I let my winners run and cut my losers quickly. Therefore, the profit I generate from wins typically outperforms the capital loss I incur from losing trades. This allows me to come out with a profitable month even when I win less than 50 percent of the time.

It took me quite a while to get to this level. When I started trading, I was rushing into trades left and right! After some experience, I realized this was not the proper approach, and began to slow things down a bit. I am now at the level where I am very comfortable with a position when I begin entering.

My style of entry on equity swings and long-term investments took me a while to perfect as well. I started off going all-in when I saw something I liked. This is not optimal. My approach now is simple, consisting of six steps:

1. Find an attractive setup and establish a direction to pursue.
2. Exhaust analysis to ensure I am comfortable with the entry.
3. Establish the amount of capital I want to put into the position.
4. Start with one-fifth or one-quarter of that capital and enter the position.
5. If the price action, volume, and/or technical indicators remain favorable after a reasonable period of time in relation to my time horizon on the trade, add another one-fifth or one-quarter to the trade.
6. Repeat step 5 until fully vested.

It's a simple strategy called averaging in, and it can greatly diminish losses in the long run. I'm not a one-trick pony when it comes to trading. I do it all. When trading futures, I rarely hold overnight. I also day trade equities and options from time to time, but my day trades primarily consist of futures since the extra leverage provides ample opportunity to bank coin in the short time frame.

My time horizon on options plays tends to be no longer than three months. I most frequently sell front-month vertical spreads (credit spreads) and front-month iron condors, but will enter a butterfly, straddle/strangle, directional put/call, or double diagonal from time to time.

I often use options to complement an existing equity position. For example, I'll sell front-month strangles against an equity position as long as I'm comfortable taking on more shares at the short put strike price (less premium received) or selling shares at the short call strike price (plus premium received). I also sell calls against underlying positions to generate income, and sometimes buy puts or put spreads for protection if I'm feeling short-term bearish about a long-term bullish position.

FLAG AND PENNANT FORMATIONS

Flag and pennant (F&P) formations are my favorite setups, the reasons being that they are common and they work very well if you know what you're doing.

A flag and pennant formation can be either bullish or bearish, depending on the direction of the flagpole. The initial move is a swift high-volume spike in price action to the upside (bullish) or downside (bearish). This quick high-volume move, known as the flagpole, can be attributed to a number of things. It can be related to an earnings report, news driven, short covering, institutional buying, and so on. The reason for the move is not as important as the price action that follows.

The flagpole is followed by consolidation on diminishing volume. Price action during consolidation can take the form of a rectangular consolidation pattern (flag) or triangular consolidation pattern (pennant). This is consolidation is generally referred to as a breather or an opportunity for the stock to catch its breath. If the flagpole is an upside move, this breather indicates that although the stock is not continuing to go higher there is still enough interest at the price level to provide support, which could mean there is more upside potential. If the flagpole is a downside move, this breather indicates that there is not enough interest at the diminished price level to pick the stock back up, which could mean there is more downside pressure to come.

The next move is key. There must be a breakout in the direction of the flagpole coupled with a nice spike in volume before I will enter a trade based on this price pattern. Force confirmation prior to pulling the trigger on entry! If you enter this trade prior to the high-volume continuation breakout, your odds of success are greatly diminished. Hence my previous quote: "Force confirmations, not trades." Following these words will improve your success rate, hands down.

I digress. Let's assume the initial move (flagpole) was an upside spike and the high-volume continuation breakout has taken place after some rectangular consolidation (flag). After the confirmation breakout takes place, I'll enter a bullish position.

So what's next? Next we have to understand how to manage the trade. First, we must know what to expect with regard to profit potential. This is simple; the move is measured by taking the height of the flagpole and adding it to the price point where the confirmation breakout occurred. For example, if the flagpole started at 80 and finished at 90, it has a height of 10. If the confirmation breakout took place at 90, the measured move is 100 (90 + 10). Therefore, my target on that trade is 100.

Now we need to know where to cut losses if the trade goes against us. Again, it's simple. Flag and pennant formations are considered null and void if they retrace 38.2 percent of the flagpole. Therefore, my stop will be placed just below the 38.2 percent retracement level.

The reward-to-risk ratio is typically just over 2:1 with these price patterns, so the trade makes sense 100 percent of the time as long as you wait for the confirmation breakout.

EXAMPLE

The YRCW six-month bar chart in Figure 24.1 presents an excellent example of flag and pennant formations.

FIGURE 24.1 YRCW Consolidates after a Big Move, Daily Chart
Source: © StockCharts.com.

Note the swift upside move coupled with a strong spike in volume. After that, we get the sideways action with diminishing volume followed by a continuation breakout move to the upside with strong volume backing the move.

YRCW was a trade I actually participated in, and obtained a profit of 40 percent as a result. That said, I tend to stay away from stocks below $5 per share. I couldn't pass this one up, though.

WORDS OF WISDOM

Life is short. I constantly try to increase my wealth and improve my situation. I've always loved a quote I heard back in college: "Shoot for the moon. Even if you miss, you'll land among the stars." I try to live my life with that quote in mind. Now, this doesn't mean I'm a crazy risk taker. It simply means I'm more prone to go for it when it feels right and makes sense from an intellectual perspective. I'm young and hungry, and intend to stay that way (at least the hungry part).

CHAPTER 25

The Birth of a New Trend

Ivaylo Ivanhoff, @ivanhoff

Ivan just keeps getting smarter faster than most. He is working harder than most as well. He integrates earnings and price momentum in order to find stock ideas one after another. He approaches momentum in a sophisticated way that is soundly reasoned and deliberately modeled, so I have come to trust his judgment. His work on the StockTwits 50 is unparalleled in terms of weekly trade idea generation for those who want strong stocks with the best odds of moving higher.

Reaction to news is more important than the news itself.

—Todd Harrison

THERE IS NO SUBSTITUTE FOR EXPERIENCE

In the summer of 2010, I joined StockTwits Inc., where I helped create the StockTwits 50—a proprietary momentum algorithm that ranks stocks based on relative strength, earnings and sales growth, earnings surprises, industry relative strength, and many other factors that historically have proven to precede big price moves. The purpose of the StockTwits 50 algorithm is to catch the next move in an already established trend. In this chapter, I reveal how I spot the beginning of the trend—what happens before a stock becomes a momentum stock.

My path to stock trading was an unusual one. I was born and raised in a country where stock market culture simply does not exist, a place where almost no one keeps their money in equities, as the local market is underdeveloped and most people know nothing about publicly traded companies. I was just out of high school and a business major at the university when I was reading on a regular basis a weekly computer magazine, whose name I don't even remember. Oddly enough, the magazine always had two pages devoted to the performance of Internet stocks. I found myself spending an exorbitant amount of time on those two pages. The U.S. stock market was in correction, so most of the stocks that were featured were down 70 to 80 percent from their peaks.

Without any experience or a well-defined approach, I opened an account and started buying Bulgarian stocks. Luck was on my side, as everything went up, every day. The only thing I disliked about the local market was the lack of transparency and the illiquidity, which caused wild ranges and huge bid-ask spreads. I wanted to learn more about the art of stock trading, and there was no one to teach me. I decided that the best place to learn about it was the United States and I moved here to study finance. Honestly, my university education did not help me at all to understand how the stock market works, but at least now I was in a place where the stock market culture was ingrained in many people's minds.

It did not take long for me to realize how little I actually knew. I made all the trading mistakes that could be made and then some more, several times, putting my own money at risk. I could say that probably I even invented some new ways to lose money in the stock market, but I realize that this would not be true. Since financial markets exist, the same mistakes have been made for the simple reason that there are human beings involved and our nature hasn't changed for thousands of years. We are emotional creatures who believe that everything should be symmetrical and balanced as it is in nature. Financial markets are very different from the linear world. They are a place where mean reversion is often delayed long enough to bankrupt the rational thinkers; they are a place where "once in a hundred years" events happen every five years.

I am wrong about 50 percent of the time and I still consider myself a good trader. Learning to accept losses as part of the game and cutting them short is the single most important step toward becoming consistently profitable. It sounds simple, but in reality is extremely difficult for everybody. Why? Because we've been taught that giving up is for losers and we should fight until our last breath. I certainly agree that you should not give up quickly, but you should stay with something only if you can influence the end result. Let me be clear: A stock doesn't know that you own it and it doesn't care that you cannot afford to lose money. The market will strip your last penny if you don't know how to manage risk. You have to understand and accept your power. You cannot move the market. You cannot tell Mr. Market where to go and how fast. This is why so many people who are successful as entrepreneurs and engineers have trouble breaking even in the capital markets. It takes a special kind of person—someone who can forget his or her ego and concentrate on what actually works. Very few people are able to reach that level and to distinguish their trading lives from their personal lives.

Trading or investing is a skill that can be learned. There are two ways to learn a new skill in general: through the school of hard knocks and through the mentorship of others who have the gift of teaching. To become a successful trader, you need to somehow implement both approaches. Nothing can replace personal experience. You can hire the best mentors in the world to teach you and purchase the most expensive equipment and trading software, but this is not going to be enough for you to build a new skill. Skill building is governed to eternal physical laws. There are a hundred billion neurons in your brain. For every skill that you possess (e.g., speaking a language or driving a car), there is a certain combination of connections between some of your neurons. To build a new skill, you need to build a new net of connections. This is why every beginning is hard; this is why big changes do not happen overnight. You have to establish new connections, which takes hard work via repetition and visualization.

People trade their beliefs. This is why it is so hard to trade someone else's market approach. You just don't trust it enough. I have found out that the best way to build a solid market understanding is to devote effort to studying past winners. I meticulously study the best-performing stocks at different time frames (weekly, monthly, quarterly, and annually) and try to figure out what most of them had in common before they made their big moves. Such an approach helps me to focus on the factors that are truly driving prices.

WHEN ELEPHANTS DANCE, THEY LEAVE TRACES

Financial markets move in cycles that are defined by institutional capital allocation. When institutions buy or sell, they do so in volume and leave clear traces for the experienced eye. The market is healthy a few times a year when stocks just want to go up. In such periods, it is fruitless to fight the momentum, as it feeds on itself. Higher prices boost risk appetite, which attracts fresh capital, which boosts prices even further. This is the time when breakouts work all over the place. My goal is to spot those periods and take maximum advantage of them.

The real money in the market is made at the two extremes—value and momentum. I believe in momentum. The stock market reflects our collective expectations and perceptions about the future. Prices change when expectations and perceptions change. The latter two change under the pressure of external factors, which have the potential to start a process of major repricing—a new trend or a continuation of an existing trend.

Price trends are fueled by catalysts. The most powerful catalysts always have an element of surprise ingrained in them. The best-performing stocks in any given year are the ones that manage to surprise the most often and by the highest margins.

The stock market constantly strives to discount events that haven't happened yet. As a result it often discounts events that will never happen. This is why in the near-term perspective price is the ultimate leading indicator. Price trends are born and sustained by catalysts—earnings-related catalysts. Behind each earnings trend there is a social trend that makes it possible.

HIGH VOLUME RANGE EXPANSION

The bulk of the directional market moves tend to happen in just 10 to 15 percent of the trading days. The rest is nothing more than noise in a range. I am looking for the event that signals the beginning of a powerful new trend. How does this signal look? Simply said—it is high-volume price expansion:

- High volume (at least three times the 20-day average daily volume).
- Price expansion (at least two times the average true range for the past 20 days and a minimum of a 10 percent move).

Such a combination of price and volume action guarantees institutional involvement. My logic is simple: When institutions buy, they leave traces. They are heavy, slow buyers; therefore, I have enough time to enter and exit as they build their positions.

I look for stocks that are breaking out of long sideways range. The longer the sideways move, the better, as the duration of the consolidation is highly positively correlated to the potential of the upside move after the range is broken. A breakout to a new six-month high (a new three-year high is preferable) improves the odds of success. At such a level, almost everyone who owns the stock is a winner, which will naturally decrease the supply of the stock. Therefore, the accumulation will be difficult, which will allow for even the slightest demand to sustain new price highs. There is very little originality on Wall Street, and price is often the leading indicator. Volume and risk appetite follow price.

Keep in mind that no setup works all the time. The success rate of any setup is a derivative of the current market environment. During severe market corrections most upside breakouts fail. Participants sell first and ask later. In such periods, it is important to protect your capital and your confidence.

LIQUIDITY FOLLOWS PRICE

On February 9, 2010, OpenTable Inc. (OPEN) reported quarterly earnings per share (EPS) of 14 cents versus analysts' consensus estimate of 7 cents. Year-over-year sales growth was 32 percent, representing a significant acceleration compared to the previous quarter. This type of surprise has the ability to start a powerful new trend, especially in a stock that is neglected in terms of average daily volume and price range.

In the stock market world, reaction to news is more important than the news itself. I saw OPEN appreciating by 8 percent in the after-hours session. It was trading at a new six-month high and had a serious earnings catalyst behind it. I immediately put it on my watch list, knowing that it had the potential to start a big move (see Figure 25.1).

Before the earnings release, the average daily traded volume in OPEN was about 109,000 shares. Many market participants limit their trading universe to stocks that trade at least 500,000 shares a day and disregard everything else as too illiquid. Liquidity runs in cycles. An event that changes the perception of value usually leads to tremendous price appreciation in a short period of time. Volume often follows price. Fast-forward a few months later, and OPEN is now trading 790,000 shares per day.

I started to accumulate OPEN after it broke above its premarket session high the next day, February 10. In two different purchases, the average entry price was 29.

FIGURE 25.1 OpenTable Inc. (OPEN) Daily Chart, Daily Volume at New All-Time High Levels
Source: © StockCharts.com.

I always like to initiate a position with a pilot buy and then add to it after my thesis is confirmed.

The stop-loss level for my position was the low of the day for OPEN, $27.99. In my experience, the strongest earnings gaps never revisit this level. The overall risk was 2 percent of my capital.

At the end of the day I sold half of my position at 31.10. I always like to lock in partial gains on the day that I entered. This puts me in a position of strength, which helps me to ride the remaining trade for a longer period of time. I am not concerned that I might miss out on part of the potential profit. After such a big one-day move, the probability of consolidation is high and I have no guarantee that the stock is not going to give up half of its gains the very next day.

It is natural to assume that after such a strong move in a short time frame, there will not be many buyers. The reason is simple. Psychologically it is very difficult to buy a stock that appreciated 20 percent in two days. Mean reversion is the normal state of mind. This is why momentum traders are the true contrarians, as they are willing to engage in a stock at price levels that are mentally uncomfortable for the average human being.

The high volume price expansion put OPEN on the radar of many institutions and retail traders who would love to get on the train, but not at this price level. I knew that they were likely to patiently wait for the stock to correct and form a base. I waited for the stock to form a bullish flag, planning to increase my position on a 3 percent or more bounce from the 5-, 10-, or 20-day rising simple moving average. There is nothing magical about the major moving averages. They just look like a natural zone of support for the simple reason that they have played this role for so many other stocks in the past that over time market participants have become conditioned to think of them as a zone of potential support. When enough people act on their beliefs, their expectations turn into a self-fulfilling prophecy and the stock bounces again. In the case of OPEN, I added to my position at 34.45 on February 24.

When a stock closes below its relevant moving average, this is a clear sign that the easy money has already been made. In my dictionary, a relevant moving average is the one that has been a line of support during the recent price run. A break below this line indicates that the stock is probably entering into a consolidation stage and only a new catalyst can help to defeat the gravity of the range—a catalyst such as new earnings surprise, raised guidance, industry move, general market move, or new contract. In the case of OPEN, I exited my position in its entirety on April 4 at 37.00—on the day after it closed below its 10-day moving average for the first time since the earnings release.

In hindsight, my exit was premature. It doesn't bother me that OPEN went on to more than double after my initial exit. I have defined myself as a trader who is looking for multiple 15 to 20 percent gains and not so much for a home run.

The goal for each trader is to optimize capital allocation. Put money at risk only during clear trends, and omit consolidation periods as they only bring frustration and missed opportunities.

THERE ARE NO PERFECT SETUPS

No matter how successful you are at trading, you should never stop learning. The only constants are the change and the uncertainty. The markets are always evolving and if you don't evolve, you will be left behind. Past successes mean next to nothing. Every day is a new battle.

There are at least a hundred potentially profitable market setups for free in the public domain. Of course, they are profitable only in the right hands. Why then are so few of the active market participants consistently profitable? For one simple reason: Successful trading is 90 percent psychology and 10 percent knowledge about the underlying forces that drive price. Most people defeat themselves. Everyone knows the basic rules: cut your losses short, let your winners run, and review your trades; and yet so many struggle. At the end of the day, consistent success is not defined by how perfect your setup is. There are no perfect setups. It is about how you manage your position.

CHAPTER 26

The Trend Intensity Breakout Setup

Pradeep Bonde, @*stockbee*

Pradeep is one of the hardest-working traders I know. His extensive knowledge and passion about the markets are reflected in everything he does. He believes in the concept: "Give a man a fish and you feed him for a day. Teach a man to fish and you feed him for a lifetime." So true.

I trade on my own information and follow my own methods.

—Jesse Livermore

LEARNING WHAT WORKS AND WHAT DOESN'T WORK

I entered the stock market actively at precisely the wrong time—right at the beginning of the bear phase in 2000. During the raging bull dot-com era, I was busy working for a start-up and my involvement in the market was sporadic. My interest in trading was initially sparked by the majority holder in our dot-com. He was an avid investor and he tracked his portfolios all the time. As the stock market peaked, the investors in the company started to lose money and as a result the funding for the business dried up. That's when my real journey toward successful full-time trading began.

Like most other traders, I was lost at the beginning. I was buying or short selling stocks at exactly the wrong time. Determined to make trading work, I exhaustively studied the equity markets by reading up on successful traders and their methods. During 2000 and 2001 I spent over $100,000 buying every book, course, software, and research I could find on stock trading.

All this study and exposure to research was enhancing my market knowledge tremendously. Two years into trading, I was learning what works and what does not work, but I was still disappointed with my bottom line. Then in 2002, everything I knew came together thanks to a book titled *The Hedge Fund Edge* by Mark Boucher

(John Wiley & Sons, 1998). In this book, Mark Boucher describes a short-term trading method based on momentum. The basic idea is to find runaway moves in stocks with momentum and to swing trade them for 3 to 10 days. I combined his approach with my previous research and started trading it. To date I continue to trade a momentum-based swing trading method that tries to capture momentum bursts. Over the years I have refined and simplified it several times, but the basic logic remains same.

In 2002, I discovered another very profitable trading strategy based on earnings. I read *Frank Cappiello's New Guide to Finding the Next Superstock* (Liberty Hall Press, 1988; pap. ed., International Marine Publishing, 1990) over a weekend during earnings season. The book talked about stocks that had outsized earnings growth and how they outperformed the market over many months or years. That concept sounded appealing to me. I researched the earnings topics further and found out about the post-earnings-announcement drift (PEAD) anomaly. PEAD is the tendency of stocks that beat earnings forecasts to continue to drift higher and outperform, and for stocks that miss earnings to continue to drift lower and underperform.

Armed with this insight and understanding, I was ready to put my new knowledge into practice in the earnings season. And as luck would have it, I found a small, neglected company called U.S. Laboratories, Inc. (USLB), which announced surprisingly good earnings. I bought it on the day it announced and pyramided my position. In the next seven or eight weeks, it went from 5 to 15, and in the process I more than tripled my money. I started looking for similar earnings plays and found more such ideas that year on stocks like MTON, BPRX, DYII, and so on. Over the years, I have perfected this setup and developed detailed guidelines to find such opportunities. Earnings breakout has continued to be a very profitable strategy for me year after year since then.

In 2002, I also developed a market-timing model based on market breadth and incorporated that into my overall trading plan. The market-timing model identifies good times and bad times for my style of trading. It has consistently kept me out of bearish periods and helped me avoid big drawdowns.

That year was also my first consistently profitable year in which I put all the elements of my trading together. The core strategies of trading momentum and earnings breakouts continue to be the same, and the only difference is the experience I have gained over the years.

LOOKING FOR ENDURING STRUCTURAL EDGES

Markets exhibit certain structural behaviors repeatedly. If we understand those structural anomalies and gain expertise in trading them, then we have an edge. Enduring structural edges, when combined with a proper risk management approach, allow me to make consistent profits year after year. In order to convert an understanding of an edge into a trading profit, you need to develop setups based on that edge. Once you have a setup, you need to become expert at trading it. Momentum and earnings are two such structural edges. The stock market exhibits good momentum characteristics during certain periods. For example, stocks that have outperformed during the prior 3 to 12 months tend to further their momentum. The same thing happens on the bearish side during bearish momentum periods.

On a day-to-day basis I trade five setups—three setups on the long side during bullish periods and two setups on the short side during bearish periods:

1. Stockbee Trend Intensity breakout long.
2. Stockbee Trend Intensity breakout short.
3. Stockbee episodic pivots bullish.
4. Stockbee episodic pivots bearish.
5. Stockbee IPO breakouts bullish.

Stockbee Trend Intensity breakout long is a momentum-based swing trading method. It looks to buy a breakout on a stock with a quarterly momentum. The objective is to capture part of a move in a trending stock.

Stockbee Trend Intensity breakout = Momentum
+ Pullback/Consolidation/Sideways move
+ Breakout

Stockbee Trend Intensity is a measure of the momentum of a stock. The higher the Trend Intensity number, the faster the stock is moving up. It is calculated using the following formula in the TeleChart software program:

100*AVGC7/GC65

where AVGC7 = the 7-day simple moving average
AVGC65 = the 65-day moving average

Figure 26.1 shows an example with BSQUARE Corporation (BSQR) stock, which has a very high Trend Intensity value of 184, meaning its 7-day average price is 84 percent above its 65-day average price.

If you look at Figure 26.1, you will see that BSQR made an explosive move in a range of a few weeks. Such stocks are great candidates for swing trading as they offer big profit opportunities in short periods of time.

Stocks with low Trend Intensity are stocks in a bearish trend. For example, look at China Bio Energy Holding Company (CBEH) in Figure 26.2.

In the Stockbee Trend Intensity breakout long method, I am looking to buy 4-plus percent, high-volume breakouts on stocks with 105-plus Trend Intensity value. Stocks with 105-plus Stockbee Trend Intensity are showing above-average momentum.

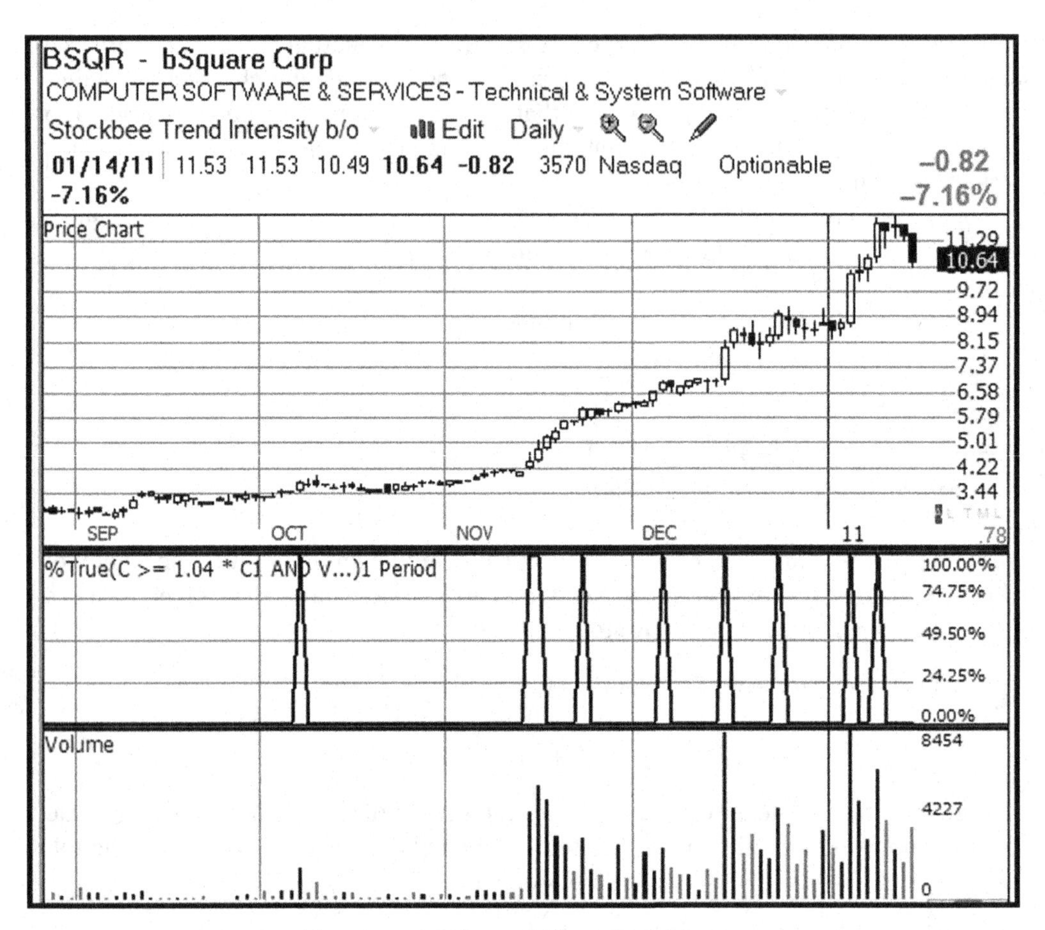

FIGURE 26.1 The Stockbee Trend Intensity Value of BSQR
Chart courtesy of Worden Brothers, Inc., www.Worden.com.

The essence of swing trading is to capture explosive moves after a brief sideways consolidation and sell into strength. Short-term momentum swings in stocks are driven by supply/demand imbalances.

When a stock gains momentum, it attracts more speculators. After a big move, many stocks tend to pause in a range defined by the new supply/demand dynamics. Any small catalyst can lead to a breakout from the range. Many market participants assume that the already established trend is likely to continue, and they enter in expectation of a breakout from the range, hoping to capture the next part of the swing. This often leads to momentum bursts lasting 3 to 10 days.

The underlying cause of stock momentum can be fundamental driven, news driven, sector driven, or often sentiment driven. Once you understand this structural phenomenon of momentum bursts, you can exploit it to capture short-term swings of 3 to 10 days. Those swings offer 10 to 30 percent opportunities in a short period of time.

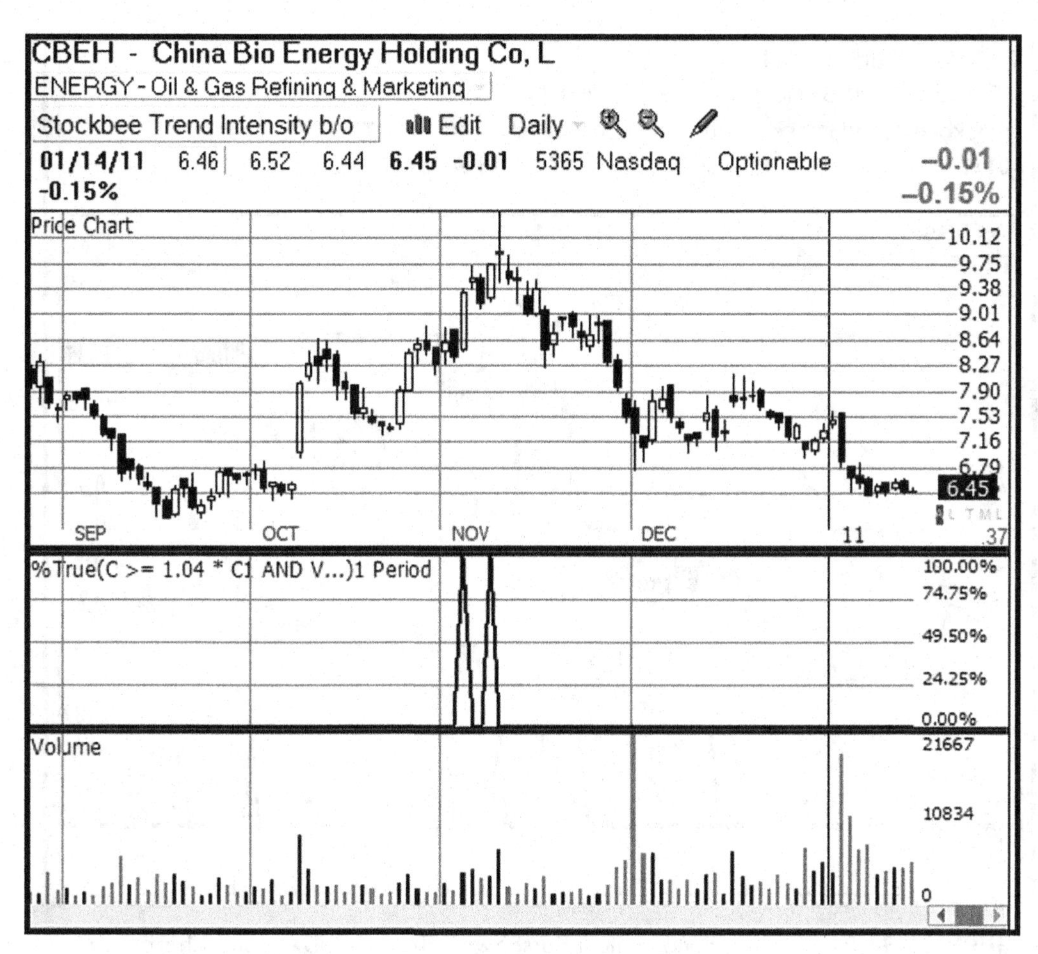

FIGURE 26.2 CBEH Has Trend Intensity of 82 and Is in a Downtrend
Chart courtesy of Worden Brothers, Inc., www.Worden.com.

CAPTURING A SWING

The example of a momentum burst swing trade on Puda Coal Inc. (PUDA) will show you how this works. In a span of seven trading days this stock went up from approximately $9 to $14 (see Figures 26.3 to 26.5). That is an approximately 55 percent move. These kinds of explosive momentum bursts of 10 to 40 percent are common in the market during an uptrend phase.

The stop on this trade would be at the low of the breakout day (Figures 26.4 and 26.5), and the risk would be between 0.5 and 1 percent, depending on market conditions.

For exits I use a variety of rules depending on how the stocks act after the entry. I exit 50 percent of the position on the third day at the close if a stock achieved my target profit. From the third day after the entry, I strive to protect profit by moving the stop to

FIGURE 26.3 Example of a Momentum Burst Swing Trade, PUDA Daily Chart
Chart courtesy of Worden Brothers, Inc., www.Worden.com.

25 cents below the high of the day. When swing trading, it is critical to take profits into strength. Such momentum bursts typically last for 3 to 10 days. If you overstay the trade, then you can end up giving up the bulk of your profits.

How much should you invest in a swing position is a function of your risk tolerance and market conditions. I am an aggressive trader, looking for big returns, and as a result I risk 1 percent of my account on swing trades during favorable market conditions. If the conditions are not favorable, I decrease my risk to 0.50 or 0.25 percent.

I trade the Stockbee Trend Intensity long breakout method only when the stock market is in a confirmed bullish mode as indicated by the Stockbee Market Monitor. You can selectively trade the method in bearish periods, but then you need to be more selective in choosing the right breakouts and risk less.

This is my primary bread-and-butter swing trading method. In 2009 I made 90 percent and in 2010 I made around 74 percent using the same method. To trade this approach

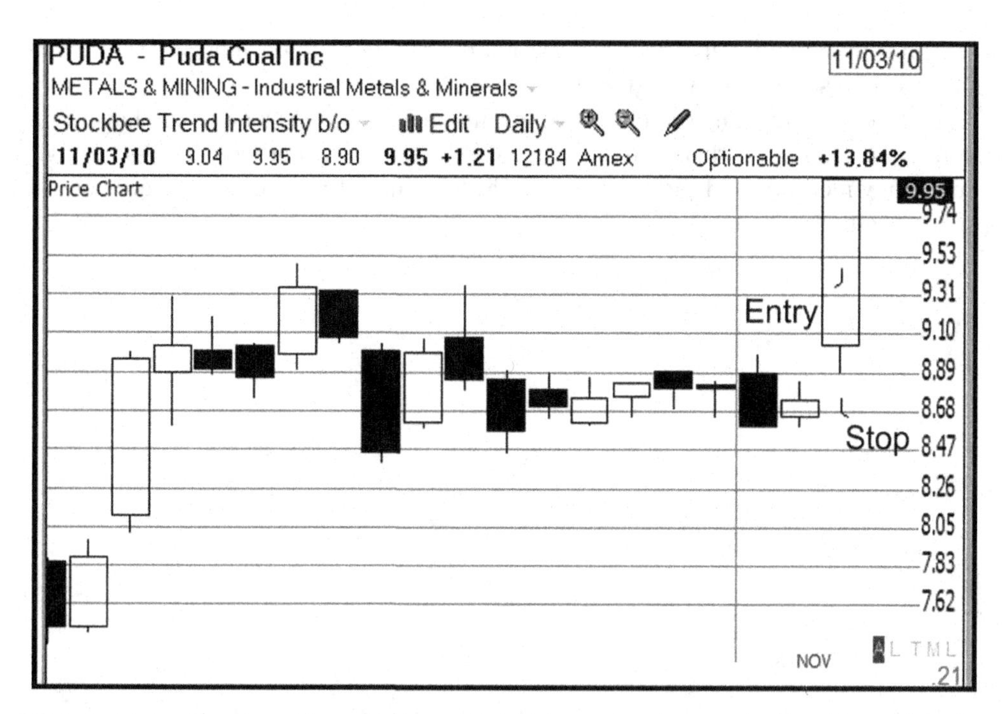

FIGURE 26.4 The Entry Signaled by a High-Volume Breakout in the First Hour of Trading
Chart courtesy of Worden Brothers, Inc., www.Worden.com.

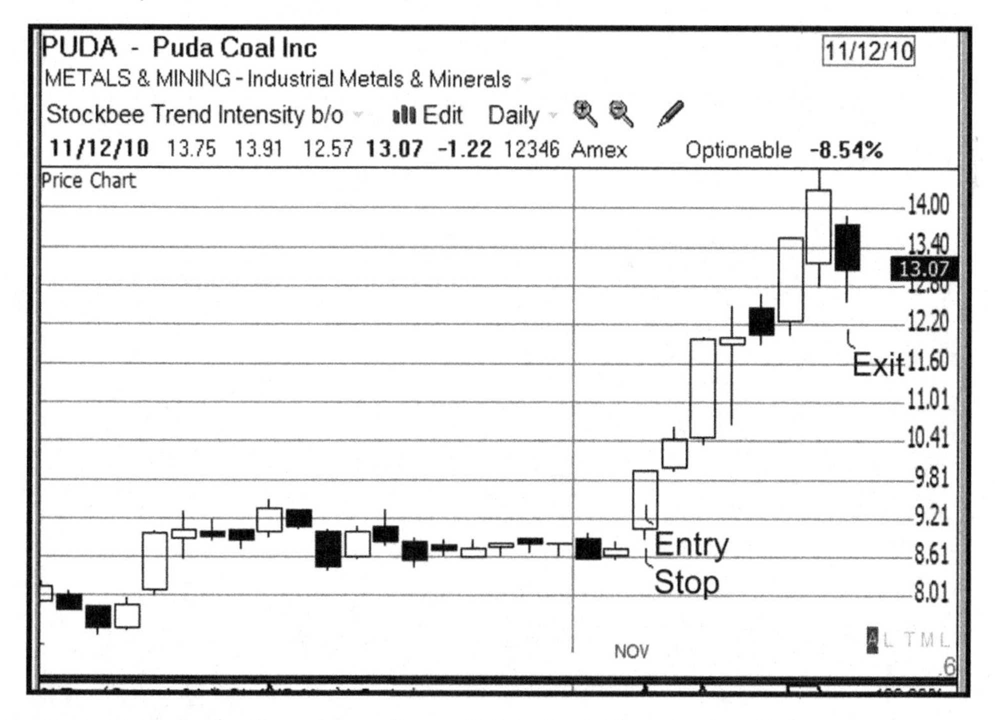

FIGURE 26.5 In the Next Seven Days, PUDA Stock Went Up by 55 Percent
Chart courtesy of Worden Brothers, Inc., www.Worden.com.

successfully, or any other approach for that matter, you need to develop an expertise in identifying good setups and a solid trading process.

The market offers many opportunities for momentum swing traders who have well-defined methods. The markets are not controllable, but your methods are. As a trader I focus on my methods and their execution. Profit is an outcome of such a methodical approach. Methods trump markets.

PART V

Options Trading

CHAPTER 27

Unusual Options Activity

Joe Kunkle, *@OptionRadar*

Joey is pound for pound one of the greatest traders on StockTwits. He throws out so many actionable ideas in such a timely fashion that he must have the distinction of being king of the shout-outs. We created StockTwits for people like Joey to come and share in real time. He makes us feel smart.

Perfection is not attainable, but if we chase perfection we can catch excellence.

—Vince Lombardi

HACKING MY PARENTS' TRADING ACCOUNT

I am an active trader in the equity markets with a focus on event-driven options trading. I use a combination of fundamental, technical, and options activity analysis to seek out stocks setting up for a big move.

I started trading when I was 15 years old. I hacked into my parents E*Trade account while they were on vacation. Although the act was looked down upon, it was hard for them to punish me when they saw what I had accomplished in the markets in just five days of trading. My first trade was buying shares in MicroStrategy (MSTR) around $18 per share and watching it go parabolic (to $1,500 by early 2000).

I became obsessed with the stock market. I would come home from football practice and instead of taking a nap, I would turn on CNBC and absorb as much information as possible.

I guess some of it was in my blood. My great-grandfather worked on Wall Street for many years and, combining that with my attraction to the gambling nature of the stock market, I had the urge to pursue trading as a career from a young age. I was playing blackjack with my grandparents at the age of 10 and was betting on horses at the track when I was 13. I was a natural fit for the stock market, which was going through the tech bubble when I first began to study and grasp the concepts of trading. I was a math wizard from the day I was born, so my learning curve was very short and that really helped along the way.

I took it upon myself to read as many money investment books as possible, beginning with mostly fundamental analysis of investments—the building blocks—and taking on technical analysis and options trading later on.

I attended Bentley University from 2001 to 2005 and received a bachelor's degree in finance. Bentley has a state-of-the-art trading room on campus, where I really started to fine-tune my trading skills. I took every trading-related class I could and attended the special one-hour trading room seminars, learning all of the software and every aspect of the equity and bond markets. When I wasn't in class, I was trading the markets. My trading skills continued to get better and at some point I was able to start putting money toward my tuition (although the IRS rained on my party when I received a lesson in capital gains taxes).

I took my first job with Investors Bank, as a corporate actions analyst, basically focusing on mergers, acquisitions, and other corporate events. It was not challenging, but gave me plenty of free time to trade during the day and also offered a tuition reimbursement program. Just a few months out of college I decided to attend Boston University because it offered a program like no other—a master of science in investment management (MSIM). The MSIM program was fantastic, a must for anyone looking to get into investment management and network with people in the industry.

I next decided to take a job with Thomson Reuters to be part of a team working on a brand-new product launch, Thomson Squawk Box. Timing was an issue and the product never really had a chance to get off the ground, as market conditions deteriorated fast and budget cuts put this project to bed less than a year after launch. However, during that year I was actively following and studying the markets on a daily basis, working 14 hours a day, and learning the ins and outs of technical analysis, as well as other valuable tidbits from my co-workers. Reuters was the place where I really found an interest in studying unusual options activity, because time after time I would see takeovers and other news moving stocks for big gains just days after I had noticed active options positioning.

After I was let go, I decided to start my own company: OptionsHawk.com, a web site specializing in options analytics that provides live market coverage with option strategies, technical analysis, fundamental analysis, and much more on a daily basis. I put my full efforts into launching the business, and it was the best decision I ever made. I was not made to wear a suit, nor work under anyone, so despite the long working hours it is fulfilling at the end of every day to know that I started a company from scratch and became profitable within three months. I also had multiple offers from hedge funds to trade funds in a backer arrangement. The ability to run a business and also trade daily is the best job I could ever have hoped for.

SEVEN SIMPLE STEPS

My trading philosophy is a combination of several different approaches—fundamental, technical, and options flow analysis. I can break down my trading style into seven simple steps:

1. *Market direction.* I always have to have a feel for market direction, taking into account economic data, the Standard & Poor's (S&P) technicals, and market sentiment. There is no use trying to be a superstar and be long a stock you see as a great buy in a downtrending market, nor short a stock you see as awful in an uptrending market. Nobody needs a hero, and fighting the direction of the overall market is a losing battle.
2. *Options flow and volatility analysis.* I monitor options activity every minute of the trading day because the "smart money" traders are using options to trade, as you can make a lot of money faster and with a smaller capital allocation. Without going into the intricacies of my analysis, I look for unusual options activity in stocks with upcoming catalysts (earnings announcements, Food and Drug Administration [FDA] approvals, investment conferences, etc.), as well as any abnormal volume activity. Monitoring the changes in volatility is key in my analysis, and I use options flow as an idea-generation tool—the first step in any trading process.
3. *Technical analysis and reading the tape.* Once the unusual options activity screen leads me to a select few stocks, I monitor time and sales to see if there are any big buyers or sellers in the name. I use fairly simple technical analysis (trend lines, moving averages, support/resistance breaks, Fibonacci lines, Relative Strength Index [RSI], Commodity Channel Index [CCI], and moving average convergence/divergence [MACD]), as I feel that if you get too fancy, you can make a bearish or bullish case for any chart.
4. *Fundamentals.* I will then check the selected stocks' basic fundamental metrics (P/E, P/S, P/FCF, margins, and short interest) to determine if the other indicators align with the technical picture. If I am looking for a quick in-and-out trade, I will let bad fundamentals slide sometimes, but the fundamentals are still a factor when determining trade size, and for swing and longer-term trades. I have always had a good eye for under-the-radar companies, and have been fortunate to be invested in many stocks that were acquired.
5. *Trading strategy.* I am a directional trader, and although I do use option strategies to trade volatility mispricing and some delta-neutral strategies, I prefer to make a call on the direction and magnitude of the move via simple calls/puts or spreads. If the options are illiquid, as is often the case, I will trade the underlying equity.
6. *Position size.* The size of a position depends on the preceding five factors and the confidence in the play based on those factors. I run an options portfolio and have

a set of rules, such as never being more than 75 percent long or short, and I use a value at risk approach when determining the position size, based on where my stop loss is set.

7. *Monitoring and control.* The last step in my trading approach is to continuously monitor positions in case any of the determining factors for making the trade happen to change. Removing emotions from the trade and using discipline will let you sleep better at night, and also will benefit your portfolio.

ALIGNMENT OF TECHNICALS, FUNDAMENTALS, AND OPTIONS FLOW

My favorite setups are when the options flow, technicals, and fundamentals all lead to the same conclusion, whether a buy or a short, which I refer to as "all the stars align" in a trade.

As for risk management, I am a "swing for the fences" trader, willing to lose 100 percent on some of my trades because I often reap 200 percent profits on a single trade in a single day. It is all about having a high hit rate, and I have maintained a 70 percent win rate on trades, so I can maintain high returns. The trades I am willing to lose the full premium are almost always event-driven plays, where either you are wrong or you are right. On technically driven and other driven trades I adhere to much stricter risk management. For most people I recommend that an options portfolio be dedicated to no more than 30 percent of your entire portfolio, and generally use a 2 to 3 percent weighting per position. I usually determine stops and targets of option positions by first determining a stop and a target on the underlying equity, usually technically driven. From that I can calculate the target and stop of the options position, but also have to take into account time decay and volatility changes. The use of options allows you to lock in gains when stocks hit your target, but also keep some money on the table, whether it be taking off a percentage of the position or legging into spreads.

Most of my trades are on a 3- to 20-day time horizon, although I do use certain strategies to play longer-term moves, often on overreactions due to earnings, using LEAPS and risk reversals. If a stock is not moving in the planned direction within three days (aside from catalyst trades with an exact date), I find it best to take the position off and look elsewhere, or else you will fall into a loser's trap of always thinking the next day could be the day it reverses.

On a higher level, my market philosophy is that markets are not efficient, as information flow is not distributed equally, and there are multiple ways to gain an edge and trade with an advantage. Although quantitative (robot) trading is taking a lot of the edge away, I refuse to agree with conspiracy theorists who believe that there is no way to actively trade and beat the returns of the broader markets. As Thomas Edison said, "There is no substitute for hard work," and I believe that working hard and sharpening your skills will lead to a successful career trading the markets.

KELLOGG IS IN TROUBLE

A recent trade that serves as a good example of my trading approach is Kellogg. On July 15, 2010, shares of Kellogg were trading at \$51.60 and I began to see 6× daily put volume trade and buyers in August \$50 puts, including a block of 1,500, showing institutional interest. The chart in Figure 27.1 shows shares making a double top around \$55 from the 2008 highs and losing momentum, so the technicals looked bearish. As for the fundamentals, shares traded 27× free cash flow, which is high for a cereal maker, and I was also noticing the prices of grains (wheat, rice, corn) starting to break long-term downtrends and realizing that these higher input costs could hurt Kellogg and its peers. With the earnings announcement set for July 29, I had the catalyst for a big move in shares, which is

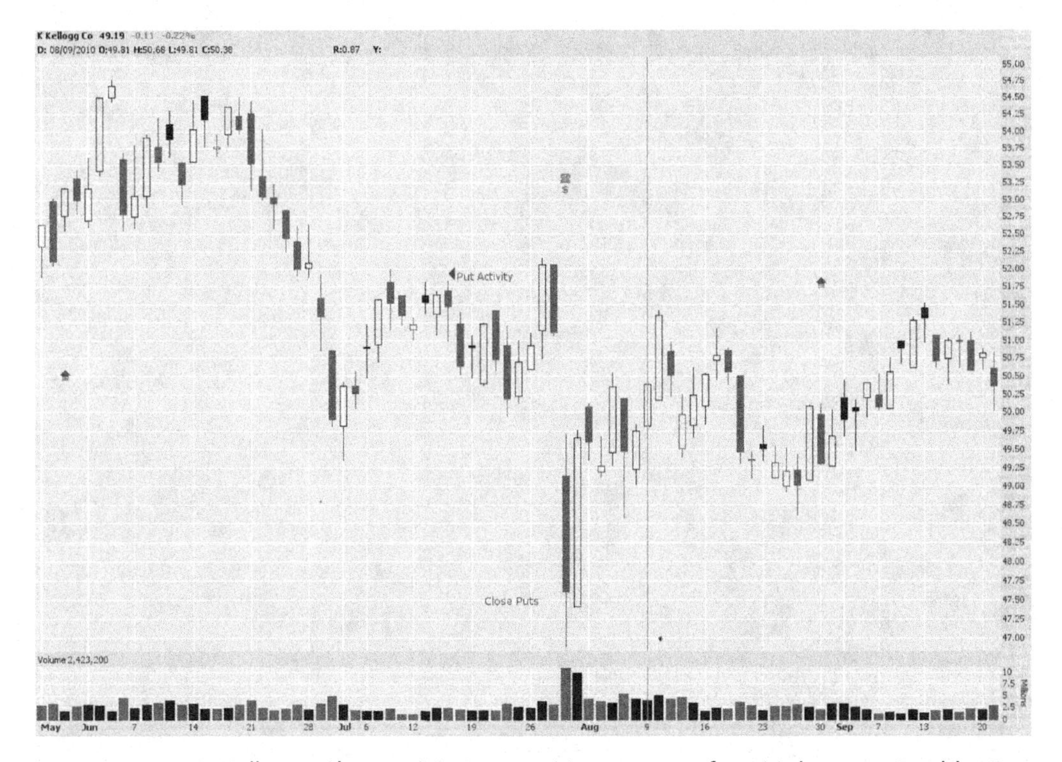

FIGURE 27.1 Kellogg Shares (K) Losing Momentum after Making a Double Top around \$55
Source: © TD Ameritrade, Inc. Used with permission. For illustrative purposes only.

key in trading options. On that day (July 15) I recommended buying the August $50 puts at $0.70.

Kellogg reported earnings and gave a bleak forecast, causing shares to drop from $51.75 to $47.75, a 7.7 percent move for a stock that generally trades quietly as a low-beta, slow-growth consumer goods name. The August $50 puts climbed to $2.35, a solid 235.7 percent gain for a two-week holding period. This is not out of the ordinary, as I see this happening all the time throughout earnings season, and in this case all the stars aligned and resulted in a big winner of a trade.

CHAPTER 28

Put Ratio Spread

Jared Woodard, *@condoroptions*

Trading options demands a deep understanding of markets and a mastery of the subtleties of the relationship between price and time. The incredible thing about Jared is that he is able to clearly communicate such complexities with every nuance still intact. Not surprisingly, he expresses trades with similar elegant precision. Jared, an early StockTwits adopter, has modeled the highest standard. The lessons in this chapter are some of the most challenging to grasp but they are rewarding as well.

IMPORTANCE OF A NONFINANCIAL BACKGROUND

One of my schoolteachers introduced me to finance and investing, and it was a kind of hobby for some time before I started taking it seriously in college and thereafter. In 2007, I started the Condor Options newsletter, because I was really dissatisfied with the level of education about complex option spreads that was available online at the time. We have since expanded to offer custom historical research, a newsletter teaching time spreads, and mentoring and individual education. In 2009, I registered as a licensed commodity trading advisor (CTA) to manage client accounts.

Any financial expertise I have was gained through experience and private study; my academic training is in logic and philosophy, not finance. I've noticed that some of the most creative and effective market participants have backgrounds or interests in other fields—not that there's anything wrong with studying finance in a formal setting, if that's where your interests really lie. But if forced to choose, I think that capacities for critical thinking and intellectual rigor are far more useful than knowing the intricacies of pricing formulas and volatility models. You can learn details anytime, but it's hard to learn how to learn.

Financial markets are crowded, mostly with herds of people doing similar things, and the only way I know to develop a reliable edge is to pay attention to new or unusual information. Two habits that have helped me quite a lot in this regard are (1) reading as much as possible and (2) being extremely selective about what I read. The reason for the first habit should be self-evident: If you aren't constantly learning, you're eventually going to become irrelevant (not to mention missing out on a huge part of what it means to be human). The second habit arose out of necessity. I used to skim many hundreds of RSS feeds on a daily basis, but I found that staying on the Internet treadmill made it harder to devote time to the long-form, meaningful research that I actually cared about. Pruning my RSS reader and my list of must-read people on Twitter cut out all of the noise with virtually no loss of substance. Some of my most productive days happen with the Internet connection shut off entirely.

A major turning point came when I started learning about and trading options. Many investors are first attracted to options because of the leverage involved—they like the prospect of making 30 percent on an options trade that might only yield 3 percent if implemented with stock. I was attracted not by the leverage available but by the increased control and precision that options provide. If taking a position in some asset is like expressing an opinion in a language, then the language of long/short stock and futures trading can be a relatively crude language: Unless you get into pairs trading or complex position sizing, you can say only two things. A multilegged options spread, however, allows you to express views about time, price, and the rate of change of price (i.e., volatility); that's a more nuanced language. So my interest in options was primarily about increased potential for risk management and for expressing market opinions more clearly.

THE MARKET IS IMPERFECT

I have a pretty unromantic view of markets in general and financial markets in particular. Markets are good at rewarding innovation and at processing large quantities of data, but even mainstream economists agree that markets are inept when it comes to public goods. Empirically, insufficiently regulated markets fail constantly (often spectacularly so). Economists Hyman Minsky and Steve Keen are really essential on this point. The 2007–2008 financial crisis was one bit of confirming evidence for those of us who are willing to take a critical look at the value of market-based systems, but it was also just another data point in an already abundant historical record.

I take it that the textbook view on the purposes of financial markets is that they connect investors holding idle capital with companies that can put that capital to good use and that they enable participants to transfer risk. I find it hard to believe that capital raising and risk transfers account for more than a small portion of what I see happening daily on public exchanges. If that doubt is well-founded, then even if the financial crisis had never happened, the financial sector would still be imposing costs on society that outweigh its benefits. A better route to an understanding of financial markets is, I think, through the literature on market failure. If we focus on things like imperfect competition, externalities, and informational asymmetry, and then survey the bargaining power and behavior of the major market actors, the picture becomes a little clearer.

One incredible irony is that so many traders sympathize intellectually with the basic tenets of neoclassical economics, when their behavior says otherwise. Speculation in financial markets is incompatible with a belief in the strong version of the efficient markets hypothesis (EMH): If you have such a firm opinion on something that you depart from an approach that only buys and holds diversified indexes, then by definition you think that the market hasn't priced some asset correctly.

To focus on more vulgar, practical matters: Successful financial speculation is entirely about identifying and exploiting situations in which an asset has been priced incorrectly. Profits and losses incurred via speculation, then, are a record of whether you have identified any genuine, exploitable opportunities or are merely trading the statistical noise. But the limits of arbitrage are also much greater than many participants realize such that even if you are able to discover and define a genuine edge, it's entirely possible that it will be impossible to exploit (for more information, read "A Survey of Corporate Governance" by Andrei Shleifer and Robert W. Vishny, *Journal of Finance* 52, no. 2, 1997). The conclusion I draw is that any trade or strategy that can't satisfy some basic statistical criteria is a waste of time. Many (or even most) of the trades taken by individual investors, in this view, never rise above the level of gambling—in the sense of having negative expectancy over time. Subjective technical analysis strikes me as particularly hopeless, since it creates openings for any number of cognitive biases and unexamined assumptions. Finding a genuine edge is hard enough without also imposing the condition that you first somehow become a steely-eyed, emotionless, perfectly rational exemplar of *Homo economicus*. Objective and quantitative analysis of price data, on the other hand, is still an interesting and promising area of research, subject to the noise and arbitrage constraints I mentioned earlier.

MANAGING PUT RATIO SPREADS

I prefer strategies that aren't aggressive with respect to price forecast—not because I never have opinions about market direction, but because I think that there's more potential in strategies that take long and short positions on volatility. I suppose I'm best known for trading and writing about iron condors, one such type of spread. But instead of repeating analysis given elsewhere, I'll look at a different example: the put ratio spread.

A put ratio spread is constructed by trading put options in the same expiration cycle at two different strike prices. Where strike price K_a is higher than K_b, a trader would buy some quantity of puts struck at K_a and sell a greater number of puts at K_b. This is often done on a ratio of 1:2 or 2:3 for simplicity (e.g., selling two 90 puts and buying one 100 put). Because more puts are sold than are bought, if the strike prices are

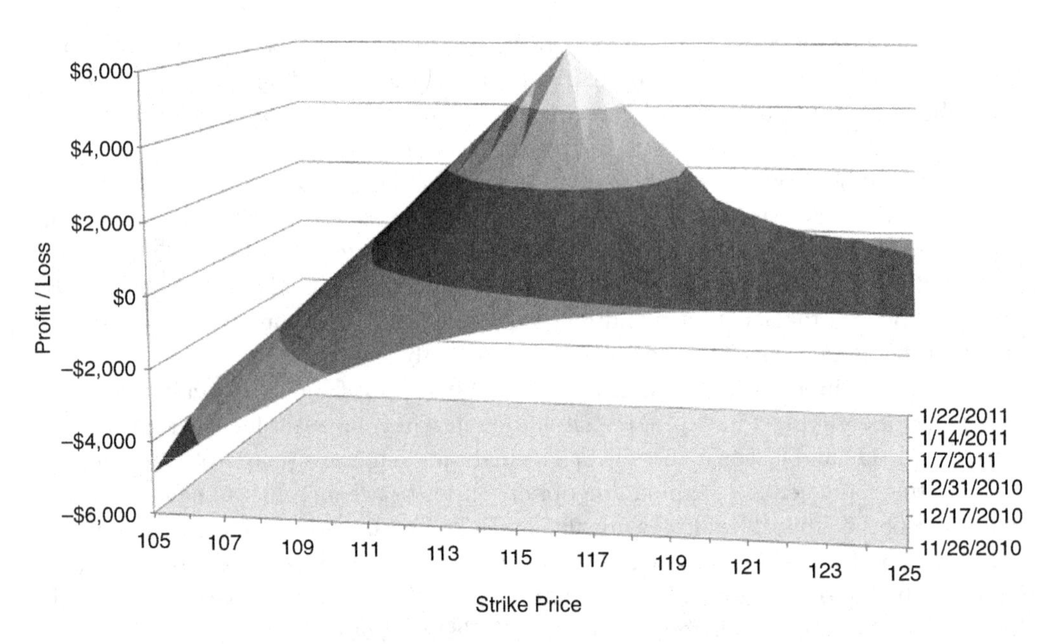

FIGURE 28.1 Put Ratio Spread

sufficiently close, the position may sometimes be opened for a net credit, although this is not a primary concern. The risk profile of a typical put ratio spread is shown in Figure 28.1.

The price of the underlying asset is displayed on the x-axis, with profits or losses at expiration shown on the y-axis. If the underlying closes anywhere above the higher strike price at expiration, any initial credit will be retained as profit or (in this case) the initial debit will be forfeited. If the underlying declines modestly, large profits will accrue: the maximum profit is earned if the underlying is slightly above the strike price of the short puts at expiration, since the short puts will expire worthless while the long put will achieve its maximal gain in relation to the overall spread. The break-even formula for a spread like this, again where strike price K_a is higher than K_b, is:

$$\text{Break-even point} = K_b - (K_a - K_b) - \text{Opening debit or credit}$$

That is, the break-even point will be the lower strike price minus the difference between the two strikes, minus the opening credit or debit. Below that point, potential losses are unlimited. From a directional point of view, this sort of trade is poised to achieve very minimal profits or losses from any positive or neutral price movement and will achieve substantial profits with modestly lower price movement.

However, a bearish price forecast isn't the only reason someone might consider a put ratio spread. In equity and equity index options, implied volatility (IV) tends to be higher at lower strike prices than it is at higher strike prices. This phenomenon—known as volatility skew or vertical skew—is the result of investors seeking protection for long stock portfolios by buying out-of-the-money (OTM) put options and being more willing to sell OTM calls. Demand for puts and the supply of calls pushes put prices higher and call prices lower (in implied volatility terms) than they otherwise would be. Sometimes, the skew is sufficiently elevated to provide an opportunity for traders who wish to exploit this difference.

Put ratio spreads are one way to trade the volatility skew. The higher number of OTM puts sold means we're selling options at high levels of IV and buying options at lower levels of IV. If overall volatility declines or the skew flattens, the value of the short puts will decline more than the value of the long puts, resulting in net profits. One important decision is whether the spread will be managed as a pure volatility play or as a combination play on price and volatility. Hedging delta (directional price) exposure on an ongoing basis will reduce the potential profit of the trade, but with the benefit of less risk and clarity in forecasting—it is easier to be right about one forecast (volatility alone) than about two forecasts simultaneously (price and volatility).

Here's a simple four-point checklist for entering and managing a put ratio spread:

1. Identify assets with liquid options whose short-term (two-month) implied volatility skew is significantly higher that their medium-term (four-month) mean.
2. For every 50 delta (at-the-money [ATM]) put purchased, sell two 25 delta (OTM) options.
3. Size the position so that you're comfortable risking a dollar amount equivalent to 40 percent of the maximum potential profit on the trade.
4. Exit the trade if the underlying trades below the break-even point (at expiration) of the position.

I'll review each of these steps in turn.

Trade Candidates

As with any options spread, it is important to restrict the scope of potential trade candidates to underlying assets with sufficiently liquid options. Look for average daily volume of at least 10,000 contracts. For individual stock and exchange-traded fund (ETF) options, bid-ask spreads have narrowed down to a few pennies in most cases; for futures options and index options (e.g., SPX, RUT), it is necessary to negotiate the spread a little more carefully.

All volatility skews are not created equal. Sometimes the options in a single stock or ETF will exhibit volatility skew because of a pending news announcement or expected event. A ratio spread entered under such conditions may amount to a bet on the magnitude of a postevent move, which is a very different kind of trade from the structural and index-based motivation discussed here. Put ratio spreads on individual stocks and sectors can be desirable trades, but some extra work is needed to ensure that all relevant fundamental factors have been accounted for. When first learning how this sort of trade behaves on a daily basis, it is probably wise to trade only index products.

Given my earlier comments about the importance of a well-defined edge, it would be inconsistent if I didn't mention why someone might be inclined to put on a trade like this. It's fine to know that put ratio spreads let us trade the volatility skew, but assuming that the options market isn't completely broken (i.e., that arbitrage opportunities aren't just lying around everywhere as if a trading piñata has just exploded), then we have to wonder under what conditions the volatility skew warrants attention.

A complete answer would extend beyond the scope of this chapter, but a reasonable first step is simply to note that, like volatility in general, volatility skew tends to be characterized by mean reversion in the short term. So when we see that skew has risen substantially, a volatility trader might want to express the view that skew is likely to fall. A fully developed strategy would include precise conditions for entering and exiting these ratio spreads based on changes in volatility skew, and arriving at a (profitable) set of rules like that would require some historical testing in and out of sample. Figure 28.2 displays the volatility skew in two-month SPDR S&P 500 index ETF (SPY) options since 2005, normalized for the absolute level of ATM implied volatility and observed bimonthly.

I've overlaid an eight-period exponential moving average, which covers about four months of prior data. If volatility skew really is mean-reverting, then observations that

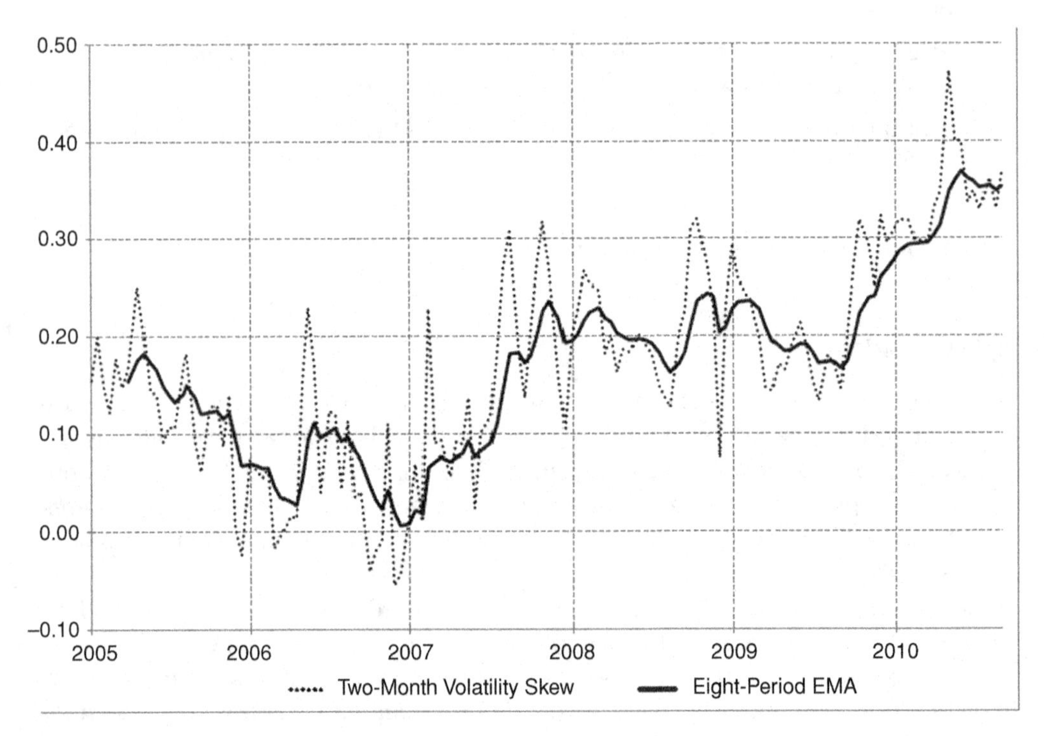

FIGURE 28.2 Two-Month S&P 500 Implied Volatility Skew
Data source: Condor Options and thinkorswim.

are significantly higher or lower than this short-term average might be situations in which trade opportunities exist.

Strike Selection

In the presence of some opinion about future price levels, the strike prices for the spread can be chosen based on that opinion. However, a volatility trader is likely to be rather uninterested in specific price levels and more interested in delta values. Selling short options with 25 deltas and buying options at 50 delta ensures that the trade will be relatively cost-neutral; that is, the price of the long put will be somewhat close to the price of the two short puts. Other combinations of deltas can certainly be used; the purpose is just to leave a wide zone of potential profitability while not incurring a large debit up front.

Another consideration when choosing strikes is the fact that implied volatility does not change uniformly across the curve: Because the vega (sensitivity to changes in implied volatility) is greater at-the-money (ATM), selecting short strikes that are too far OTM may result in a position that is insufficiently sensitive to changes in skew. If we bought one 50 delta put and sold five 10 delta puts, for example, we would be likely to witness a situation in which the value of our long ATM put decayed faster than the value of the short OTM puts.

Position Sizing, Risk Management, and Exit

Risk management for a trade like this depends in part on whether you're going to hedge your price exposure: For a trader who just wants to enter the spread and leave it alone, one reasonable exit condition would be if the underlying trades below your break-even point. Unless the trade is near expiration, if the lower break-even point is violated, the mark-to-market loss might be as large as 40 percent of the maximum profit potential for the trade. That's a good rule of thumb for position sizing, too: 40 percent of the maximum potential profit should be the amount you're willing to lose on the trade.

Alternatively, even a relatively lax delta hedging regime will allow you to tolerate more downside movement, since you will be selling shares into weakness. Participants trading smaller or fully allocated accounts may find dynamic hedging too capital-intensive and may prefer the break-even stop-loss method mentioned before. This position can be closed by buying back the short options and selling the long put option.

SETUP APPLICATION

For instance, looking at Figure 28.2, we can see that there was a sudden spike in the volatility skew in early November 2007. Price action in recent months had been tumultuous, and there had been two single-day declines of more than 2 percent in recent weeks, so traders were likely nervous about additional shocks. On November 5, SPY

TABLE 28.1 Prices and Implied Volatility for SPY December 2007 Put Options

Strike Price	Bid	Offer	Delta	Implied Volatility
140	1.96	2.01	−23	26.62%
141	2.14	2.19	−25	26.10
142	2.33	2.39	−27	25.55
143	2.54	2.60	−29	24.99
144	2.77	2.84	−31	24.46
145	3.00	3.10	−34	23.87
146	3.25	3.40	−37	23.31
147	3.55	3.70	−40	22.75
148	3.90	4.00	−43	22.18
149	4.25	4.35	−46	21.57
150	4.60	4.70	−50	20.82

Data source: thinkorswim.

closed at $150.05. The implied volatility for OTM puts expiring in December 2007 is shown in Table 28.1.

The volatility skew in these options is evident if we compare the implied volatilities of, for example, the ATM (50 delta) and 25 delta options—there's a difference of 5.28 percentage points. A put ratio spread designed to profit from this volatility skew will need to buy options that are closer to the money and sell a greater number of options out-of-the-money. For this example, we'll use the 50 delta and 25 delta puts:

Buy 10 SPY December 150 puts for $4.70.
Sell 20 SPY December 141 puts for $2.14.
The net debit is $0.42.

The lower break-even point for this trade will be 141 – (150 – 141) – (–0.42), or 132.42. Since this trade was opened for an initial debit, we'll lose $420 if SPY closes above 150 at expiration. The maximum profit of $8,580 will be achieved if SPY is slightly above 141 at expiration.

The position saw a positive early start, as prices declined to 141 over the first three weeks of the trade (see Figure 28.3). Additionally, by the end of November the difference between the implied volatility of the short and long puts was only 4.27, which was a favorable result. The put ratio spread was priced to close at about $1.75, for a gain of $1.33 or $1,330, and the results of weekly delta hedging netted an additional $338.

By December 18, the underlying had rallied and was at about 146, and the value of the short 141 puts had dwindled to just $0.23, making the trade functionally a directional bet in the form of the long 150 puts. Hedging that exposure was becoming more capital-intensive, and since the position had achieved its purpose, it was time to close it. The closing price for the put ratio spread was $4.29, for a net gain of $3.87 or $3,870 on

FIGURE 28.3 SPDR S&P 500 ETF (SPY), Price History
Data source: Commodity Systems Inc.

the 10 × 20 contracts we used for this example. Hedging costs were $905, so the total gain on the trade was $2,965.

WORDS OF WISDOM

It is easy to be narrow-minded, self-interested, and greedy. It is easy to be a capitalist; being human is hard. When it seems like every force in the world is aligned to push us to seek our own individual advantage, the only interesting and worthwhile action is to insist on our obligations to one another.

CHAPTER 29

Know What You Don't Know

Adam Warner, @*agwarner*

Adam is one of the most experienced options guys on StockTwits. He has seen it all and knows the nuts and the bolts of countless options strategies, the names of which I can't even remember. Adam's generosity with students and good causes has earned our deep respect.

OPTIONS TRADING WAS A BIT OF A FAMILY BUSINESS

I have traded options for almost half my life now. (Wow, scary thought.) I started as a market maker on the American Stock Exchange (AMEX) in February 1988. We stood in trading crowds with only our buy and sell pads to protect us. We got a roughly 300-pound package of position and valuation sheets each day that we got from our clearing firm. And unless you could commit it all to memory, you carried them with you all day.

Trading was not the career I had planned. My dad had traded options on the AMEX in the 1970 s and early 1980 s, and one of my brothers-in-law soon followed, so it was a bit of a family business. After a couple of summer jobs on the floor, I took the GMAT and applied for all sorts of Wall Street jobs, and ended up working for a firm called the Options Group. They provided a (then) state-of-the-art online options pricing system for predominantly nonequity options. The firm was terrific, but my job (tech support) was not. My dad suggested I trade on the AMEX. It was 1988, and while I had intended to take my career in another direction.

I didn't take to the trading life at first, but grew to love it and hung in until 2001. Part of my love involved simply happening on a great trading spot. On the AMEX you basically set up camp in a trading crowd and made markets in the options in front of you. Back then you just physically could handle only so many (handhelds were not invented yet). I had about four or five I could manage; the busiest was the old USX Corporation. At the time, USX owned both U. S. Steel and Marathon Oil. The hook here was that Carl Icahn owned size and pressured the company to split into two. The option flow got us wildly long calendar spreads, and as luck would have it Icahn's agitating hit a crescendo right around the expiration of the short side of our calendar, so the position worked. I was in my early twenties and mistook some good fortune for genius. By the time the Internet bubble hit almost a decade later, I realized that your success in the biz really lies at the intersection between smart trading and good fortune.

I ultimately left the AMEX because increased automation reduced the need for a sole proprietor to actually remain a floor member. And the advent of multiple listings in every listed option basically eliminated the bid-ask spread that provided our lifeline. So, 13 years later, I picked up my laptop and my handheld and my cell phone and moved to an off-floor location to trade, ultimately working from my house.

It was a different game off-floor. As a market maker, the system basically handed you enough trades with edge in them that you could afford to pay the piper on the occasional smart-money disaster you had to make good on the other side of. Off-floor, the only pick-offs are the ones you do to yourself. But gone too are the built-in edges.

I added option writing to my day in 2003. I responded to an inquiry at a site called StreetInsight. com, later known as RealMoney Silver. I co-wrote its options column for about a year, and then moved on to Minyanville. com. I also started up my own site, Daily Options Report (http://dailyoptionsreport. com), which I believe is the oldest options-centric blog in continuous existence. Over the years I've guest-written Barron's Striking Price and appeared on myriad other spots such as MarketWatch, TradingMarkets. com, and InvestorPlace. I also wrote a book for McGraw-Hill titled *Options Volatility Trading* (2009).

ON AND OFF THE FLOOR

As a floor trader, I had no say whether I net owned or net shorted options. We simply had to take the other side of public order flow, then hedge accordingly. I could always lay off my delta (share equivalent) exposure. But at the time I couldn't easily offset my vega (volatility exposure). And at the time, that was pretty much one-directional. The public by and large would sell you call after call. They would buy puts, too, but not in nearly the same quantity. I could go short the stock to hedge my share position, but it left you net long options on paper. Sometimes there was an enormous amount of paper, and as a member we had special margin treatment that allowed us to take down those positions.

That part by and large worked out okay, as the late 1990s saw generally uptrending volatility.

At the end of the day, an option affords you the ability to make a two-pronged bet—one part directional and one part volatility. You can win directionally and lose on volatility quite easily. Say you buy calls for a lift in the stock, but it doesn't happen with enough time or enough magnitude to win. That's not a bet I liked, even though you can occasionally win quite large.

Once I left the floor, I didn't have to buy every call in sight anymore. And I still don't. My basic strategy revolves around option sales, most frequently puts, put spreads, or iron condors (put and call spread shorts of the same expiration in the same name).

I don't have a particular market philosophy other than maybe "know what you don't know." In my case, that's fundamental valuation. My definition of value is the price I see on my screen right now. Frankly, I add nothing to the table analyzing a company. I do look at charts, though I am not exactly a technician.

SELLING PREMIUM IN MOMENTUM NAMES

The major ingredients of my favorite setup consist of a modest decline within a generally uptrending name. For example, take a look at Figure 29.1.

Clearly the stock has found a groove. But I am not a momentum trader per se; I want to go long on pullbacks, not breakouts. So I take action on those pauses and drifts toward the 20-day moving average (MA) like in early October, as well as early November.

FIGURE 29.1 BIDU Consolidates, Daily Chart
Source: © StockCharts.com.

I initiate short either puts or put spreads. I always leave room for more. In other words, if I intend to short 20 puts or put spreads, maybe I start shorting four, and then short four more into the next batch of weakness. And so on.

I stick to nearer-term options. Rarely do I go beyond two months out. Why? Partly because the bet I want to make is a combination of the direction and the near-term volatility of the underlying, not to mention the exponential increase in option decay as an option approaches expiration. Go out further in time and the bet becomes more about the implied volatility of the option itself.

Once I finish legging, there are several possible outcomes. To simplify, though, we can narrow them down to two. One possibility is they expire worthless, and painlessly. That is, the stock either goes up or doesn't not decline enough to really threaten that the puts expire with any value. This sort of outcome manages itself. I most likely take no action, though sometimes I simply close out the puts or put spreads for a profit. Or if I feel it has gone too far the other way, I will "condor" it. By that I mean I short some sort of call spread in the same name with same expiration cycle. I can max out profit and collect both that premium and the put premium if the stock expires higher than the put strike I sold and lower than the call strike I sold.

The second possibility is that the stock continues to decline and threatens my put or put spread sales. There's now a huge distinction between the two plays. The put spreads have defined risk; the loss maxes out at the width of the strike prices of the spread minus the premium you took in. Say, for example, I sell AAPL January 260–250 put spreads for $2. If AAPL closes over $260 in January, I pocket $3. But if AAPL closes at $250 or below, I lose $10 – $3, or $7. That's a lot, of course, relative to the premium I took in, but it's defined, similar to a stop-loss level. I may short stock into the weakness so as to defend my position or I may do nothing. It's a case-by-case basis.

If I simply sold naked puts, though, I would really have to take some sort of action. That might involve buying them back for a loss, buying a cheaper strike put and turning the position into a spread, or shorting stock into weakness.

So I guess I have a second trading philosophy after all. The best way to make money in options is to not lose money in options. You'll take countless small hits, but I'm talking big money.

Last, don't complain about things beyond your control. Bush, Obama, the Federal Reserve, the plus tick rule, leveraged ETFs, high-frequency trading (HFT) machines, and more have been blamed for a poor economy for the past two years. At the end of the day, none of them make trading decisions in your account. *You* do. If you believe whatever prevents stocks from ever going down again, don't whine; go long. If you believe some evil cabal of hedge funds, fueled by the ability to short stocks on minus ticks, has caused a spike in volatility, here's a thought: Don't sell volatility.

Complaints waste time and energy better spent analyzing and adapting to the current trading backdrop.

CHAPTER 30

There Is Always an Option

Steven Place, @stevenplace

Steven is a StockTwits veteran. He is only 12. I'm kidding. But young Steven is far too wise for his age. Options can be simple or complex. Steven is working hard daily to make them simple and profitable for people. His readers are loyal and love him. You will, too.

Enhance returns, reduce risk, print money.

—Steven Place

LEARNING THE RULES OF THE GAME

While I've always had a passion for finance and markets, my focus of study was electrical engineering. I developed a proficiency in software, statistics, and stochastics; these disciplines helped me to find my edge in the markets from both a quantitative and a perceptual aspect.

During my time at college, I developed a self-study of finance. While interning at a major defense contractor, I would be plugged in to Bloomberg Radio. In between being president of a fraternity and my other coursework, I would head to the library and read trade and business magazines like the *Harvard Business Review*. I went through dozens of finance books and began taking a special interest in equity options. The pricing and behavior of options resonated strongly with me and grew out of my expertise in statistics and probabilities. As I had a full ride to university, the college fund became my initial trading capital.

Postcollege, I was living in Orlando, Florida, during the real estate boom. My friends were getting real estate licenses, pricing for single-family units was absurd, and I was renting an apartment from a group of engineers who thought their investment would fund their kids' college tuitions. I had not yet read how manias and bubbles developed, but that experience had a profound impact on me, as it revealed how extended things can get and how rational behavior is a myth when money is involved.

I feel very fortunate for two things: the crash of 2008 and the rise of social media. Living through that bear market, I gained a much firmer grasp on risk management than I did during easier markets. While the economy ground to a halt, I was learning lessons and techniques that provide significant gains to me as a trader.

FOLLOW THE INTERMARKET FLOW

I synthesize several different types of market information across three time frames, including market structure, volatility analysis, and sentiment analysis. Time frames include very short-term, intermediate, and macro.

I like the phrase "think macro, trade micro." I analyze how various markets are interrelated; a move in one asset class often affects others. For example, if oil inventories see a higher draw than expected and there is a pop in crude futures, we may see a run-up in equities as they are on the same risk conveyor belt.

Markets cycle by both price and volatility and I usually trade based on an integrated analysis of these two factors. I identify where we are in both of these cycles and structure options trades around the cyclical thesis. For example, if the trend has changed from down to neutral but volatility is still high, I will be a net seller of options into that fear. Conversely, if the trend goes from neutral to down and volatility is low, I will be a net buyer of options.

When stock is traded, the only risk concerns price and where the market goes. But when options are traded, you have to know where the market is going, when it will get there, and how fast the move might be. So there are times when I can get the direction right but the option strategy wrong. My job is to carefully select a strategy that will enhance returns, reduce risk, and print money.

I actively employ options hedging strategies in order to clearly define risk. I may use index options to accomplish this or look for fresh short opportunities. As a result, my strategies tend to perform better in mean-reverting markets and I lag during prolonged market low-volatility uptrends.

Nevertheless, all trends end, good times do come to an end, and a new volatility cycle presents me with my bread-and-butter opportunities.

HOW OPTIONS WORK

One of the beauties of equity options is that you don't have to get the direction of the price right to make money. Instead, you can bet on volatility, which is a function of how fast the stock moves and how strongly in a direction. So when we look for violent rejections, we are bullish on volatility.

The screening selection for this trade is relatively simple. Since it is a fairly advanced options trade, it's best to select names that have liquid options. Also, high-priced, high-beta names work best, as we are looking for fast movement on both a percentage and an absolute basis. High-profile names will work best as those levels tend to be cleaner. These parameters will leave you a list that you can monitor every few days, looking for critical levels that may be retested.

If you think a stock will be violent, you can buy a straddle. A straddle is a combination of a put buy and a call buy, at the same strike price. It is a limited-risk, limited-reward trade that makes money as long as the stock sees a strong movement either way. For you to make money, you have to see a very fast movement in either direction. But if the underlying stock doesn't move, the position will decrease in value due to the time decay of being long options. In this particular case, time is not on your side.

The choice of the straddle is more of an art than a science. What we see in the options market is a constant trade-off between risk and premium, and between speed and time decay. Essentially, the closer an option is to its expiration, the more time decay will come out, as short-term risk is well known. But with that elevated time decay, you end up with higher-gamma trades. Gamma is essentially the acceleration of a position. So if you are long gamma like a straddle buy, you become "more right" in a position.

I tend to trade front-month options when it comes to the S/R (support/resistance) straddle buy. Many option traders don't recommend being a net buyer of near-term options, but I prefer to play on the edge of the gamma knife, as I see higher gains in terms of risk.

The major risk of this trade is if the stock doesn't see a strong move and stays around those levels, as the time decay will come into options. Because of this, it's best to have time stops available. I generally get impatient and cut a position after five days (one week) of trading. I've often seen a stock break big after I exit a position, so I will sometimes take on a half position and add full risk if the time decay puts the position in a drawdown. Note that this isn't averaging down, as I am not adding more risk than I planned.

The hardest part of this trade is taking profits. Due to the time risk, you want to see a very, very fast move off that level—and if you get it, you don't know if it is going to mean revert or if you will see larger profits. There's no easy answer to taking profits, but I will often have a price target based on market structure, or will use the average true range (ATR) to dictate my exits.

PLAY THE BIG MOVE

This setup is called the S/R straddle buy. It is one of my favorite setups due to its high expectancy and simplicity. When a stock tests a support or resistance level, that means the price is coming into an area that was very, very unstable the last time. If a stock is rallying and then stops and reverses, that indicates buyers were not willing to purchase shares at that price, and the market had to auction lower to find fresh buyers.

I look for violence at a level. Imagine an National Basketball Association (NBA) game where the point guard runs to the hoop to make a layup, but when the ball leaves his hands, this hulking seven-foot-tall center comes in to block the shot—and not only blocks it, but swats it into the cheap seats. You will see that in price action as well, when a stock rises or falls to a level and then is violently rejected and returns to where it came from. That's the price action you want to see. If the market runs into a technical level and then stays there, that tells us there wasn't a swift rejection of prices. It is a weak level. We want to see a strong level.

When a stock comes to retest a violent level, it will often see sharp price action. Either the stock will break that level swiftly and run outside of its recent range or it will see that level hold and reject price. We don't know which way the stock will go, but the odds are high for a fast move one way or the other.

The chart in Figure 30.1 shows the daily price action of GOOG during the summer and early fall of 2010. Notice that when 510 was first tested, a significant sell-off

FIGURE 30.1 510 Was a Major Resistance Level for GOOG, Daily Chart
Source: © StockCharts.com.

occurred. The second time the stock came to retest that level, it was violently rejected and saw a 30-point move in two weeks. The third time it tested, it broke to the upside, and saw a 25-point move in a little over a week.

THE SETUP

In the summer of 2010, Priceline (PCLN) had been trading in a band between 175 and 200 for about a month. Figure 30.2 shows the third retest of 200, and I felt that it was either going to break big here or get rejected and head back down to 190. Note that playing this band with an S/R straddle buy at the highs and the lows of this band would have been profitable the past three times, so I felt that this strategy would most likely continue to work.

FIGURE 30.2 PCLN in a Band between 175 and 200, Daily Chart
Source: © StockCharts.com.

Because the stock was trading closest to 200, I decided to look at the front-month 200 straddle. There were only nine days left to expiration, which meant time decay would really be against me, so I needed to see a very fast move. The straddle was priced at 9.50, so I needed to see that move in the name to break even. Considering that PCLN had been at 190 just a few days before, I felt that was possible. Furthermore, if the stock broke out, the measured upside move would be in the magnitude of that 175 to 200 range, or 25 points.

Although this trade should never be held to maximum risk, it's best to determine your position size on the assumption that it could go to zero. Off a model $40,000 portfolio, I rarely put more than 10 percent at risk on a position. So that means a maximum risk of $4,000, and the current PCLN straddle was going for $950. At maximum risk, I could have put on four straddles, but I opted for three.

For this particular example, there was a very tight time stop of only three days. In other words, if the stock didn't see significant price movement away from this level within three days, I would exit the trade for a loss.

Figure 30.3 shows what happened to PCLN into options expiration.

FIGURE 30.3 PCLN Breaks Out above 200, Daily Chart
Source: © StockCharts.com.

It hit the top of my 25-point upside target, and I closed the trade on a break above 210 for a very nice profit. In hindsight I could have held for more profits, but there was risk that it could revert and retest that level—which would be disastrous for the position. In this type of trade, there will always be a trade-off between letting your winners run (betting for more upside) and having the risk of reversion, which reduces your position value due to the time decay. At expiration, the straddle was worth 18.00 (an increase of 8.50), so the position maxed out with a gain of 89 percent, or a profit of $850 per straddle.

This strategy can be very simple to begin with, but many more advanced trades can be extrapolated from it. For example, you could trade stock against your position, a technique known as gamma scalping, or you could hedge by selling straddles on an index, a technique known as dispersion trading. These techniques are frequently used by hedge funds and equity derivatives desks, but I believe that retail traders also can easily grasp these concepts and add them to their own strategy set.

WORDS OF WISDOM

I believe that overconfidence can lead to complacency, which then leads to poor risk management. I will always be a student of the markets, learning new trades and concepts as this market requires a very high level of adaptability.

CHAPTER 31

Selling Premium

Darren Miller, *@attitrade*

Darren is proving that all shrinks look like Phil Pearlman. With respect to trading, Darren loves to share ideas, keeps things honest, and adores options. No fear.

SECTION 1256 CONTRACTS

I have been actively trading since finishing graduate school in 2002. I currently manage the model portfolio at 6040 Financial and serve as the director of education. My strategy focuses on selling option premium in the broad-based indexes and options on futures (Section 1256 contracts). Typically there is about a 3 percent premium built into options when comparing the statistical volatility of the S&P 500 (SPX) versus the market expectation of the next 30-day range (volatility) of the S&P 500 (the VIX). This difference can fluctuate, but in general the implied volatility is higher than the realized volatility.

I trade Section 1256 contracts because of the 60/40 tax rule, which increases returns based on favorable tax treatment. For example, assuming a tax rate of 35 percent, the taxes on a $10,000 capital gain would be $3,500. Using the 60/40 rule, 60 percent of the capital gain ($6,000) would be taxed at 15 percent and 40 percent of the capital gain ($4,000) would be taxed at 35 percent. That works out to a $900 tax for the long-term gain and a $1,400 for the short-term gain, which totals $2,300. If the gains were taxed 100 percent as short-term gains, then I'd be looking at $3,500. The overall tax rate for this example of the 60/40 rule is 23 percent [(60% × 15%) + (40% × 35%) = 23%]. That works out to be 12 percentage points less than the 35 percent rate for short-term capital gains and represents paying roughly one-third less in income taxes by trading SPX or mini-futures of the SPX (ES) rather than the S&P 500 ETF (SPY).

HISTORICAL FOUNDATION

My market approach is based on various statistics derived from historical market data. I watch the seasonal tendencies and look for exceptions. Abnormal moves should correlate with higher volatility. If I don't see the correlation and take the trade anyway I assume more risk since premiums aren't elevated even though fear is. At this point I either look at different strikes or wait a day to see the elevation in premium before making a trade.

As a simple example of historical data, I look at the prior six option cycles and the range that they produced. For example:

July 72.33
June 120.32
May 80.23
April 163.90
March 61.04
February 83.82

If I take a simple average of the ranges, I come up with 96.94. This average takes into account one earnings season and several instances of economic reports like nonfarm payrolls, the consumer price index, numerous housing-related numbers, and so on. I then attempt to recollect any unexpected events that may have occurred such as a Federal Open Market Committee (FOMC) announcement. In this example, April had a large range that merits a closer look as part of my due diligence.

Once I have an idea of the average movement over the period that I studied, I will turn to the actual month I'm trading. Here is the September seasonality of the option cycle moves (keep in mind that this isn't a calendar month but rather the option cycle month) over the past decade:

2009 = 76.61
2008 = 415.57
2007 = 75.83
2006 = 61.93
2005 = 69.71
2004 = 40.76
2003 = 63.43
2002 = 118.05
2001 = 141.32
2000 = 161.98

The 415 range sticks out, and that was the financial crash, which involved unprecedented events. Such events cannot be predicted before I sell premium, so proper hedging and adjustments need to be made. With the exception of 2008, September appears to be a rather mild month in terms of a price range. However, I also notice that the further back in time, the larger the ranges were. In looking at the SPX price chart, I can see that the overall market during that time was in a downtrend. Therefore, a larger range in a downtrending market tends to be the rule rather than the exception.

The average of the range for this period (10 years) is 122.52. If I take out the outlier (September 2008), I get an average of 89.95 and a pretty good idea of an expected range for the September 2010 cycle. I will use this information as I move to assessing technical levels in the price action.

TECHNICAL FOUNDATION

Turning to a more traditional candlestick chart, I begin to assess technical levels in the SPX. So far the August low has been 1,056.88 and the high has been 1,129.24. I like to start with a weekly candle to get an overall idea of trend and levels of support and resistance (see Figure 31.1).

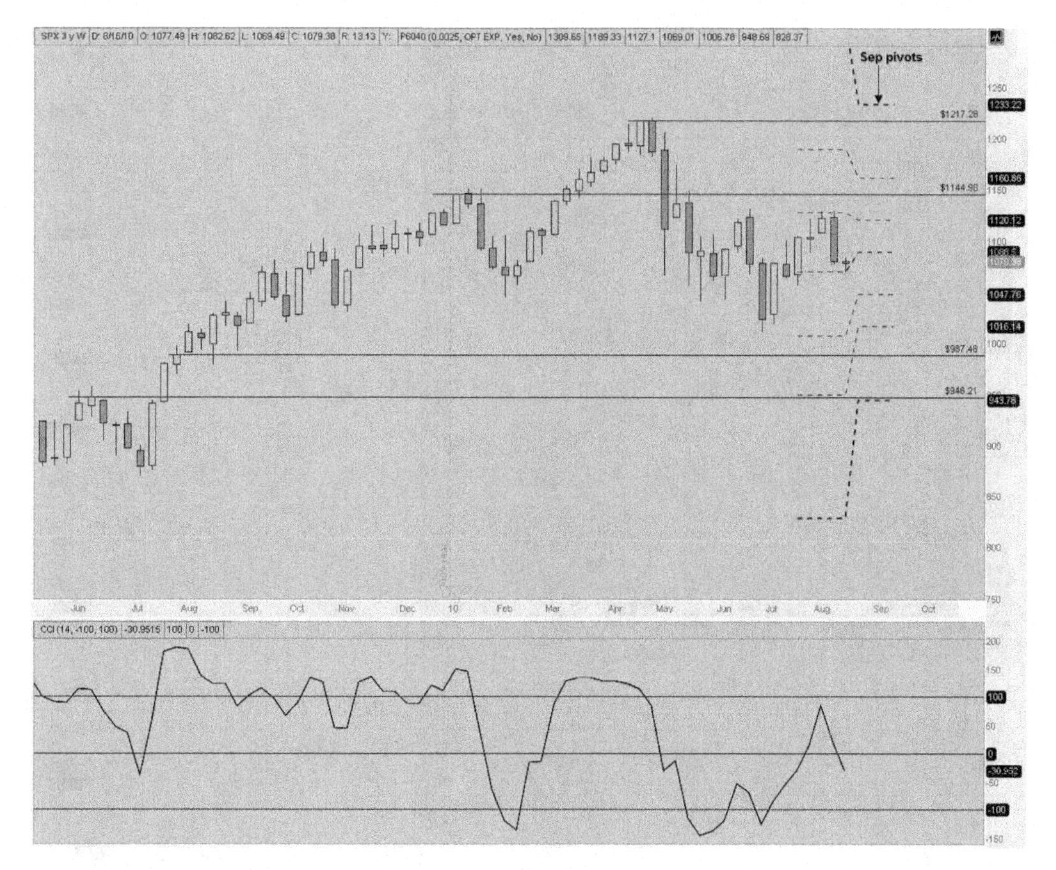

FIGURE 31.1 SPX Pivot Points, Weekly Chart
Source: TD Ameritrade. 2010 © TD Ameritrade IP Company, Inc.

I prefer to use the body of the candle rather than the actual wicks or shadows as both buyers and sellers agreed on that closing price. These levels are the first step in technical analysis and where I'd like to see a confluence of other levels if possible. The dashed lines on the chart are the option cycle pivots that show both the August and September levels. The first thing I notice with the pivots is that they have come in quite a bit, which suggests the SPX traded in a narrow range for August.

The dashed line shows the September pivot at 1,088.50. To the upside are resistance levels R1, R2, and R3 at 1,120.12, 1,160.86, and 1,233.22, respectively. On the downside are support levels S1, S2, and S3 at 1,047.76, 1,016.14, and 943.78, respectively. The support level that is sticking out for me is the 987.48, which is below S2 by nearly 30 points.

So far my analysis is suggesting that September is expected to be a narrow-range month. If I take the range between the R2 and S2 levels, I get a 144-point range. This range falls within the historical price action for September that was discussed earlier. Things are beginning to take shape, but I want to look at multiple time frames here to make sure I'm well informed.

In the daily chart in Figure 31.2 I can see that the CCI is bouncing as the SPX itself if basing just above the August pivot. I also notice that a recent uptrend has been broken,

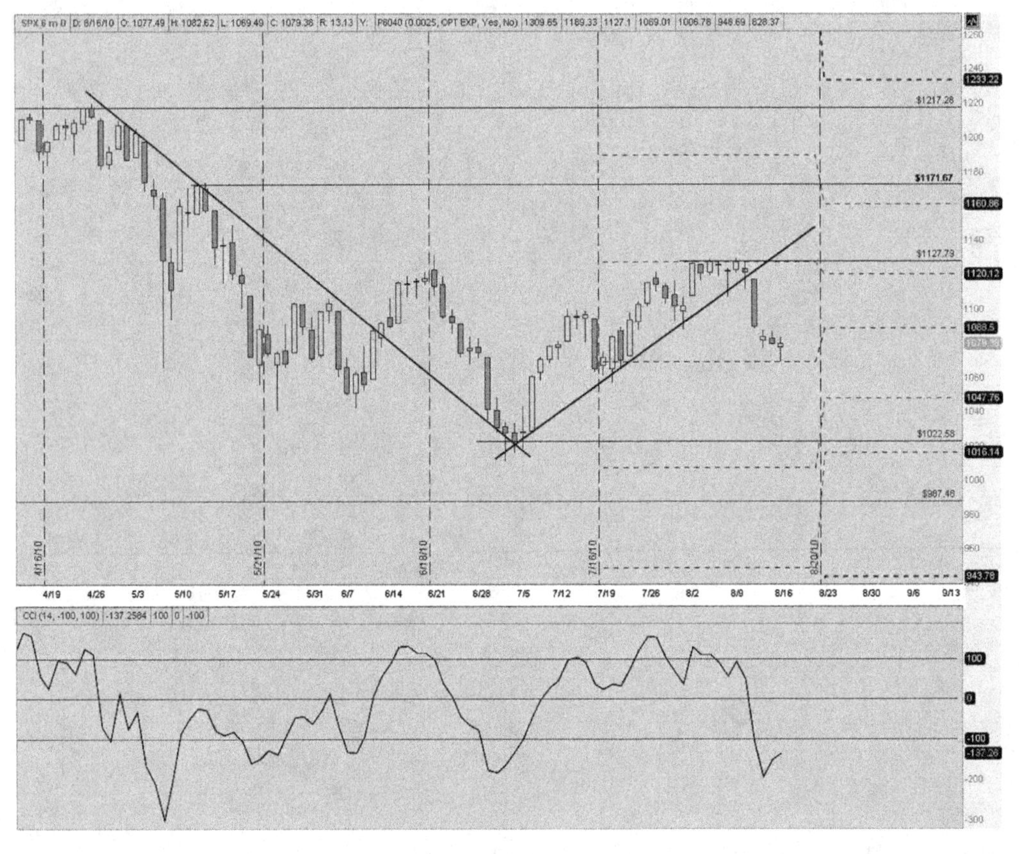

FIGURE 31.2 SPX Pivot Points, Daily Chart
Source: TD Ameritrade. © 2010 TD Ameritrade IP Company, Inc.

and it appears to be a solid break as evidenced by the size of the candle. This suggests a few things to me: namely, that there were quite a few stops under that uptrend support as well as some sell-to-open orders for a new short position. In other words, it suggests an area of sentiment for the future.

One other level I notice is the prior resistance at 1,171.67. This level is about 11 points above the R2 level of the option expiration pivots pointed out on the weekly chart (Figure 31.1). I also make note of the near-term support level where the downtrend ended and the uptrend began (1,022.58) and the fact that it isn't quite beyond S2. However, the 987.48 level from the weekly chart is beyond S2 by nearly 30 points and that is worth noting. These two levels (1,171.67 and 987.48) will be a great starting point for me as I delve into the chains to check premiums.

CHOOSING STRIKES

Now that I've got a decent historical perspective and solid technical levels to work from, I want to see what premiums are out there for strikes near my comfort levels. There are a few rules that I follow when deciding which strikes to sell:

- I don't want to own more than 10 percent of the open interest.
- I'd like to take in a 0.50 or better credit for the spread.
- I *never* sell naked options but rather spreads, which defines my risk (remember 2008).

In Figure 31.3, I can see that the calls offer very little in the way of premium for out-of-the-money strikes. This is in line with the overall near-term trend of lower highs and lower lows seen in my technical analysis. I know through the historical analysis of range that I can write any of the calls in the gray box and the odds (acceptable by me) are in my favor that they will expire worthless. This doesn't mean I just jump in and start selling at the first strike but rather start looking there.

I can see from the put chain shown in Figure 31.4 that there is far more interest in the downside, when looking at the premium being paid for out-of-the-money strikes. My analysis suggests that I can write any of the strikes that are outlined in the gray box. However, I also look at the probability of reaching a strike and the probability of it expiring worthless. I like the probability of reaching a strike to be under 20 percent and really prefer to sell around that level. The 950 put has a 20.84 percent probability of being touched during the September cycle, and that is a good starting point.

This strategy focuses on time decay (theta erosion) and not so much on volatility or other Greeks. However, that doesn't mean I don't look at them. In the chart shown in Figure 31.5, I can see that the 30-day historical volatility (HV) has been on a steady decline since the June expiry. I also notice that the implied volatility (IV) has recently seen a nice pop since crossing over HV in August. As a premium seller I like to see the

CALLS										Strikes: ALL	
Option Code	Open...	Volume	Theo ...	Impl Vol	Delta	Theta	Prob....	Bid X	Ask X	Exp	Strike
SPX100918C1...	21,675	0	37.20	23.16%	.59	-.45	85.00%	36.20 C	38.20 C	SEP 10	1065
SPX100918C1...	28,087	2,709	34.10	22.89%	.57	-.45	90.10%	32.90 C	35.30 C	SEP 10	1070
SPX100918C1...	50,273	10,681	30.95	22.48%	.54	-.45	95.30%	29.90 C	32.00 C	SEP 10	1075
SPX100918C1...	32,512	7,701	28.05	22.16%	.51	-.44	99.28%	27.00 C	29.10 C	SEP 10	1080
SPX100918C1...	24,395	153	25.30	21.85%	.48	-.44	93.36%	24.30 C	26.30 C	SEP 10	1085
SPX100918C1...	28,467	1,248	22.65	21.50%	.45	-.43	87.39%	21.60 C	23.70 C	SEP 10	1090
SPX100918C1...	23,775	102	20.25	21.23%	.42	-.42	81.39%	19.20 C	21.30 C	SEP 10	1095
SPX100918C1...	174,194	47,461	17.40	20.48%	.39	-.40	74.86%	16.80 C	18.00 C	SEP 10	1100
SPX100918C1...	27,084	34	15.75	20.58%	.36	-.39	69.29%	14.70 C	16.80 C	SEP 10	1105
SPX100918C1...	42,195	3,052	13.30	19.87%	.33	-.36	62.67%	12.70 C	13.90 C	SEP 10	1110
SPX100918C1...	24,155	36	12.00	20.03%	.30	-.35	57.57%	11.00 C	13.00 C	SEP 10	1115
SPX100918C1...	26,409	96	10.30	19.70%	.27	-.33	51.80%	9.30 C	11.30 C	SEP 10	1120
SPX100918C1...	62,675	5,282	8.50	19.12%	.24	-.30	45.63%	8.30 C	8.70 C	SEP 10	1125
SPX100918C1...	13,124	603	7.45	19.14%	.22	-.28	41.03%	6.50 C	8.40 C	SEP 10	1130
SPX100918C1...	7,841	50	5.85	18.40%	.19	-.25	34.87%	5.30 C	6.40 C	SEP 10	1135
SPX100918C1...	13,063	881	5.25	18.67%	.17	-.24	31.53%	4.50 C	6.00 C	SEP 10	1140
SPX100918C1...	12,971	451	4.40	18.51%	.15	-.21	27.43%	3.60 C	5.20 C	SEP 10	1145
SPX100918C1...	80,587	1,205	3.45	18.04%	.12	-.18	22.89%	3.00 C	3.90 C	SEP 10	1150
SPX100918C1...	2,426	21	2.90	18.00%	.11	-.17	19.80%	2.10 C	3.70 C	SEP 10	1155
SPX100918C1...	11,907	1,612	2.35	17.81%	.09	-.15	16.67%	2.20 C	2.50 C	SEP 10	1160
SPX100918C1...	4,664	56	1.90	17.67%	.08	-.13	13.98%	1.35 C	2.45 C	SEP 10	1165
SPX100918C1...	13,441	3,200	1.53	17.53%	.06	-.11	11.63%	1.00 C	2.05 C	SEP 10	1170
SPX100918C1...	59,880	6,481	1.15	17.21%	.05	-.09	9.23%	1.10 C	1.20 C	SEP 10	1175
SPX100918C1...	10,387	2,367	.88	16.98%	.04	-.07	7.34%	.55 C	1.20 C	SEP 10	1180
SPX100918C1...	5,056	32	.90	17.72%	.04	-.08	7.22%	.70 C	1.10 C	SEP 10	1185
SPX100918C1...	6,854	368	.70	17.57%	.03	-.06	5.82%	.40 C	1.00 C	SEP 10	1190
SPX100918C1...	7,018	1,451	.60	17.72%	.03	-.06	5.02%	.55 C	.65 C	SEP 10	1195
SPX100918C1...	86,391	2,198	.47	17.64%	.02	-.05	4.06%	.35 C	.60 C	SEP 10	1200
SPX100918C1...	4,590	2,980	.50	18.37%	.02	-.05	4.09%	.30 C	.70 C	SEP 10	1205

FIGURE 31.3 SPX September 2010 Call Options

elevated level of implied volatility, as it means traders are willing to pay more for their options. Elevated levels of implied volatility are nice, but they also suggest that there is some pending event (real or imagined) that is causing the rise. Therefore, I need to have a handle on macroeconomic and geopolitical issues that can impact the market.

PROACTIVE TRADING

By this point I have a good understanding of where I'd be comfortable selling premium and have some strikes picked out. I may choose to watch certain spreads during the day to see what the volume looks like or maybe an individual strike in order to leg into a spread. Believe it or not, historical data suggests that there are better days and weeks to sell premium. While it's not absolutely necessary to sell during these times, doing so has proven to produce higher premiums.

For the most part I focus on the $10 spread, as that allows me to define my risk at a level I'm comfortable with. So, depending on how much premium I take in, I'll know

Strikes: ALL						PUTS								
Exp	Strike	Bid	X	Ask	X	Option Code	Open...	Volume	Theo ...	Impl Vol	Delta	Theta	Prob....
SEP 10	895	1.45	C	2.50	C	SPX100918P895	641	0	1.98	37.25%	-.04	-.16	9.77%
SEP 10	900	2.15	C	2.80	C	SPX100918P900	118,771	689	2.48	38.03%	-.05	-.19	11.60%
SEP 10	905	1.80	C	2.95	C	SPX100918P905	119	2	2.38	36.77%	-.05	-.18	11.47%
SEP 10	910	1.95	C	3.20	C	SPX100918P910	3,159	48	2.58	36.45%	-.05	-.19	12.32%
SEP 10	915	2.15	C	3.40	C	SPX100918P915	2,006	17	2.78	36.08%	-.05	-.20	13.18%
SEP 10	920	2.20	C	3.80	C	SPX100918P920	2,826	24	3.00	35.74%	-.06	-.21	14.13%
SEP 10	925	2.40	C	4.00	C	SPX100918P925	30,533	2,097	3.20	35.29%	-.06	-.22	15.01%
SEP 10	930	2.70	C	4.30	C	SPX100918P930	3,142	1,303	3.50	35.05%	-.07	-.23	16.21%
SEP 10	935	2.90	C	4.50	C	SPX100918P935	638	9	3.70	34.53%	-.07	-.24	17.12%
SEP 10	940	3.20	C	4.80	C	SPX100918P940	7,059	179	4.00	34.19%	-.08	-.25	18.35%
SEP 10	945	3.50	C	5.10	C	SPX100918P945	10,940	14	4.30	33.80%	-.08	-.26	19.58%
SEP 10	950	3.80	C	5.40	C	SPX100918P950	86,973	8,252	4.60	33.37%	-.09	-.27	20.84%
SEP 10	955	4.20	C	5.80	C	SPX100918P955	208	0	5.00	33.09%	-.10	-.28	22.38%
SEP 10	960	4.60	C	6.20	C	SPX100918P960	4,513	137	5.40	32.74%	-.10	-.29	23.94%
SEP 10	965	5.00	C	6.60	C	SPX100918P965	666	4	5.80	32.36%	-.11	-.31	25.53%
SEP 10	970	5.30	C	7.20	C	SPX100918P970	5,066	446	6.25	31.99%	-.12	-.32	27.25%
SEP 10	975	5.70	C	6.90	C	SPX100918P975	46,554	10,176	6.30	30.97%	-.12	-.31	28.03%
SEP 10	980	6.30	C	8.20	C	SPX100918P980	1,996	258	7.25	31.26%	-.14	-.34	31.03%
SEP 10	985	6.80	C	8.80	C	SPX100918P985	4,367	31	7.80	30.89%	-.15	-.35	33.09%
SEP 10	990	7.40	C	9.40	C	SPX100918P990	7,561	21	8.40	30.53%	-.16	-.37	35.28%
SEP 10	995	8.10	C	9.30	C	SPX100918P995	776	22	8.70	29.73%	-.17	-.37	36.87%
SEP 10	1000	9.20	C	9.80	C	SPX100918P10...	131,672	5,372	9.50	29.52%	-.18	-.38	39.58%
SEP 10	1005	9.50	C	11.50	C	SPX100918P10...	239	30	10.50	29.45%	-.19	-.40	42.68%
SEP 10	1010	10.30	C	12.30	C	SPX100918P10...	18,315	160	11.30	29.09%	-.21	-.41	45.42%
SEP 10	1015	11.00	C	13.20	C	SPX100918P10...	10,877	510	12.10	28.67%	-.22	-.42	48.21%
SEP 10	1020	11.90	C	14.10	C	SPX100918P10...	14,501	68	13.00	28.28%	-.24	-.43	51.23%
SEP 10	1025	12.90	C	15.10	C	SPX100918P10...	74,614	2,303	14.00	27.92%	-.25	-.44	54.45%
SEP 10	1030	14.00	C	16.20	C	SPX100918P10...	36,326	2,178	15.10	27.60%	-.27	-.45	57.89%
SEP 10	1035	15.20	C	17.30	C	SPX100918P10...	24,453	5	16.25	27.25%	-.29	-.46	61.45%
SEP 10	1040	16.40	C	18.50	C	SPX100918P10...	40,405	64	17.45	26.87%	-.31	-.47	65.13%
SEP 10	1045	17.60	C	20.00	C	SPX100918P10...	10,835	548	18.80	26.55%	-.32	-.47	69.06%
SEP 10	1050	19.10	C	20.50	C	SPX100918P10...	180,335	26,424	19.80	25.85%	-.34	-.47	72.74%
SEP 10	1055	20.50	C	22.90	C	SPX100918P10...	4,272	176	21.70	25.83%	-.37	-.48	77.31%
SEP 10	1060	22.20	C	24.40	C	SPX100918P10...	20,847	5,647	23.30	25.47%	-.39	-.48	81.68%
SEP 10	1065	23.90	C	26.10	C	SPX100918P10...	24,197	291	25.00	25.11%	-.41	-.48	86.20%
SEP 10	1070	25.80	C	27.10	C	SPX100918P10...	45,907	2,754	26.45	24.46%	-.44	-.48	90.76%
SEP 10	1075	28.00	C	29.90	C	SPX100918P10...	71,718	14,276	28.95	24.54%	-.46	-.48	95.71%
SEP 10	1080	29.80	C	32.00	C	SPX100918P10...	42,235	9,460	30.90	24.09%	-.49	-.48	99.33%

FIGURE 31.4 SPX September 2010 Put Options
Source: TD Ameritrade.

exactly how much capital I have at risk. As mentioned earlier, managing risk by selling spreads can keep me from blowing up my account. However, that's not the only or even the best way to manage risk.

Another way I proactively manage risk is by limiting the amount of capital allocation each cycle. I start by committing 40 percent, leaving 60 percent to adjust if needed. In most cases, I'm selling the next cycle before the current cycle ends, so there's a window of about a week in which I have 20 percent for adjustments.

Hedging my position is done as technical levels are broken, not breached. In other words, if I'm short the 1,150 strike, I'd need to see a break through that level followed by a test of that level as new support. I'll typically look to buy back a portion of the short

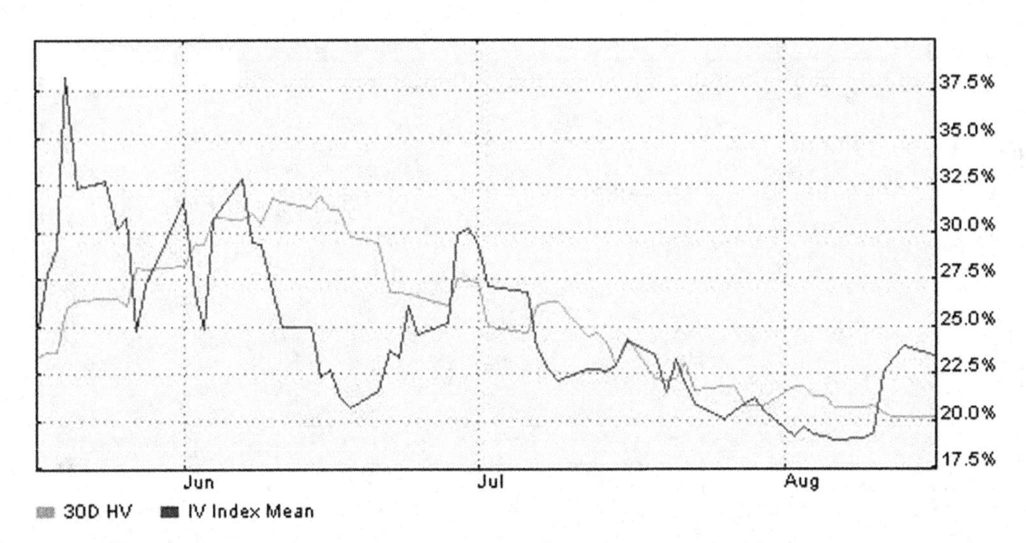

FIGURE 31.5 SPX Daily Three-Months Volatility Chart
Source: IVolatility.com.

strike first and then work with the delta from that point. If there is a highly sentimental level such as a large round number or prior intermediate high or low, then I prefer to adjust my delta in favor of an advance to that level.

The use of both historical patterns and technical analysis is typically enough to allow the spread to expire worthless. However, if an unforeseen event occurs and price moves beyond (by $10 or more) the short strike, I attempt to roll up and out. This process involves moving to a weekly, quarterly, or monthly cycle (out), and further out-of-the-money strikes (up). While this isn't the ideal scenario, the occurrences are rare and the adjustment can usually be placed for a credit.

CHAPTER 32

The New High Dip

Chris Stauder, @BuyOnTheDip

Chris loves to leverage his trading ideas via options, but he also knows how to manage risk. He is smart enough to be based in San Diego, and his tweets are often funnier than mine.

Dip him in the river who loves water.

—William Blake

THE MORNING PAPER

My infatuation for the stock market started at the breakfast table with my dad, reading the newspaper. I was probably 10 years old at the time, eating Wheaties at 5:30 A.M. My dad left for the station every day at 6 A.M. sharp. This, 30 minutes a day, Monday through Friday, was my introduction to stocks. On the porch: the *Oakland Tribune* and the *San Francisco Chronicle.* Dad would always start with the business section; me, sports. I loved our hometown Oakland A's and the Boston Red Sox—an odd combo, but I thought my Dad looked like Wade Boggs, Hall of Fame Red Sox third baseman, with his classic 1980s mustache. After I finished the box scores and scanned the league leaders, we'd switch. Dad would hand me the business section and ask, "What looks good? I'll give you $5,000 play bucks. Pick a stock."

I remember staring at letters and numbers, looking for something familiar. In those days the paper would show the company name slightly abbreviated, the ticker symbol, the previous day's closing price, and the 52-week high/low, and then there was a little up or down triangle if the stock was at a 52-week high or low. The paper would also boldface the company name when it was at a 52-week high. Since I knew little about the world of business and nothing about the stock market, what stood out were those bold names and the little up triangles. In the second column, the Bs, I saw this one name—it was bold, had an up triangle, and had a huge price tag. With most stocks having a one-, two-, or at best a three-digit price, this four-digit monster obscured the newspaper's column alignment with its size. I looked up to my father with a confused grin and said, "BerkHa?" He replied, "Berkshire Hathaway." There weren't many down triangles, yet tons of bold company names with up triangles. It must have been a great bull market at the time.

That $5,000 stock made sense. It fit with my personality. I was always, as my elementary school teachers would say, "extremely talented, but we wish he'd apply himself more"; a class clown with an insatiable thirst for attention; and selfishly lazy, yet successful. So with $5,000 to spend, I could buy the most expensive stock on the page, satisfying my will to be weird. It was the outlier, a rebel among commoners, an anomaly. Also, I didn't have to do a lot of complicated math—one share. Simple. It was easy to track gains and easy to find on a page full of tickers, percent signs, triangles, and seemingly random numbers. Over the next few months, I watched BerkHa go from being bold with a triangle to not bold and no triangle. After a few days or weeks, it would be bold again and that little triangle would appear, signifying a new 52-week high. The stock was making new highs, pulling back, and then making new highs again. This realization would eventually become my go-to strategy, the new high dip.

By 1989, BerkHa was trading at $8,000 per share. And 20-plus years later, BerkHa is now at $125,000 per share. I still follow Berkshire Hathaway, BerkHa (BRK. A), and Warren Buffett. I've never owned a real share and I no longer care for the Red Sox or Wheaties. I learned a lot from my dad and the morning paper. I still wake up at 5:30 A.M. and scan for leaders.

VAK TRADING

The V is for visual. I've always been a visual person. Charts are naturally appealing to me. I love watching lines and numbers move. Red, green, red, green. Stocks go up and then they go down, and then they go up, then down, then back up. It's a game of dips and rips, highs and lows, breakouts and breakdowns. You need a strategy. One tool you have is your *eyes*. You can watch the tape or use technical analysis through charting. I can't speak on reading the tape, as I don't know enough about it. I have a better eye when it comes to the charts. It's about previous points of interest—noting how stocks respond to certain price levels and round numbers and how they move around market events. The main thing I take from a chart is direction. Is the stock in an uptrend or a downtrend? The key to the new high dip strategy is to buy dips in an uptrend.

The A is for auditory. Listen, discuss, and engage. It almost sounds like a political slogan, but it's the world we now live in: the social society. Auditory learning involves listening: to spoken (and written) words, from self or others. We live in a unique, unparalleled time of real-time information. Stock quotes are real-time; market reactions and commentary are real-time. Whether you "heard" it from Jim Cramer on television, from a twitterer on StockTwits, or while reading the financial blogosphere, it's all opinion until price confirms. And with stocks and the market, you have to have a bias to make money. You have to have an opinion. My advice is to *listen* and *filter*. Collect the data, make your own assumption based on the information you have, and pick a side. Do you think the market will go up, down, or sideways? Once you have your opinion, how are you going to play it? There are many vehicles, methods, and instruments: stocks, options, exchange-trade funds (ETFs), bonds, futures, forex, and so on. Where is your best opportunity? How are you going to profit from your opinion? How much capital will you invest? This is a game of opportunity cost. Wikipedia defines "opportunity cost" as *the cost related to the next-best choice available to someone who has picked among several mutually exclusive choices.* You can leave your $10,000 in cash or risk that same $10,000 in the stock market. The opportunity cost in investing examples can be determined only in hindsight. Review your trades and listen to the opportunity.

The K is for kinesthetic—the physical: touching, feeling, doing, hands-on experiences. You have to make actual trades to make actual money. Order entry is one aspect of trading that gets little attention. You have a choice: call your broker and verbally place an order or facilitate the purchase yourself via online brokerages. If you're reading this, you've probably already set up a personal trading account and make your own trades. Market or limit orders? How are you going to establish your position? What is your stop loss?

I use market orders only when I'm chasing a stock or option. This is about buying dips, so we will only use limit orders in this strategy. Now the question is position sizing and portfolio allocation. Let's feel out a few examples. With $10,000 you can buy 10,000 shares of a $1 stock, 1,000 shares of $10 stock, 100 shares of a $100 stock, 10 shares of a $1,000 stock, or some mix in between. Remember that 10 percent is 10 percent is 10 percent. If a $1 stock goes up 10 cents, that's 10 percent. If a $100 stock goes up $10, it's 10 percent. It starts with a goal: I want to make X amount by Y date and am willing to risk Z capital. Do you want to turn your $10,000 into $11,000 or into $111,000? You'll need a very different approach to accomplish either. You can't make a 1,000 percent return in one year buying 100 shares of IBM at $100; the stock may double (100 percent return) in a year, but even that's generous. The average return is around 10 percent annually on a buy like that. Personally, I'm not interested in making 10 percent on a $10,000 initial investment over one year. That doesn't excite me enough to risk the capital. I'd rather just hold the $10,000 in cash if 10 percent were my maximum potential return. How about the 10,000 shares of the $1 stock? That can work, but now we're talking low float, low volume, near penny stocks. That's just too risky to be a core strategy. I like the 1,000 shares of a $10 stock. Stocks from $4 to $16 are a challenge and hold great opportunity. For my risk appetite, though, they take too much patience and time. Waiting for the hard-to-time spike from nowhere requires too much screen staring. So where is the opportunity?

THE NEW HIGH DIP STRATEGY

Let's review what we know. We are looking for high-priced stocks in an uptrend making new 52-week highs. The next step is to identify the pullback, *the dip*. In the new high dip strategy, we are looking for a 5 to 10 percent pullback in liquid, optionable stocks. This works best in high-volume, big-name blue chips. In this example we use a recent trade in AAPL (Apple).

The common math is as follows: \$10,000 buys 33 shares of AAPL common; \$300.98 × 33 = \$9,932.34 (plus commission). If \$AAPL goes to a new high—let's say \$330—that's approximately a 10 percent move on a \$9,932.34 investment, or a \$993.23 gain (minus commission). That's not a bad trade; most money managers don't return 10 percent a year.

FIGURE 32.1 Pullback after a Strong Run, AAPL Daily Chart
Source: © Stockcharts.com.

And there are five chart visuals to notice from Figure 32.1:

1. Stock in uptrend, with recent new high of $319 in mid-October.
2. A 5 percent to 10 percent sell-off/pullback.
3. Lighter volume during pullback (good sign).
4. The 20-day simple moving average support.
5. High liquidity and optionability.

With our initial stock criteria met, the next step is deciding on month and strike price for our option purchase. I recommend buying one month out (not the current month, but the following one). In this example that would be December, not November, calls. You are basically buying yourself more time to be right and more time to let the purchase work for you. Deciding on strike price is simple. Pick the closest strike that would equal a new high. In this example it's the December 320s. With $319 as the mid-October high and an available strike at $320, that's your strike. Use a limit order and buy on the dip!

MY OPTIONS APPROACH

The sum of $1,200 buys two call contracts of the AAPL December 320 call; $6.00 × 2 contracts (100 options per contract) = $1,200. The call options gained 100 percent in four days, while the common hit new highs, gaining 6 percent over the same time period. The common strategy yielded $1,000 on $10,000, whereas the options strategy yielded $1,200+ on $1,200. With the same $10,000 of original capital, you could have 10 plays like this on your book.

Note in Figure 32.1 that AAPL hit $321.04. What was our strike? 320. I often preach taking profits as the common reaches the strike price. From out-of-the-money to in-the-money! Strike prices are nice round numbers and make for good sell points. It's not a profit until you take it. Use your strike price as an initial profit objective. Set a limit order to exit the trade and split the bid-ask spread if necessary.

Like many traders, I find that my best trades are instantly profitable. You know that buy, the one where you are in the green within minutes and the position never looks back. Those "pure bliss" trades are nice, but we have to prepare for losses as well. With options I've found it best to take the loss the same day; if you're not up on the trade by 30 minutes before closing time, start entering your exit order, and take the loss. It's really that simple; just sell it and take your remaining capital. If you don't, you'll wake up down another 10 percent or more, and that's not risk management—it's portfolio suicide and a sure way to blow up your account.

Go find a stock you like that's on its 52-week high, wait for your 5 percent to 10 percent pullback, stalk your strike price, set some limit orders, and *buy on the new high dip!*

PART VI

Forex Trading

CHAPTER 33

They Call Me Mrs. Cable

Lydia Idem, *@faithmight*

From my meetings with Lydia and following her writing, I believe she has great trading instincts and much to offer traders at all levels. The currency markets are an extremely challenging world to trade—the leverage alone is difficult to understand but also the markets are always open and active! I am fascinated by the trend followers and traders who aim to master them.

If you want to be a successful trader, you have to learn to read the tape.
—Ilian Yotov

FINDING MY TRADING STYLE

They call me Mrs. Cable; this is because I trade almost exclusively the British pound/U. S. dollar (GBP/USD). The GBP/USD currency pair earned the nickname "cable" from the time when an underwater communications cable synchronized the stock quotes between the London and New York markets. Before I specialized in this pair, I traded different asset classes and currency pairs. I began participating in the markets by investing in equities back in high school. My mother opened my first trading account. Then during my senior year in high school, my economics teacher taught the class how to read stock tickers out of the business section of any newspaper. I was fascinated. The next week, I went to Charles Schwab, spoke with a broker, and placed my first orders on some mutual funds. What started as a trade in my mind grew into a 12-year investment. I tried to trade individual stocks, but commission costs didn't make sense to me when I held no-load mutual funds. The next time I made an actual trade it was in the foreign exchange (forex) market. I have traded no other market since.

I entered the forex market in late 2006. My parents had watched an infomercial about trading foreign exchange. I had just moved back home to California when they invited me to attend a seminar about it. Initially I was skeptical, but when I learned about this super-liquid, multitrillion-dollar market in which you buy *and* sell, I was hooked.

I began my forex trading career as a scalper. Scalping is a very short-term trading style based on minute charts like the 1-minute or 5-minute chart. I entered trades with a target of 10 to 20 pips with stops based on a 1:1.5 risk-reward ratio. I traded the entire market, including the EUR/USD, GBP/USD, USD/CHF, USD/JPY, USD/CAD, EUR/CAD, EUR/JPY, GBP/JPY, AUD/USD, EUR/GBP, and NZD/USD. I traded almost all time frames, including the 10-minute, 30-minute, 60-minute, 180-minute, 720-minute, daily, weekly, and monthly charts. I would trade the Asian session, the European session, and, of course, the New York trading session. It was very haphazard and completely unsuccessful. After three months of demo trading, I went live and found out very quickly that I had much more learning to do. I still wasn't a successful trader. But I was not discouraged. I listened to hours of forex traders radio every day, filling large notebooks cover to cover with handwritten analysis of my trades before I finally went digital. I continued learning everything I could about trading currencies.

Like most new traders to the forex market, I was taught and encouraged to scalp and trade short-term time frames. I was taught that holding positions longer than a day was for more advanced traders. In hindsight, I was trying to trade a method that simply did not suit my personality. This was what crippled my trading success. But I had no idea at the time, and I continued to struggle.

I defiantly listened to the advanced traders programs to learn. This is when I met my mentor, Ilian Yotov, when he took over as broadcaster and teacher of an advanced forex radio show. His programs are for longer-term swing traders. Though I was a newbie, I really enjoyed Ilian's teachings. I had finally found a trader who didn't exclusively scalp the markets. All the forex trainers for new traders were scalpers. But within three months of listening to Ilian and studying his teachings, for the first time I began to really learn how to trade the forex market. Ilian taught me two important lessons:

1. How to trade according to my own trading psychology.
2. How to read the markets for myself.

Upon suggestions from Ilian and other listeners of his forex radio show, I read the book *Trading for a Living* by Alexander Elder (John Wiley & Sons, 1992). It was from that book that I learned the very foundations of trading psychology and how it applied to my own trading. I began to realize that my poor performance was most attributed to *not* trading my own style. I am not a scalper. I don't like to trade the shorter time frames, and I'm terrible at reading the price moves that occur on those tiny time frames. More important, a scalper is only looking to grab 10 to 20 pips of any move. Well, this type of reward does not satisfy my ego. I will overtrade in order to get the number of pips that my ego can consider a good day of trading. I learned from Dr. Elder that overtrading is a very common pitfall for the individual trader and I was falling prey to it every day.

THE ROAD TO SUCCESS IS IN SPECIALIZING

The more I traded, the harder it became to keep abreast of all the different countries' economies, politics, and geopolitical connections. Trading all the major pairs at that time meant that I had to keep track of events in the United States, Great Britain, Switzerland, Australia, New Zealand, Germany, Italy, France, Japan, and Canada. Ten countries! The information flow became overwhelming. While I was watching one trade, I was missing three other trades and it would really frustrate me. That frustration led me to chase trade after trade and mount loss after loss. So I made the decision to follow another piece of advice from my mentor: "Choose your bread-and-butter pairs. Those pairs you get to know so you know how they move and why they move."

I took a close look at all the currency pairs in my journals and realized that my best analysis was on GBP-related pairs. I love the GBP. It is my currency of choice because it is liquid and volatile, and it exhibits very technical price moves. The natural choice was GBP/USD being a USD pair. Against the USD, the GBP moves very technically and really respects the Fibonacci retracement levels. In case the GBP/USD presented no trading opportunities, I wanted to have an alternative pair to trade. I chose the EUR/GBP because it moves very slowly, as opposed to the GBP/JPY, which is hypervolatile. It is also a very technical pair, and I like the slow nature of the EUR/GBP currency pair in a market where assets can literally move hundreds of pips in a matter of minutes. Trimming my focus down to two currency pairs was very difficult in the beginning. I felt like I was missing out on every trading opportunity in the market! It was hard not to jump into a trade, but I stuck to my plan by trading only the analysis that I had written down. And since I had done analysis only on the GBP/USD or EUR/GBP, I was less tempted to jump into a trade on another currency pair. I always follow a written plan before placing a trade. My first concrete trading rule was formed out of this focused approach to my trading. Most important, the more I get to know the personality of each pair, the more successful I become at understanding how each pair moves. My efforts are focused, and the outcome is much more successful.

I love the macroeconomic element to trading the forex market. I never enjoyed the microeconomic view in trading equities. There is too much information over too many different stocks, which doesn't match my trading psychology. My simple approach allows me to study just four countries for fundamental developments. With the forex market, I enjoy learning about the different economic releases and geopolitical gossip from around the world and watch how different countries are faring and affecting one another. Ilian taught me how to recognize fundamental shifts in the market and use that analysis in addition to technical analysis.

THE TRANSITION FROM DEMO TO LIVE TRADING

Under Ilian's tutelage, I began trading the Quarters Theory and using Fibonacci retracement levels to determine entries. I did a written analysis on each pair that I traded. I submitted those analyses to Ilian to be critiqued during the Q&A segment of his radio show. I waited to see if he would read my analysis live over the air. I remember the first time that happened I was so honored that I downloaded that episode to my computer. I was never shy about sharing my analysis. Rather than the praise, I wanted to know what was wrong with it and where the holes were. Ilian was firm, too. It was one thing to listen to a guru on how to trade the markets. There was quite another feeling of accountability involved when you have that guru criticize your trading decisions and rationale live for thousands of other traders to hear. It wasn't long before the feedback on my submitted analysis was exemplary and Ilian, my mentor, would agree completely with my entire analysis. I was ready to make the transition, once again, from demo to live trading.

Learning to read the tape and follow price action, even without looking at charts, was a major turning point in my career. I learned how to read regular charts and price and use Fibonacci retracement levels and became a trader of my own analysis.

KEEPING IT SIMPLE

My approach to the markets is simple. I don't use many indicators or time frames. I trade three currency pairs now on only three time frames. I believe that fundamentals are the root cause of price action in the forex market. As a result, I believe that a combination of fundamental and technical analysis is very important to trading the forex market. I love to find a budding new trend and ride it until my targets are hit. The goal is to get on the trend at the right price headed in the right direction. In order to do that successfully, it is important to understand the personality of the currency pair that you are trading.

Different currency pairs move and react very differently in the markets. Pairs exhibit a unique market psychology due to the juxtaposition of cultures exhibited in a currency pair. Technically, markets tend to move in 250-pip increments. These 250 pips are marked by what are called the large quarter points. Price moves in any direction from one large quarter point to the next. This is the premise of the Quarters Theory. I learned the Quarters Theory from Ilian and after years of my own testing and trading in the markets, I believe this theory to hold true. Given this, I concentrate my analysis on how a pair is moving within that 250-pip range.

My market analysis always starts at the daily chart. The daily chart is my foundation and becomes the basis of all of my trades and trading decisions. I scan the daily chart for the long-term, medium-term, and short-term trends. Once the trend is determined, I want to know its duration. A newly developing trend has different trading opportunities than an old trend that has lasted for several days, weeks, or months. I determine the duration of the trend by using a variation of the Elliott wave theory called the Quarters Theory trend waves count.

Once my wave count is complete, I will calculate Fibonacci retracement levels on the most current trend wave on the daily chart. The Fibonacci levels signal a reversal or a continuation. Any correction that exceeds the 61.8 percent Fibonacci level (the golden mean) is my signal of a reversal. The daily chart Fibonacci levels set the course for the rest of my trading analysis.

I then drill down to the 60-minute chart. I use the 60-minute chart for an overview of intraday price action. Despite the overall trend on the daily chart, the 60-minute chart tells me how the pair is moving in the current trend. I will calculate Fibonacci retracement levels on the intraday move on the 60-minute chart. If the intraday move is in the same direction as the trend on the daily chart, I will set limit orders based on the Fibonacci retracement levels to enter the market in the same direction as the trend. If the trend is old and the price moved countertrend, then price action validates that the trend is coming to an end and I will set limit orders based on the Fibonacci levels to enter the market against the trend on the daily chart. Intraday price action must confirm what I am seeing on the daily charts. If they don't correlate, then there is no trading opportunity for me.

I will also use the 100-day and 200-day simple moving averages on the 60-minute chart to see where price will move intraday and help time my entries into the market. Price tends to find resistance and support at these moving averages. If price manages to break through the 100-day simple moving average on the 60-minute chart, I can expect price to move toward the 200-day simple moving average. Using the additional information provided by the moving averages helps me remain patient until price provides a much better entry level.

After the 60-minute chart, I like to look at the 5-minute chart to see what price is doing in real time. The 5-minute time frame is my smallest time frame, though I don't use it to make a trading decision. I use the moving averages on this time frame as well. I can use these two moving averages on the 5-minute chart to see how price moves in real time. This real-time look at prices is helpful to determine entry and reinforce patience with price action.

Those are my three time frames. Occasionally, I will look at the weekly and monthly charts, though I will never look at time frames smaller than the 5-minute chart. Again, limiting the number of time frames I use in my trading focuses my efforts. If I don't see a trade setting up on my time frames, I simply will not take a trade.

The last thing I do in my market analysis is to take a purview of the fundamental landscape. Since I believe that fundamentals do drive the currency markets, I am sure to be aware of any news that may affect my trades or even provide a catalyst to set up identified trading opportunities on the daily chart. I always want to look over the economic calendar for the week and pay attention to days that have news events that can produce highly volatile price moves. News can change trends or reinforce them, so it is important for me to be aware of the fundamental landscape for any given currency pair.

RISK MANAGEMENT

Price points are very important to my trading plan. Price points reveal the direction the currency pair will go and how much of that move I can capture. So I pay very close attention to the entry and exit of a trade. My entries should be the maximized point in a window of validation on a trade setup. Many price points make up this window because my entry must fall between the Fibonacci retracement levels. Ideally, entries are taken between the 50 and 61.8 percent Fibonacci retracement levels. A more aggressive move for me is between the 38.2 and 50 percent Fibonacci retracement levels. I spread my risk over multiple price points by scaling into and out of positions using bracket orders. I prefer to use smaller lots per trade and build into a position. There is not just one price that is optimal but always a range of prices. I like to take advantage of as many of those opportunities as my total risk will allow. Ideally, a majority of those price points will be reached building a position of multiple trades. I believe it is much more prudent to scale into a position with smaller lots than to choose one price and enter with multiple lots on that one price. The market may determine that the one chosen price is not the best-timed price, and with multiple lots at one price a few pips against you could blow your entire account. So I am much more conservative and will always build a position in the market by scaling into it.

I calculate the loss (risk) and profit (reward) based on specific entry and exit price points. I target between 50 and 200 pips on a single trade. The large quarter points of the Quarters Theory determine my targets. I also establish targets based on support or resistance levels. My risk-reward ratio must be met in order for me to take a trade. I will not enter a trade that does not meet my target, because the risk-reward ratio is no longer in my favor. Rather, I will wait for more ideal setups and then look for an entry at that time.

I scale out of my positions as well. I prefer to scale out of a position mainly for psychological reasons. I trade better when I have pips in the bank to evidence a successful trade. As profit targets are met, I continue to remain in an astute mind-set to continue trading. Met targets enhance your mind-set, just as losses hinder your mind-set. I have also seen many times when my target was missed by a few pips, only to turn around and reverse on me. Scaling out of my position, I have at least captured some of the trade instead of settling for breaking even or, worse, taking a loss.

APPROACHING THE MARKET

My favorite setup is one based on the Fibonacci retracement levels. Anticipating moves can be dangerous in the forex market because moves have the potential to whipsaw a trader in a matter of minutes. In addition, if you are not mindful of the economic calendar, a trade can go against you or become invalidated very, very quickly. To avoid this adverse action, unlike many traders, I love to take a trade *after* the market makes a major move. After that major move, I know that the market has decided which way it wants to move. Though I may miss the initial breakout, I know the direction so I can jump in on the continuation with certainty in a higher-probability trade. Since I trade only the GBP, I know it is very good at continuing a move in the direction of a breakout, especially early in the trading day during the European trading session.

Once an intraday price move has occurred, I will calculate Fibonacci retracement levels on the 60-minute chart. I am looking for the area to which price will pull back and correct before continuing on in the direction of the intraday trend. I will set limit orders with a stop and target already defined. Because my target determines my stop, my entry is very important to the success of any trade I take. I determine a stop using a 1:1.5 risk-reward ratio. So I must know my target to make this calculation. I compare the resulting price from this computation to important price levels on the charts in all three time frames. Already for me, the point of validity is beyond the golden mean. If my computed stop loss is beyond the point of validity, then I have confirmation that my entry is a good one and my timing is good. If my stop loss falls ahead of the point of validity, then I won't take the trade. The timing is too early to enter the trade, thereby decreasing the probability of success for that particular trade.

When managing a trade, I will add to the position using the same premise as when I first entered the trade. However, my stop is very tight, as opposed to using a 1:1.5 risk-reward ratio. Any additions to a position are treated as free candy, and as such if the timing is wrong (because the trend is coming to an end or news causes a reversal), then this free candy won't turn into a cavity. Therefore, I keep the stop very tight on any trades that are adding to an already open position.

This approach works best for me because I know my psychology as a trader. Larger profit targets keep me in trades longer and prohibit me from overtrading. This method does not require me to be in the markets all the time at all hours. My approach to trading works for my psyche, and that is why it is successful for me.

PUTTING IT INTO PRACTICE

Now I have laid out my approach to the market and my trade setups. But knowing my approach and executing it are two different things. I am always perfecting my craft. Taking a trade at the right time, allowing that trade to develop, and then being patient enough for my targets to play out are things that I am constantly working on as a trader.

My market approach checklist looks like this:

- ☐ Study the daily chart for long-term trends and important price points.
- ☐ Study the daily chart for short-term trends in the vicinity of those important price points.
- ☐ Drill down to the 60-minute chart for intraday trends and current market psychology.
- ☐ Calculate Fibonacci retracement levels on both the daily and the 60-minute charts to determine entry.
- ☐ Calculate the risk-reward ratio.
- ☐ Study the fundamentals.
- ☐ Answer the question: "Is this a high-probability trade?"
  - ☐ If yes, enter the market.
  - ☐ If no, find another opportunity.

FIGURE 33.1 A Look at the Long-Term Trends, GBP/USD Daily Chart
Source: OANDA Corporation's fxTrade platform.

Now let's examine a specific example of a possible trade using my rules by taking a look at cable, my favorite currency pair.

Starting with the daily chart in Figure 33.1, I review the past year to see the long-term trends in the GBP/USD currency pair. I see that though cable was in a downtrend starting in November 2009, it has been in an uptrend since May 2010. This current bull trend is a near reversal of the previous bear trend. The current trend is still clearly to the upside.

Zooming in on the current price action on the daily chart, I want to determine how old the current trend is. Trades taken in the direction of the trend have a higher probability of success when the trend is relatively new. A new trend is in a first or second trend wave. An old trend provides different trading opportunities. An old trend is in a third or more trend wave. To determine the age of a trend, I count the waves within the trend. Unlike Elliott wave theory, the consolidation corrective wave is not counted in my wave count.

We can see in Figure 33.2 that despite the strong uptrend, the current trend is old. As I stated before, an old trend provides different trading opportunities. I can wait for the correction to take place and take a trade in the direction of the trend. Or I can take a countertrend trade and play that corrective price action. I will take the trade that has a high probability of success and provides the risk-reward ratio that I require. The fundamental landscape will determine that.

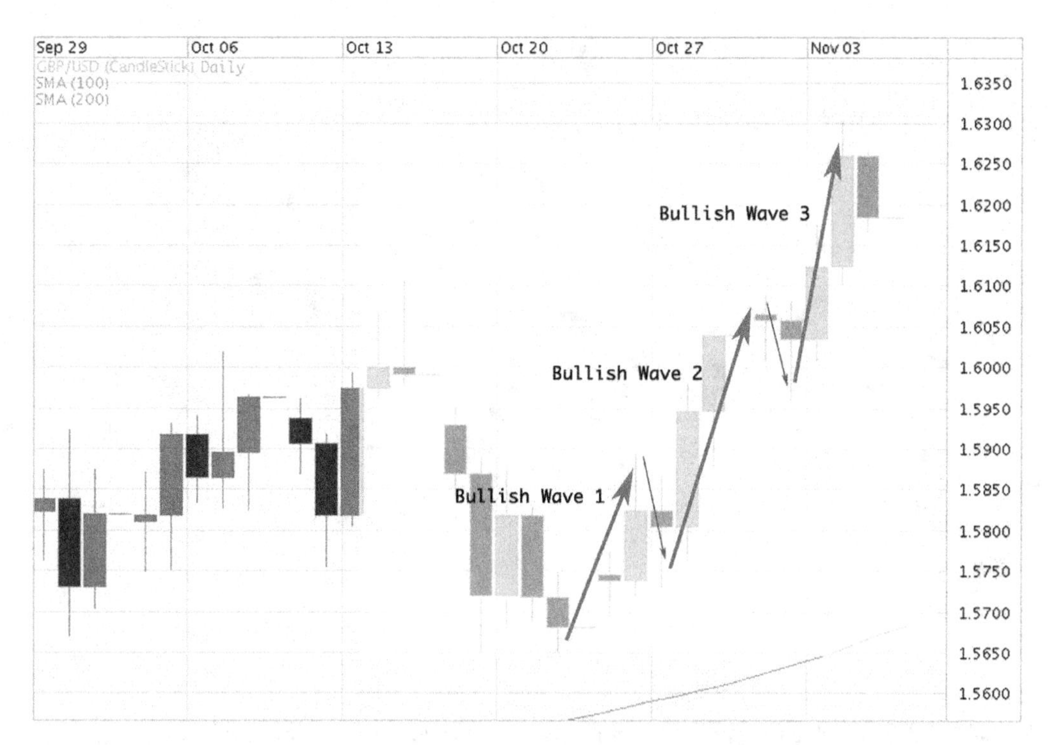

FIGURE 33.2 Counting the Waves in the Current Trend, GBP/USD Daily Chart
Source: OANDA Corporation's fxTrade platform.

Now the trend here has come to an end and cable is correcting off the highs. When I see price has rolled over and started to pull back, that is when I will calculate the Fibonacci retracement levels to see where price might fall before it turns around and continues on in the direction of the trend.

I calculate the Fibonacci levels on the current trend wave first. I can see that the market has already corrected 38.2 percent, so it is possible that the GBP/USD could turn here and head higher (see Figure 33.3). However, the recent fundamental developments in the strong U. S. payrolls reported in November 2010 may induce a more substantial correction. With that possibility in mind, I also figure the Fibonacci levels on the entire trend. Therefore, if the fundamentals do cause a more significant pullback, I am already aware of levels where price may find support. I am also aware of levels that may mean a reversal is truly under way.

Within the context of this correction, I look for support and resistance levels that may be of significance as the pair retraces. I find two support levels here and mark them on the chart as well. To learn just how important these levels are, I look back over the past year to see if price has respected these levels before (see Figure 33.4).

It is very interesting to see that price has respected both price points at 1.6100 and 1.6000 as support and resistance in the past year. So I know that these levels are important levels where price could find bids and start to rise again in the direction of the

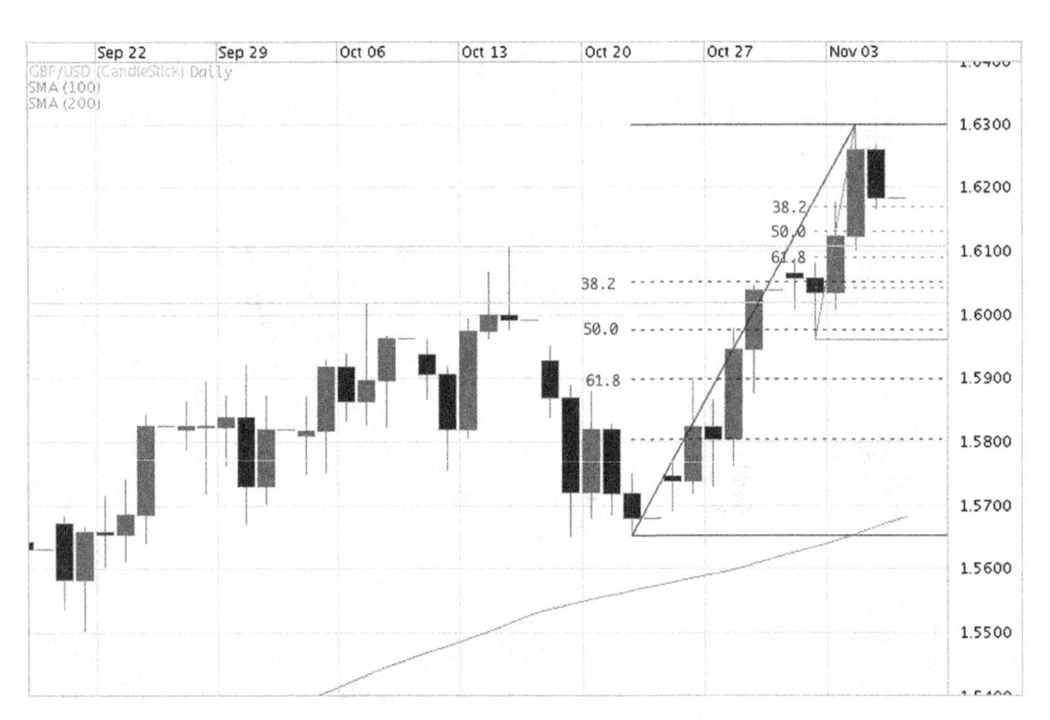

FIGURE 33.3 Calculating Fibonacci Retracement Levels, GBP/USD Daily Chart
Source: OANDA Corporation's fxTrade platform. © 2011 OANDA Corporation. All rights reserved.

FIGURE 33.4 Marking the Support Levels, GBP/USD Daily Chart
Source: OANDA Corporation's fxTrade platform. © 2011 OANDA Corporation. All rights reserved.

FIGURE 33.5 Finding an Entry, GBP/USD 60-Minute Chart
Source: OANDA Corporation's fxTrade platform.

current trend. It also suggests that if price breaks below these levels, the prevailing trend has indeed ended and the pair may be working on a reversal of the short-term uptrend.

Now that I can see my important levels, the prevailing trend, and the current price action, I am ready to determine my entries (see Figure 33.5). Since I know that this uptrend is old, the GBP/USD may stage a more significant correction of the *entire* trend. Therefore, I want to be prepared to sell rallies (depicted by the gray squares) near the highs. Using the Quarters Theory, my target is in the vicinity of 1.6000. Calculating my risk-reward ratio, the prices above 1.6200 result in stops that are well above the highs on the chart. Given the two failures at the highs, I can even set my stops much tighter but still above the highs. If I am short and price turns against me, my losses will be small and quick. But if price does continue lower, then my reward will far outweigh the risk on the position.

I still respect the long-term uptrend, and fundamentals still favor the GBP over the USD. So I have buy orders in place (depicted by the dark squares). I determine these entries just like I would any trend-following trade. On the GBP/USD, ideally I want to scale into a position between the 50 percent and 61.8 percent Fibonacci levels. Cable is very capable of producing corrections of that magnitude. I am aware of the moving averages on the 60-minute chart in particular. Cable respects these levels. If price finds support at the 100-day simple moving average, then the correction is over sooner than I expected and I need to manage any trades accordingly. However, a break below the

100-day simple moving average signals that price will fall further toward the 200-day simple moving average. If that is the case, then I want to get in long ahead of that 200-day simple moving average in case price finds support there and reverses higher. But I must be aware that a major support level at 1.6100 is between the 100-day and 200-day simple moving averages, and price may just stall out there. If a breach of that level occurs, then I will watch the Fibonacci levels on the entire trend and scale in accordingly. My long trade becomes invalid once the 61.8 percent level on the entire trend is breached.

WORDS OF WISDOM

In the early years in my trading, I was more concerned with methodology, as I think most traders are. But recently, my interest has turned toward the psychological aspect of what we do. Swing traders must master patience, as impatience is a far greater hindrance to performance for a swing trader than for a scalper. We *must* wait for setups, and then once in a trade we *must* wait for that trade to develop. My worst losses come on the back of haste. I rush to get out of a trade. Then I rush to get back in a trade. Then I rush to get back out of that trade, only to rush back into another trade. In between those hasty decisions is hurried research and analysis. This is no way to trade. On top of that, my psyche can't trade well at all in hurried circumstances. When I am on a losing streak, it is almost always due to a lack of patience. I know this about my trading now. All traders must discover how to keep their egos in check. Once a trader can master her own ego, the pips will indeed follow.

CHAPTER 34

The Mind of a Chartist

Raghee Horner, @ragheehorner

Raghee has a tremendous grasp of the markets. She continues to work hard every day, and her work ethic is an inspiration for everyone. She is an excellent teacher, and the StockTwits community deeply treasures her contributions to the forex conversation.

The key to effective entries is understanding the psychology of the market.
—Raghee Horner

THERE MUST BE A WAY

I was introduced to trading by a client of mine when I worked as a Divemaster in college. This singularly changed my mind about the types of things people could do to earn a living. Even at a young age, freedom was number one on my list of priorities. Trading was that one thing where I saw both freedom and the potential for unlimited income. This was in 1991. I was 19 years old, impressionable, already a business owner, and on my way to law school. The fact that I had met a trader (he traded bonds) showed me that it was possible. That really was all I needed.

I began trading end-of-day commodity futures. My first 18 months were very successful; therefore, when I had my first series of losses into my second year of trading, it was mainly due to arrogance and breaking my rules. I think we tend to think we are bigger than the market when we are successful for a long period of time. This was in the early 1990s, before the Internet as we know it now, so I received paper charts in the mail each Monday that I would update by hand until the next week. I had the luxury of slowing down and taking my time and looking closely at my trades. With intraday data bombarding traders today, slowing down is a tough thing to do. My indicators were calculated by hand and therefore not a huge part of the decision process; that's where I became reliant on price action. Getting up-to-date fundamentals was not a reality, so I really was not ever reliant on that type of information. I did, however, get a DTN satellite dish set up in the mid-1990s, and that opened my eyes to the fact that while I did not use fundamentals to make trading decisions, I had to respect them.

My main struggle early on—like most traders I see today—was trade management. I think entries are the easy part of the trade in many ways in that we usually follow our process when entering a market: aligning all the stars and making sure the reason for entry is valid. However, I noticed something in myself and also found as I began teaching others to trade at a young age that I was not alone. The wheels come off the wagon for most people when it comes to following through on exits. Profit targets and stops are very difficult for most traders. They often don't know where a trade is no longer valid (what I call a point of validity), and they don't know where to realize their initial profit target—which is important because that's where their trade turns into a winner and therefore the stops can be moved to protect gains. I think exits for many traders are knee-jerk reactions to profits or losses. It was not this way in the early part of my career and, interestingly enough, I think it was an advantage for me not to have access to tick-by-tick intraday data and only end-of-day prices that I would get by phone from my broker. Once I got streaming data, it was almost like another short learning curve because of the price information I now had. It was right about that time that I added day trading stocks to my commodities trading. That would have been in mid-1996.

My second struggle came from one of my favorite and most profitable strategies, which was identifying a trend and then waiting for corrections in the trend in order to trend follow. I call this swing trading. The swings are the bounces and pullbacks that we call corrections or retracements. This was also the time I began teaching myself more about Fibonacci levels. I had been using 50 percent retracement without really understanding that it was based on Fibonacci ever since I had begun trading, but I dove deeper into more levels and understanding which rallies and sell-offs to use to get the most accurate levels. Fibonacci is incredibly subjective and therefore difficult to learn at first, but the accuracy it offers in the support and resistance levels it projects is absolutely worth it. Between my 34-day exponential moving average (EMA) (34 of course being a Fibonacci number), psychological level, and Fibonacci retracement and extensions I now have an excellent idea of where support is waiting in an uptrend and where resistance is waiting in a downtrend.

CHARTS ARE MY LANGUAGE

My philosophy on how I perceive the markets working comes from the view of being a chartist. I know I will never be privy to all that moves a market, and even if I were, understanding and applying it quickly would be a challenge. Price allows me to measure where a market has been and to interpret what sentiment is being reflected, whether that sentiment has enough organization to create momentum, and then in turn whether the momentum can transition into a trend. Price-based analysis—for me—means that all the news and fundamental information in the markets have been "baked into the cake." Therefore, price is really a measurement of psychology to me. I am trading opinions and emotions. Price is market emotion. To me, trading is about nothing more than understanding fear and greed. The key is market trends and whether I see a sideways or trending market on whatever time frame I am analyzing. I truly feel that as long as I am respectful of the volatility that fundamentals present to a market, price will give me all the insight I need into sentiment, momentum, and trend.

DOW THEORY

The idea behind market trend is nothing new; in fact, it's really 100-year-old Dow Theory. The term was coined posthumously, but Dow Theory includes the philosophy and strategies that Charles Dow outlined in his newsletters in the early 1900s. One of the concepts was the idea that markets move in different phases. Of the six popular principles, the idea that market trends have three phases has been the most important in my own trading. Market trends, according to Dow, are composed three distinct phases. When the market is moving in a quiet, less volatile price range it's said to be in an accumulation phase. This phase is characterized by a narrow sideways range. It lacks momentum and will often have predictable support and resistance. There is little overwhelming sentiment in any direction and therefore no momentum; however, once momentum affects this narrow sideways range, prices will then transition to the second phase, known as a markup or a markdown. While Dow did not necessarily speak of a markdown phase, it's especially important to understand that financial markets are cyclical and trend in both directions.

Trending markets are unbalanced markets. Overwhelming supply indicates the downtrend and overwhelming demand indicates an uptrend. Consider that the only reason the market moves higher is because traders and investors are willing to pay a higher and higher price. Alternatively, the downtrend occurs because traders and investors are willing to sell at a lower and lower price. The imbalance comes from the market sentiment and momentum favoring either the bulls or the bears.

Trending markets are often the most difficult for traders and investors to handle because there is always the urge to follow the momentum, when in fact healthy trends correct and it's at these corrections that the best price and the lowest risk can be taken.

If there's a market phase that I would call "account killer," it would have to be the distribution phase. Distribution is characterized by high volatility, a wide and often unpredictable trading range, and exhaustion at the floor and ceiling of the range. Identifying this market is challenging; trying to differentiate it from accumulation is often where traders will erroneously identify this market simply as a nontrending environment. Oftentimes traders will see a rally toward the ceiling and mistake it for a trend, only to watch prices then exhaust and reverse. Momentum players will see prices reach the ceiling, oftentimes piercing it as well, and expect momentum and follow-through, only to watch prices exhaust and reverse. Distribution can be characterized by confusion. Confusion carries with it unpredictable momentum and a lack of organized sentiment.

Simply knowing that these phases exist can open the discussion to how to identify one from another and how to select the most effective entry strategy to manage the underlying psychology and price movement of that phase. In my experience, trading is less about a specific entry strategy and much more about risk management. Every entry strategy has a market environment that it was designed to capitalize on. Trend traders, in my opinion, can look for trend continuations, trend corrections, and trend reversals. Which of those three will actually occur has to do with how strong the trend is, where the market can correct to without reversing the trend, and where the trend will be defined as broken. The most difficult part of trend trading for many traders is knowing the difference between corrections and reversals. In a trend, a correction can be an entry point, while the error of assuming a reversal is still within the area of a correction can be a disastrous entry.

For nontrending market movement, there is either a quiet, sideways organization of the accumulation phase or the volatile, wide range of distribution. Momentum traders would do best to capitalize on breakouts and breakdowns from accumulation, whereas traders who like to capitalize on the exhaustion of an oversold or overbought market within a wide range can thrive in a distribution market. Let's examine how specific indicators are also more effective in different market environments. Take, for example, the accumulation phase, where traders waiting for a breakout through resistance or a breakdown through support can use a moving average convergence/divergence (MACD) histogram to confirm market momentum and the likelihood for follow-through. In a distribution phase, traders looking to capitalize on exhaustion at ceilings and floors can utilize a stochastic to confirm whether the market can stall and reverse.

FINDING THE RIGHT APPROACH

Using just a single entry strategy or indicator is like thinking you can use a hammer to fix everything. Knowing this and identifying these market phases were things that I had not seen in any books I read, videos I watched, or seminars I had attended. This is when I began experimenting with three exponential moving averages based on the Fibonacci number 34; it would change my trading forever.

There are two basic principles to using what I now call the 34EMA Wave. First is the market memory or lookback, and the second is the idea of clock angles.

What we view on our charts is the data—the price action—that measures market sentiment, momentum, and trend. How much of this data we view will shape what our opinion is of market direction, so I make sure to use a market memory or lookback to keep a uniform view of each time frame's price action. This allows me to view the recent rallies, sell-offs, highs, and lows that will determine the touch points of trend lines, as well as horizontal support and resistance levels. Too much data, and I will be in danger of including data that may not hold relevance; too little data, and I could miss out on important clues on the chart. The time frames I watch with the most frequency are the 15-, 30-, 60-, and 240-minute charts, and the daily chart. The market memory or lookback on the 15-minute chart is three to five days, for the 30-minute it's one to two weeks, on the 60-minute it's three weeks, for the 240-minute it's four to six weeks, and on the daily it's one year.

This amount of data also allows me to determine the clock angle of my 34EMA Wave, which is the 34-period exponential moving average on the high, the low, and the close. These three individual EMAs act as dynamic support or resistance in trending markets and they also—by the angle at which they are traveling—tell me the market trend that a specific time frame is currently in. The market trend that is measured by the angle of my 34EMA Wave will determine which entry strategy I will use (see Figure 34.1). Simply put, there are five things a market can do: correct within a trend; continue the trend; reverse the trend; move in a wide, volatile sideways direction; or move in a narrow, less volatile sideways direction. I have to have a strategy to handle each scenario. But the first step is always determining whether the market is moving up, down, or sideways.

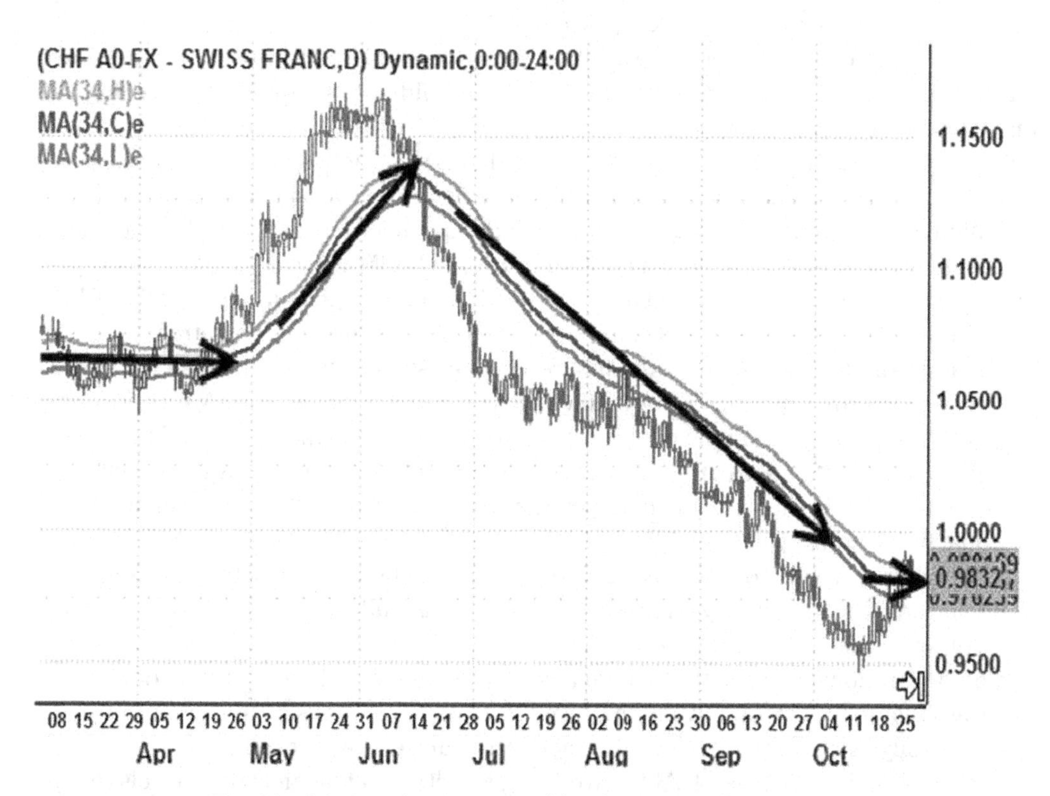

FIGURE 34.1 The Market Trend Is Measured by the Trend of My 34EMA Wave, CHF
Source: © eSignal, 2009.

CAPITALIZING ON CORRECTIONS WITHIN THE CONTEXT OF A TREND

If the 34EMA Wave is traveling at a twelve o'clock to two o'clock angle within market memory (uptrend or markup phase), I will use the 34EMA Wave as well as Fibonacci retracements to determine where support may be waiting and where I could enter a swing buy. Swings to me are the corrections within a healthy trend. When the market is moving higher in an uptrend, I would much rather position my entries at support and expect a resumption of the trend. Using the dynamic support of the Wave (with secondary confirmation from Fibonacci levels or psychological levels) identifies where buying support could hold the correction.

As mentioned before, one issue traders often have is differentiating a correction from a reversal. I hear statements like "The EUR/USD is reversing" but I find that to be incorrect or incomplete unless the specific time frame is being discussed. Oftentimes these supposed reversals are simply bounces within the context of a trend. The most psychologically significant trend is that of the daily chart, so that should be considered even when intraday time frames may actually be reversing their intraday trend. A reversal is defined as when the 34EMA Wave is no longer acting as support in an uptrend or resistance in a downtrend (a four to six o'clock angle).

Knowing where the correction transitions into a reversal is at the heart of swing trading, because without this distinction, lower lows should not be bought into and higher highs should not be shorted.

Consider that there are basically only three things price action can do at any support or resistance level: stall, accelerate, or reverse. When prices are in an uptrend, the expectation is that support will cause a stall and a move back higher from the floor. The challenge is often to determine which floor. With the 34EMA Wave, the floor in an uptrend would be the area between the 34-period EMA on the high and the 34-period EMA on the low. This area acts as a cushion if the trend is healthy. In a downtrend, the 34-period EMA on the low would be the first level of resistance and the ceiling area would extend higher to the 34-period EMA on the high (the top line of my 34EMA Wave).

Notice in Figure 34.2, in the twelve o'clock to two o'clock uptrend on the 240-minute EUR/USD, how many times prices traded lower (corrected) to the 34EMA Wave or very close to it before buying support held and the trend resumed higher. This can apply to any time frame and any market.

One filter that can be used is the direction on the daily chart. If the daily chart is in an uptrend, the overall psychology of that market is bullish and therefore it is more prudent to follow the trend by positioning entries at levels of support both intraday and end-of-day. Although shorts can be taken even when the overall market direction is up, be aware that these are usually going to capitalize on corrections of the larger uptrend, and when buying support eventually is reached, the uptrend will resume.

When the support of the 34EMA Wave overlaps with psychological price levels (numbers that end is "00" and "50"), there is secondary price-based support. The same applies

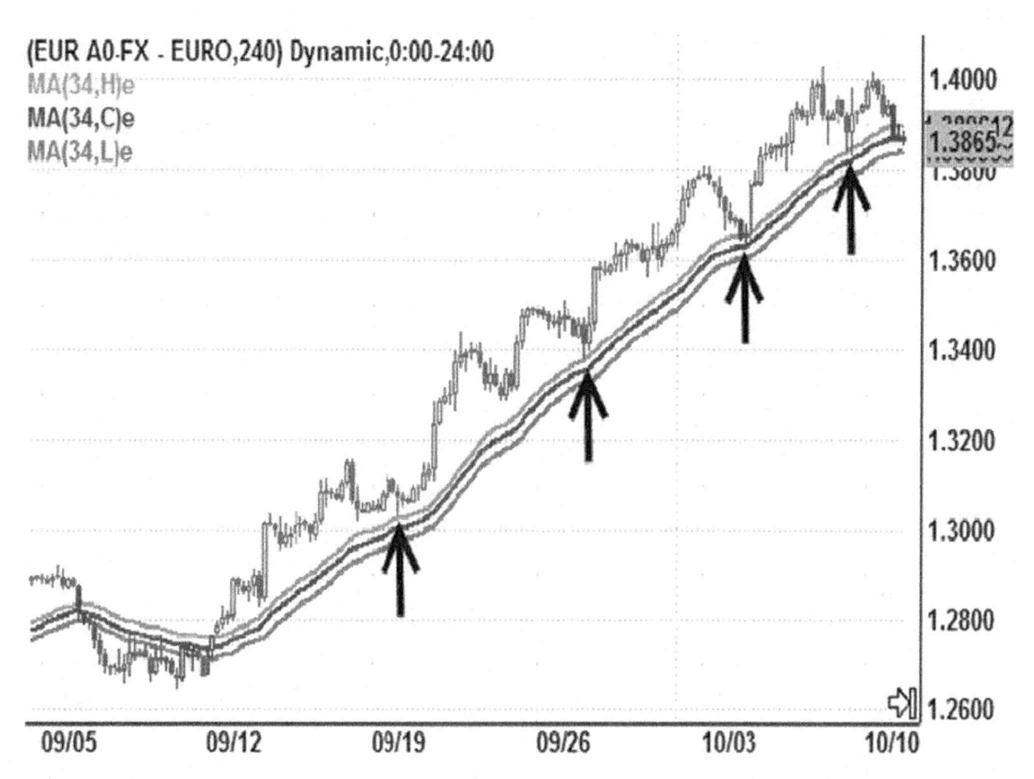

FIGURE 34.2 The Uptrend Is Supported by the Rising 34EMA, EUR/USD 240-Minute Chart
Source: © eSignal, 2009.

to these levels when there is resistance. The reason for this is that orders tend to congregate at whole, round numbers and these levels can create support when traded down to and resistance when traded higher to. It's also important to remember that there is usually a five-tick/pip/point cushion above and below these levels. So if prices begin to break through a "00" level, there could be momentum waiting as the orders are filled and acceleration builds.

The trend entry criteria are as simple as identifying the market trend with the 34EMA Wave, noticing whether the Wave has been respected on past correction (if applicable), and entering on a correction to the dynamic support of the 34EMA Wave in an uptrend or the dynamic resistance of the 34EMA Wave in a downtrend. The validity of the trade (think stop loss and risk management) is therefore dependent upon the 34EMA Wave holding.

In an uptrend, the 34-period EMA on the high will be the first entry trigger; therefore, if prices break five pips/ticks/points below the 34-period EMA on the low, the swing buy is no longer valid. In a downtrend, the 34-period EMA on the low is the first entry trigger, and if prices rally higher than five pips above the 34-period EMA on the high, the trade is no longer valid.

PART VII

The Art of Trading

CHAPTER 35

Trading Is an Art

The Fly, *@the_real_fly*

The Fly is one of my favorite reads on the Internet—not always clean, but always passionate. The Fly has a tremendous feel for the market and it shines through in his writing. He writes about the inevitable bad trading streaks, which makes his winning streaks even more fun to follow. Behind the aggressive chatter and style lies a trader with deep insight who respects the market and its mechanisms and always stays in the game.

Death is nothing, but to live defeated and inglorious is to die daily.
—Napoleon Bonaparte

BORN TO WIN

In high school, I won a writing contest with a heartfelt article about a tragic occurrence that had happened to me and my family when I was just five years old. It was a big deal, as my work was published in the local New York City rag and ABC News visited my house for an interview. A mutual fund manager from Seligman & Company must have been touched by my story, because he contacted my school and asked to see me. Upon meeting him, I was offered a summer internship. At this internship, my job was to open his mail and organize his things. This was before the wonderful invention of e-mail, so he was absolutely inundated with wirehouse research. I read it all. From that point on, I was obsessed with stocks.

After college, I entered the money management business. At the beginning it was tough, especially for a kid from Brooklyn with no well-to-do contacts. However, with a little hard work and some space-alien magic I made enough money to build a pyramid made of gold.

On a serious note, the difference between me and everyone else I know is this: I try harder. Plus I am smarter (intelligence truly is a factor). Some people focus their energy on climbing absurdly dangerous cliffs, picking up girls at sleazy bars, or hitting baseballs: I am great only at buying and selling stocks, with the marked exception of keeping eloquent journals at iBankCoin (http://ibankcoin. com), of course.

KNOWING WHEN TO PRESS A BET

My philosophy is to assume that most traders get it wrong, so I bet against them. Essentially, I am a contrarian at heart, but utilize algorithmic software to stay focused on what is working. Throughout the years, I've learned to minimize my risk during times of uncertainty while pressing my bets on high-percentage moves. This is a skill that can only be considered an art as it is very hard to explain but is easier said than done.

I am an ardent disbeliever in the church of technical analysis. I believe technicians use charts as a crutch to avoid doing proper research. A great man once said, "A man and his charts is an idiot with charts, indeed." I subscribe to that way of thinking without any reservations. However, I do appreciate the power of program trading when trying to identify high-probability setups. Because of this belief, I've developed my own proprietary software that helps me achieve market mastery without having to book countless hours doing slave work—sifting through balance sheets and Securities and Exchange Commission (SEC) filings. Computers: they're a beautiful thing.

SCALING IN

Generally speaking, I go into every trade with the idea that I will be wrong about the entry price. If I am interested in building a position, I will stagger my buys over days or weeks, rarely months. My typical position size is 2 to 8 percent of assets. However, downside hedges can get as big as 25 percent and cash is always north of 10 percent. When I build long-term portfolios, I adhere to the strictest asset allocation methods from the ground up. I select five stocks from the 10 principal sectors of the S&P 500 index and track them closely, solely based on performance and weighting. For example, if I decide to allocate 10 percent of assets into basic materials, and my basket of stocks gets obliterated, sending my weighting down to 7 percent, I will buy more to fulfill my 10 percent quota. On the flip side, if my technology holdings soar, I will pare them down to get back in line with my target allocation.

To be honest, this is all meaningless drivel, since I haven't really done this in over two years. Since the beginning of the end of the world in 2008, I have shelved my asset allocation practices in exchange for more flexible trading strategies, using my proprietary algorithmic software. In other words, I no longer enter the war by way of a tank. I have opted for the trusty sniper rifle, with an egregious scope and silenced muzzle.

My trading is assisted by an analytic engine named The PPT. Basically, the software my partner and I have developed scans every stock and exchange-traded fund (ETF) that is publicly traded and grades them using all available fundamental and technical data available to humankind, which then translates into a buy or sell recommendation—kindly provided by our trusty computers. The true power of our software is the high level of accuracy that it achieves at inflection points, identifying tops and bottoms. Granted, it has not been around a long time (a little less than two years); but the results speak for themselves. Over the past two years, the markets have never been more volatile and my performance has never been better, returning more than 60 percent in 2008 and 90 percent in 2009. As of August 2010 I was up approximately 40 percent.

My style of investing is difficult to explain in one short article. Despite the obvious stringent parameters that I just outlined, I view investing as an art form, not a skill. I am very flexible to the point where I never give stock advice to people at cocktail parties or to family members—due to the fact that my opinions change so often. If you really want to know how I tick, read my blog; it's free.

RIDING THE VXX

My most recent successful trade was in VXX from April to early June 2010. At that time, volatility was at 52-week lows and people were elated to be long equities in the midst of a worsening credit crisis in Europe. This was a classic contrarian trade, buying VXX from 25.00 down to as low as 18.50. My strategy was to leg into the position, assuming my trades would be wrong—due to the bullish nature of the market. By early May, my cost basis on VXX, thanks to my patience and methodical buying programs, was in the low $20s. As the market dumped out, volatility spiked and I booked profits on the position, which constituted a record 40 percent of assets due to my conviction (I rarely, if ever, build positions bigger than 20 percent of assets). I ended up making approximately 40 percent on that one trade, putting my year-to-date gains well above those of my peers.

CHAPTER 36

Embrace the Tape

Quint Tatro, *@tickerville*

Quint loves the markets as deeply as kids love their home sports teams. He's smart, passionate, and hardworking, and luckily for us, he enjoys being a mentor. If you spend any time following his stream, you will be hooked. You might even want box seats and season tickets.

NEVER AGAIN!

The cold, crisp air did nothing to alleviate the feeling in the pit of my stomach as I walked around the outer bounds of the corporate office complex. To the casual observer I would be viewed as someone out for a morning stroll, stepping away from the desk to enjoy the brisk sunshine, when in reality I was a person toiling with the reality of having just lost hundreds of thousands of dollars in client money. The words still rang in my ear: ". . . and with that we believe it will be much easier for Winn Dixie to handle its current debt issues while under the protection of bankruptcy."

How could this be? I had done all the proper due diligence. I had pored over balance sheets, studied income statements, analyzed margins, and talked to management. This small grocer was going places. Sure, the stock was bleeding to death, but wasn't that the time to buy more based on your homework and conviction? We started with a measly 1 percent; however, by the time it was finished, we had lost 3 percent of the portfolio in that swift blow I'll never forget.

It was somewhere between the second and third loops as I began to sweat, regretting the bottle of wine I had enjoyed the evening before that, when I vowed never again to be the sucker in a stock trade. Something was missing, and I was determined to find out what it was.

Like most, my foray into active trading came with an introduction to Jim Cramer. After a Charter Communications here and a Lucent there, I quickly moved on. Don't get me wrong; Cramer has been and always will be a pioneer in this industry, but his style was eerily similar to what I was trying to avoid. I had no desire to buy low, lower, and even lower.

Stock market analyst and educator James "RevShark" DePorre, on the other hand, preached a different mantra—one that I could understand, one that I could relate to, and one that I had to learn. His style was unemotional, objective, and above all flexible. It seemed as if he didn't care which way the market went; he simply wanted to be on the right side. After devouring all I could of his writings, I reached out and with a bit of hustle and luck, I was soon working elbow to elbow with the trading legend, who began pouring his vast knowledge into me, building the foundation for what would become my own personal style.

After a few years under Rev, I once again ventured out on my own, spreading my wings, prepared to soar. My eye was sharp and my understanding of market movement vast; however, my consistency—well, let's just say it was slightly lacking.

My strategy was more artistic than scientific. While my approach to trading remained objective, my entries and exits became rather emotional. I would trade off of feel much more than the technical read. It led to significant and staggering runs, which I thoroughly enjoyed; however, quickly thereafter it would always lead to a drawdown that was beyond reasonable. The erratic swings were enough to bald any man, and yes, I attribute my balding to that, but in hindsight the foundation was there; it simply needed to be refined.

Over the years, I set off on another course to implement consistency into my trading. It has been a personal exploration and one that I don't ever believe will end. I now utilize a journal for each trade, outlining my read beforehand such that I have something to follow once the emotions creep in. My risk is quantified on each trade, and my exit strategy is consistent. The results have been mind-blowing, as I have now produced a consistently rising equity curve that my partners and I can be proud of.

THE GAME

For my style I must remember that the market is nothing more than a game: traders versus traders, all attempting to take money from one another. When the bell rings, he or she with the most wins, well, wins. Most people struggle with trading when they bring into the game any outside opinion or idea that may bias them in any way. At times, I am guilty of this and it is a lifelong struggle to set these ideas down daily.

Market movement is nothing more than a vast number of individuals acting based on their beliefs. My job is simply to find a small edge and seek to exploit that edge over and over again.

FADING THE OBVIOUS

My early trading education was primarily based on traditional technical analysis. Lately, however, I have seen a vast shift in that traditional technical analysis has become so popular that the real moneymaking opportunities lie in trading the traders who are trading traditional technical analysis.

Let me give you a specific example. In early 2009, after the general market had started pursuing a historic run, the averages carved out a head-and-shoulders pattern on the daily time frame. Traditionally this pattern is one that is developed when a market or stock is topping out. The psychology is that the market has a subtle top and rolls over, which marks the first left shoulder. Shorts, which have entered appropriately, use this peak as a stopping point while bulls may use this key level as a buy point. Following a brief decline, the market breaks this key level, subsequently going on to new highs. Unfortunately for the bulls, this crescendo does not continue and selling once again sets in. This movement creates the head, and solidifies the psychology that sellers are taking over. Shorts that were stopped out on the formation of the head are now emboldened and reenter with a new stop being that of a break of the highs. Longs that entered on a move over the left shoulder are stopped out and discouraged. As sentiment shifts from bullish to bearish, the market attempts yet another rally, this time being turned back before new highs, establishing the final piece of the picture, the right shoulder. The pattern is complete and insinuates the possibility for much more weakness to set in. The traditional trigger point of the pattern is when the lows of the left shoulder, head, and right shoulder, traditionally known as the neckline, are all broken.

In early 2009 this pattern was developed beautifully except for one variable. It was probably the most talked about, publicized, and traded pattern in the history of trading. It was bound to fail, and when it did, it kicked off the second leg of an even more powerful rally led by what in hindsight is clearly one of the biggest short-covering squeeze fests we've ever seen.

I had had inclinations prior to this event that traditional technical analysis was no longer as viable as before, but this event solidified my thoughts greatly. Now I no longer look for just the traditional setups, but for those change-in-character setups that allow me to fade the traditional style of play.

A SYMPATHY PLAY

One of the areas in trading I tend to favor is sympathy plays. Many traders stick with the best of the best in terms of winning stocks inside a hot sector. While there are times I manage to find myself in these names, I also like capitalizing on what may move next or in essence thinking one step ahead of the masses. In the past, I would pile into a sympathy idea with überconfidence, thinking that I would be proven right in due time. It worked out on occasion but when it didn't, I was stuck holding a losing position with absolutely no momentum whatsoever. As I have matured as a trader I have learned that an idea is nothing without an edge. I have learned to be patient and stalk my prey and that simply observing the right area while being prepared to pounce still puts me a step ahead of the rest.

Recently this happened with a trade in U.S. Global Investors, Inc. (GROW). For several years now, I have seen a correlation in movement among mining stocks and U.S. Global due to the company's primary business being that of a mutual fund manager over mining funds. Of course, the correlation hasn't led to the secular bull market in GROW as it has in many mining names, but typically when the group is moving it is only a matter of time until traders seek out GROW and bid it higher. Furthermore, due to its thinness, it tends to have incredible moves that can tack on excellent gains if timed appropriately.

As the dollar has declined and precious metals have taken center stage, mining stocks have been all the rage. Many have had exceptional runs, and when they began I once again had a feeling it was only a matter of time until U.S. Global (GROW) caught the sympathy bid. Around August of 2010 I began watching GROW with interest, not wanting to overanticipate the move (see Figure 36.1). On one particular day in August, the 18th to be exact, the stock started to percolate but for whatever reason didn't quite feel as if it had the legs to keep going. I wish I could quantify why I felt that way, but I cannot. Luckily I took a pass on the play, as the stock reversed and went on to come within a few pennies of 52-week lows a few days later. Finally, in September, the stock once again started to consolidate after clawing its way off the deathbed and looked ready to move.

On October 5, the mining stocks were all the rage. We entered the day with the dollar getting smashed and hitting new lows, while gold and silver ran. Momentum was hot and heavy, and I suspected it was time for U.S. Global (GROW) to participate.

It was at this time I decided to take a position. The offer stood at 6.70 and it was my read that if the day low of 6.34 was broken, I would not want to remain in the trade any longer. Calculating a stop of 0.40, or 6.70 – 6.30, I took the appropriate number of shares in order to risk my desired amount.

Now, my strategy is a little different than most in that I typically will book gains as the stock moves to my advantage, at various levels of my initial risk. For example, since my risk was 0.40, then when I reached a 0.40 profit per share, I would sell one-third and raise my stop.

The timing was perfect, as GROW ran, closing up 7.55 percent on the day—however, not quite at my first profit target of 7.10, or 6.70 + 0.40. The following day the stock followed through, advancing over 14 percent on a volume surge and allowing me to book multiple levels of profit. Of course, rather than keep even a small piece, I subsequently sold all the shares and moved on to the next trade. Let's just say holding on to winners isn't a strong suit of mine.

Whereas U.S. Global was proper execution followed by a positive result, successful traders will tell you that sometimes you can swing the bat just perfectly and still strike out. This happened to me recently as I looked to short Halliburton (HAL) on a wedge break follow-through. Let me explain the setup. Since mid-August 2010 Halliburton had

FIGURE 36.1 U.S. Global Finally Follows the Strength in Mining Stocks
Source: © StockCharts.com.

been following a strong uptrend, moving from the mid-20s to the mid-30s (see Figure 36.2). However, on October 18, Halliburton had a price break after its earnings release, sending the stock down through the uptrend line on heavy volume. This in itself was not a reason to short the stock; however, it did put the pattern onto my radar for further observation. As the next several sessions unfolded, Halliburton began shaking off the postearnings drop, wedging back up toward the previous highs. The move to me was suspect, however, as volume continued to decline, and each time it looked as if the stock was really going to accelerate, a large seller stepped in and sold into strength.

I waited patiently until the right opportunity emerged. What I was looking for was a price break below the current rising wedge, thus giving me a prudent short entry with a stop at recent highs. The trade is rather textbook in nature, but with such a bullish tenor in the environment, I was willing to give it a shot.

Finally, on October 27 Halliburton cracked the shorter-term wedge. The stock showed visible weakness and I took my cue, moving in for a short. Because I was a

FIGURE 36.2 Halliburton Breaks Down from a Bearish Wedge, HAL Daily Chart
Source: © StockCharts.com.

bit overly sensitive about shorting in such a strong environment (the general market had been up significantly for several weeks), I used the current-day high as my stop in calculating my total risk and subsequent share count. I wasn't going to fight a strong trend in the event the break did not follow through but would rather stop out and reenter on another opportunity.

As the day continued, my Halliburton ebbed and flowed and would not break. By day's end it was within 5 cents of my stop, so rather than hold the shares I decided to surrender the short and move on.

Now, most traders would roll over in pain observing what HAL did the very next day, but I just chuckled and moved on. Even if I had kept the stock into the following day, my predefined stop would have grabbed my shares in the first hour of trading. Any other method would have been undisciplined and a very dangerous road to begin traveling down.

Sometimes you line up the bat and swing with perfection, but it just doesn't go your way. Welcome to trading.

WORDS OF WISDOM

Embrace the tape. Not a single person knows where the tape will move on any particular day. Sure, we all may make an educated guess and plan accordingly, but we truly have no idea; and those who pontificate as if they do are lying. It is not our job to determine where the market or life will go, but to roll with the punches as it develops. As a proud father of two children, I have started to experience the ebbs and flows of a wild and crazy ride. If I wasn't flexible and humble, I would definitely not be enjoying the ride. Playing the market successfully is all about handling whatever comes your way with a confidence that, right or wrong, you can keep moving forward.

CHAPTER 37

Macro Setups at the Crest of Structural Change

Gregor Macdonald, @GregorMacdonald

Gregor is a great friend, a huge brain, and a fantastic writer. He can be structurally bearish but maintain a long portfolio. He can look at the world's serious problems and see the possible outcomes that produce simple portfolios and low turnover. I believe you have to keep it simple when investing. Low turnover is of the utmost importance, and trend following with consistent risk management can produce superior portfolio results. Gregor's research and portfolio allocations are things I watch closely.

BEGINNING OF PEAK OIL

In the spring of 2004 a young woman would appear most mornings on Bloomberg Television to explain why oil, should it ever rise as high as $40 a barrel, would quickly fall from such a level as the world would surely pump like crazy to capture those prices. What the young oil analyst from Boston did not understand was that roughly two years earlier a broad but imperceptible shift had taken place, which we now understand as the transition from cheap oil to expensive oil. In the early part of 2004, however, because the global oil supply had indeed made such a big upward move coming out of 2001, it was understandable that oil industry veterans thought that would continue. But consider this: As oil *prices* were trading in the 30s in the spring of 2004, and as the Russian government made its first move against Yukos, sending oil through $40, oil *production* was reaching a plateau. This plateau would maintain itself over the next six years, and is still in place today. Surely we can't blame people on financial TV for not seeing that in 2004. Or can we? Had there been ways to piece together the big shifts taking place in the oil market, despite the conventional wisdom of the time?

Here in the autumn of 2010, in the midst of an ongoing bull market in gold, let's consider yet another endless stream of vapid, lazy commentary that has attempted for the past year to explain why gold is in an unsustainable bubble. Uninformed, and riddled with cliché, this nay-saying caucus is eerily reminiscent of the reaction to oil's move above $40 a barrel in 2004. What does it tell us, for example, that a range of economists and finance professors are given editorial space to write high-school-level essays on gold as a bubble? Essays that could be written in any decade, about any asset, regardless of important shifts taking place in the market? These are exactly the type of editorials that were being written in the preceding decade about oil. And why was so much ink being spilled over oil last decade, and over gold this decade? Because when price begins to move outside of its historical range, it attracts a lot of attention. Unfortunately for the general audience, but happily for the trader, this attention nearly always comes wrapped in emotion and reactivity rather than understanding. And that provides an opportunity.

MACRO SETUPS

Most traders often think of setups on a short-term technical level. However, in my own trading history, I have generally used big, macroeconomic themes to provide a framework for my setups. And here's why: I like the time frame of a macro trade much better. It gives me time to think, and it gives the trade time to develop. Generally, because the time frame is much more forgiving, any mistakes I make will involve exiting the trade too early. Although the opposite problem, exiting the trade too late, is also possible in a macro trade (especially if one is using options), it's much less common. Indeed, as many macro trend traders will acknowledge, it's necessary to be willing to lose 5 to 7 percent at the end of the trade in order to have stayed the course for many months, accumulating gains far in excess of a final tail that trims the gains.

The setup in a macro trade, therefore, is essentially about a very broad misunderstanding. Back in the 2003–2004 period, interest rates had been kept very low in the United States and this had helped to accelerate growth in the developing world. But this had also caused the U.S. dollar to come down from its big 2002 highs. By 2003, the dollar was in a well-established downtrend and the world economy was starting to grow. And yet the media and the New York financial sector was stuffed with observers who expected oil, the primary energy source for the world and input to all industrial economies, to stay flat. Did that make sense? No, of course not. And why did they expect oil to stay flat? They had a million reasons, but none of them had anything to do with oil. In truth, nearly all commentary could have carried the same title: *I Am Confused by These Changes; Therefore, the Changes We Are Witnessing Must Be Temporary.*

THE RIGHT VEHICLES TO PLAY PEAK OIL

When the attack from Moscow on Yukos lifted oil above $40 per barrel in the late spring of 2004, I knew that such developments would be taken back quickly by the futures market and were not sustainable. At this time another set of conditions in Nigeria, rebel attacks on oil infrastructure, was also putting upward pressure on oil prices. How could rebel attacks in tiny Nigeria, a small oil producer, and a political attack on Yukos in Russia affect the price of oil if the world had loads of spare capacity? It became increasingly obvious that oil was set up for a structural move higher. And yet, a stony edifice of oil experts was adamant this was not the case. Perfect! I set out to find the best trading vehicles to express my view.

Unsurprisingly, I found that the same deep skepticism about oil was impacted, like a bad molar, in the share prices of the large integrated oil companies. And when I looked at the implied volatility and premiums on their call options, I was stunned! They were trading like call options on a sleepy trust or master limited partnership, with the expectation of no underlying price movement at all. In late spring, I began scooping up batches of autumn, winter, and following-year call options on British Petroleum, Royal Dutch Shell, Petrobras, TotalFina, and ConocoPhillips. These were being given away for pennies as the market believed even 10 percent moves higher in the big integrated oil names were impossible. Six months later, a number of these had made at least 10 to 15 percent moves. By 12 months later, stocks like Conoco were nearly 50 percent higher.

GOOD MACRO INVESTORS ARE CONTRARIANS

The exact same setup appeared not once, but twice, in global gold and silver mining stocks over the past decade. The most recent opportunity occurred following the 2008 crisis, when gold bullion fell back below the all-time nominal high. Once again, it has been the large-capitalization senior names like Barrick, Gold Fields, AngloGold, and Newmont that have struggled against years of investor disgust and bewilderment as their share prices have slowly creaked higher. The economists, investment bank analysts, and TV talking heads who spent each day shouting down oil last decade appear to have resurfaced en masse to try their hand again, this time at gold. The same calcified misunderstandings abound this time as well. But just as with oil last decade and gold this decade, the skepticism has not been borne exclusively by the ignorant.

Don Coxe, the veteran market watcher and investor, has a perfect saying that describes these macro setups: "The greatest gains are possible from a sector when those who know it best love it least." And that has certainly been true for energy and precious metals. The 25-year underperformance of both sectors did not produce merely a short-term period of disbelief. Decades of punk returns produced an entire generation of oil analysts, business school professors, and mining executives who eventually would create an entire belief structure around the underperformance of commodities. The experts grew to distrust their own industry. Meanwhile, the prestige of paper currencies and the perma-cheap pricing in resources would eventually be taught as a theory in business school. An army of the skeptical was born.

Setups in macro trading are therefore about finding a discrepancy between price and belief. This sounds unremarkable, but what's different is that the belief structure tends to be almost philosophical and the pending trend change tends to be structural. On the spectrum between precision and scope, therefore, macro setups are less concerned with precision and instead try their hand for a big goal: scope. What's exciting about these trades is that even in the macro space itself, many traders and large institutions will still be addressing themselves on shorter time frames. In other words, they too will be trapped by *precision* and the demands of their clients to produce returns on a 30- to 90-day basis. As is so often the case with all trading, leveraging the narrow-mindedness of the other players is necessary. When you see the entire media and financial complex trying to beat back an emerging structural change, you will likely find that the cost of expressing an opposing view is so cheap that most of your gains will be made by your ultralow cost of entry.

CHAPTER 38

Broken Butterfly Formation

Anne-Marie Baiynd, *@AnneMarieTrades*

In the era of the social Web, a person's reputation does not have to come from personal meetings. The time line of ideas, a person's consistency, and owning up to losses as well as wins are what matter most. While I've not met Anne-Marie, her reputation for good ideas is second to none. She offers up complete and detailed ideas around her strategy and then follows up with commentary on how trades performed.

MAJOR CORNERSTONES

I see a number of events as cornerstones in my career. The first was learning to understand market internals—the heartbeat of the market—UVOL, DVOL, TRIN, ADVN, DECN, VIX, and (most important) the movement of the E-mini futures. Without monitoring these elements, much of my trading day would be a miss.

The second high-impact event was my introduction to Brian Shannon through a Web search years ago, while I was striving to understand how the market works. He had a monumental effect on my trading career—from the volume-weighted average price (VWAP) to multiple time frames, from understanding stages that a stock goes through to paying attention to reports coming out. He taught me that in order to trade well, you must always be in a state of discovery and interpretation, and be willing to change your mind. I never realized how little I knew before becoming familiar with Brian's work.

The most recent major event in my trading career came with the discovery of the Fibonacci retracements and the notion of forward pricing. Once I taught myself Fibonacci, trading became a very personally and financially rewarding experience.

Here's something funny. I worked in recruiting for 14 years, and when I was ready for a change, I was looking for an occupation that had nothing to do with people, only machines. I'm a bit of a loner and I thought trading could employ my love of mathematics, pattern recognition, and mechanics in general. It would be a bonus if I could get a break from people. Though I think many might not admit this, I would also say that it seemed cool and exciting. I was quite sure that anyone who traded was a bazillionaire, and I was intent on amassing more.

The particularly relevant question might be: What has kept you trading? Getting into trading is easy; staying there is not. Trading is an enterprise for the toughest and the most resilient minds, as it is fraught with disappointment and dismay as we learn to trade. There is no occupation on earth that I know of that can make you feel like you are on the top of Mount Everest one day and at the shore of the Dead Sea the next like trading can. Absolute euphoria, bone-chilling fear, abject hopelessness and defeat—all are emotions that the real trader (the one doing it for a living) feels at some time in his or her career, and I was no different. But in spite of that, the more I learned about the markets, the more I grew to love every aspect of their movements. The more I learned the game, the easier it was for me to get up and try again the next day. Other than refusing to fail at anything, I would say that it is my love for the markets that has kept me in the game.

Let's just say that I spent a very long time in unconscious incompetence. I don't think I had stages, because getting it was a bit like a lightbulb coming on. It was like walking from the dark into the light—the proverbial penny drop. Maybe it was gradual, but I didn't notice it, and my accounts didn't show a gradual move, either. It was a V-shaped recovery.

The turning point came with the understanding of the need for risk management and scaling.

I struggled for a couple of years before becoming consistent in my picks and wins. I lost copious amounts of cash. It was very hard for me to learn trading, probably because I failed to stop and learn the lessons the market was trying to teach me. But I decided I was not going to lose the fight. That is the attitude I kept until what I believed about my ability became reality. Truly, I say all the time that the main reason I got it was because I was fortunate enough not to run out of money before the light came on. But it was the will to keep going in the face of defeat that gave me new life every day.

When I started trading, I could barely spell the word *stocks*. I knew *nothing* about the markets, so I started from ground zero and learned about economic reporting first. Little by little, I added to my knowledge base, studying technicals and relative strength indicators. When I discovered how mechanical the markets were at certain times, I was certain I had all the tools to perform. But that's sort of like saying that because I have fingers, I can sit down at the piano and play a concerto.

Everything I had trouble with was psychological. Psychological dysfunction caused execution catastrophes. I discovered I was constantly contrarian until I realized that working in the market means, as a technical momentum trader, you never side with the underdog. I traded scared, and that would make me enter late and leave late. I cut my winners and let my losers run. I would choose arbitrary entries and exits, and I traded impulsively. I took dreadful risks and never considered what I could lose, only what I could make. I began to think I would never make a good trader and I would defeat myself mentally before the start of the day. I traded angrily. I traded news late, stepped in front of earnings, and chased stocks as they ran, never knowing where I was going. To say I overcame an incredible number of struggles would be putting it mildly. I am pretty certain that there are very few mistakes I did *not* make in my journey to accomplishments.

PREPARATION IS ESSENTIAL

My market philosophy is simple. Know what economic news is coming and try to stay out of the way when it comes. Wait for the market conditions you want before you risk any capital. Let someone else step up and take those first risks. Just follow after and pick up your Benjamins along the way. Never try to catch a bottom or a top. Trade with the trend so the wind is at your back. Trading into a headwind is just asking for trouble.

Honestly, I am a simple girl. I don't pretend to know how the market works. I absolutely do not. What I do understand are the charts and what makes sense from a fundamental perspective. I do not trade instruments that I do not understand. What makes me a good trader now is a blend of common sense, strength in technical analysis, the willingness to admit what I do not know, and the gumption to go out and work until I learn it. I stay away from people with opinions alone. I am always on the hunt for empirical evidence. Opinions are noise for the most part. As Joe Friday would say, "Just the facts, ma'am."

Prepare for the day. Prepare so much that nothing is a total surprise. Expect the unexpected and plan every trade like it is going to go against you. This approach helps me manage risk well. I trade only a small basket of stocks, so I watch for them to move. When the market is trending, I'll look for the appropriate setups. If the market is flat or lacks momentum, I will sit on my hands. I wait for trades to come to me. I choose my exact entry price and my exact exit price. I stalk my trades. If there are lots of economic news releases, I try to stay out of the market. And I never try to predict how the market will react; I just wait for it to react and then I just follow. Or that's the plan I start with every day. Sometimes, the human element causes the occasional glitch.

TRADING FIBONACCI RETRACEMENTS

The setups I am looking for involve stocks setting up to cross a golden ratio. The golden ratio region represents the Fibonacci levels between 38.2 percent and 61.8 percent. If the trend is strong, I will watch the stock to test on a smaller time frame than I usually trade. It normally tests, rejects, and then breaches, and potentially comes back to test. At the retest I will enter in the direction of the trend up through or down through the golden ratio.

Why should it work?

Stocks generally behave the same way around important levels of support and resistance. Fibonacci retracements find these areas quite quickly and we can trade off of them easily.

APPLICATION OF MY SETUP

On August 17, 2010, I went short NFLX at the open via long puts and short stock. Why? A broken butterfly formation identified by the Fibonacci had indicated it was time to short. I had then waited for days for the stock to show weakness, but it never did (see Figure 38.1). Patience is the number one reason I make money every day. After three days of waiting to short this stock, August 17 began with an exhaustion gap, and this alone was a great clue for the short I had been waiting to execute. The moment it rolled over on the chart, I went short at 140.16. This trade was countertrend because the market really roared that day, but the formation was too solid to miss. I closed the short stock

FIGURE 38.1 Waiting Patiently for NFLX to Reverse, Daily Chart
Source: © StockCharts.com.

position the same day at 133, and rode the puts down to 126.50 on the following day for huge returns.

The market is rhythmic, and patterns break the way they are supposed to if they are well identified. Don't exit a trade until the trade tells you it is broken according to formation.

Screening is very simple for me. I trade the same high-beta, highly liquid stocks every day. I don't have to search for something moving, as something is nearly always moving in my basket; but if nothing is moving, I am content to wait.

Trade exits are customarily preassigned. I always know where I am getting out of my core holding. Sometimes if a stock breaches my levels and it seems to be in a continuation, I will move to one-quarter size and watch it attempt to test the next Fibonacci level. I spend a lot of time scaling in and out of positions as they hit and pull back from Fib levels.

RISK MANAGEMENT PHILOSOPHY

Have you had three bad trades in a row? Stop trading!

Something is broken and you need to find it and fix it. This is the only thing I will say to myself if I have a string of losses. I allow myself only three consecutive losses. Either my perception is skewed, or I am off my rhythm, or I am simply blind to very obvious facts because I am trading with preconceived notions. Whatever it is, I fix it and resume. If a fourth bad trade occurs, I stop trading for the day. A trader can never deliver his or her A game every day. It simply is impossible. It is a part of being human.

Here's another way I manage my risk. I ask myself three questions:

1. What is the range of possibilities for this trade?
2. What is the appropriate stop loss or the most I can lose here?
3. If the wheels come off the bus, how will I manage the impending crash?

Way too many novice traders don't ask these questions, so they run out of money before they learn to play the game. Poor risk management is the single cause of most trader failure. You could trade on a coin toss and still survive if your risk management rules are solid.

A lot of people have well-defined stops, and by and large if you are not trading in a precise system, then using something like an average true range or something you have determined as support is a fair thing to do. My philosophy is a bit controversial because all I use are mental stops. Now, does that come back to bite me in the you-know-where? Absolutely, but more times than not, it keeps me in the good trades and quickly out of the broken ones. I adopted the mental stops process when the market spent its days with extremely long wicks day after day many months back. I decided on smaller size so I could stomach the drawdown. I assumed, correctly for my style, that it would be a better remedy than having a stop that gets blown out all the time.

It is all about relative lows, so my mental stop involves looking at the landscape for clues on support in the near term. I tell folks all the time: Price does not stop arbitrarily—there is always a reason, and that reason is usually support and resistance nearby, or far away.

Because my trading mechanisms are precise, I do not hedge as a rule. If I feel there is going to be trouble, I simply get out. If I am wrong, I'll get back in. My rule is the well-worn one: When in doubt, stay out. You don't have to play every day.

I rarely use more than 4 percent of my operating day-trading capital on any one position. If I find myself more than 40 percent invested in the market during the day, I will not trade anymore. I am extremely conservative with my money, with rarely more than 20 percent invested in any positions overnight. Call it skittish, but after 2007–2009, I'll call myself once bitten, twice shy. Does this cause me to miss moves sometimes? Yes, but for me, there are so many setups and so many trades available with my system that it is never about missing the big one. It is all about trading with probability on my side, taking a little bit every day, being consistently positive, not taking too many unnecessary risks, and living to trade another day.

I do not trade on margin, ever. This I can say I have never done (probably the only mistake I have never made).

CHAPTER 39

Always Happy, Never Satisfied

Joshua Brown, @reformedbroker

The investment management business is ruthless and almost always about returns, but Josh shows that you can be a successful student of the markets and still care about your clients. Doing the right thing matters and Josh always does the right thing. He brings insights, links, missives, and laughs to our streams, and the StockTwits community loves and respects him for that. He's also a loyal friend and fantastic writer who calls me the "Blog Father," so I had to include him in this book.

MAKE ALL YOUR MISTAKES EARLY IN YOUR CAREER

I'm a fee-based financial adviser in New York City. I work with high-net-worth individuals, corporations, institutions, and charitable foundations. My job is to truly understand clients' objectives and risk tolerance, which enables me to allocate their investable assets with the most efficient risk/reward balance possible. Contrary to what some professors tell their students, trading and investing are as much art as they are science, and experience counts a great deal.

I began my career as a stockbroker at the end of the 1990s when everything was going up, everyone was trading, and brokers were rock stars. As a rookie, I witnessed the most parabolic stock boom in history as the tech-heavy NASDAQ took out 5,000 and captivated the world. I then had a front-row seat for the denouement as all the gains were given back, margin wiped out the reckless, and the dreams of the buy-and-holders were shattered. My entire career thus far has been spent in the shadow of those wild days, but the harsh lessons of loss and risk during my formative years have been invaluable. I can recognize a bubble but still be smart enough to be in it for the fun part. I can also recognize the need for humility and the requisite stops and hedges that go along with that.

I'm down to run with the bulls or the bears, but not if I don't know where the exits are.

I arrived at the majority of my market knowledge the hard way—I've made every mistake in the book and some that don't even appear in the book just yet. The legendary hedge fund pioneer Michael Steinhardt counsels that we should make all of our mistakes early in our careers. After more than a decade fighting it out on The Street, during a cyclical bear market no less, I finally feel as though my biggest errors are behind me. Probably.

What is left of me now that the rough edges and imperfections have been chipped away? Not exactly Michelangelo's *David*, but I can certainly say that I've acquired a sturdy foundation.

There are rules to this game, but the catch is that the rules for every investor are different. Investors can't develop their own set of rules until they know victory and defeat firsthand. They must learn for themselves through trial and error, through all different market environments. These rules are merely the principles that one chooses to follow, accepting the fact that they will not always limit risk and may often force one to miss out on profitable opportunities. I have to let enticing trades go all the time because the wounds from when I've dropped my guard and abandoned my discipline are still so raw.

And in the absence of so many mistakes, the game becomes easier—and more lucrative.

THINK MACRO, TRADE MICRO

My approach as an investor is to isolate long-term themes that have the potential to ride out shorter-term volatility. I look for megatrends and my job is to drill down and find the best stocks, bonds, or funds that will allow me to express the trade.

I also try to base my allocations on the macro picture, something I barely cared about until 2008. The first judgment for anyone in stocks right now has to be whether equities as an asset class are in favor. My next judgment revolves around where the strength is likely to be over the intermediate term. Which sectors are likely to outperform and, within those sectors, which industries? Finally, I'll begin looking at the stocks within that sector or the exchange-traded funds (ETFs) and mutual funds that will enable me to get the type of exposure I want.

To recap: the asset class, then the sector, then the industry, then the stock. You don't buy the best house on the worst block in real estate; you buy the hovel in Beverly Hills. The stock market is the same—the majority of your performance or risk will come from the market itself and then the neighborhood in which your stock resides.

As of this writing, bottom-up stock picking has become an exercise in futility, with some of the greatest fundamental stock pickers of all time retiring and complaining in the media about the hypercorrelation of the moment. This will pass at some point, but I play the hand I'm dealt, not the hand I used to be dealt or I wish I would be dealt.

THINKING A FEW MOVES AHEAD

My favorite setups vary depending on what the market is offering me at any given juncture. I try to keep up with what's working, but rather than chasing the current trends I start thinking about what may work next. There is an element of chess involved here. I'm really good at seeing the next move or two ahead and determining the reactive events that will result from different market developments. This is ironic, as I'm a terrible chess player.

THE GOLD/SILVER RATIO

An example of this anticipatory style would be my very early affinity for the silver stocks (see Figure 39.1). Regular readers know that I'm not one of these end-of-days guys with the hoard of gold coins and the fallout shelter in the woods somewhere. But the rally in gold had been going on for eight years before anyone really started talking about it, so the table was set to get involved.

The layup trade was to figure out what else would work in the mid to late stages of a gold rally, and silver fit the bill perfectly. There is a historic gold-to-silver price ratio that, while not consistent, allowed for something called the slingshot effect. The basic premise

FIGURE 39.1 The Gold/Silver Ratio, 20-Year Chart
Source: © StockCharts.com.

was that gold would move first, but ultimately silver would snap forward to catch up and ultimately overshoot the gains in gold. This is precisely what has taken place over the past few years. Gold has done well since late 2008, but silver has done incredibly well. I was talking about stocks like the miner Silver Wheaton (SLW) as an even more aggressive way to play the gold-silver slingshot back in early 2009. We caught an easy triple simply by determining the reaction to a gold rally and seeing a few moves ahead.

WORDS OF WISDOM

Everyone who has found any kind of lasting success on Wall Street has the same thing in common—a lack of complacency. This is different than plain old ambition. We're talking about the ability to make yourself uncomfortable and unsatisfied, regardless of past and even current levels of achievement.

This way of thinking is hard to understand for a lot of people, but on The Street the need to move up is so deeply ingrained in us that to think otherwise is almost heresy.

CHAPTER 40

One Step Ahead of the Herd

John Benedict, @*geckojb*

John is a real professional, which is obvious from everything he does. His attention to detail and his disciplined investing approach make him an invaluable asset for the StockTwits community.

A FINANCIAL ADVISER FOR OVER 12 YEARS

My career started off in the late 1990s at a major brokerage house. From there I moved on to a large broker-dealer that specialized in financial planning. I started like many others in the industry by being an asset gatherer and letting the investment departments at the broker-dealers I represented help me manage the client assets.

It was the same mantra everywhere. You cannot control the markets, so just worry about bringing in assets and we will tell you how to manage the money. The strategy was simply to sell product and keep clients invested no matter what. You are trained from day one that markets cannot be timed and that over 90 percent of your returns are derived from asset allocation.

The turning point of my career came in the 2000–2003 bear market when my clients lost 30 percent or more of their life savings. This affected me emotionally. Watching retirees and those close to retirement lose money weighed on me each time I reviewed their monthly statements. Holding clients' hands while uttering "Hold on for the long term" did not seem like a viable strategy. The investment departments were hard at work churning out brochures and other sales material reminding everyone that markets have always gone up. Other material would discuss how the stock markets had survived other major events like world wars, oil embargoes, and crashes and always resumed their upward trends. This was the point I started to question the system.

There seemed to be no price at which these investment departments would recommend to sell. I thought there must be a better way. I had a deep desire to seek the truth by researching other methods to help clients invest money. My journey led me to a few in my profession who were doing something called technical analysis. From 2003 to 2005 I slowly absorbed various methods. Technical analysis gave me the feeling of being more in control than the "buy and hope" method did.

JOINING NAAIM

In 2007 I joined the National Association of Active Investment Managers (NAAIM). Being surrounded with other like-minded financial professionals propelled me into designing our firm's own proprietary indicators. In 2007 I started work on our Risk Controlled Investment (RCI) index. The RCI index is a tool that helps me to determine the risk/reward profile on a macro level. From there I choose our positions using a relative strength methodology. I am a trend follower at heart.

By late 2007, our RCI index and other research started to indicate that the stock markets were exhibiting exhaustion. We had a model now, but my plan of attack was still evolving. Would I sell everything right away, reduce by half, or short stocks? From late 2007 on we were reducing stock allocations down from the 80 percent level to around 30 percent by September 2008. My original plan was to reduce stock allocations by half once our model gave a sell signal. In late September 2008, prior to the Troubled Asset Relief Program (TARP) vote, I started to sense that we could be on the cusp of a major dislocation simply because no one was looking for it. I decided that I needed to do whatever it took to help protect my clients' assets and thus went to 100 percent cash by October 1, 2008.

WHY TECHNICAL ANALYSIS WORKS

My general philosophy in managing money is to have a risk management strategy in everything I do. The systems and models that I have built look at capturing intermediate-term trends. However, my persona and gut instincts have tendencies that can be more contrarian and mean-reversion focused. Intersecting the two becomes the challenge.

Everyone has a buy discipline and can tell you what they like, but almost nobody will tell you when or what they will sell. Having a risk management approach means being able to plan for the unexpected outcome. We all expect our trades to work, but what will you do when they don't? Having a disciplined approach to investing, and incorporating risk management, allows me to not be afraid of failure.

I believe that technical analysis works because investors are driven by emotion. Human emotion has not changed since our prehistoric days, and is still driven by the basic fear-greed and flight-fright responses. I believe these emotions can be captured in stock charts and then viewed using patterns, cycles, and indicators, and charting of price.

Because investor behavior tends to repeat itself, I believe that one can recognize these behaviors and possibly even attempt to predict how price may be affected. There are several ways this can be done.

We run several different types of portfolios in our firm. These include a growth and income stock portfolio, a momentum stock portfolio, an alternative model, and a mutual fund/exchange-traded fund (ETF) model. These strategies are all different but the way we think about managing the risk is the same.

Since no one strategy can work all the time, I am a believer in diversifying among strategies. On one end of the spectrum you have trend-following systems. These are the most popular and most widely used. On the other end you have mean-reversion systems. Each of these two systems can then be classified into short-, intermediate-, and long-term time frames. For further diversification you may also include other strategies such as seasonality, event driven, and cycles. Thus far my early work has focused on the greed and herding instincts of investors that produce trends based on relative strength or momentum that last several weeks to months.

BEATING THE HERD

One of my favorite setups involves finding sectors, or stocks within a sector, prior to their next intermediate-term advance and before others find them. If I can get in prior to when the herding instinct kicks in, I can drive big gains early on and be in a better position to exit with those gains once the trend is exhausted. This is a pattern that may take longer to develop as it often occurs right before the trend starts. I have very specific ingredients that I follow for this setup.

The primary ingredients for finding an intermediate-term winner prior to others are:

- *Thesis.* What is your thesis for wanting to invest in this stock or sector? You don't necessarily need a thesis for entry but it can be helpful.
- *The weekly chart.* First view the selected sector or stock on a five-year weekly time frame. Look for horizontal support and resistance on the chart. A chart that is pulling back to five-year horizontal support is a definite candidate for more study. I have found these patterns the past two years to often lead to big winners. These horizontal areas of support and resistance often can be places where buyers and sellers have met in the past. It's where emotion meets price.
- *The daily chart.* Once support has been found on the weekly chart, the next step is to review the daily chart. Here I am looking at two things. First I am drawing trend lines. Is the stock at or near a trend line on the daily chart? Next I am looking for chart patterns such as ascending wedges, cup and handles, and so on. A chart pattern does not need to exist for an entry; it only helps to offer me more evidence.

Once I have determined that the sector is a viable candidate based on the weekly and daily charts along with any price pattern, I then look at the 50-day moving average.

Is the stock above or below the 50-day moving average? I am looking for stocks that have just risen above the 50-day moving average. Next, is the 50-day moving average trending up or down? I will need to see the 50-day moving average flat or rising.

The last thing I do is look at the stock's Relative Strength Index (RSI) and moving average convergence/divergence (MACD). I will never make a decision based on these, but they can aid in identifying low-risk entry points. I look for two things here. The first is a daily RSI rising above 30 or exhibiting positive divergence. Either is fine but oftentimes when trying to find a sector that is poised for an intermediate-term advance it's an RSI rising from a low to above 30 that is the buy signal. I will also look for daily MACD to be rising above the zero line and giving a buy signal where the fast line is rising above the slow line.

MY DBC TRADE

In early September 2010, whispers of a potential quantitative easing (QE II) were making the rounds in the blogosphere. No word had reached the mainstream press yet. I thought that if QE II would happen, this would drive the dollar lower while driving up commodities. Commodities could be a big winner.

I first looked at UUP, a proxy for the U. S. dollar, and the chart pattern confirmed that the potential for a large swing to the downside could happen. Next I started to flip through various commodity charts using a five-year weekly time frame. This allows me to gain a longer-term perspective.

Let's focus on DBC (see Figures 40.1 and 40.2). DBC had been a laggard compared to other sectors the previous year but possessed what appeared to be a potential bottoming pattern (May to July 2010). This is a very strong confirming pattern to my thesis and my risk management approach. Precious metals had been in a very strong uptrend but had recently pulled back to trend line support and offered a nice low-risk entry point.

As for the secondary ingredients, DBC had been vacillating above and below a flat to sideways 50-day moving average for the past two years. Each time DBC had made it above the 50-day moving average it had run into overhead horizontal resistance causing it to fall back below the 50-day moving average.

RSI weekly gave a buy signal on June 1, 2010. This prompted me to now place an alert for the next time it went above the 50-day moving average. RSI daily was forming a positive divergence from the bottom in late May until DBC finally broke above the 50-day moving average. This was a very positive development. MACD was also building a positive divergence along the same time frame.

Last, let's look at position size. Once it has been determined to buy a position, I typically use a very simple dynamic position size calculator. The calculator answers the question: *How many shares of a stock should I buy if I know what I am willing*

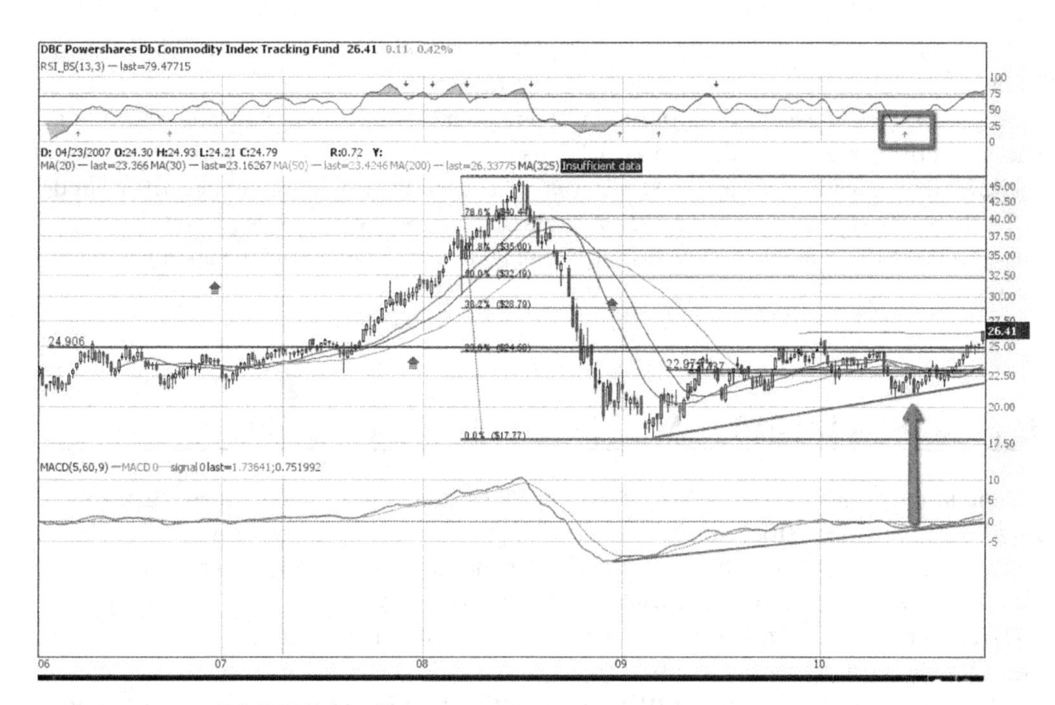

FIGURE 40.1 DBC Weekly Chart
Source: © TD Ameritrade, Inc. Used with permission. For illustrative purposes only.

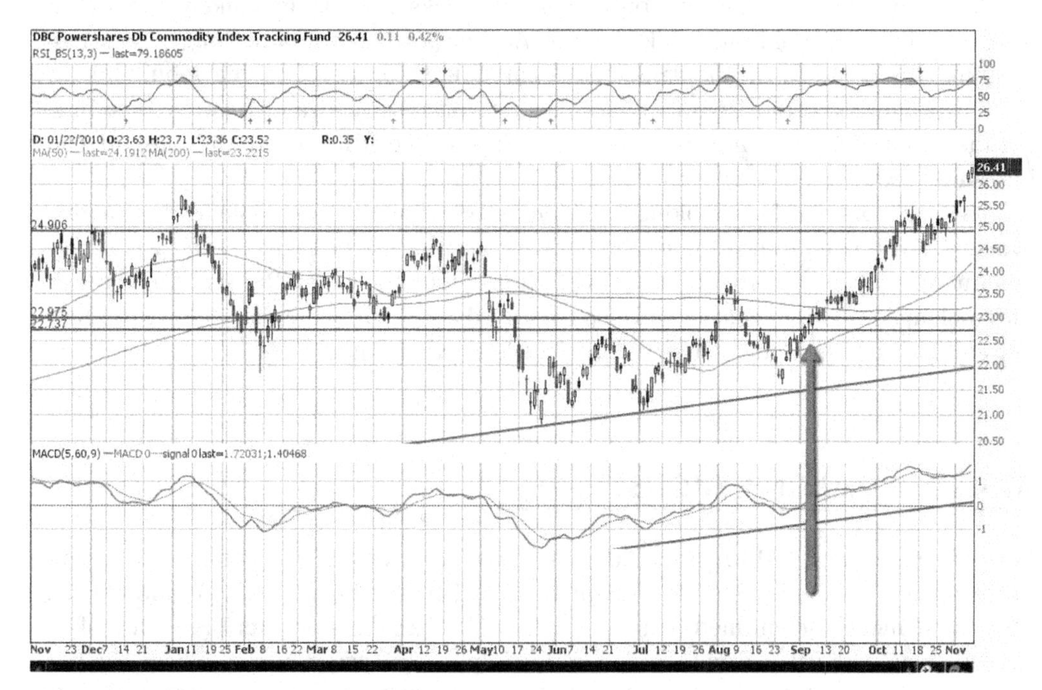

FIGURE 40.2 DBC Daily Chart
Source: © TD Ameritrade, Inc. Used with permission. For illustrative purposes only.

to lose and the price change from X to Y? Most position sizes are in the 3 percent to 5 percent area.

Based on my thesis of a more precipitous dollar decline along with the bottoming pattern in the stock, RSI daily and MACD positive divergences, and now price above a rising 50-day moving average, the stock was purchased in early September 2010 around $23 a share. My stop was placed at $21. A trade down to $21 would have placed the stock in a new downtrend making a lower low, bringing it back down below the 50-day moving average.

BUYING ON A LARGER THAN NORMAL PULLBACK

Buying momentum stocks can sometimes be rewarding and at other times frustrating. Buying a momentum stock at the wrong moment can lead to large drawdowns. Most will not have the patience to sit through the sometimes large temporary dislocations momentum stocks can bring. I avoid this situation by buying a current or former IBD 100 stock on a larger than normal pullback using some but not all of the ingredients I described in my first favorite setup.

Look for a current or former IBD 100 stock that is still displaying high earnings per share (EPS) and has undergone a large pullback.

A weekly chart is not needed for momentum stocks. It is highly unlikely that a solid momentum stock would pull back that far. At that point it would no longer be a momentum type of stock. On the daily chart I am looking for a stock to have built a base at or near an area of horizontal support. A more aggressive strategy can involve buying the stock at intermediate-term trend line resistance if no horizontal support can be found.

Other factors that I am looking for: Is the stock above or below the 50-day moving average? I will need to see the 50-day moving average flat or rising. Last, check your confirming early indicators, RSI and MACD. It is helpful to see the RSI rising along with the stock making higher highs. I will also look for daily MACD to be rising above the zero line and giving a buy signal where the fast line is above the slow line.

ATHEROS COMMUNICATIONS

Former highflier and IBD 100 stock Atheros Communications (ATHR) was hit 40 percent in the span of five months (May to September 2010) (see Figure 43.3). A quick check of its fundamentals confirmed that ATHR was still a growth story. Its EPS still looked strong, along with sales growth. I also noticed that ATHR was building a base right at a horizontal support and a prior breakout from July 2009. The 50-day moving average that was declining with the stock finally reversed and started to flatten in October 2010.

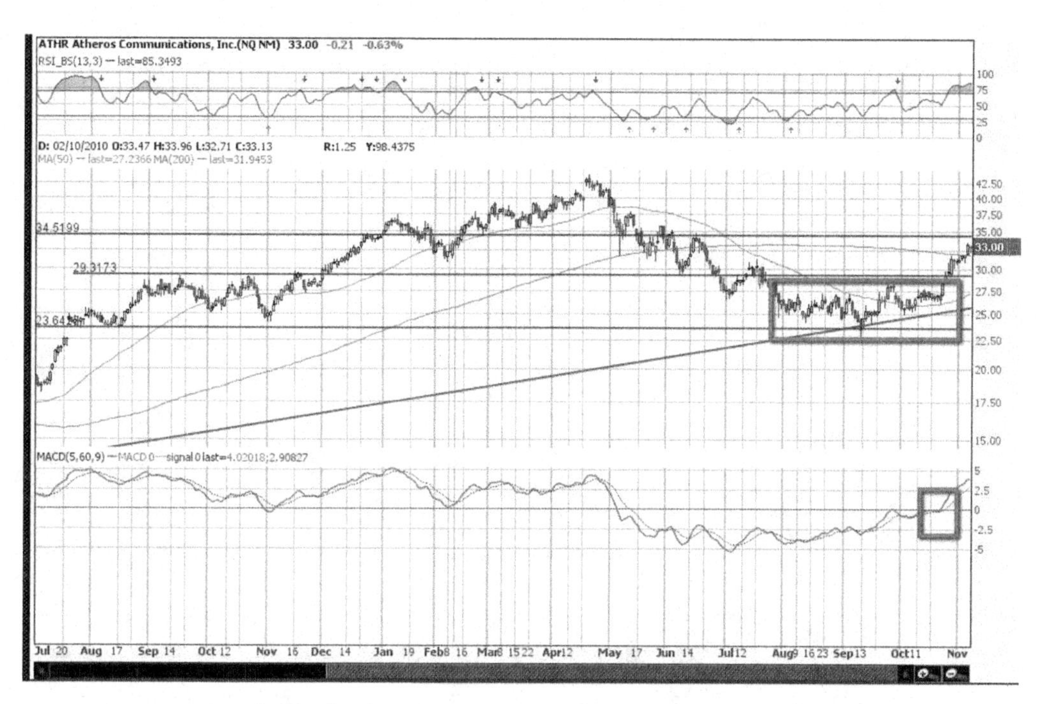

FIGURE 40.3 Breaking above a Rising 50-Day Moving Average, ATHR Daily Chart
Source: © TD Ameritrade, Inc. Used with permission. For illustrative purposes only.

MACD started to turn up and head above the zero line. The same month, the stock broke above its rising 50-day moving average and successfully tested it. In my book, this is considered a buy signal.

HAVE A PLAN AND TRADE YOUR PLAN

The most successful traders and investors I know are the ones who have the discipline to stick to their plans. Also, there is no substitute for just putting in the time. Recent research suggests that it takes up to 10 years to master something. Here is advice for anyone looking to start investing.

- Learn from others.
- Failure will happen often, especially early on. Be prepared for it.
- Don't fear failure; embrace it.
- Do what works for you. Over the course of time you may try to copy and emulate other traders, but you will learn you won't have the same success.

CHAPTER 41

Change Is the Only Constant

Steve Gomez and Andy Lindloff, @*todaytrader*

Steve Gomez is a great guy and a friend living his version of the American dream. He lives in California, trades, and has a motorcycle. Steve was an early adopter of StockTwits. He is a generous trader, sharing ideas and trades with a large following.

Remember, it [the market] is designed to fool most of the people most of the time.

—Jesse Livermore

IT'S A METHOD, NOT A SYSTEM

This is the answer people usually get when they ask us about our trading style. Both my business partner Andy and I have been trading equities since 1998. In fact, we met on a retail trading floor once known as Cornerstone Securities. Together, we cut our teeth in a group trading environmental stocks back in the days of the tech bubble. The allure of trading with direct access to the markets without having to move to the big city was a calling that neither of us could pass up.

Since we were both new to the game of direct access trading, we were learning to trade a popular style of buying pullbacks and adding to those positions as they went through new highs. For all we knew, this was how you made money trading in 1999. Some of the veteran traders had been doing this in their accounts since 1995. They literally became programmed to trade this way for big profits, for a long time. It was the only way they knew.

All that changed in March 2000. Abby Joseph Cohen at Goldman Sachs was making a major call to lighten up on equities. This was not what a nervous and overbought market needed to hear. From that point on, it was a new game and those that adapted would go on and find a new way, a way to adapt to change.

Some big traders from other offices around the country used to love to come to San Diego to vacation in the afternoon and trade the early hours of the Pacific time zone. During this time we came to study their methods and quietly observed the tremendous success they had leading up to the turn of the millennium. Buying pullbacks and then buying more at highs just kept on working for them. But when the market turned, it seemed some of these guys had a hard time adjusting. Andy and I were still relatively new to trading, so we had not yet formed dogmatic habits or opinions. As it turned out, the greatest lesson that some of those traders gave us was to accept the fact that no matter what we had learned in the past, nothing lasts forever.

Fast-forward a few years and we were surprised to learn that a few of those traders who had run up really nice accounts had given back 95 percent of that money by fighting the changing markets. Many went on to join proprietary trading firms and began the process of rebuilding their trading methods. The major lesson for us at the time was to recognize that change does not come easily, even for some of the great traders we had once held in high regard.

One of the best ways to prepare for market changes is to have a sound money management rule. This was something that we both fortunately developed a respect for early on. Having seen people blow up perfectly good trading accounts in a short period of time just seemed insane. There had to be a simple way to control incremental losses to your capital as an active trader. The 20 Percent Rule was a simple rule that we came up with during the corrective phase of the markets after March 2000.

This simple money management rule acts as a circuit breaker for your active trading capital. Let's face it; every active trader has a bad streak from time to time. The good traders often find a way to correct what is wrong or not working. During that time is when traders can do the most damage to their accounts if not checked. Having a rule that says, "I will not lose more than a certain dollar amount per day" is a wise rule. Pitching coaches take pitchers out of the game when they do not have their normal stuff working. A good trader needs to know to pull himself or herself out of the game, as there is no coach to do it for you.

What is a good level of pain to use when setting a daily downside stop-loss level to your trading account? That is certainly a subjective question, as everyone has a different level of pain tolerance. If you have anything more than a 2 percent daily risk to your trading capital, I would evaluate how that is working for you. Some people can mentally take more of an intraday drawdown than others. If you are the type who is not so cool under pressure and tend to make irrational decisions in this state of mind, 2 percent might even be too high. If you are one who may not trust yourself enough to implement this rule, call your broker; most of them are happy to lock you out on their end. This way, you never have to fight the urge. The system locks you out until the next day.

Many traders just focus on managing the down days and forget about the painful prospect of giving back the good days. Protecting your upside days with a good money management rule is just as important. The 20 Percent Rule, as we call it, reminds us to not give back more than 20 percent of gains on the days of solid performance. Ideally, this profit target number for traders should be at least two times greater than the daily stop-loss number for bad days. Maybe three times greater could be a better risk/reward profile for more aggressive traders to follow. The idea is to manage the downside while still giving you the opportunity for further upside. On the days you are really seeing and participating in the moves, you don't want to slow down. You don't want to say, "I will stop trading today if I can just make a certain dollar amount; then I will quit." Obviously you are trading well, so why not make hay while the sun is shining? The next bad day will be back soon. But if you manage the bad days and let the good days run, things start to add up better at the end of the month.

ABILITY TO ADAPT TO CHANGE

Early in 2009 we noticed that there was a major change in the market dynamics. Stocks begin to trade more erratically, and intraday 5-minute charts started to become less predictable. We knew there was something strange going on besides the current volatility in the marketplace. We had heard that computerized trading was infiltrating the markets on a micro level but weren't aware of its magnitude. Stocks were still getting from point A to point B on the daily charts, but the intraday action was morphing into something different. What used to be a graceful waltz of price action was turning into a mosh pit. After talking with other experienced and successful traders who were also having trouble banging out profits, we knew this was a major change and would be a tough hurdle to overcome. I noticed that my swing trading was outperforming my day trading for the first time in 10 years. I continued to day trade full-time, but my profits were not what I had been accustomed to.

By late 2009 high-frequency trading (HFT) was in full effect as more participants entered the arena. Unfortunately, it is here to stay and we have adapted by removing ourselves from the micro-level playground it has come to dominate. Playing smaller sizes, scaling in and out of positions, and using longer-term charts (10-minute and daily) have helped in this endeavor. But our biggest adaptation was our concentrated efforts to focus more on daily setups and swing trading. We believe it is more beneficial for the beginning or average trader without professional help to concentrate his or her efforts on short-term swing trading.

Somebody once said, "The policy of being too cautious is the greatest risk of all." We often tell our subscribers about how in nature, penguins will tend to stand and watch the one in front as it jumps into the water and swims to another location. They do this to try to make sure it is safe before they will follow and dive in. Unfortunately, they are usually the ones that are most likely to be attacked by a predator. This is the herd mentality a trader needs to avoid to be successful. As humans, we are wired to want to follow the herd, and that instinct is hard to overcome.

Now more than ever, it seems the market enjoys shaking the trees, trying to catch people leaning around support and resistance levels. Buying breakouts is old school and may have worked in the good old days but not in a range-bound market. I believe it is crucial to take a calculated risk when swing trading. This may mean buying stocks when the charts and price action are telling you to sell. Successful trading is all about the entry. I will often see a stock flirting with a multimonth high and set an alert well below looking for a four- or five-day pullback (you would be surprised at the number of them that go off).

The logic is that many traders will be entering the trade near highs or chasing highs looking for a breakout. If it fails (and in most cases it does), the stock will pull back as frustrated longs cough up their shares until the selling is exhausted and the stock starts to stabilize. This represents a good risk/reward opportunity. Once my alert goes off I will stalk the stock, closely watching price action, support and resistance areas, and volume. When I feel the selling is abating I will enter a one-half position with a tight stop in case I am too early. If I am right and the stocks bases and moves higher, I start to look for a place to add to my position. This is the key to maximizing profits. You often hear about adding to winners. and this is the way we like to do it at TodayTrader.

LOOKING FOR RELATIVE STRENGTH

A solid setup that we like to look for is a stock showing relative strength in a bearish tape or relative weakness in a bullish tape for short setups. For simplicity we will use the relative strength scenario. If a stock is holding up well (going sideways) or creeping higher in a market that is selling off, it is a great candidate for a strong upward move once the market gets a bounce. Not only are buyers intent on buying the stock at this level, but you will also have lots of traders on the wrong side shorting and looking for a break as the market continues its slide lower. We use our stock watch list (about 200 stocks) and nightly scans to find these setups. The risk is easy to define, because in most cases buyers have been supporting and accumulating a stock at their price and the overall market has been selling off. If we are wrong, we will be stopped out shortly below the lows of the range minus a little wiggle room. If we are right, then the short sellers are caught leaning and competing with fresh buyers to cover their losing positions.

A great example of this is a trade we made for our subscribers in RAX (see Figure 41.1).

On August 24, 2010, while going through our stock watch list, we noticed that RAX was holding up really well, basing and refusing to go to monthly lows even though the SPDR S&P 500 ETF (SPY) had gone from 110 to 105 and was battling from going to yearly lows. We were really salivating on this one because RAX had about a 30 percent short interest at the time. On August 25 we noticed some volume (our number one indicator) coming into it and took a one-half position at 18.70 with a stop at 17.95. It had a nice little move and when overall market bounced on September 1 we felt that we had a good

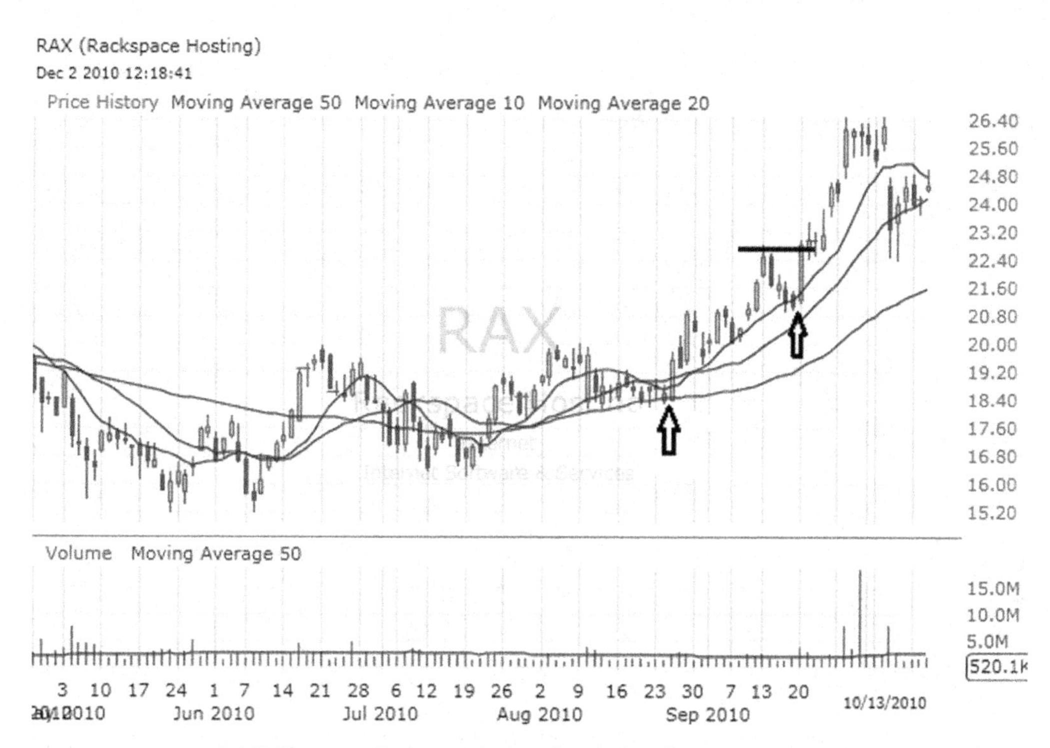

FIGURE 41.1 RAX Showing Relative Strength, Daily Chart
Chart courtesy of FreeStockCharts.com. © FreeStockCharts.com.

trade and started to look to add to it. We got that opportunity on September 17 when it had had four days of pullback and we added another half on the daily 10-period moving average at 21.40. The next day it had a big move higher and we sold half the following day (September 21) at 22.85 to lock in some gains. A couple of days later it started what was to be a parabolic move for four days, and we sold the second half of our position, closing it out at 25.89 after good news and an upgrade.

When something has the feel of going parabolic, it usually doesn't last long before the musical chairs game is on. Hindsight, of course, is always 20/20, but it's also nice to sell when you can, not when you have to. Having to sell a great winner when everyone else is rushing to the exits at the same time is never fun. Eventually, the cloud computing stocks had their day of panic-driven profit taking on October 6, 2010, and it was nice to be already out and on to the next trade.

CHAPTER 42

The Kirk Report

Charles E. Kirk, @thekirkreport

I love this chapter, and I knew I would. I have been following Charles's blog for years. He believes as I do that there is a method to the madness of the markets and mentoring is very important. If you are taking your first steps in trading and investing, make "The Kirk Report" a daily read and dig into his archives.

When all the criteria are in balance, do the thing you least want to do. You have to decide early on whether you're playing for the fun or for the success. Whether you measure it in money or in some other way, to win at trading you have to be playing for the success.

—William Eckhardt

MY JOURNEY

I live in a small college town named Cedar City in southern Utah. The markets have been my passion for almost 20 years.

My journey in the markets began shortly after graduating from college, getting married, and going to work as a private investigator for a law firm. My wife and I were starting our lives together, and I decided to learn how to invest with the money that we were trying to save for our future. Neither of us had any real experience with investing or the markets, so we had a lot to learn!

After asking questions and seeking out advice from others concerning investing, including paying for advice from two financial advisers, we soon realized that most people didn't seem to know much about investing, either. Like many people back then, we started by investing our hard-earned money in several actively managed mutual funds, and it didn't take long to recognize the stupidity of doing so. Once we both discovered that most mutual funds and money managers underperform a low-cost S&P 500 index fund most of the time, we thought we could at least do better than that—or at least give it our best shot.

While working as a private investigator, I spent the next three years learning everything I could get my hands on about investing and the market. At first it was just a hobby, but the more I learned, the more I wanted to learn even more. During this period, I read over 500 books on investing and trading. I also opened up a brokerage account with a $2000 starting balance with money we put aside for a rainy day.

What was a very part-time hobby back then soon turned into a full-time passion when I decided to go to law school in 1996. It was at that same time I became very active in the markets. The era of low-cost online trading was just starting and my interest in the markets continued to grow. In fact, while in law school I was both a full-time student and a full-time trader, often skipping classes or using the law library's computers equipped with broadband Internet to trade stocks.

Although I had intended to pursue a career in law, when my father passed away a month after my graduation from law school I decided to take the road less traveled and become a full-time trader. My father, who had been a successful businessman in his own right, had told me the last time we saw each other to follow my passion and do what I love. It was clear to me at that pivotal moment what I needed to do, which was to pursue my passion in trading.

Looking back, it was not as gutsy a decision as you might believe. At the time I was already making more money trading than I would be working as a first-year law firm associate fresh out of law school. So in the summer of 1999 I asked my wife, who worked as a high school teacher, to "give me two years to prove that I can make it out on my own." My promise to her was this: "If I can't prove to you that I can make a better living for both of us *and* be a happier person in two years than working as a lawyer, I will then put our money in index funds, take the bar, and practice law." Fortunately, I never looked back, nor did I have to fall back on plan B!

Like most, the learning curve for me had its fair share of ups and downs. In fact, to this day I do not consider myself an expert of the markets, but rather I like to think of myself as a perpetual student. I'm always learning new things and getting better. A successful year for me beyond making enough money to support myself and my family is one in which I can honestly say that I've learned how to be a better trader and have helped others do the same.

Over the years, many have asked whether I was successful from the start. The answer is both "yes" and "no." At the time, with the market in bull market mode (late 1990s), it was relatively easy to make money in the markets. They say a bull market makes everyone look like a genius, and that was certainly true in my case. Even though I lacked much in skill and experience, the market allowed me to profit from my own folly. It wasn't until the years that followed that the challenge of trading consistently well became fully appreciated and respected. While I've been fortunate never to experience a down year or even one in which I haven't beaten the S&P significantly, some years have certainly been better than others.

It goes without saying that all of us have our own special skills and experiences that help us become good traders. Specifically, I have four major assets in my favor that have made a world of difference: a very strong work ethic combined with a large amount of tenacity and humility; a keen research ability developed in both college/law school and working as a private investigator; the ability to compile data and discover interesting patterns using computers; and most important, the patience and support of my family.

MARKET PHILOSOPHY AND APPROACH

My goal as a trader is to find and profit from what I call low-risk, high-reward opportunities. In essence, I'm always on the hunt for situations that have what I determine is minimal downside risk with overwhelming upside potential.

To find and trade those opportunities, my first step is to use a number of proprietary stock screens to identify potential trades. Originally, these screens were based on the strategies of legendary investors like Benjamin Graham and Warren Buffett, but they have since been modified to fit my own time frames and risk tolerance. In addition, through testing, tweaking, and use for many years, these screens have been developed to locate and target stocks and exchange-traded funds (ETFs) that have both the fundamentals and the technicals that have often produced well-above-average returns.

I currently have at my disposal around two dozen different types of screens that I track very closely and monitor daily. The reason I use so many screens is that, just like some investment strategies, some screens outperform while others underperform in different types economic and market environments. For the past decade, I've dedicated a tremendous amount of time and effort to figuring out which screens to use when and, more important, why those screens work best in certain situations. While my research on this continues, I've now reached the point where I have a good idea of what works most but certainly not all of the time. In addition, this also changes as the market evolves and the level of sophistication grows with programmed trading. In other words, what works now offers no guarantee that it will continue to work the same way in the future. The challenge we all face is that the markets are always evolving and undergoing rapid change. Those traders who can adapt their methods and focus as the environment changes are those who truly prosper over the long term.

Once I review my screens and the stocks that show up within them, I then build narrow target watch lists based on that input. I then use technical chart pattern analysis to determine when a stock offers the most advantageous entry point, which again offers the least risk with the most upside potential, and set price alerts accordingly. Price alerts set in advance often help me spot situations within my watch lists.

Ideally, when I enter a new position, I enter that stock at the point where it should prove I'm correct being long (or short) soon after my initial purchase. If the trade proves valid and becomes profitable as expected, I then scale aggressively into the position to its target allocation. Likewise, if the trade proves invalid and wrong (i.e., it moves against me), I quickly sell and take my loss. Overall, I am right more than wrong, but not by much, which is why proper risk management is so very important.

Beyond trading individual stocks in this manner—which, as you can imagine, requires a tremendous amount of patience because it isn't too often that stocks on my watch list will provide an ideal setup—in recent years to increase my returns and lower my overall risk I have been trading ETFs aggressively using technical patterns and trend analysis. This has enabled me to have most of my capital in play at all times while allowing me to stay patient looking for and scouting individual trades within stocks on my watch list, which in turn has significantly improved my overall performance.

LESSONS LEARNED FROM MENTORING

They say you learn the most when you teach others, and in my experience that has been so very true. "The Kirk Report" has been a wonderful opportunity not only to share my personal journey with others but also to learn and improve upon what I do every day as a trader. In recent years, I also began a special mentorship program that has taken my journey to a whole new and exciting level.

Here are some key lessons I've learned from mentoring and from sharing my journey through "The Kirk Report":

- People learn in much different ways, but the key toward greater success and a much faster learning curve is to have a well-documented learning plan in place and then to follow that plan religiously. As my father often said, "Plan your work and work your plan." This is something I work on closely with everyone who joins my mentorship group. With any active learning plan, it is also paramount to build in some level of accountability so that others can help you stay on track to make real progress. It has been proven by many research studies that we achieve goals more often when others hold us accountable for our actions.
- Most people think they are better traders than they actually are. This can be proven by accurate record keeping and a close evaluation of performance for multiple time periods. This is why having a trading journal is so important even though most traders do not keep one. The first step when I mentor someone is to review what they've done and figure out where they are currently. Most traders, even those who are very successful, have little insight into what they're doing right and wrong, and (even more important) why. Understanding yourself and your true strengths and weaknesses and also developing a strategy that take advantages of both is more important than most realize.
- Those who have performed the best are those who have learned methods to separate their opinions and beliefs from their trading decisions. In other words, they have improved because they no longer seek to trade their opinions (or opinions

of those whom they agree with in principle), but rather to exploit opportunities they see, especially when they conflict with their internal viewpoints. Most of the mistakes I see are made by those who try to use the markets as a means to prove how smart they are and end up figuring out sooner or later the exact opposite in painful and frustrating ways.

- To trade consistently well, you must go against every natural instinct you have. For example, many traders will tell you, "No one goes broke taking profits," but in reality that's exactly how traders go broke, as they cut winners far too short and keep losers way too long. Understanding and having strong working knowledge of both human nature and emotion combined with your own natural tendencies (both strengths and weaknesses) must not be underestimated.
- Many traders talk about the importance of finding "the hard trade" and doing things that "feel wrong" to prosper. There's a tremendous amount of wisdom in that advice. For example, I've often instructed new traders in my mentorship group to spend a month in a practice account with only two goals: (1) to lose everything in that account and (2) to lose as much money as they can as fast as they can. You will be surprised to learn what always happens. First, those traders initially often trade better and more profitably, and they soon learn and appreciate that it can often be as difficult to lose money as to make money, especially when you are trying to do it quickly. This exercise offers a tremendous learning experience and one that I highly recommend to all traders no matter their level of skill or experience. In fact, once you learn how to really lose money in the market, you learn how to improve and succeed even more. Also, this exercise will help you remove the fear of losing in your own approach. To trade well, you must learn how to use fear you feel and the fear of others to your own advantage.
- Traders who have learned to turn off and tune out of all (or most) media input (including social networking) are outperforming significantly. The performance spread between those who read a lot online versus those who don't is so significant that if you saw the difference you would radically change how you spend your own research time. While it is very important to learn from others, you must be extremely careful to manage and guard what information you consider daily to significantly outperform. Traders, for example, who spend time reading about the economy from economists and/or who attach themselves to perma-bulls and perma-bears are those who struggle the most. If your goal is to make money in the markets, stop trying to make yourself look smart, and turn off and tune out this noise.
- Proper position sizing remains one of the least respected, underutilized, and misunderstood concepts for most traders. Moreover, far too many traders still struggle with implementing a consistent stop-loss strategy as they fight the signals produced or they utilize a system that is too tight for the types of strategies they employ. I have often said (and have proven this to be true) that even the best trader can trade the worst stock or ETF profitably. As an exercise of sorts in my mentorship group, we often have weekly face-offs where I and other traders will trade

the same stock or ETF for an entire week. Those who have good risk management skills always outperform in this exercise. In fact, too many think that success is dependent upon finding good setups or good stocks, when in reality that has very little to do with it. Proper risk management will determine your success as a trader more than any other thing.

- Those in my mentorship group who have been focusing on developing one method/one strategy are faring far better than those who manage multiple systems. Those traders who have a tendency to switch and constantly tweak their systems and approaches often underperform during multiple time frames. It is imperative that every trader develop what I call a bread-and-butter strategy that the trader can use and that will generate most of his or her profits. I find that too many traders know a lot of things but are not expert in one thing, and that's to their key disadvantage. To have any edge in the market, you have to be a true expert of your own strategy. And, remember, if you don't know what your strategy's weaknesses are, it isn't because they don't exist, but rather you simply haven't discovered them yet.
- A wise man once said, "Making the simple complicated is easy. Making the complicated simple is brilliant." The same is true in trading. Simple strategies that can be explained to a 10-year-old work far better than those that are complex and extremely difficult to explain and use. In my experience, traders go through a bell curve of sorts where they start with very little knowledge and few skills and then as their knowledge improves they begin to add layers of complexity to their systems. This complexity, also by the way, doesn't usually help. Then over time they learn to break that down again and make their system straightforward and simple and matched to their own personality. If you can, avoid the temptation to add layers of complexity and indicators to your approach. Adding them won't help the bottom line; it will only make the system extremely difficult to manage when the pressure is on and will delay you from being more successful. In trading, making the complicated simple for you is the way to go.
- No trader can truly copy another trader's strategy. One of the reasons I focused on education rather than advice at my site is because I've learned that most of us have to go our own way. How I trade personally cannot be repeated by another trader because no one is like me, nor do they have the skills I have, the weaknesses I face, or my temperament. So many traders waste years and thousands of dollars to find other traders or investors to copycat rather than using that same time and energy to develop their own unique approach. However, I'll let you in on a little secret. Every single successful trader I know has at one time figured out sooner or later that the path to success resides within himself or herself and cannot be purchased from other human being. Yes, learn all you can from those who surround you, but ultimately you must carve your own approach and go your own way in the market. Your destiny and future success already reside within you; you just need to find them.

- The most important factor that will determine your success will be whether you utilize a strategy that suits your personality and skills the best. It takes years to do this and to acquire the level of skills and experience you need for trading successfully. In case you are curious to know, the learning curve never really ends, but for most it takes seven years or even much more to do consistently well in the markets. As you might guess, most people don't have that kind of tenacity and capital to outlive the long, arduous learning curve; but for those who do the markets offer truly wonderful opportunities. I can't think of anything I'd rather do, and I'm grateful to have the opportunity every day to do what I love.

CHAPTER 43

Stick with Names You Know

Ronald Roll, *@gtotoy*

Beneath Ron's gruff exterior there is a sophisticated market technician, and he masterfully wields every tool and every indicator. He is incredibly generous with his time and expertise, helping novices find their footing.

BUYING MY FIRST STOCK

The long and sordid road to my success as a trader probably began on my eighteenth birthday. That was the day I was first granted access to some funds that had been put away for me. I had already been operating a profitable landscaping business for several years; so money of my own was no mystery to me. But this was definitely more money than I was accustomed to playing with, and you'd better believe I was ready to get my game on. The big event of the day was picking up my tricked-out '78 Trans Am. I'd put a down payment on a full-works customization the month before and she was ready and waiting for me—the single most beautiful thing I'd ever seen. I tore ass out of there and headed for home. Halfway there, I'm barking the tires going real fast, when she slips on me and we eat a telephone pole. Happy birthday to me!

Not three months later, I'm chatting up my grandfather for some assistance in making the smart play and initiating a serious investment. The party was legendary, but it'd run up a hell of a bill and it was time to wise up. Of course, being the ornery old guy Gramps was, he wasn't about to just do something for me. He agreed to help me on the condition that I had to pick the company to invest in and it had to be one that I personally believed in. At the time I had an Apple IIe computer. Since I did honestly believe that we were only just beginning to see the early stages of what became the personal computing revolution, I was pretty confident that AAPL at $7 a share was a solid buy. So, I stated my case and Gramps obliged in assisting with executing the transaction. Voilà! I was a bona fide shareholder. After launching a new landscaping business with most of my remaining loot,

I got so busy that I rarely even thought about those shares. "It's a long-term investment. Forget about it," I'd tell myself.

When it did pop into my mind and I checked the numbers, it usually just pissed me off; so I decided that it didn't matter and I stopped thinking about it. It wasn't until almost 10 years later in 2000 that I was sitting in a waiting room at the dentist's office and picked up a newspaper to pass the time. AAPL was at $35 a share! #@%! Then and there, I was sold on the idea of becoming a trader. Funding my new obsession-to-be with six figures set the hook deep, real deep.

PREPARATION, PREPARATION, PREPARATION

My initial strategy was that of a part-time swing trader since I still had a business to manage and was pressed for time during the day. I was cautious at first because I knew the AAPL call was a fortunate coincidence at best. I also recognized the fact that it took almost a decade—and really, my forgetting about it—for it to fatten up the way it did. And aside from obvious clichés like "Buy low, sell high" I didn't know anything. So, I played it safe and just dipped my toe in. Well, I didn't have any discipline; so that didn't last long. Despite my obvious shortcomings, I actually did quite well out of the gates. It took only about two months to double that account. Of course, I only got more "cowboy" and put the pedal to the metal. And almost as quickly as it came, it was all gone.

That's when I realized what I needed to do. I paper traded while I learned anything and everything I could about the fundamental nature of the equities market and how to decipher the technical data left in its wake. Now, there are a lot of naysayers when it comes to the value of paper trading. Some casually dismiss it as a potentially useful tool because it somehow can't evoke the "real" emotion of trading; you need to feel the risk. That's just silly, as is the idea that emotion somehow even has a place in a successful trading strategy. It doesn't. In fact, emotion is probably the ultimate culprit for 99 percent of the accounts that blow up. And therein lies the rub. Trading is an intensely emotional activity. After blowing up my first account, I stuck to paper trading for a full year.

What I discovered through that experience was that my single greatest obstacle to pulling off successful trades wasn't my interpretation of the technical data I was relying on for the setup; it was the constant bombardment of all kinds of emotional impulses we all experience every day as human beings. And giving in to emotions tends to lead to some rationalization or another for deviating from the original trade plan. In reality, the most successful traders operate completely devoid of emotion, like machines. Why? They *are* machines. Paper trading offers an effective risk-free method for humans to practice trading like a machine and temper the natural tendency to let emotions interfere. I highly recommend it as a prerequisite for first-time traders and any traders who feel like they've maybe lost their edge. For me personally, as a result of the foundation I laid with my paper trading, I now pull the trigger on a trade knowing exactly where I want to sell my shares and where my stop is. And more often than not, my trade orders are entered in advance and executed automatically in an effort to even further remove the temptation of emotional interference. Plan your trade. Trade your plan.

I am a technical trader first and foremost. I then consider myself primarily a swing trader first and a day trader second. My hard-core scalping days are pretty much behind me, but I have and continue to use as many tools in my box of tricks. As the market changes I change. The inability or unwillingness to adapt to a changing market seems to be a major problem with a lot of traders. They learn one style and ignore every other one. If they are disciplined, then this is acceptable. If they know when to walk away from the market for an extended period of time because they do not know how to trade it, that's great. But, let's be honest; most can't walk away, and it is at these times that they can get really hurt. The key is identifying a key change in the overall market mechanics, and trying to stay one step ahead of the sheep.

ANALYZING DIFFERENT TIME FRAMES

The core of my style has been an ongoing effort at mastering the S&P 500 through technical analysis. I believe that overall support and resistance on the equity markets rarely (if ever) changes over extended periods of time. There are always major buyers and sellers at the same places (i.e., support and resistance). Support and resistance are simply where the forces of supply and demand meet. The heart of my toolbox is rooted in the concept of supply and demand. Where there is support there is demand, and where there is resistance there is supply. For me, knowing the S&P 500 and its SPDR exchange-traded fund (ETF) (SPY) like the back of my hand has been my major breakthrough and key to my success. Everything I do as a trader is always based on what the overall market is doing. I always have a multiple time frame view: from the 6-month, the monthly, the weekly, and the 5-minute chart.

As far as individual stocks go, I am always ripping apart an equity chart over a long-term picture, sometimes as far back as 20 years. This gives me a solid feel for where the real buyers and sellers will show up. Once I have done this and identified key support and resistance levels, I leave them on my charts indefinitely. I'm not a big fan of generic scanning. In my arsenal of stocks, I have close to 300 or so that I monitor on a regular basis, and it is from these that I "scan." I believe most stocks have a mind of their own, and learning a stock's behavior over the course of time can help me in predicting its next big move. I very rarely run scans looking for the next "great" setup. I like to be in names known to me. Some stocks are known to perform better than others in, say, an overall market pullback, and the only way to know this is to have watched them for many years. Way too many traders bounce around looking for the next great play. This is not a good strategy in my honest opinion; at least it does not work for me. Stick with names you know and real companies.

I have broken down the long-term support and resistance for the top 10 of all major SPDR S&P 500 (Spy) and other index exchange-traded funds (ETFs) like IYR, IYT, XLE,

XME, and so on. It is from these that I will look for sector rotation, and focus on the one or two best setups in each one's top 10. A huge part of my success has come from simply being patient and observant. New traders have got to stop trying to make money. Trading is about fine-tuning your skills and discipline. Great traders are successful because their playbook is well stacked and they are constantly expanding and improving it. I do my best to remain calm when trading and to believe in my plan. One simple method I use is to never have my broker platforms up in front of me. I always have them minimized and only pull them up when making a new trade. This keeps my focus on the chart, not the profit and loss (P&L) column. Focusing on P&L can really interfere with my judgment. I do little things like this to eliminate micromanaging, which is a trader killer.

Success in something as difficult as the stock market does not come easily. It is always the result of hard work combined with experience and the ability to read market sentiment. Some of my personal ingredients for making consistent profits in any market include: aim big and settle for small; don't get caught in pump-and-dump stocks; analysts are meant to be faded at the top and bottom of a range; when buying the fear, meaning on known bad news that gets rehashed, step up to the plate; sell into the greed or the oncoming pump from the so-called experts; admit quickly when you're wrong, and cut losses fast! There are no successful marriages in the stock market, so don't think you can get away with it. Don't worry about fear or greed; just know that there is always someone willing to pay you a premium for being early. The market is complicated enough without adding to it; keep everything as simple as possible; remove all noise during the trading day, and that includes the television.

As far as swing trading goes, there is one basic technique I would like to share. As a trader, I am always trying to hone my entry and exit skills. This is where you can mix both styles of swing and day trading into one. For almost every swing trade entry, I take 50 to 100 percent more than what I intend to hold as a swing. So, for example, let's say you want to swing trade an equity with a price of $20 per share. You want to hold 2,000 shares. Your original plan called for a 50-cent stop loss in place. What I do in a well-trending market that day is take 3,000 to 4,000 shares. If this particular entry was good and the stock moves up around 50 cents, then I will sell the 1,000 to 2,000 extra shares and continue to use my original 50-cent stop on the remaining shares as a swing trade. This gives you cushion to protect against any overall market or equity weakness the next day. Usually the worst-case scenario is that you will get stopped out of the trade minus 50 cents, which would leave you net flat for the trade.

CHAPTER 44

Massive Trends and the Trajectory of Noise

Phil Pearlman, @ppearlman

Dr. Phil Pearlman is our community psychiatrist and therefore has the hardest and least rewarding job at StockTwits. Phil can be gentle when he needs to be and quick with the block. That is both skill and art. Phil has a fantastic eye for winners as well. I would trust Phil with my last dollar. Oddly, he trusts me with his.

Once in a while you get shown the light in the strangest of places if you look at it right.

—Robert Hunter

I began trading equities in the mid-1990s and at the time I had no idea what I was doing. I opened a Datek account with $10,000 I had won as an award teaching special education and began buying tech stocks that my brother Vic and brother-in-law Barry were telling me to buy. It was fantastic! Cisco Systems, Intel, and Microsoft were some of the names and it did not take a pro to win.

In hindsight, it worked in my favor that I did not fully understand asset allocation or risk management, as I put my whole account in just a few names and held on. If I had been allocating and managing risk better, I might not have established such a substantial account. I was getting long stocks that were moving and making a significant amount of money.

I had just moved back to Washington, D.C., to pursue a doctorate in clinical psychology, and it was fortuitous that I lived in a building with a group of people who worked at America Online (AOL). They were caught up in the excitement and I recognized that what was going on in the Internet space was profound. AOL wound up becoming my first really big winner. In hindsight, and even while I was not managing risk well, I was applying some of the same principles to that trade as I did to my largest winners that came later.

I had a good feel for what was going to be hot, and looking back this is the one feature of my market participation that has remained stable. It is all about using your strengths to establish an edge, and for me it was a sense of visualizing a large trend that was in its early stages.

By the late 1990s, I was trading more actively and was fully caught up in Internet stocks. I was learning a bit more about how equity markets worked and had a nose for a good story and the rhythm of the indexes, which, in general, was more predictable than today.

However, by the time I was finishing up my graduate work in the second half of 1999, it was becoming clear to me that the markets were in the throes of a mania rivaling the legendary tulip bubble of the 1600s. There was a striking and disturbing parallel between the speculative euphoria blossoming in those buying NASDAQ stocks and the experience of those diagnosed with manic-depressive (bipolar) disorders, which I had been studying closely.

I recall the day Jeff Bezos was named the *Time* magazine Man of the Year at the end of 1999. I was interning in Rochester, New York, and saw him on the cover and thought to myself, "Oh my God, the collective sentiment is madness!"

I sold most of my portfolio and even tried to short some stocks, quickly getting stopped as the insanity reached its zenith in March 2000. The lesson was key in my understanding of markets and motivated me to begin studying market psychology more closely.

DISCOVERING BEHAVIORAL ECONOMICS

For the first few years that I was actively involved in the markets, I was not aware that there was a branch of economics that focused specifically on the psychology of markets. Behavioral economics was a relatively new field that grew out of a branch of social psychology called judgment and decision making. The early practitioners were more focused on empirically disproving the efficient markets hypothesis and less concerned about making money in markets, which I always found a bit petty and odd.

Nevertheless, I was reading everything from Daniel Kahneman and Amos Tversky's work to Richard Thaler to Andrei Shleifer and applying theory to my view of what was playing out in the stock market. This was a huge step in my approach, as I was coming to recognize that the psychology of the individual could be applied to market experience and that many of the same common irrational tendencies were analogous to market behavior. Specifically, there is a trajectory to how a person processes and integrates new information that is imperfect and only occurs over time, which is similar to the way the collective market participant prices information and larger trends.

By the end of 2003, I had begun trading professionally at a new hedge fund in New York. We built an earnings momentum model with a fundamental analysis overlay, and the timing of this was extremely good as the market was entering a five-year bull run. The basic idea was to find companies that were beating estimates by a wide margin and to focus on getting long those with the best financials and the best story. The market only slowly and inefficiently processes news, and when the news is surprisingly good there is often a ton of upside.

IDENTIFYING MASSIVE TRENDS EARLY

While I've applied multiple strategies over the past 15 years, the one common theme and the one that has created the most wealth has been identifying massive trends that are occurring with an expansive time frame. The goal is to make an informed bet and manage it rationally over time.

The first one occurred almost accidently as I bought AOL stock before AOL bought CompuServe and held it until not long after AOL bought Time Warner. The idea was fairly simple: The Internet was growing and would have profound implications in how people find information and relate, and AOL was at the center of the Internet.

There have been others, too, including coal and BTU, GLD and the absolute devaluation of currencies, LCA Vision and the rapid growth of laser eye surgery, and Ceradyne and the huge increase in military spending.

The primary psychological component of this strategy actually has less to do with sentiment, which people most often associate with market psychology, and much more to do with conservatism of information processing, which pertains to the more experimental and less known field of cognitive psychology.

First described by Ward Edwards, a pioneer in decision-making theory, conservatism of information processing as it applies to markets refers to the tendency participants have of not fully taking into account new information as it becomes available. It just takes people a while to price in the implications of massive trends early on. This leads to a long lag time while the asset price catches up to the landscape, the fundamental value. In addition, not only does price catch up over time, but if the trend is a large one and enough people hop aboard, price overshoots sane valuations, sometimes by a lot.

Whether it is the Internet, laser eye surgery, war, or inflation, I seek to identify massive trends that are in the early stages of playing themselves out and that will grow in public awareness and intensity as they develop over the course of an extended period of time.

People are slow to process new information and to integrate it into their investments. This is the trajectory of information and noise, and it is the place where opportunity awaits. As others wake up to the implications of new trends, they jump on board. Then still more follow, and by the time the trend is fully understood by the investing public, the corresponding equities not only have gained significantly in value but have usually increased well beyond fair value.

With every new massive trend, there is often an obvious way to play it. Many times, this is just fine and plenty of wealth can be created. Often, though, the largest and most obvious plays are also the most complicated, are the first to get crowded, and have the most attention already on them.

This is why the best of the best massive trend plays go one step further to find lesser-known companies that have even a higher level of inefficiency.

As public awareness of massive trends grows, so does the noise. People come out of the woodwork across a variety of venues voicing strong opinions, usually with motivations that are disconnected from truth discovery and are inaccurate.

If you possess clarity where there is a high level of uncertainty and debate surrounding a trend, then you have a huge advantage and must then seek to express your edge in the market in a way that is profitable.

This is why experts in areas such as technology and medicine have incredible alpha potential if they focus on the massive trends in their fields of expertise and expressing those trends rationally in markets.

CERADYNE AND THE WAR ON TERROR

After the September 11 attacks, I began scouring the market for companies aside from the largest defense names that would benefit profoundly from a new era in American history. It was clear to me that with a hawkish president (and vice president) and the first significant attack on U. S. soil since Pearl Harbor, our nation was going to war at some point.

Living in close proximity to the attacks and having been shaken by them, I did not let that stop me from doing serious analysis, as I was predominantly in cash and felt that I had a good beat on the era of war approaching while others were fearful and debating.

I began buying Ceradyne stock on December 19, 2001, a few months after the September 11 attacks in New York and well before the United States formally began a war in Iraq.

Ceradyne is a maker of advanced ceramic products that has been run for its entire history by its founder, Joel Moskowitz. Moskowitz was an engineer and pioneer in the application of ceramic materials in products such as clear braces and body armor.

This was not a high-growth company but had been run efficiently and conservatively and had a solid balance sheet. It was tiny relative to major defense stocks such as Lockheed or Northrup, which I was also buying.

I read every bit of data that anyone could possibly get their hands on regarding this company, and all I found was opportunity. First, it was a solid company fundamentally and was generating cash, so I thought this alone limited downside to some extent. Second, it was the best-of-breed maker of a military-grade body armor product that would be required in an increasing supply.

I viewed it more as a call option that would not have theta. In the case that the United States entered an extended war, CRDN would be leveraged and would grow revenue well beyond expectations.

I remember one period in 2003 when the stock got hit because the company reported much lower gross margins, but I already knew that this would occur because it was expanding its capacity to manufacture body armor substantially with a new factory. I bought more. Two quarters later the company was blowing out estimates with huge numbers relative to the estimates of the few analysts who covered the stock.

Aside from CRDN being a smaller, less known stock and being levered to an increase in military activity and spending, it also benefited from a huge amount of argument and political confusion. Body armor and protecting our troops became political, and this added to the poor communication of accurate information. It increased the noise. This allowed me to trade around the position effectively, as this noise create huge swings in the stock price.

Knowing the real story was critical during these periods because it created opportunity. Nevertheless, the most difficult part psychologically was holding as the noise increased. There were front page stories in the *Wall Street Journal* and the *New York Times* that were wrong, and the price on this relatively thin issue was being bounced about like a Ping-Pong ball.

I did sell a third of the position after the price tripled, which I often regret, but I think it made it easier for me to trade the stock because I had my basis out.

I sold most of the rest near the highs and had a 15-bagger on those shares. I held a bit for nostalgia's sake, which was definitely a mistake, and still hold some for a six-bagger.

Being able to identify a massive trend is not so difficult if you think deeply for yourself and immerse yourself in the field and the available information. The tough part, at least for me, is acting rationally over time once you are in the trade and letting it play out. This is where you can make a lot of money.

CHAPTER 45

We Have Met the Enemy, and It Is Us

Abdel Ibrahim, *@RatioTrader*

Abdel is a Fibonacci expert who trades with precise discipline and respect for levels and his plan. The methodical manner in which he approaches the craft of trading helps him to sail through the harsh winds of market chaos and uncertainty.

The title of my chapter is a line that comes from the comic strip "Pogo" and was actually quoted in *Market Wizards* by Jack D. Schwager (New York Institute of Finance/Simon & Schuster, 1989). It really hits home when I think about trading.

My trading journey has been a fascinating one, to say the least. I never had any formal training in finance or economics. My background is actually in design and creative marketing. I started out as many people do—taking some money I had saved and throwing it into some stocks. It wasn't long before I was spending more time looking at my positions than actually doing design work (although I still love design). It really struck me when I was at work one day and my boss came up behind me as my screens were full of stock quotes and she was giving me this pretty nasty look. You can guess what happened shortly afterward.

So here I was, no job, and some money saved up. I had bills, rent, and I'd just met this girl, so I had to make some cash to keep up with my way of living. As I traded day in and day out, I found myself being very inconsistent. In fact, I found myself trading purely off of emotion. I was making all the novice mistakes, from not using stops to just getting out of trades for absolutely no reason. It was pretty crazy when I look back on it. I wasn't trading any better than my mom could, and I'm not exaggerating.

HAVING THE PROBABILITIES IN YOUR FAVOR

In the initial year of trading, my equity looked like a ski slope. I was running out of money when one day a friend of mine introduced me to a book called *Market Wizards*, which is a collection of interviews with some of the greatest traders of our time. What was interesting about this book was that none of the traders were talking so much about what they bought and sold, but more about some of the important mental aspects of trading. They talked about how emotional control was so important and that it really boils down to having the probabilities in your favor. I remember veteran trader Larry Hite talking about how he would trade gold and cocoa the same way. It was amazing! As time went on, I stumbled upon another book, called *Trading in the Zone* by Mark Douglas (Prentice Hall Press, 2001). Again, it was a book that had no technical or trading information, but rather dealt with how we should mentally approach the markets. The author talked about the importance of probabilities and sticking to a set trading plan. He talked about how you can have an expectation of what might happen, say, over 100 trades, but you don't know what may happen between the individual trades. At that time I was thinking to myself, "How can you approach a market in the exact same way every time?" It didn't make much sense to me then. As I did more and more reading and research, I gradually built an affinity to technical analysis.

IT'S ALL ABOUT HAVING AN EDGE

What I learned about technical trading was that it was all about having an edge. If this, then this. It's very straightforward. In fact, some traders just create algorithms and let the computers take care of the rest in an attempt to remove any emotion. I started researching different trading methodologies, and one stuck out. Fibonacci is a cool word, right? I'm not sure exactly what made me so attracted to Fibonacci numbers; maybe it was because they were derived from the Great Pyramids of Egypt, and my mom and dad just so happen to be Egyptian. I'm not really sure, but either way, I was fascinated by it. I learned everything I could learn about Fibonacci numbers. I learned about the golden ratio (0.618) and how frequently it exists in the world. It's pretty wild when you think about its existence in our galaxy, in nature, in our own bodies, and of course in the markets!

But there was a problem: Like any other trading system, you can easily get overwhelmed with information. I noticed this in many of traders I would speak to or listen to. A lot of them wouldn't have a very specific set of rules like the Market Wizards did. I soon realized that if I wanted to succeed and be a profitable trader, not only did I need to know what to do, but I needed to associate rules and then (even more important) I needed to follow those rules for every single trade. That's how probabilities are formed. If you aren't doing the same thing each and every time, then you really can't form reliable statistical data. I watch a lot of sports, and when I watch basketball, for example, and players go to the foul line to shoot free throws, the percentage they shoot is simply based on the fact that they are standing the same distance from the hoop, which is at the same height, using the same ball, and so on. So I had to approach the markets in that way. The goal was this: I had to put together a trading plan that I knew would produce a high probability of success in the markets that I traded. I knew I wouldn't win every single time. I even knew there would be times when I might experience a few losing trades in a row. I recall taking a coin and flipping it and getting heads four times in a row. This is a perfect example of knowing your probabilities, but still not knowing the outcome of each individual trade. In fact, you should try it. Take a coin and flip it 10 times a day for a month. Keep track of your results. You may find the day-to-day results surprising, but at the end of a month, you'll usually be pretty close to 50 percent.

I have found that trading Fibs with rules is a fantastic way to trade. One of the reasons I really like Fibonacci levels is because of how they are dynamic to any market and any time frame. Fibs don't disappear when markets are volatile. You can trade anything as well with Fibs. I started trading the S&P 500 futures on a 3-minute chart. Now I'm trading anything and everything that produces a signal. Stocks, futures, currencies, even options—they all respect Fibonacci levels. This brings me to my next point: which levels?

THE PULLBACK TRADE

One setup that I like to do a lot is a trade that I refer to as the pullback trade. You've probably heard of buying pullbacks, but I implement the method much differently than most. Again, I have very specific rules. Let's go though some of the basics of the trade setup.

Markets tend to move in a series of higher highs and higher lows or lower lows and lower highs. A lot of people seem to think you can just buy or sell these retracements and you'll be fine. The biggest issue I've found with doing that is that most people don't know where to place a stop, where to place a target, and which level to even buy or sell at. Because there are so many Fib levels out there, it's really easy to take something that is pretty powerful and screw it up.

So here is what I do. First, I look for an impulse leg. What I define as an impulse leg is a swing high to a swing low (or vice versa), as you can see in Figure 45.1. Once I see an impulse leg, then I look for one of five things to exist at the 61.8 percent retracement. You may be wondering, what about the 50 percent retracement? For the pullback trade setup, I do not look to buy or sell at the 50 percent retracement. I'll get to why in a moment.

So what are the things I look for at the 61.8 percent retracement?

1. *Previous structure resistance or support.* If you look left and you're going long, you'd be looking for previous structure resistance (anticipated support). If you are going short, then you're looking for previous structure support (anticipated resistance).

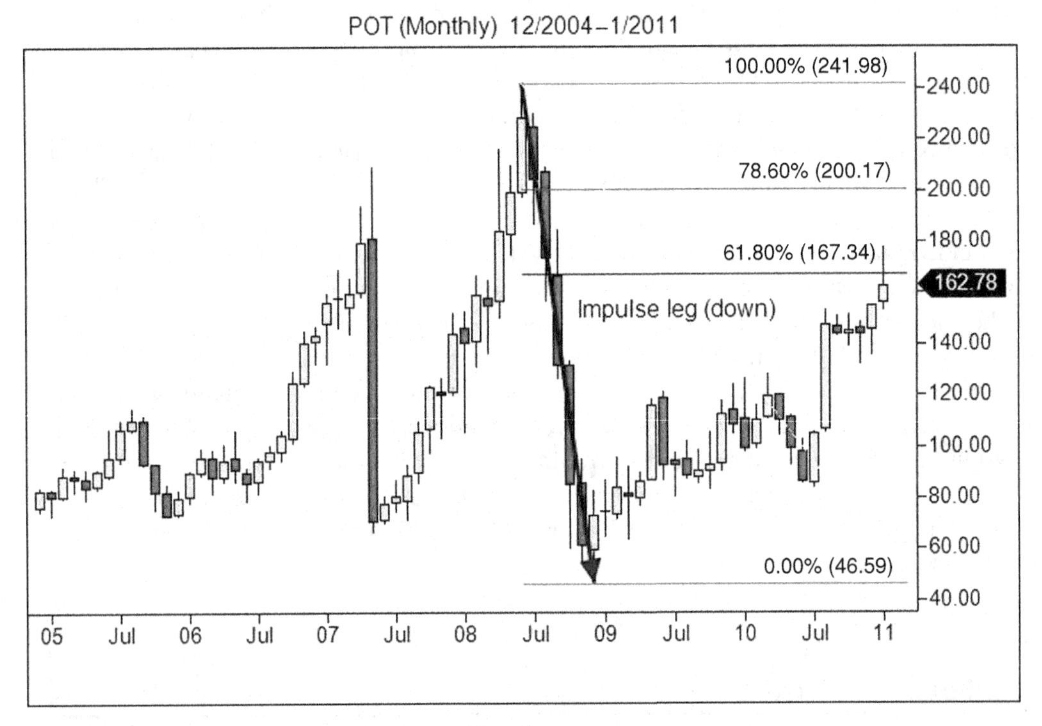

FIGURE 45.1 Impulse Leg, POT Monthly Chart
Source: NinjaTrader, LLC. © 2011 Ninja Trader, LLC.

2. *Fibonacci confluence.* Fibonacci confluence is when two Fibonacci levels (usually an extension and a retracement) meet together at the specific level. So, as an example, if the 1.272 percent extension of a smaller leg meets with the 61.8 percent retracement of a bigger leg, then that is Fibonacci confluence.
3. *One-to-one symmetry.* One-to-one symmetry is usually associated with Fibonacci confluence. When a market makes a one-to-one move, it typically does it with symmetry. Take a look at Figure 45.2.
4. *Trend line.* This is pretty straightforward. If a major trend line meets with the 61.8 percent retracement of a leg, we've got a trade.
5. *Pivot.* Depending on the time frame you're looking at, you're going to have different pivots. I tend to stick to the pivots of that time frame. As an example, I'm not looking at daily pivots on a monthly chart. Usually daily pivots are good for any daily or under time frame. Weekly pivots are good for weekly charts, and so on.

Now, only one of these five things needs to exist at the 61.8 percent retracement. If there are more, of course it helps, but only one is needed.

Going back to the point of why I use the 61.8 percent retracement instead of the 50 percent, I do so mainly for two reasons. First, 61.8 percent is the golden ratio, and

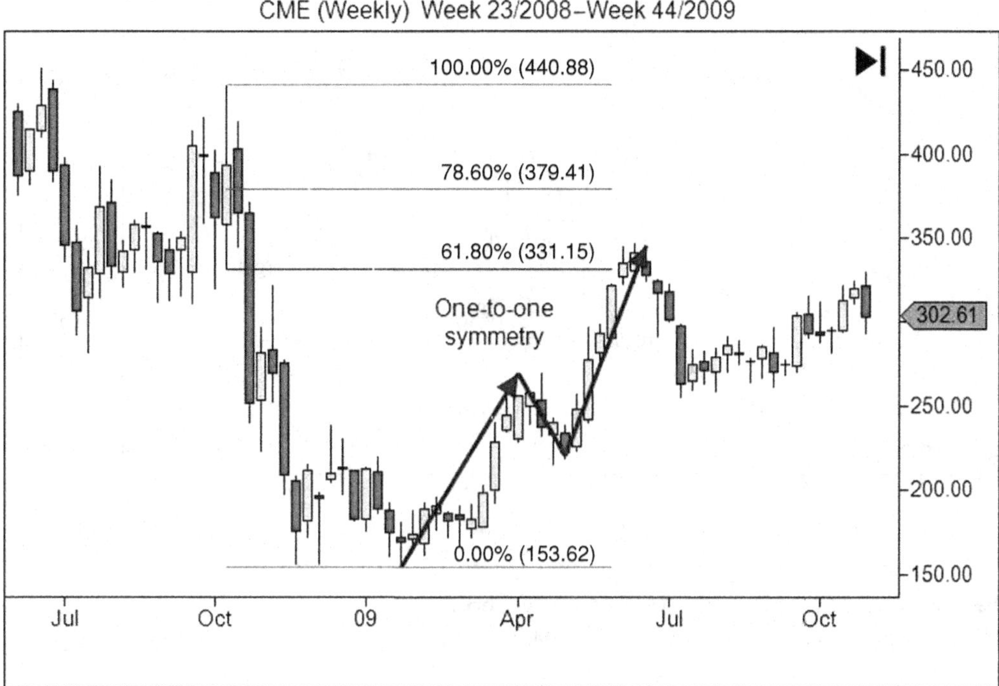

FIGURE 45.2 Weekly Pivots, CME Weekly Chart
Source: NinjaTrader, LLC. © 2011 Ninja Trader, LLC.

I would rather take higher-probability trades than a higher quantity of trades. What I've found is that although markets may not get to the 61.8 percent level as often as they get to the 50 percent, when they do get to the 61.8 percent retracement and one of the five things I look for is there, there is a 65 to 70 percent probability of success. I like those odds a lot.

As far as stops are concerned, I use the 78.6 percent retracement of the initial impulse leg, as you can see in Figure 45.3. The first target is at a 38.2 percent retracement of the retracement leg. This gives me a better than 1:1 risk-reward ratio. The second target is a retest of the high or low of the impulse leg.

So, when we step back and look at this trade, what do we have? We've got a 65 to 70 percent probability trade that offers us a better than 1:1 risk-reward ratio on our first target. It's a great setup, and going back to what I said in the beginning, it works in *any market and any time frame.*

An example we can look at is the AAPL monthly chart shown in Figure 45.4. You can see it produced a couple of the things we look for right at the 61.8 percent retracement. One of the great things about this strategy and approach is it allows you to set up the trade before it actually takes place. That is something that I truly love about Fibs. Not only that, but I can use Fibs for both my stops and my targets and find really predictive areas where markets are going. Remember, this is not 100 percent effective; it's 65 to 70 percent effective. It's extremely important to also understand that losing is something

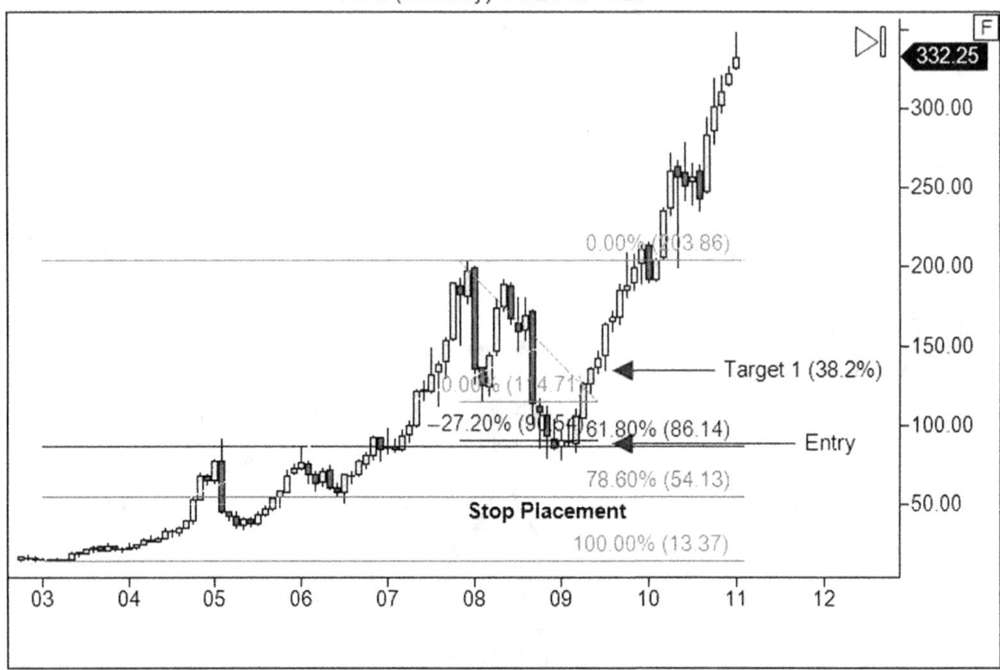

FIGURE 45.3 Price Targets, AAPL Monthly Chart
Source: NinjaTrader, LLC. © 2011 Ninja Trader, LLC.

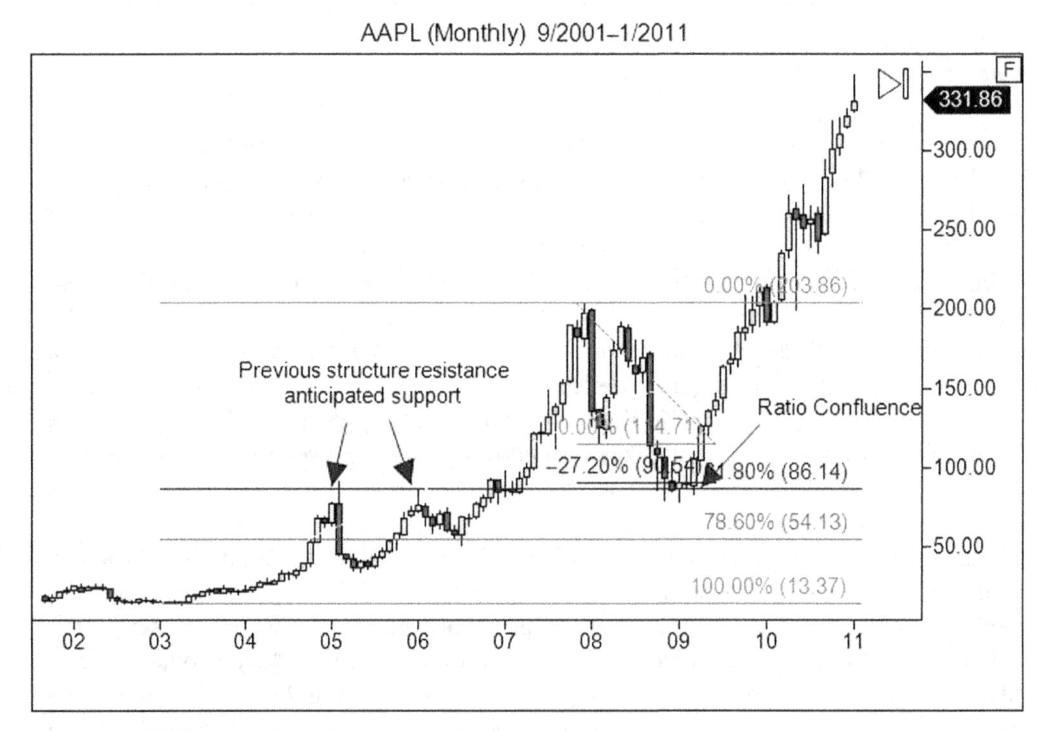

FIGURE 45.4 Fibs for My Entries, Stops, and Targets
Source: NinjaTrader LLC. © 2011 Ninja Trader, LLC.

that *will* happen sometimes. It's part of any trade setup no matter what you trade. What is more important is understanding how the repetition of this pattern will produce positive results when implemented consistently and properly.

Last, I want to remind you that profitable trading is not about having a ton of trades. In fact, it's the total opposite. It's about taking the setups that have proven to show success. The only way you can implement this is by testing it yourself. Even though I've laid out a setup that I use every day, the only way you're going to believe it works is if you test it and see for yourself. On top of that, you have to be disciplined about doing it every single day. Once again, profitable trading is not as much about actually trading as it is about discipline, emotional control, and attitude toward the markets.

CHAPTER 46

A Contrarian at Heart

John Welsh, *@johnwelshtrades*

The small-cap momentum crowd loves to hate John because he's the guy betting against them. The stock market is not about making friends; it's about making money. This is just a simple truth that John embraces. If John gets negative on a stock you are long, watch out; he's often correct in his assessment.

CUTTING LOSSES QUICKLY

I started trading in the late 1990s, during the Internet boom. All stocks went up and I was hooked. You could have thrown a dart at the board to pick a stock and still make money. Stocks would go up 50 percent in a day on news of stock splits.

I took a particular interest in the biotech stocks, because they were and are the most volatile. Over the years I have accumulated knowledge regarding most biotechnology companies and how they trade and what catalysts will move them up or down. Experience helped me internalize the buzzwords that make stocks move and attract liquidity.

My hardest trading year came in 2001, which ironically was the year after the Internet crash in 2000. It is my only losing year on record. Not a specific reason stands out, but it was the constant nonprofitable trades that wore me out while working a full-time job. I remember thinking at the time: Trading used to be easy, but not anymore; maybe it's time to cut my losses, take my capital, and move on.

The major turning point in my trading career came when I started to track my trades on an Excel spreadsheet, as shown in Figure 46.1.

I noticed I developed a problem of adding to losers, which compounded my losses. Once I began to accept losses and cut them quickly, the profits from my winning trades started to exceed my losers and the big turnaround was in place.

	A	B	C	D	E	F	G	H	I	J	K	L
2												
3												
4	Bought	Market	Time Bought	Time Sold	Date Sold	STOCK	POSITION	ENTRY	EXIT	SHARES	GAIN/LOSS	COMMENTS
5	4/29/2009	REG	12:00:00 PM	4:00:00 PM	4/29/2009	NVAX	SHORT	3.1	2.8	−10,000	$3,000.00	Shorted right near day's high after coming back from an opening dip. WHO raised the alert to level 5, could go as high as 6, but NVAX did not move much off it at all.
6	4/29/2009	REG	5:00:00 PM	5:00:00 PM	4/29/2009	SQNM	LONG	5.4	5.9	2,000	$1,000.00	Absolutely hammered down from $15 on fraud news regarding Down syndrome test. I bought it right at the low and sold before conference call.
7	4/30/2009	REG	8:00:00 AM	10:00:00 AM	4/30/2009	MGM	SHORT	9.6	9	−4,000	$2,700.00	Shorted MGM near the top of the day, almost hit $10. News on Dubai World financing shot the stock up almost 70% on the day. Was way overextended, took the cash.
8	4/30/2009	REG	12:00:00 PM	2:00:00 PM	4/30/2009	FAZ	LONG	7.75	8.15	3,000	$1,000.00	Bought FAZ near the day low after Chrysler bankruptcy. Took profit off the table before I left for the day.

FIGURE 46.1 Trading Journal

I started trading full-time in 2004–2005, after I developed enough confidence in my approach. Confidence was based on the consistency of my results, not on a daily but rather on a monthly basis. I left a six-figure, full-time job and went on my own. It was not an easy decision, but I have always hated the corporate world so much that I have never looked back.

AGAINST THE CROWD

I am a tape reader and a contrarian. I like to go against the crowd, because most of the time the crowd ends up wrong. To be a contrarian requires a unique mind-set. When everyone is yelling that the market is going up, that has to set off a mental alarm in your head that the market is probably overvalued. Of course, it's just the opposite when the sentiment is exceedingly bearish.

I estimate that over 90 percent of market participants lose money in the market. This is due to crowd mentality. When it feels like the safest time to buy a stock, it is usually a proper time to consider selling.

Prudent risk management is the key to my trading success. I am wrong at least 50 percent of the time, yet I am consistently profitable and have been six years running. It's because I cut my losses quickly. My average loss size is much smaller then my average gain. When my position goes against me, I quickly take a small loss and move on. There is no point in staying and waiting for it to come back. I can always buy the stock if it sets up again. I can always buy another stock. There are so many opportunities every day.

I have a short-term account and a long-term account. In my day trading account I rarely hold a position overnight. When I make a trade in this account, I know I have limited time to be right. When the trade goes against me, I exit immediately.

When my account balance gets too high, I take some money out of my account, save it, and act like I lost it. I trade better this way. When I think I lost money, I am more disciplined in regard to equity selection. I take less risk and have more profitable trades.

SHORTING EXTREMELY OVERBOUGHT STOCKS

I like to short the overbought momentum stocks, especially in the biotech sector. I do this around recent news catalysts. The biotech sector trades on sentiment. When a stock becomes cultlike, when the crowd thinks the stock will not go down, I come in and short. This makes me the most unpopular guy in the room.

I usually do not ride momentum on the upside. I realize that this is simultaneously a trading skill and a trading flaw. It is a skill because it prevents me from buying overvalued, overhyped, and parabolic stocks. It is a flaw because taking part of the upside is just as good as taking part of the downside.

I am not a technical trader. I trade mostly on volume and news catalysts. A few screens I use for trade ideas are the highest percentage gainers and losers for the day. Over time I have developed an understanding of many stocks and what kind of catalyst will move them.

A typical example is Rambus Inc. (RMBS), which has been a frequent visitor of highest percentage gainers and losers lists over the years. RMBS is constantly trying to sue large companies for patent violations. Over the past few years, there have been many twists and turns on RMBS. I know that any news regarding a lawsuit will increase its volatility substantially. Some key buzzwords I seek in the RMBS-related news are *delay*, *royalties*, *settlement*, and *appeal*.

SHORT, SHORT, SHORT

Again, I am not a technical trader. On August 31, MVIS (Microvision Inc.) broke out on high volume due to a rumor that its camera components would be included in the iPhone. I know the price and events history of MVIS very well and did not believe the rumor. There was to be an AAPL event the very next day in the afternoon, and I expected that there was a good chance for MVIS to continue its run on the morning of September 1, so I waited patiently. Take a look at Figure 46.2.

The conference was scheduled for 1:00 P.M. Around 12:30, I noticed that MVIS was weakening. I shorted the name into weakness before the event. The only way MVIS was going to be at the AAPL event was if they bought a ticket. I knew that the announcement

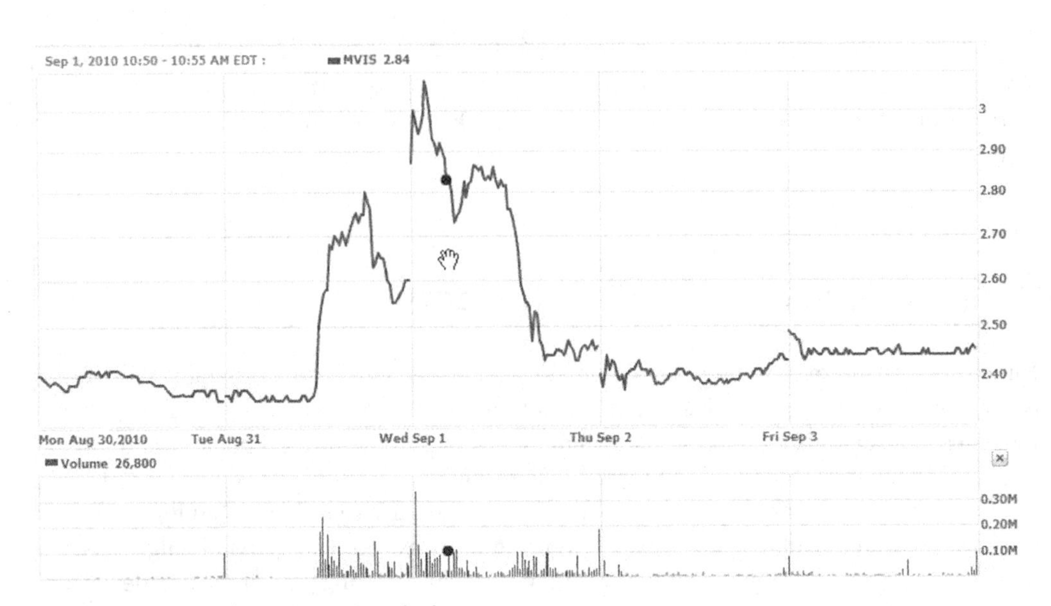

FIGURE 46.2 MVIS Goes Parabolic
Source: Copyright © 2011 Yahoo! Inc. All rights reserved.

would cause a spike in volatility and if my thesis was proven wrong, I was ready to exit immediately with a small loss. If was right, my short position would profit significantly. Essentially the setup offered a great risk/reward.

There was no AAPL announcement on September 1 regarding MVIS, and the stock sold off. I pocketed the quick dollars based on these overbought conditions going into the meeting.

Index